AFTER SCHOOL NIGHTMARE

Story and Art by
SETONA MIZUSHIRO

1

go!comi

Translation – Christine Schilling
Adaptation – Mallory Reaves
Lettering & Retouch –Eva Han
Production Manager – James Dashiell
Editor – Audry Taylor

A Go! Comi manga

Published by Go! Media Entertainment, LLC

Houkago Hokenshitsu Volume 1
© SETONA MIZUSHIRO 2005
Originally published in Japan in 2005 by Akita Publishing Co., Ltd., Tokyo.
English translation rights arranged with Akita Publishing Co., Ltd.
through TOHAN CORPORATION, Tokyo.

Visit us online at www.gocomi.com
e-mail: info@gocomi.com

ISBN 1-933617-16-0

First printed in August 2006

1   2   3   4   5   6   7   8   9

Manufactured in the United States of America.

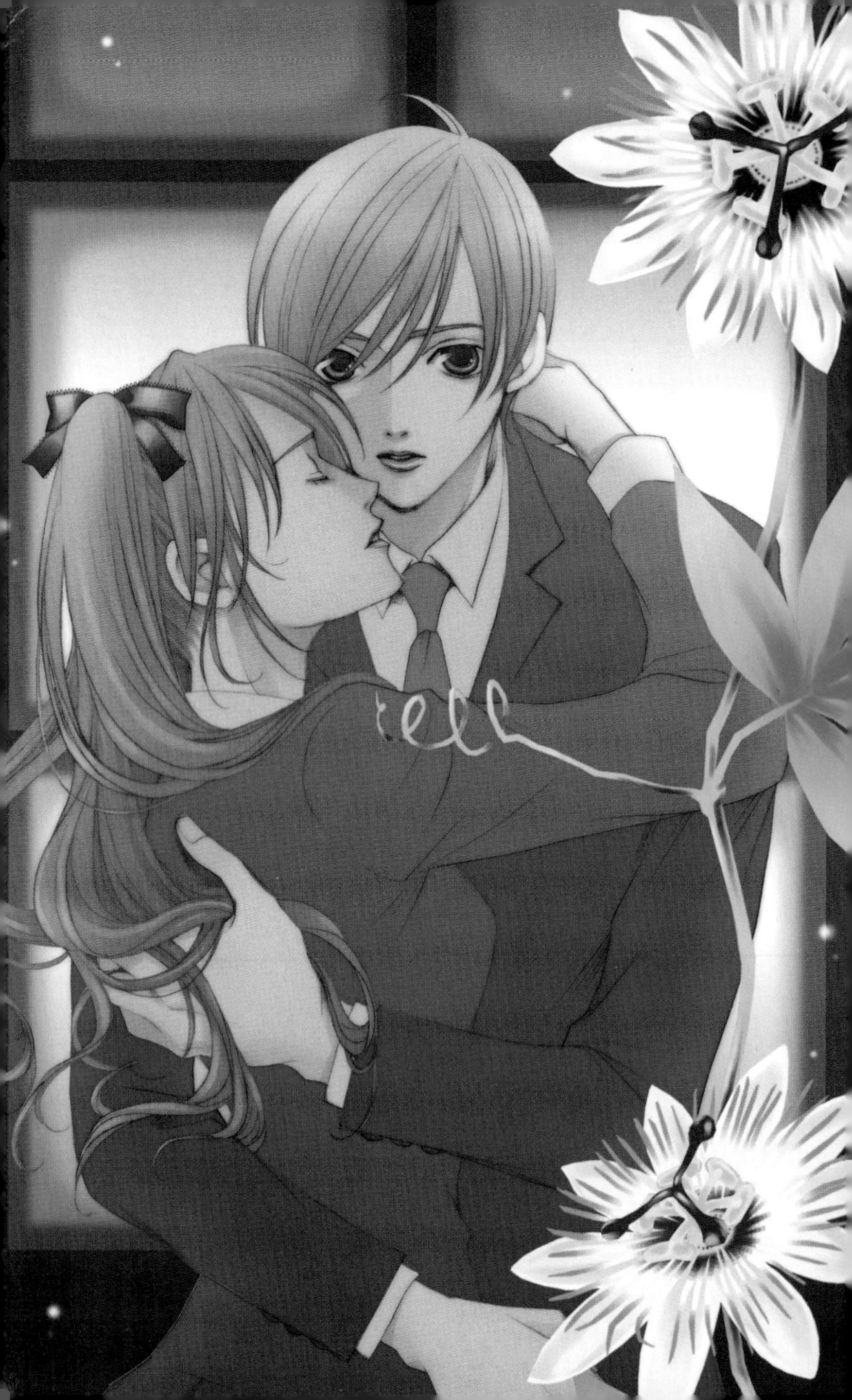
tell

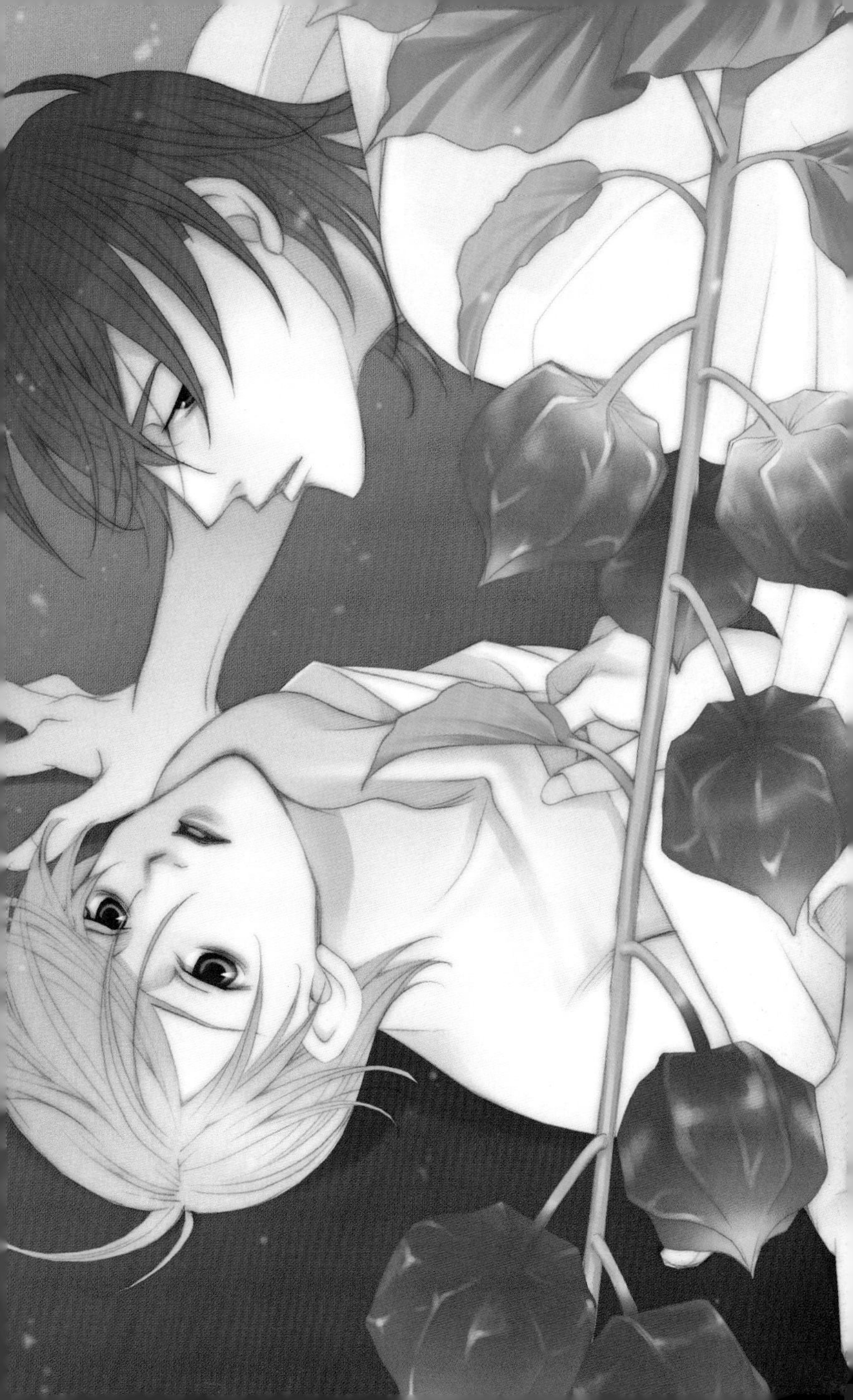

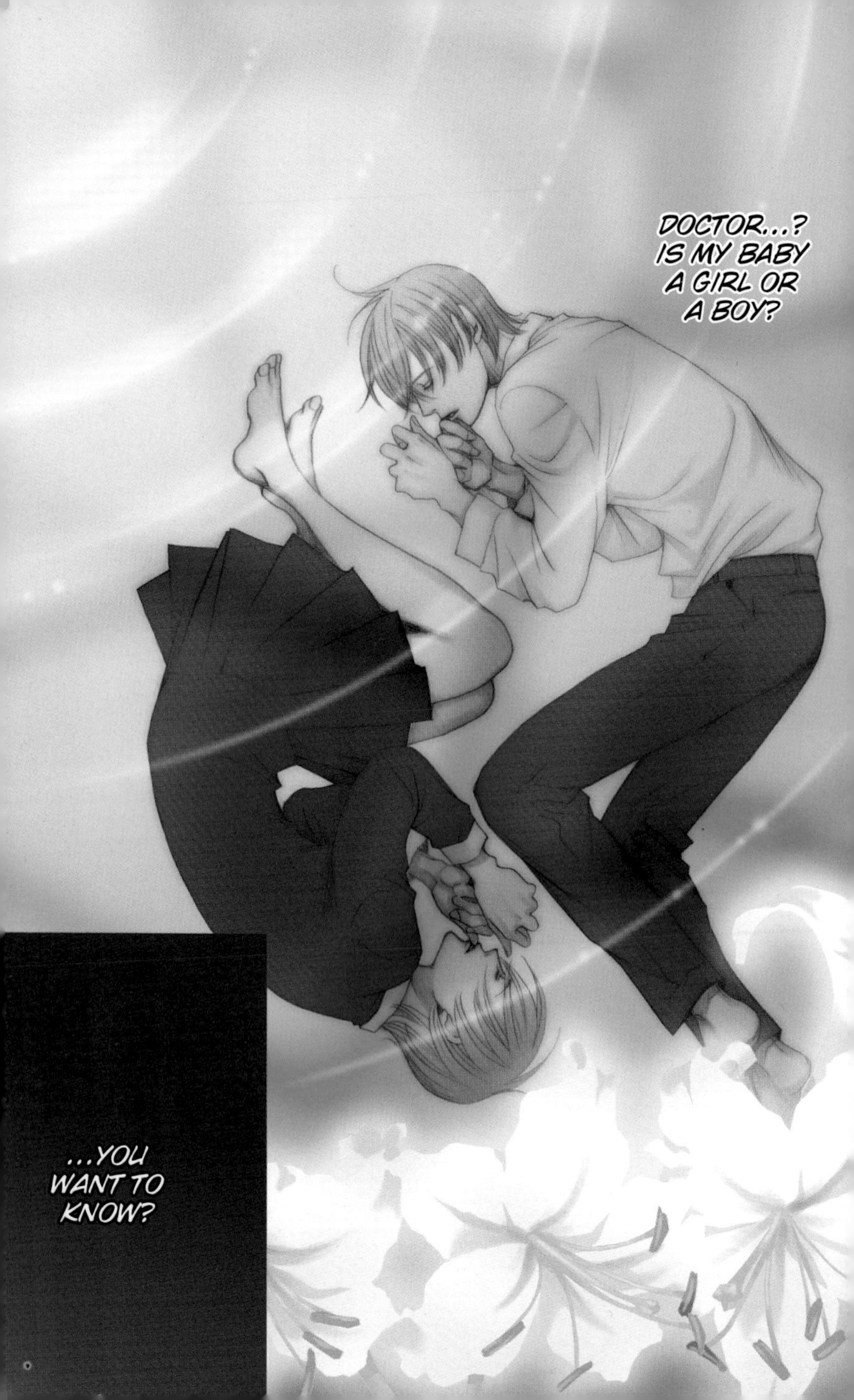
DOCTOR...? IS MY BABY A GIRL OR A BOY?
...YOU WANT TO KNOW?

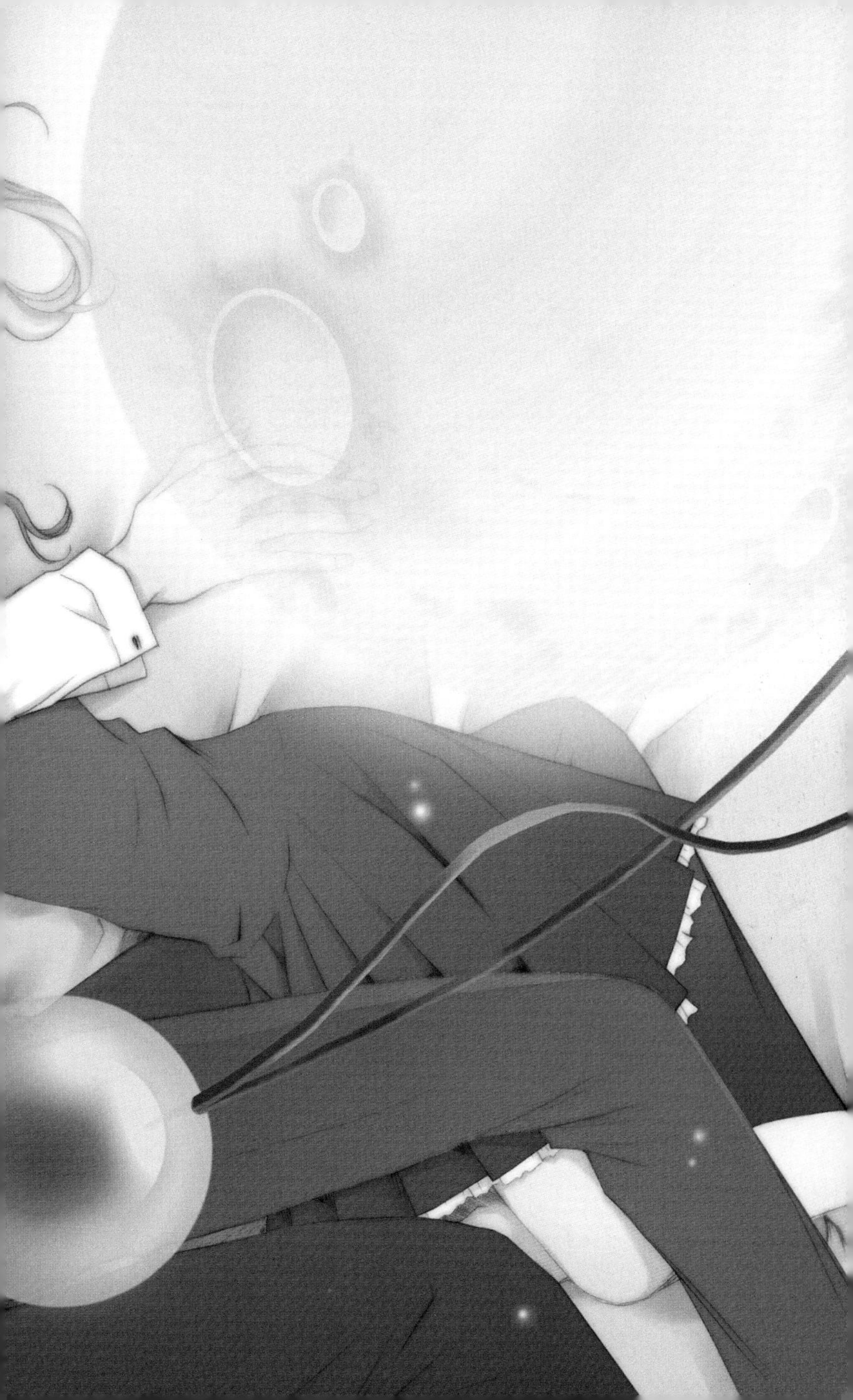

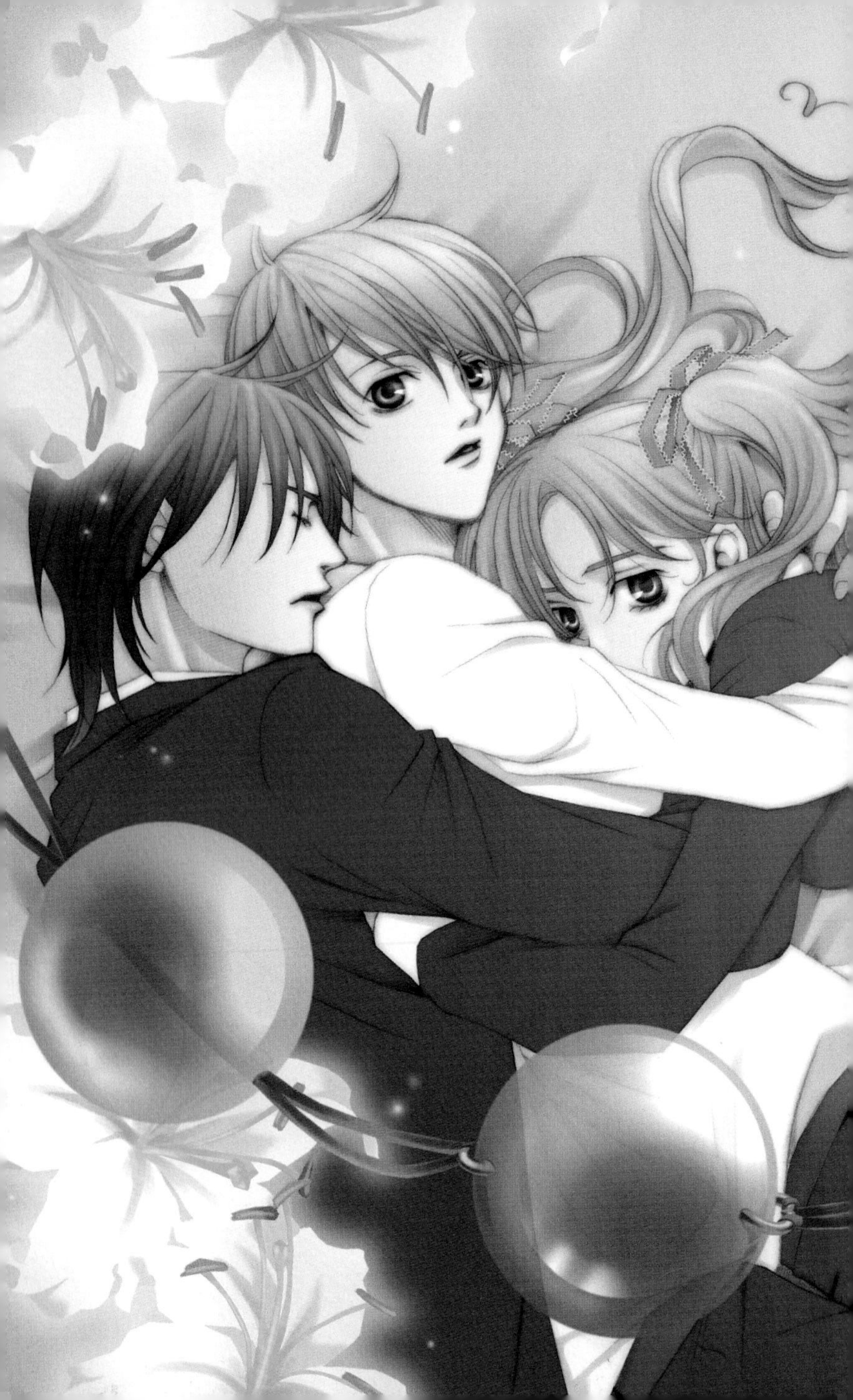

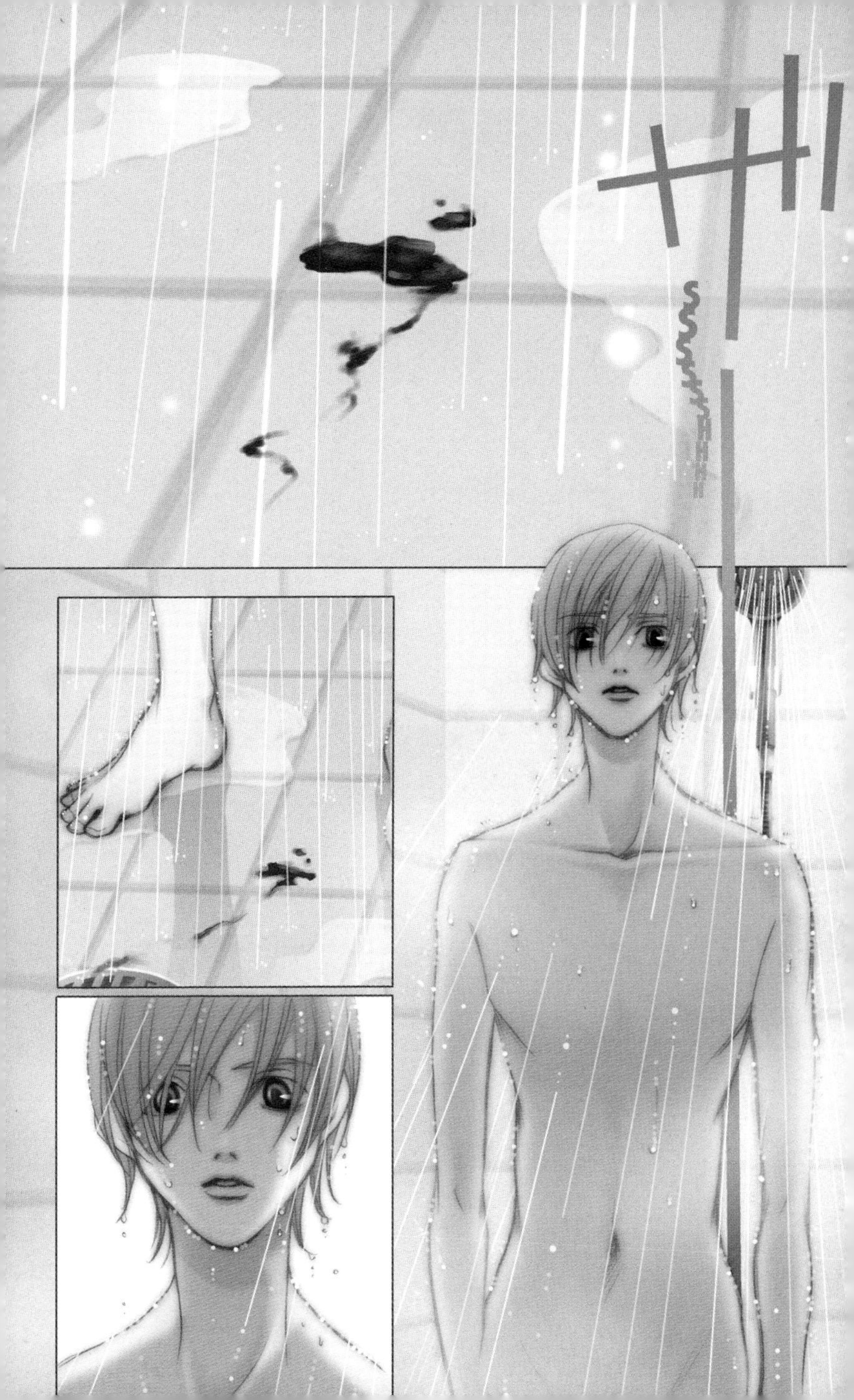
ザー
SSSHHH

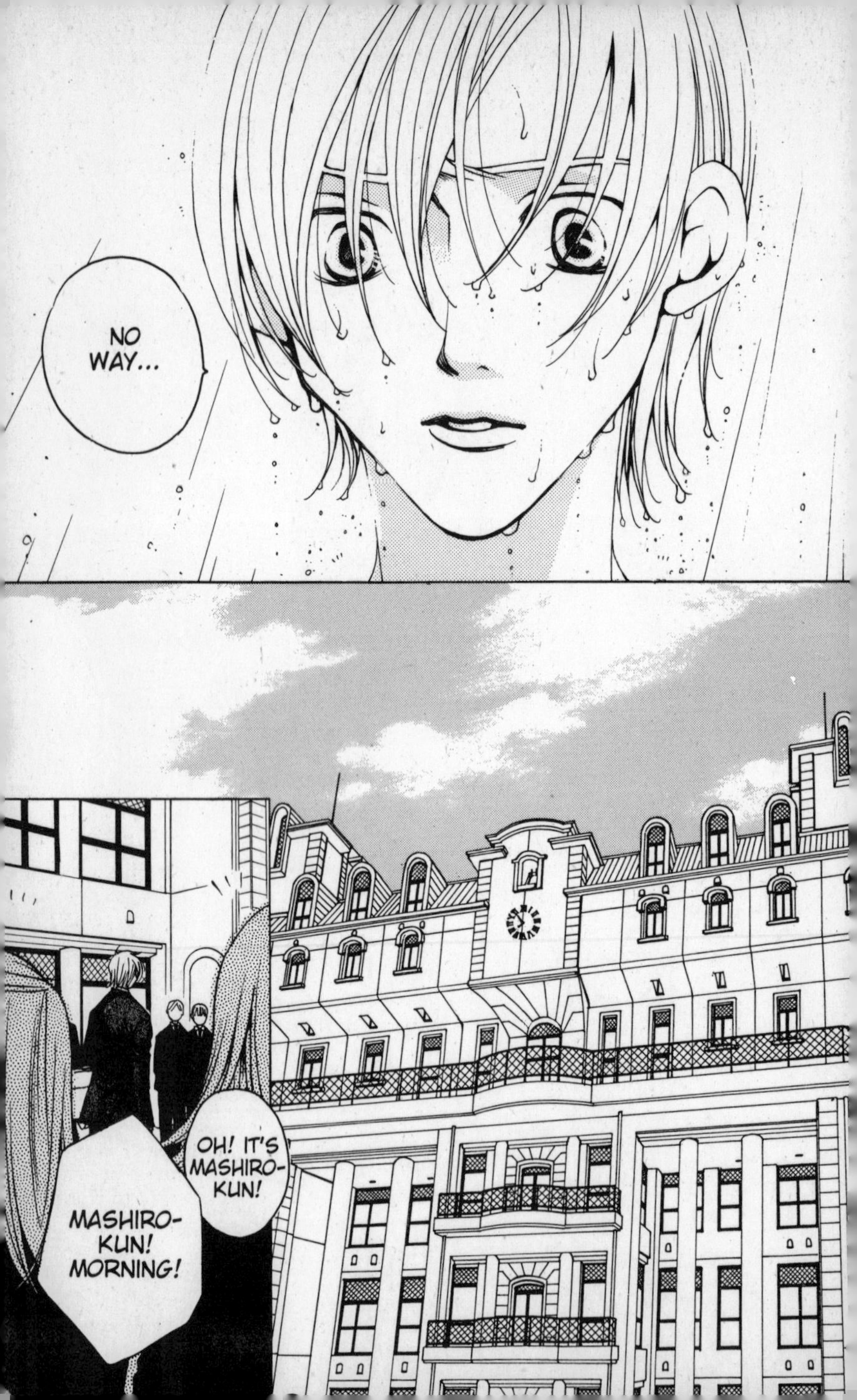
NO WAY...
OH! IT'S MASHIRO-KUN!
MASHIRO-KUN! MORNING!

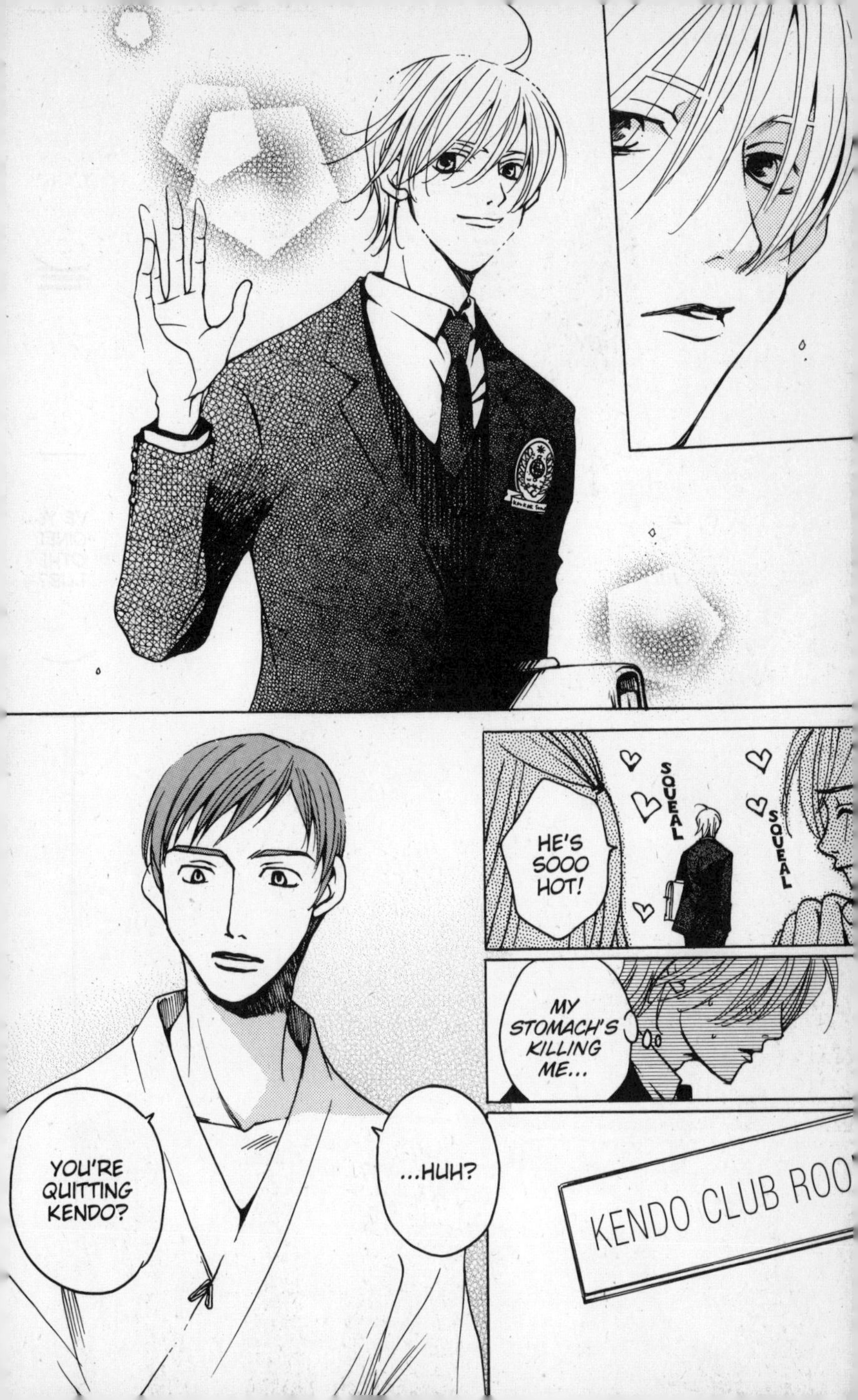

SQUEAL
SQUEAL
HE'S SOOO HOT!
MY STOMACH'S KILLING ME...
KENDO CLUB ROO
...HUH?
YOU'RE QUITTING KENDO?

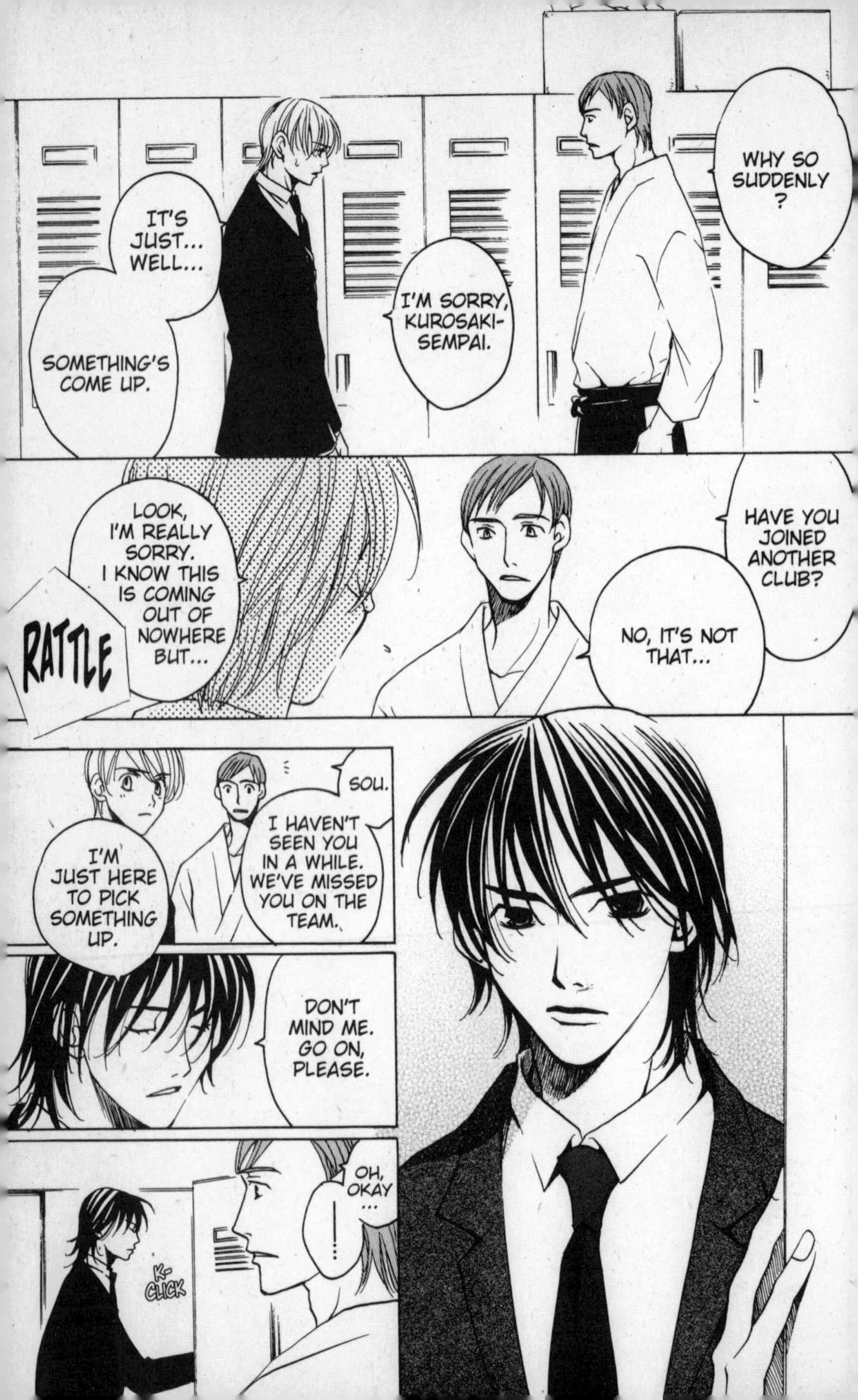
WHY SO SUDDENLY ?
I'M SORRY, KUROSAKI-SEMPAI.
IT'S JUST... WELL...
SOMETHING'S COME UP.
HAVE YOU JOINED ANOTHER CLUB?
NO, IT'S NOT THAT...
LOOK, I'M REALLY SORRY. I KNOW THIS IS COMING OUT OF NOWHERE BUT...
RATTLE
SOU.
I HAVEN'T SEEN YOU IN A WHILE. WE'VE MISSED YOU ON THE TEAM.
I'M JUST HERE TO PICK SOMETHING UP.
DON'T MIND ME. GO ON, PLEASE.
OH, OKAY ...
...!
K-CLICK

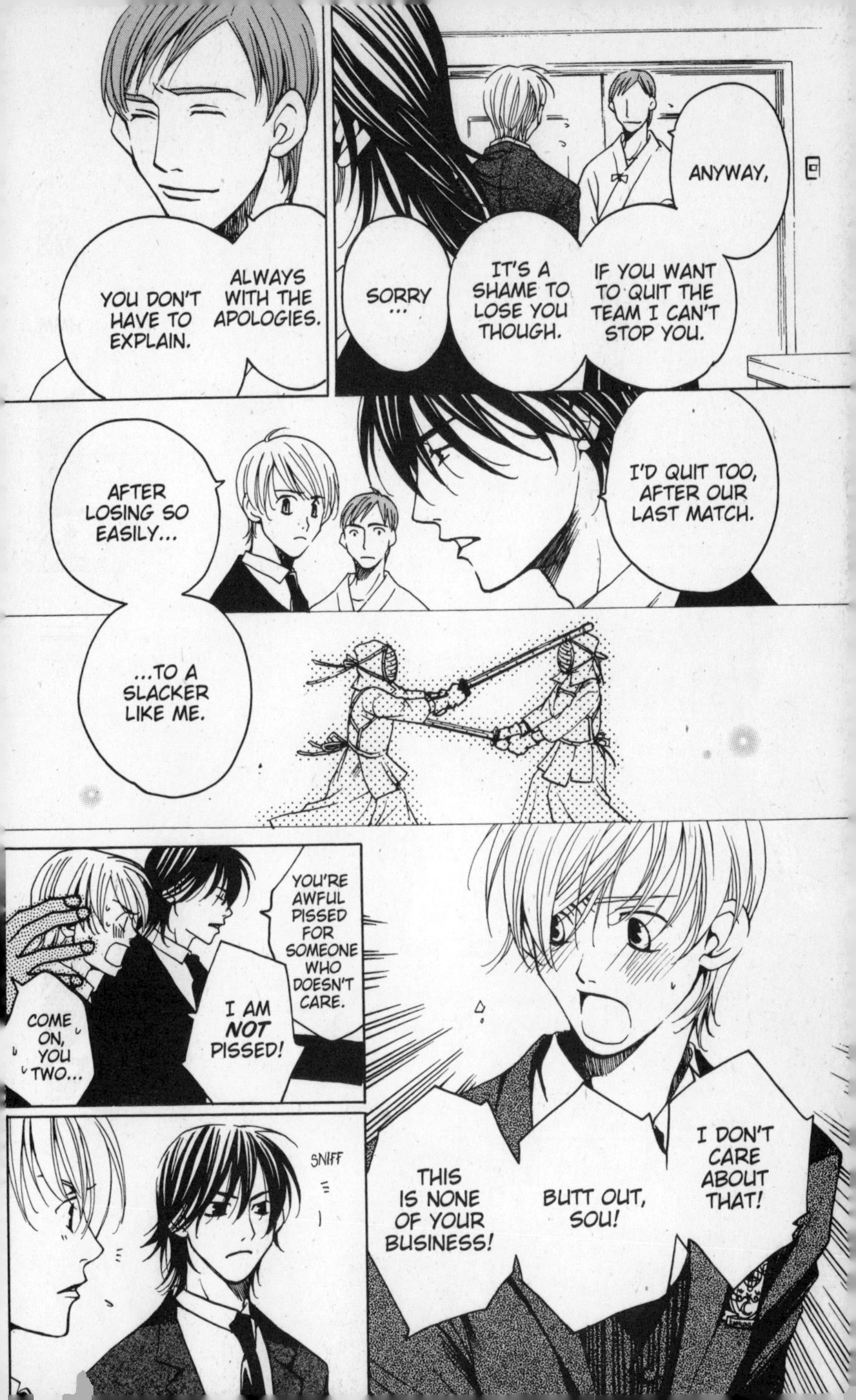

ANYWAY,
IF YOU WANT TO QUIT THE TEAM I CAN'T STOP YOU.
IT'S A SHAME TO LOSE YOU THOUGH.
SORRY...
ALWAYS WITH THE APOLOGIES.
YOU DON'T HAVE TO EXPLAIN.
I'D QUIT TOO, AFTER OUR LAST MATCH.
AFTER LOSING SO EASILY...
...TO A SLACKER LIKE ME.
I DON'T CARE ABOUT THAT!
BUTT OUT, SOU!
THIS IS NONE OF YOUR BUSINESS!
YOU'RE AWFUL PISSED FOR SOMEONE WHO DOESN'T CARE.
I AM **NOT** PISSED!
COME ON, YOU TWO...
SNIFF

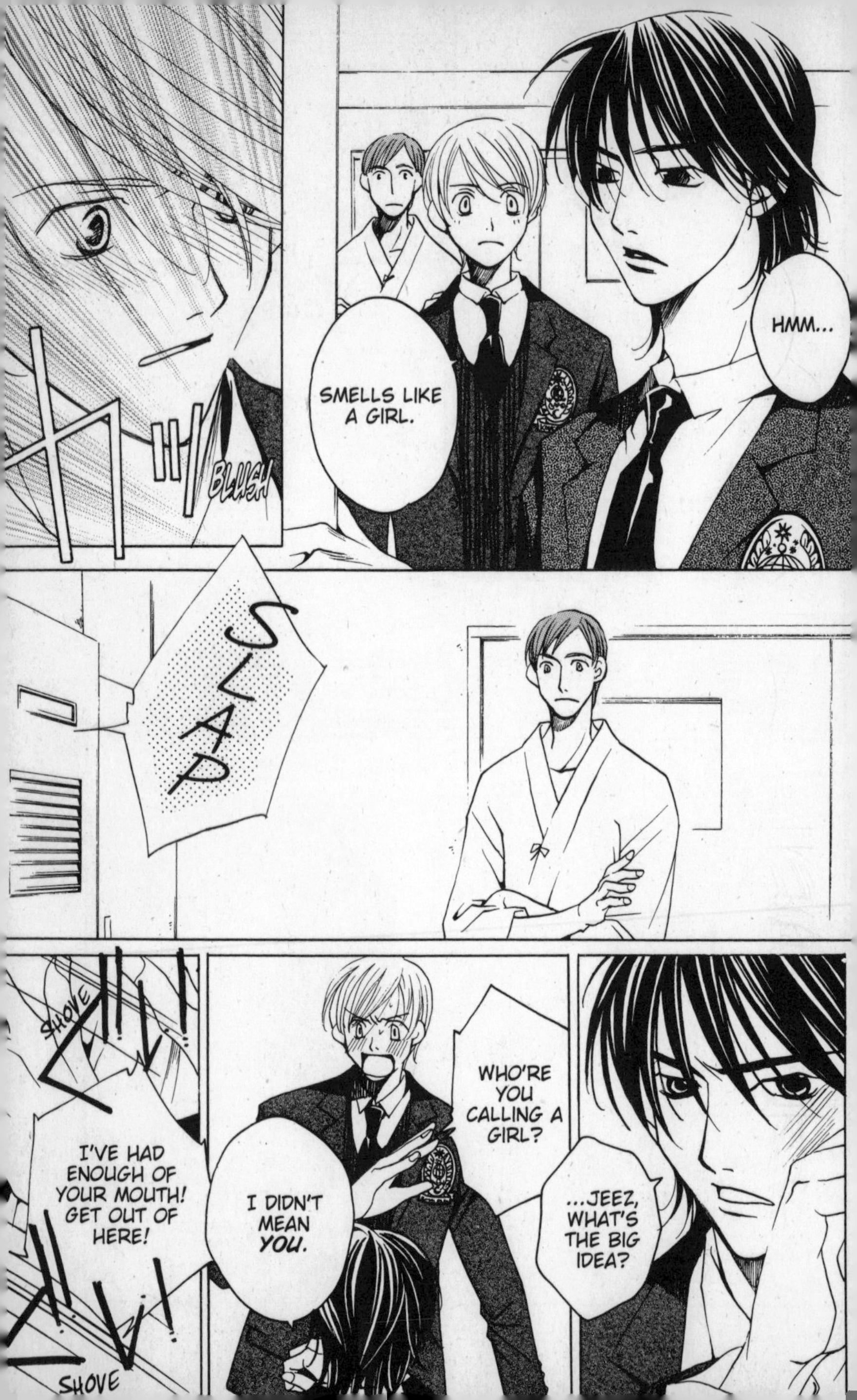
HMM...
SMELLS LIKE A GIRL.
BLUSH
SLAP
...JEEZ, WHAT'S THE BIG IDEA?
WHO'RE YOU CALLING A GIRL?
I DIDN'T MEAN *YOU*.
SHOVE
I'VE HAD ENOUGH OF YOUR MOUTH! GET OUT OF HERE!
SHOVE

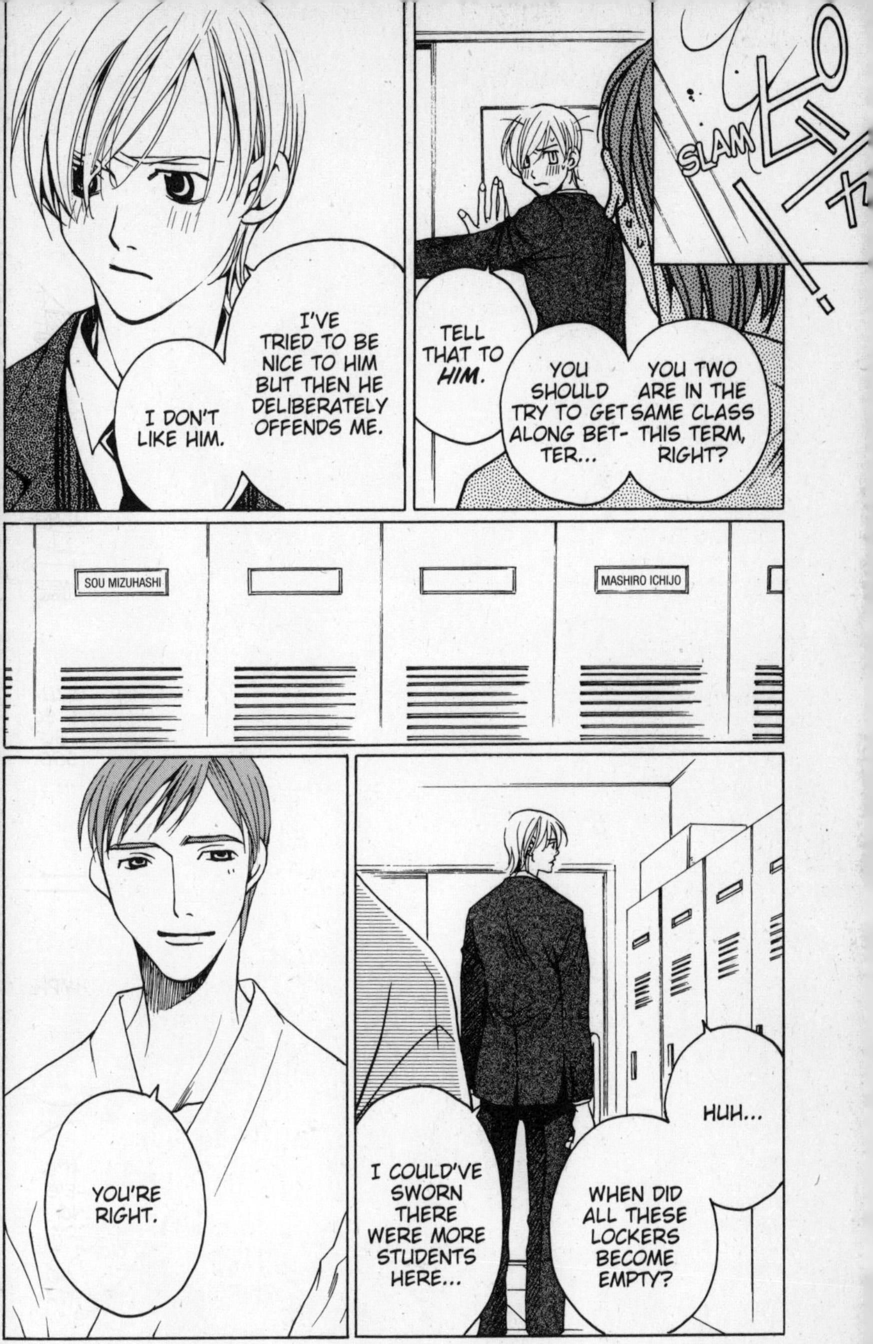
SLAM
YOU TWO ARE IN THE SAME CLASS THIS TERM, RIGHT?
YOU SHOULD TRY TO GET ALONG BETTER...
TELL THAT TO *HIM*.
I'VE TRIED TO BE NICE TO HIM BUT THEN HE DELIBERATELY OFFENDS ME.
I DON'T LIKE HIM.
MASHIRO ICHIJO
SOU MIZUHASHI
HUH...
WHEN DID ALL THESE LOCKERS BECOME EMPTY?
I COULD'VE SWORN THERE WERE MORE STUDENTS HERE...
YOU'RE RIGHT.

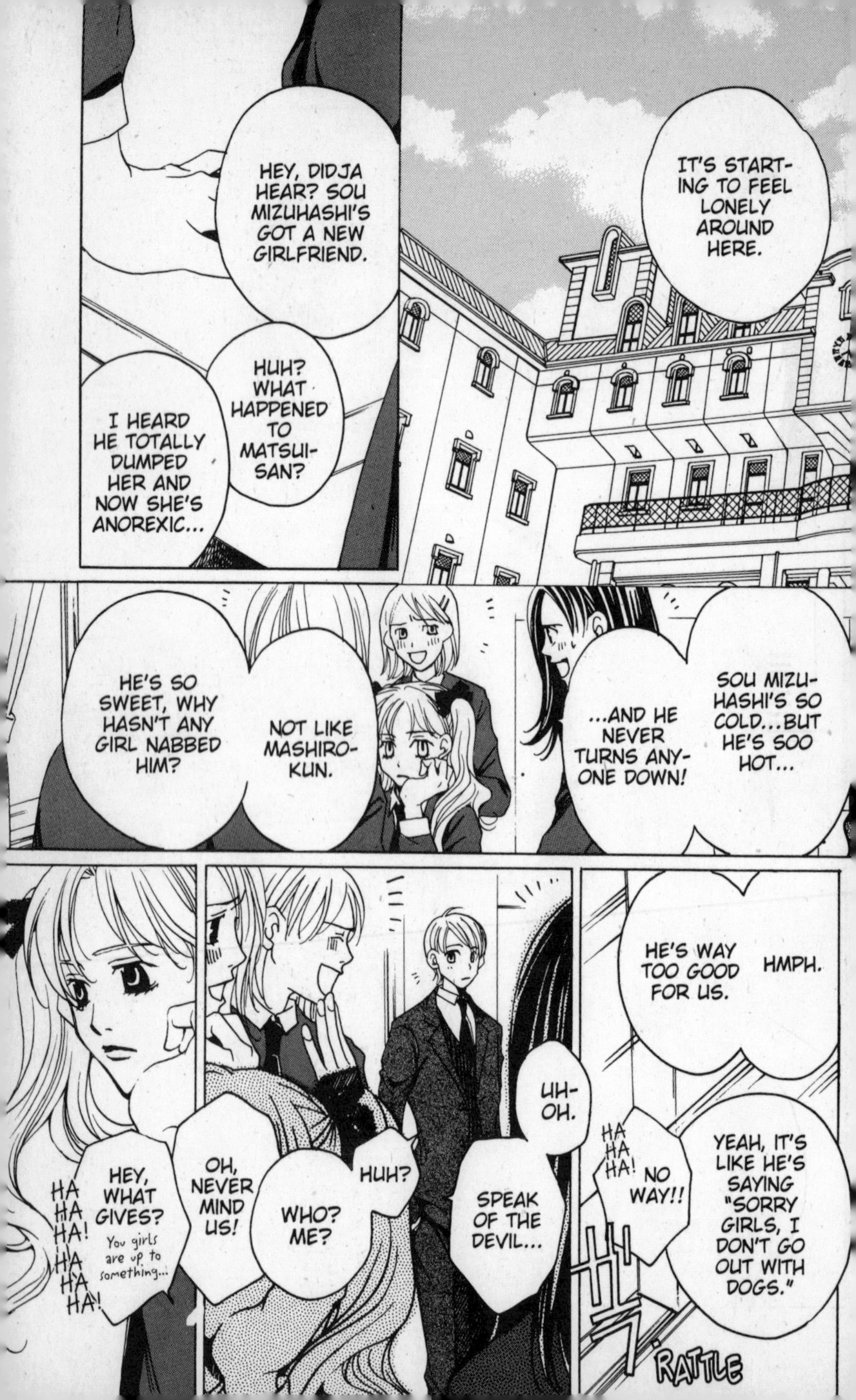
IT'S STARTING TO FEEL LONELY AROUND HERE.
HEY, DIDJA HEAR? SOU MIZUHASHI'S GOT A NEW GIRLFRIEND.
HUH? WHAT HAPPENED TO MATSUI-SAN?
I HEARD HE TOTALLY DUMPED HER AND NOW SHE'S ANOREXIC...
SOU MIZUHASHI'S SO COLD...BUT HE'S SOO HOT...
...AND HE NEVER TURNS ANYONE DOWN!
NOT LIKE MASHIRO-KUN.
HE'S SO SWEET, WHY HASN'T ANY GIRL NABBED HIM?
HMPH.
HE'S WAY TOO GOOD FOR US.
YEAH, IT'S LIKE HE'S SAYING "SORRY GIRLS, I DON'T GO OUT WITH DOGS."
HA HA HA!
NO WAY!!
RATTLE
UH-OH.
SPEAK OF THE DEVIL...
HUH?
WHO? ME?
OH, NEVER MIND US!
HEY, WHAT GIVES?
You girls are up to something...
HA HA HA! HA HA HA!

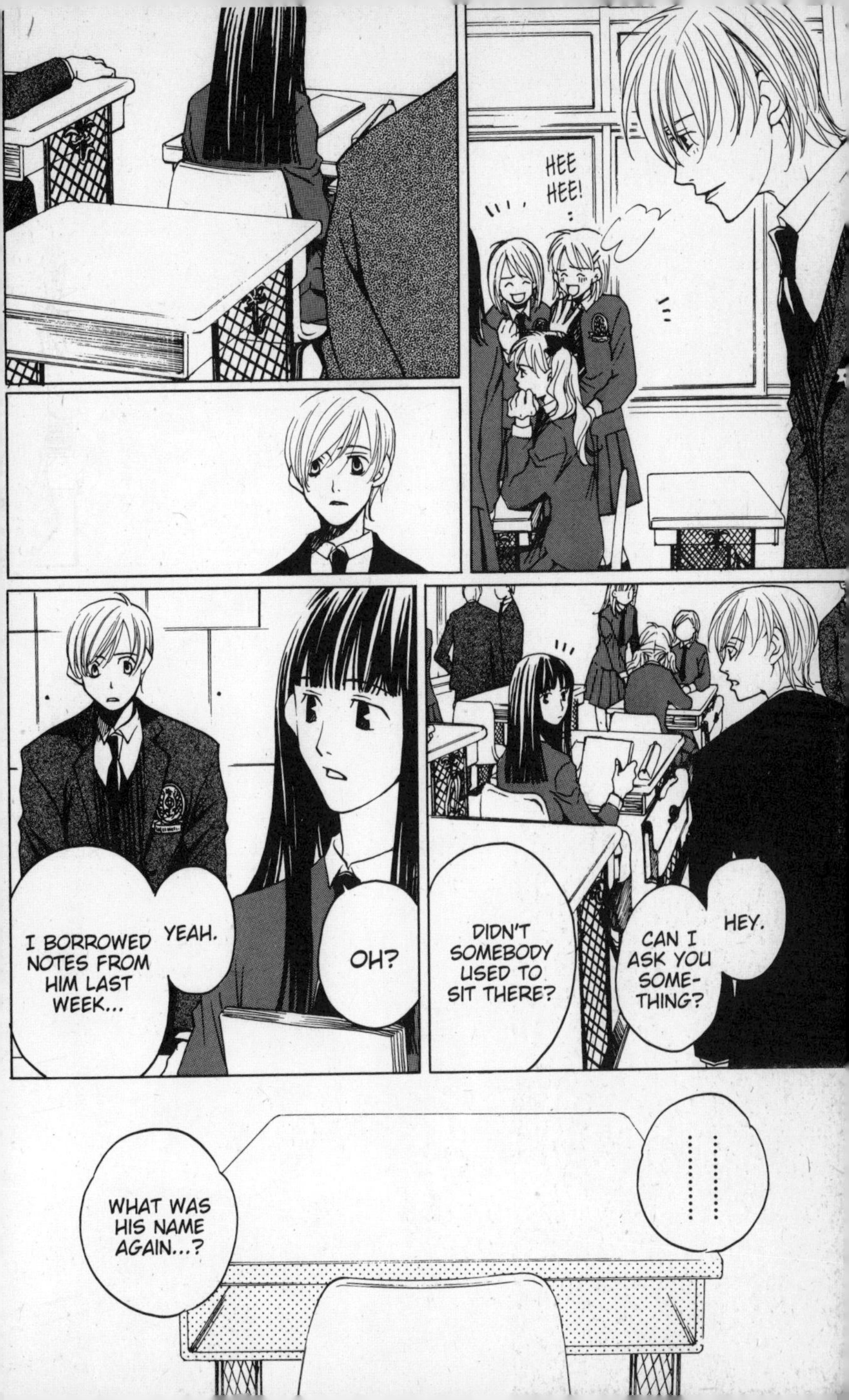
HEE HEE!
HEY.
CAN I ASK YOU SOME-THING?
DIDN'T SOMEBODY USED TO SIT THERE?
OH?
YEAH.
I BORROWED NOTES FROM HIM LAST WEEK...
......
WHAT WAS HIS NAME AGAIN...?

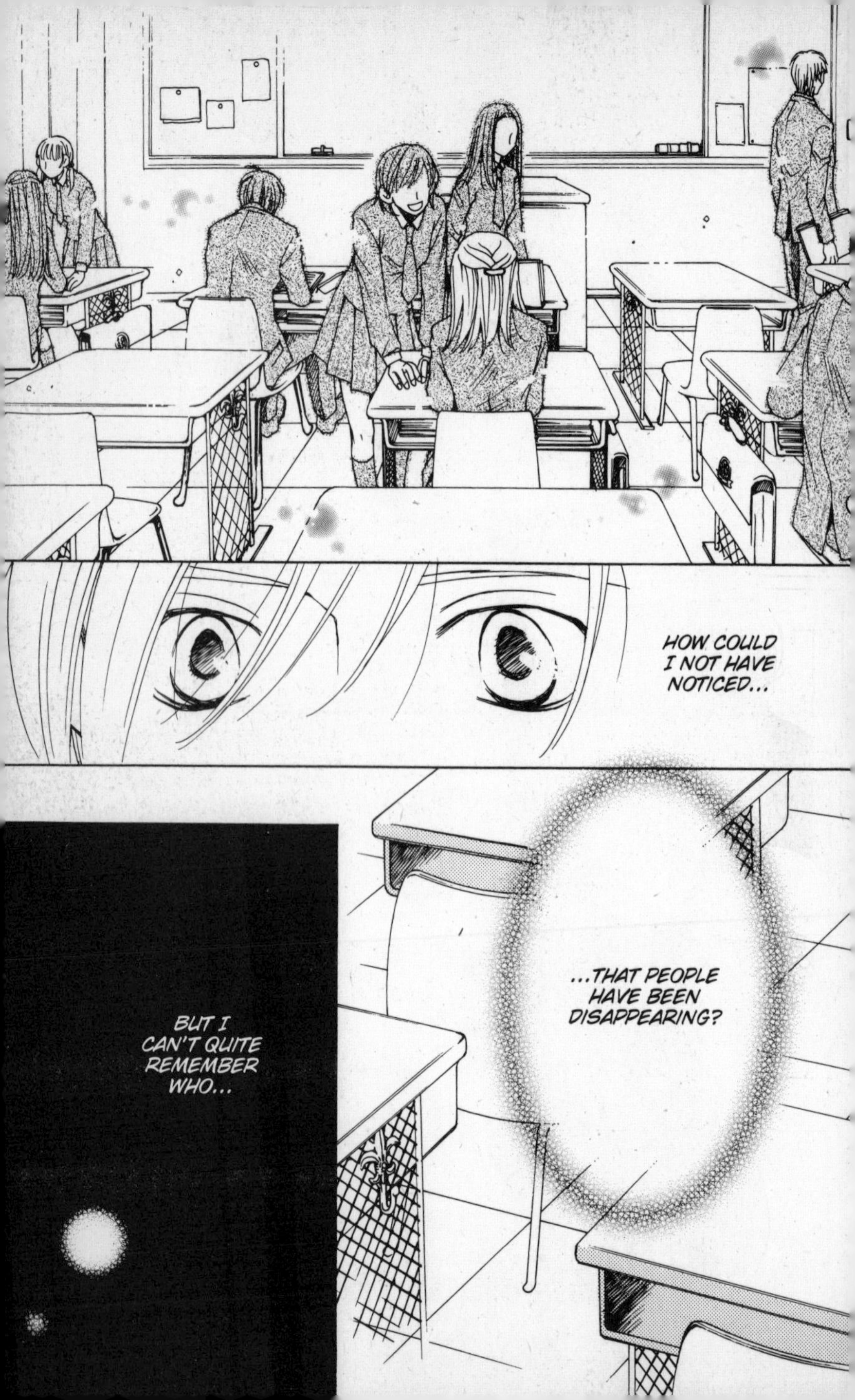
HOW COULD I NOT HAVE NOTICED...
...THAT PEOPLE HAVE BEEN DISAPPEARING?
BUT I CAN'T QUITE REMEMBER WHO...

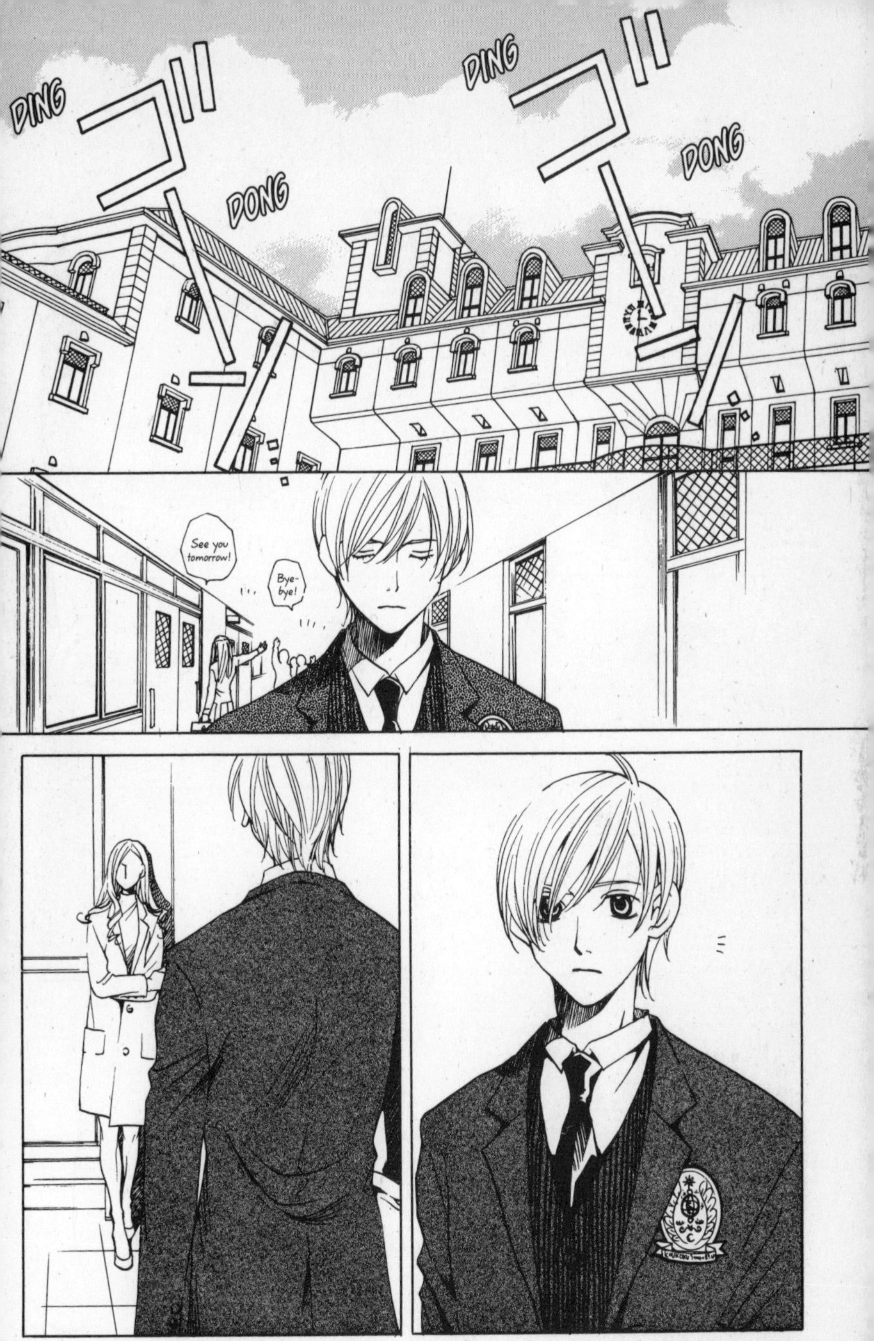
DING
DONG
DING
DONG
See you tomorrow!
Bye-bye!

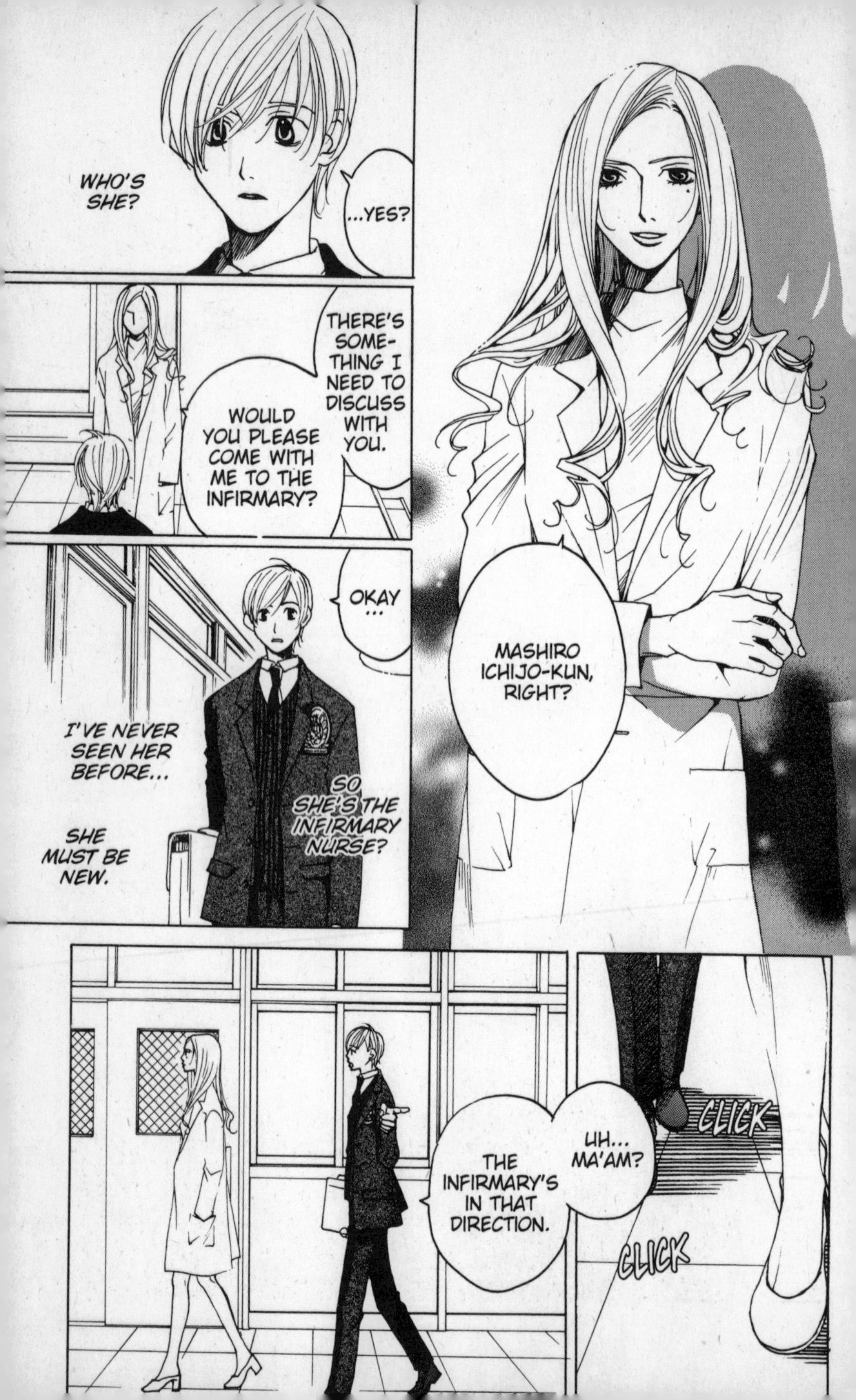
MASHIRO ICHIJO-KUN, RIGHT?
...YES?
WHO'S SHE?
THERE'S SOME-THING I NEED TO DISCUSS WITH YOU.
WOULD YOU PLEASE COME WITH ME TO THE INFIRMARY?
OKAY ...
SO SHE'S THE INFIRMARY NURSE?
I'VE NEVER SEEN HER BEFORE...
SHE MUST BE NEW.
CLICK
CLICK
UH... MA'AM?
THE INFIRMARY'S IN THAT DIRECTION.

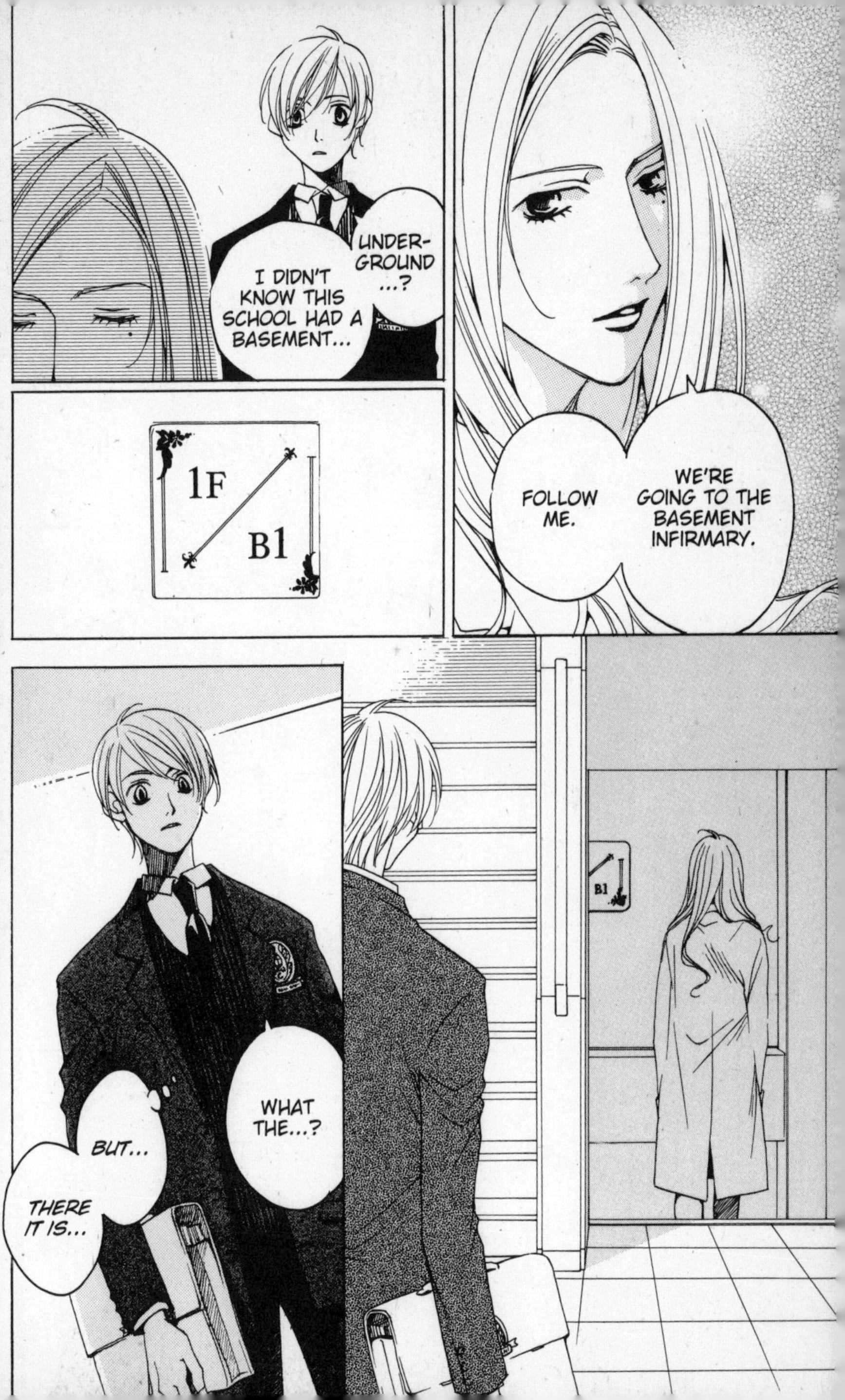
WE'RE GOING TO THE BASEMENT INFIRMARY.
FOLLOW ME.
UNDER-GROUND ...?
I DIDN'T KNOW THIS SCHOOL HAD A BASEMENT...
1F
B1
B1
WHAT THE...?
BUT...
THERE IT IS...

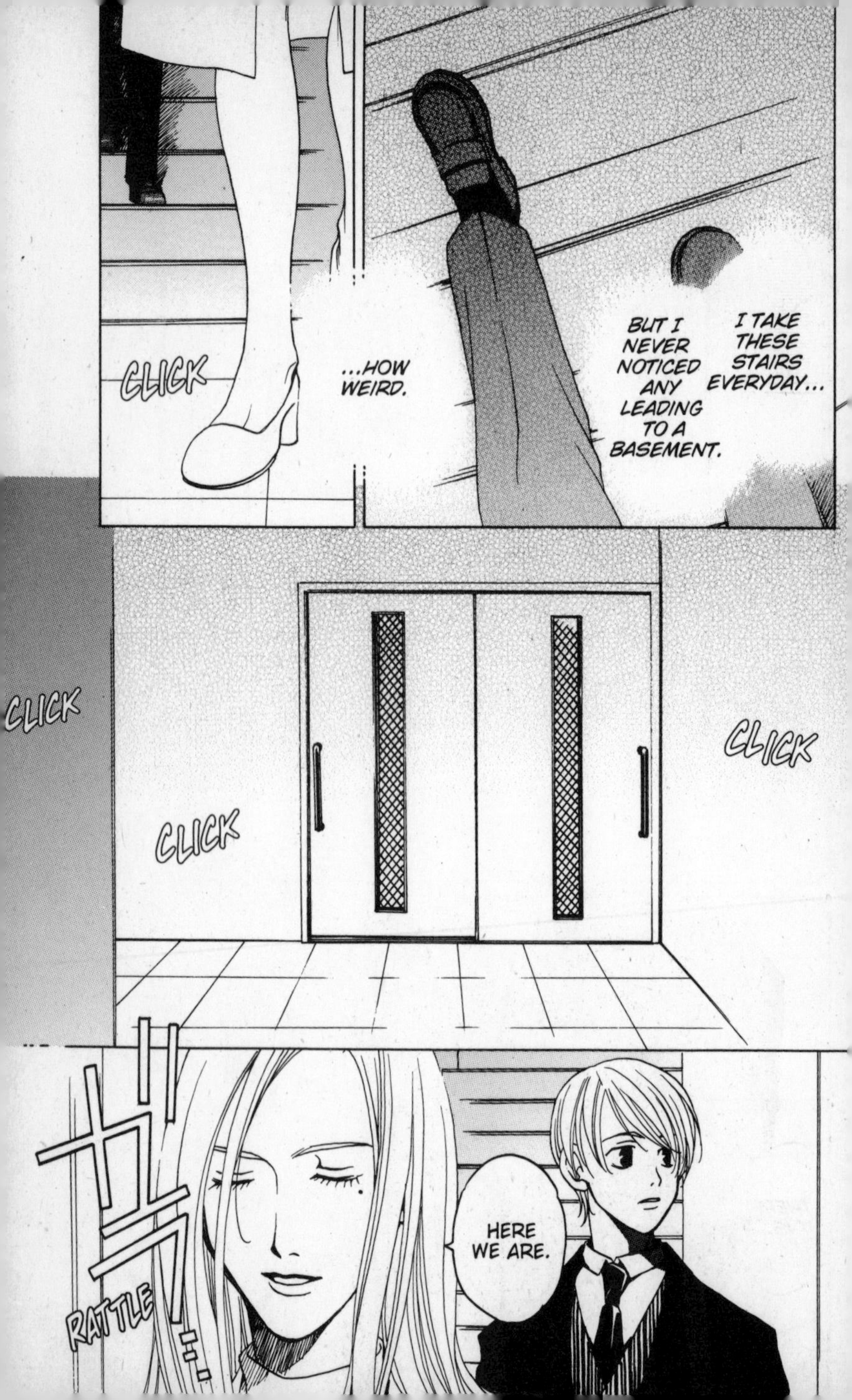
I TAKE THESE STAIRS EVERYDAY...
BUT I NEVER NOTICED ANY LEADING TO A BASEMENT.
...HOW WEIRD.
CLICK
CLICK
CLICK
CLICK
HERE WE ARE.
RATTLE

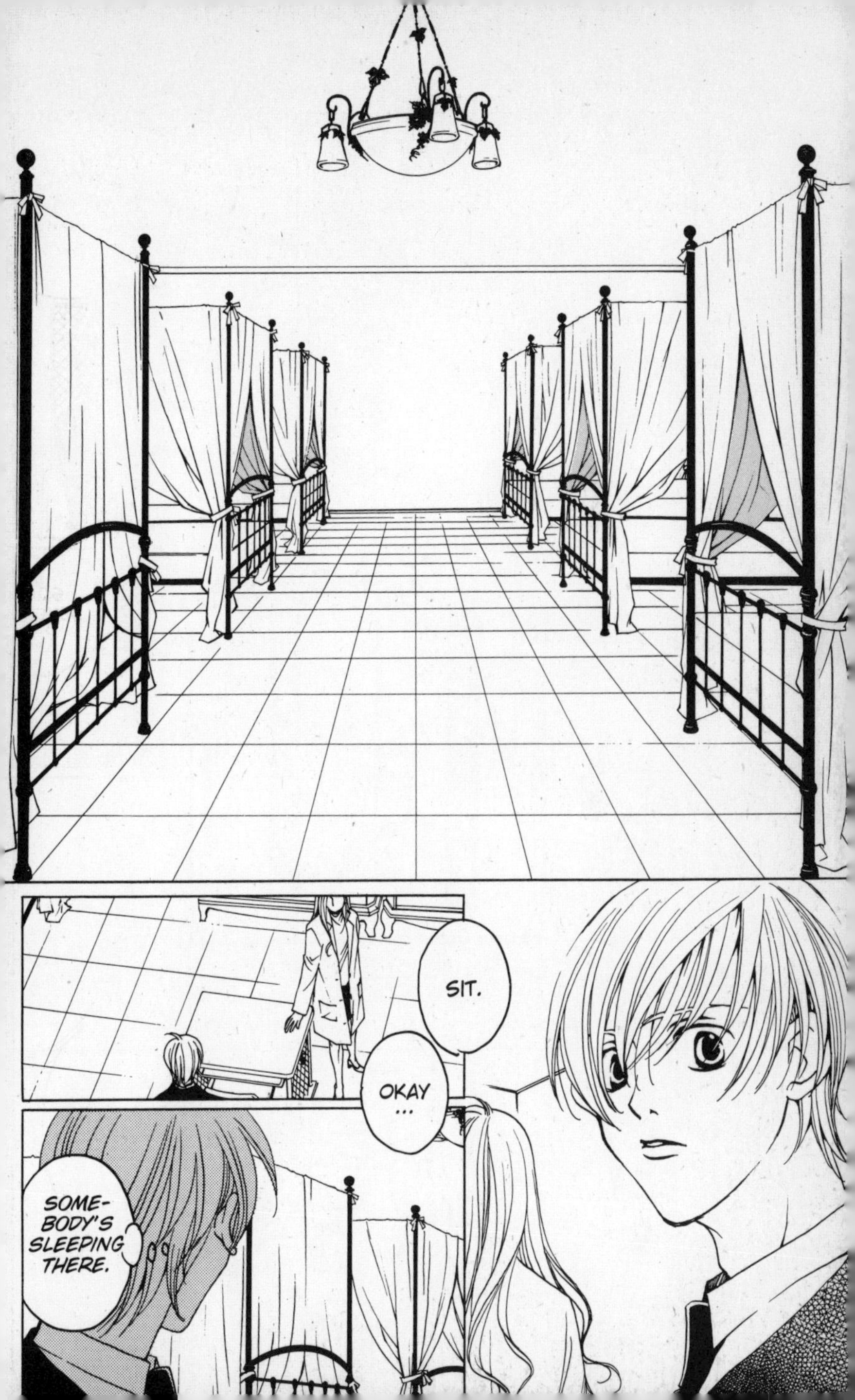
SIT.
OKAY ...
SOME-BODY'S SLEEPING THERE.

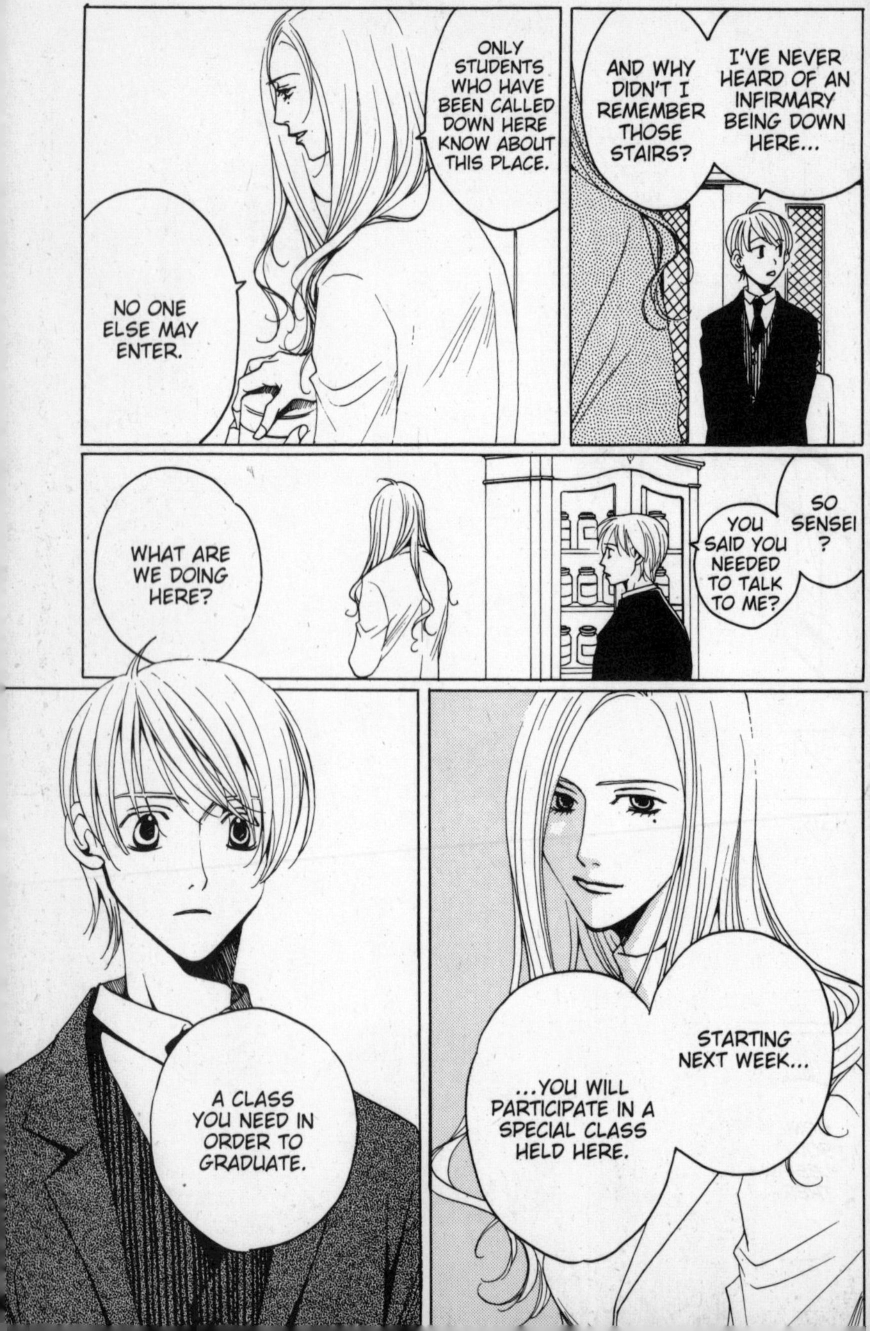
I'VE NEVER HEARD OF AN INFIRMARY BEING DOWN HERE...
AND WHY DIDN'T I REMEMBER THOSE STAIRS?
ONLY STUDENTS WHO HAVE BEEN CALLED DOWN HERE KNOW ABOUT THIS PLACE.
NO ONE ELSE MAY ENTER.
SO SENSEI?
YOU SAID YOU NEEDED TO TALK TO ME?
WHAT ARE WE DOING HERE?
STARTING NEXT WEEK...
...YOU WILL PARTICIPATE IN A SPECIAL CLASS HELD HERE.
A CLASS YOU NEED IN ORDER TO GRADUATE.

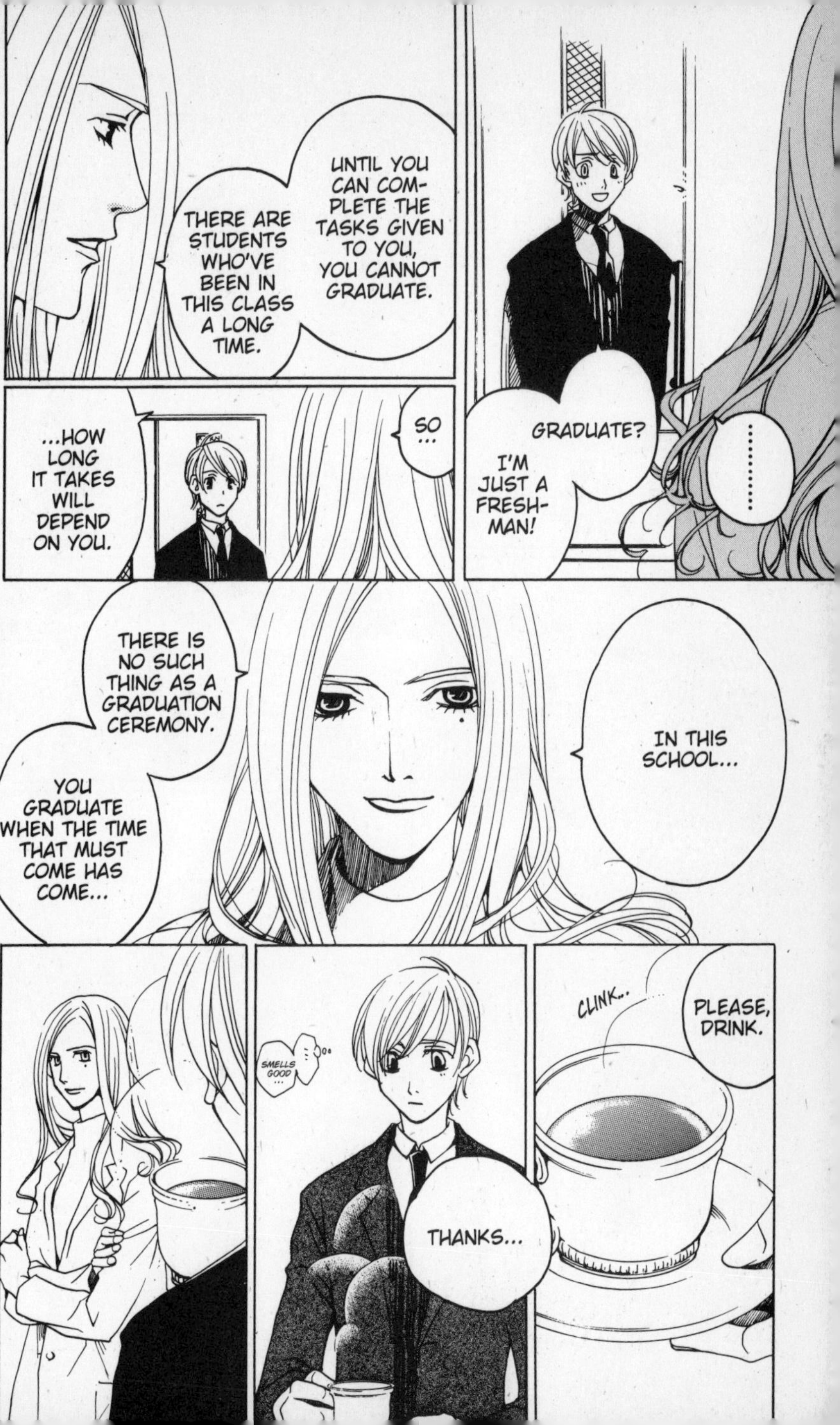
GRADUATE? I'M JUST A FRESHMAN!
....
UNTIL YOU CAN COMPLETE THE TASKS GIVEN TO YOU, YOU CANNOT GRADUATE.
THERE ARE STUDENTS WHO'VE BEEN IN THIS CLASS A LONG TIME.
SO...
...HOW LONG IT TAKES WILL DEPEND ON YOU.
IN THIS SCHOOL...
THERE IS NO SUCH THING AS A GRADUATION CEREMONY.
YOU GRADUATE WHEN THE TIME THAT MUST COME HAS COME...
CLINK...
PLEASE, DRINK.
SMELLS GOOD...
THANKS...

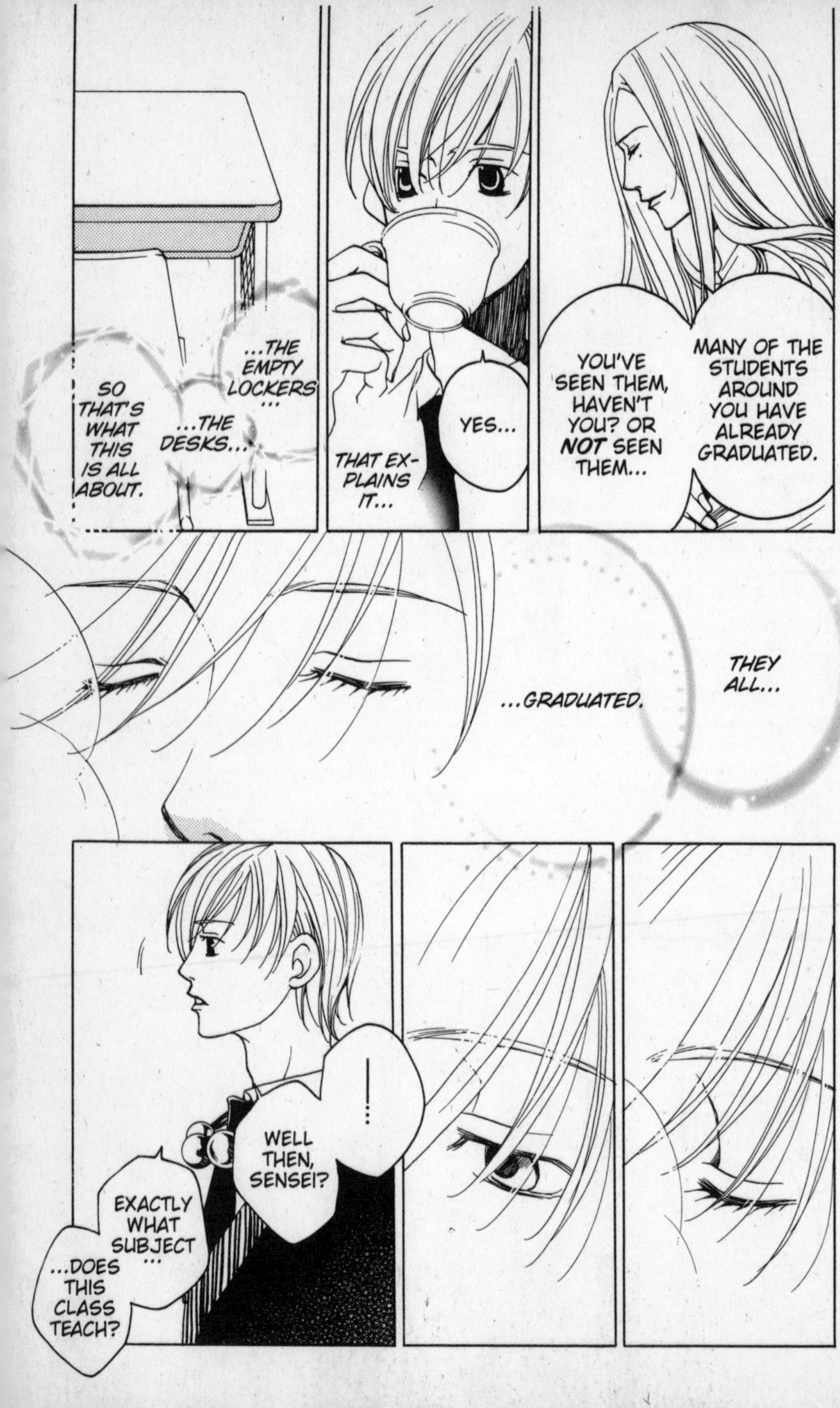
MANY OF THE STUDENTS AROUND YOU HAVE ALREADY GRADUATED.
YOU'VE SEEN THEM, HAVEN'T YOU? OR NOT SEEN THEM...
YES...
THAT EX-PLAINS IT...
...THE EMPTY LOCKERS...
...THE DESKS...
SO THAT'S WHAT THIS IS ALL ABOUT.
THEY ALL...
...GRADUATED.
!...
WELL THEN, SENSEI?
EXACTLY WHAT SUBJECT...
...DOES THIS CLASS TEACH?

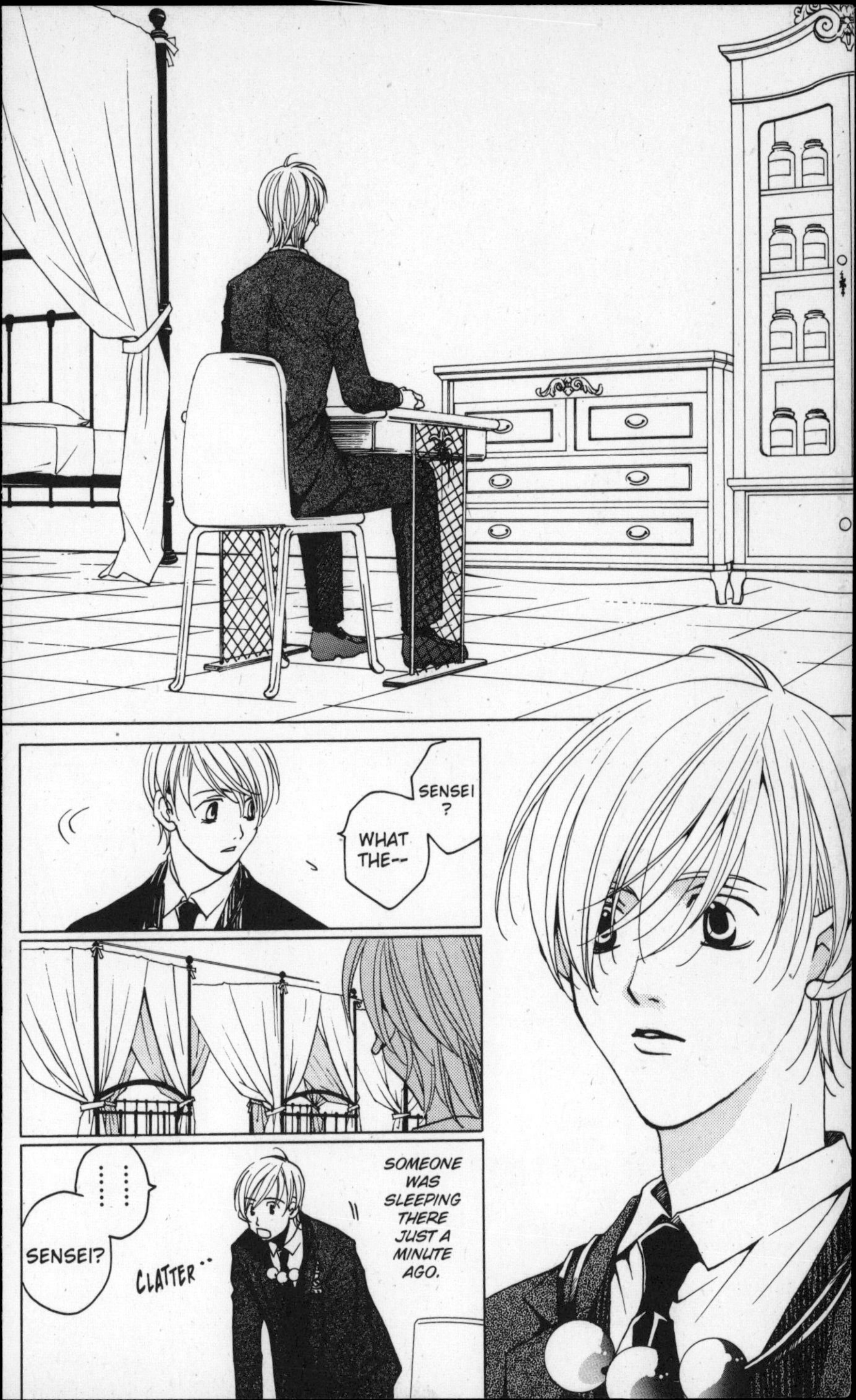
SENSEI?
WHAT THE--
SOMEONE WAS SLEEPING THERE JUST A MINUTE AGO.
......
SENSEI?
CLATTER..

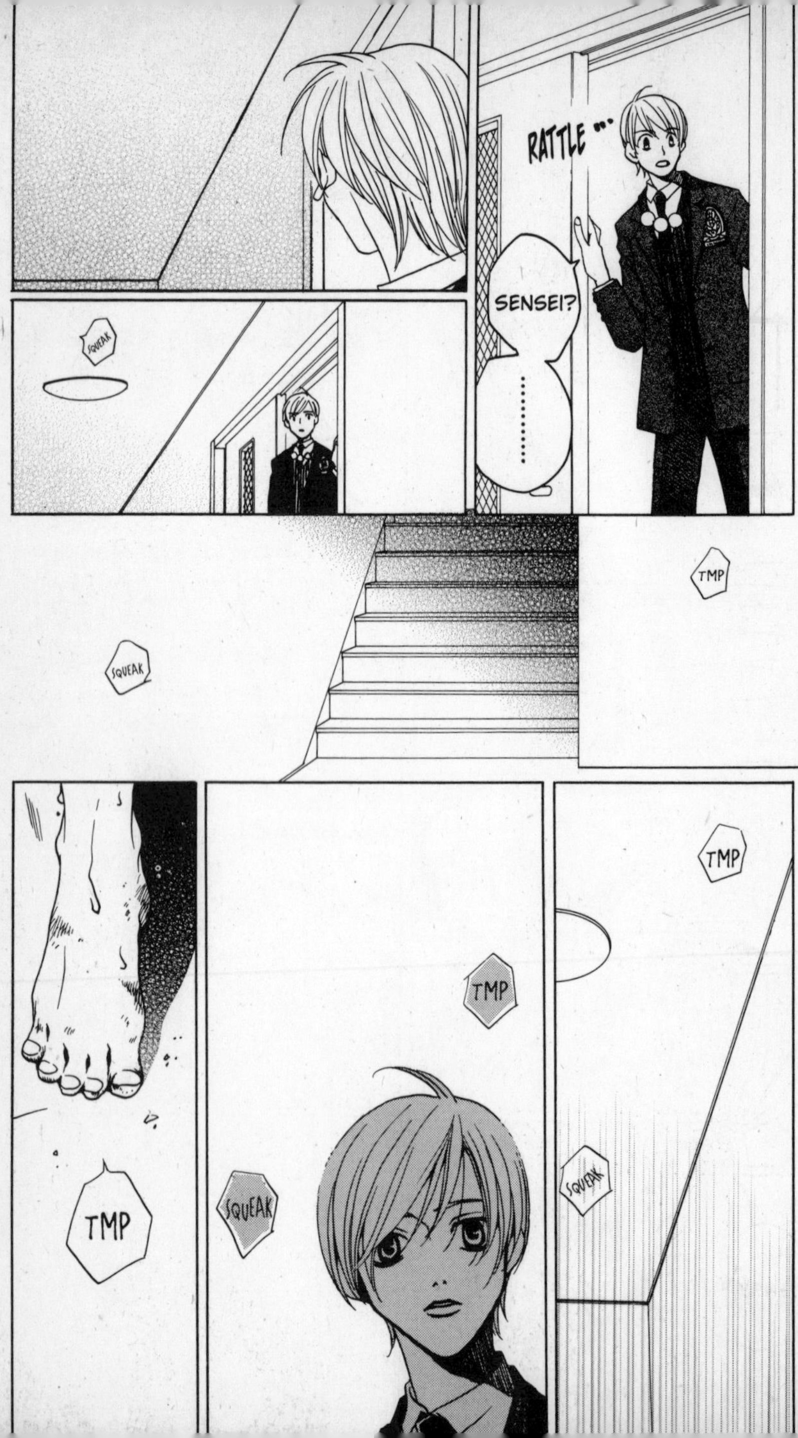
RATTLE...
SENSEI?
......
SQUEAK
TMP
SQUEAK
TMP
SQUEAK
TMP
SQUEAK
TMP

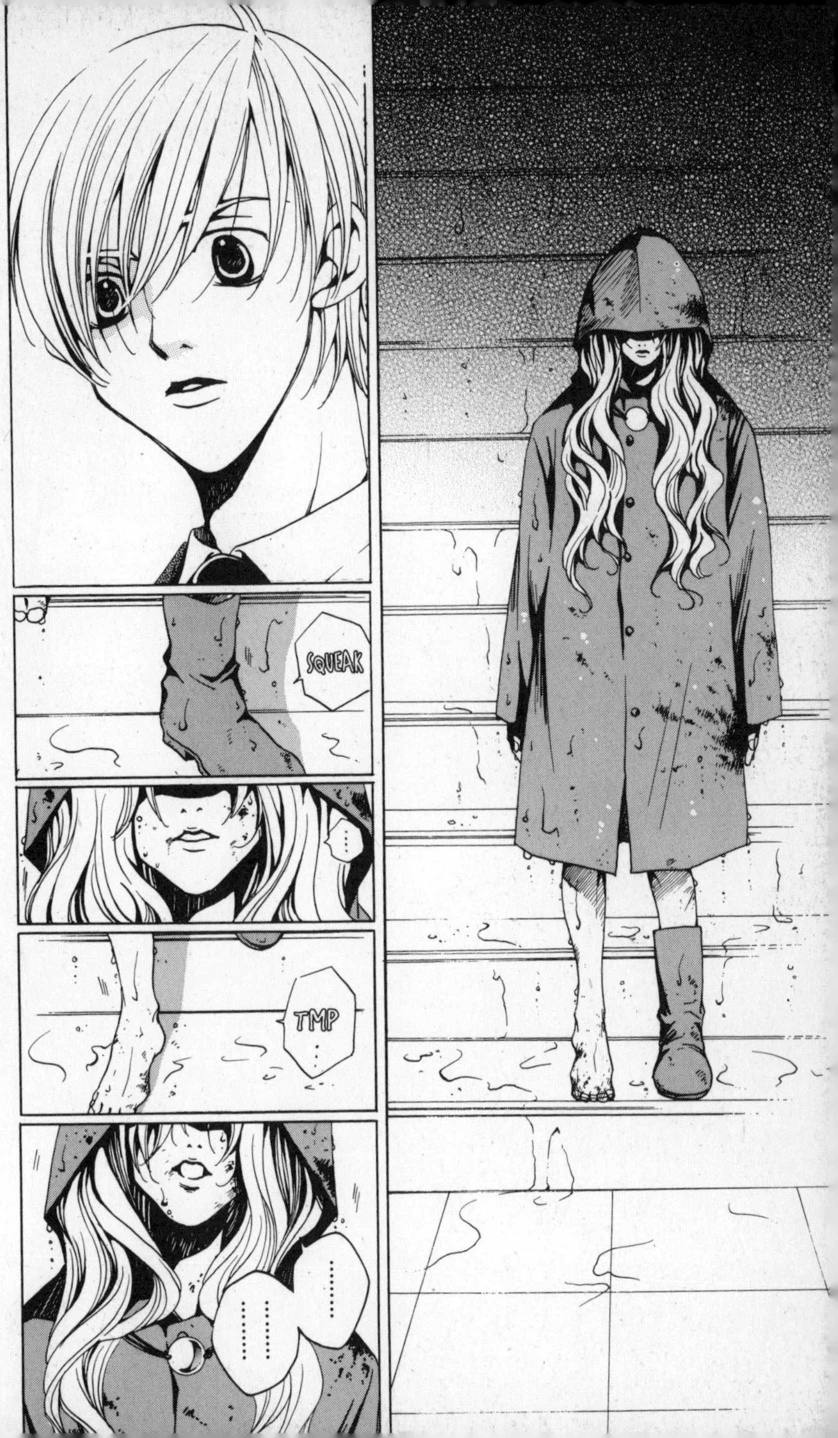
SQUEAK
...
TMP ...
......

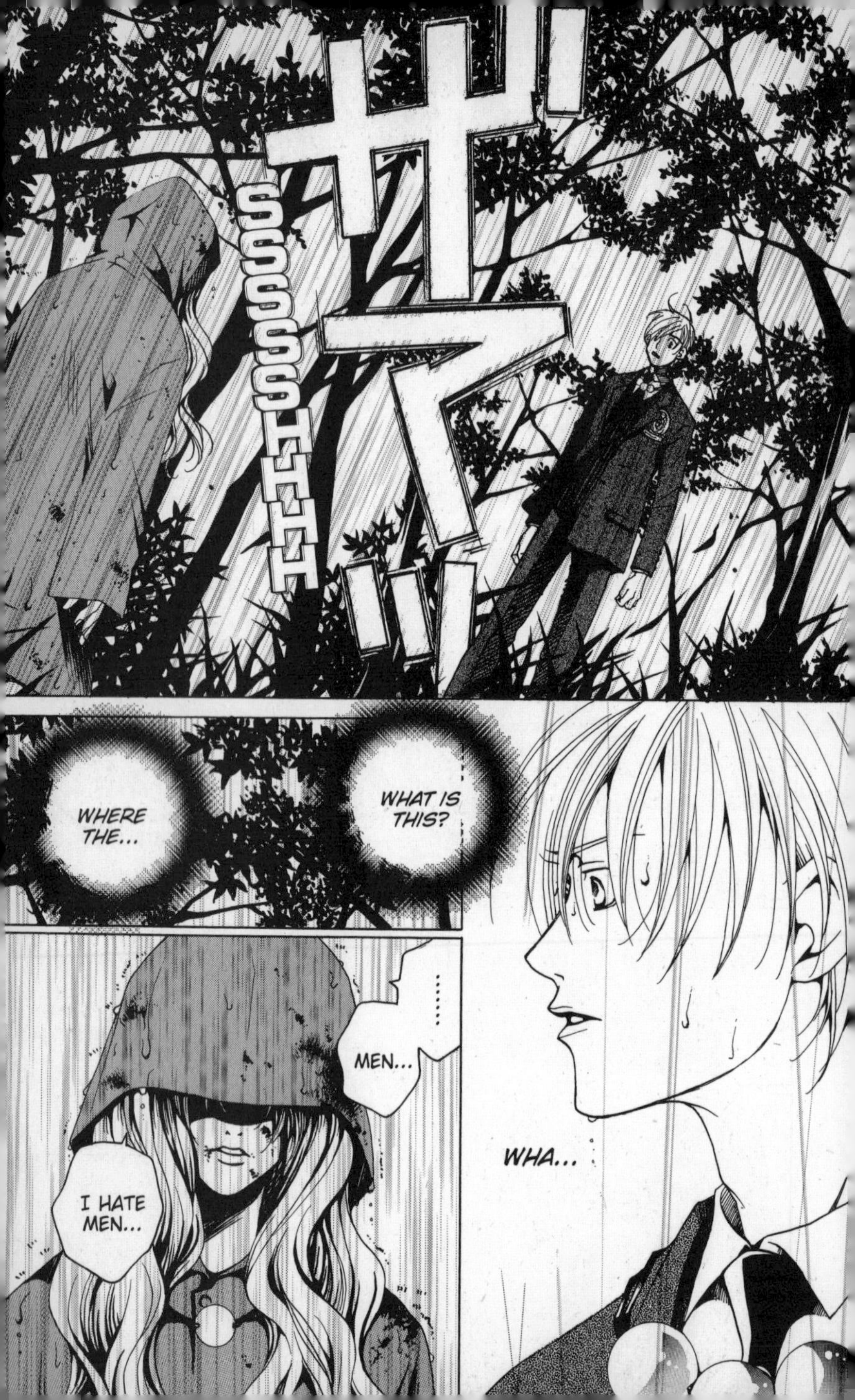
SSSSSHHHH
WHA...
WHAT IS THIS?
WHERE THE...
......
MEN...
I HATE MEN...

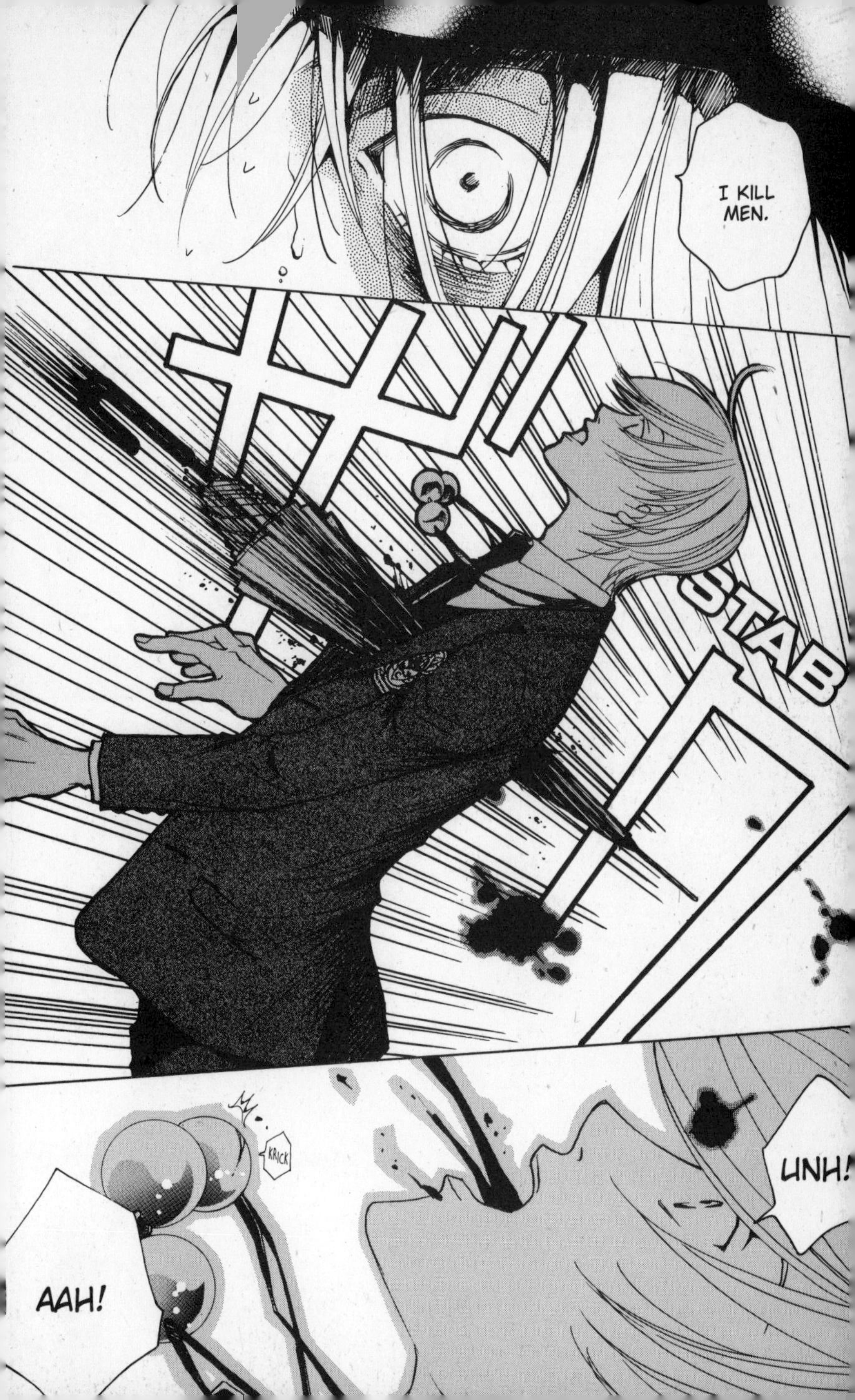
I KILL MEN.
STAB
UNH!
KRICK
AAH!

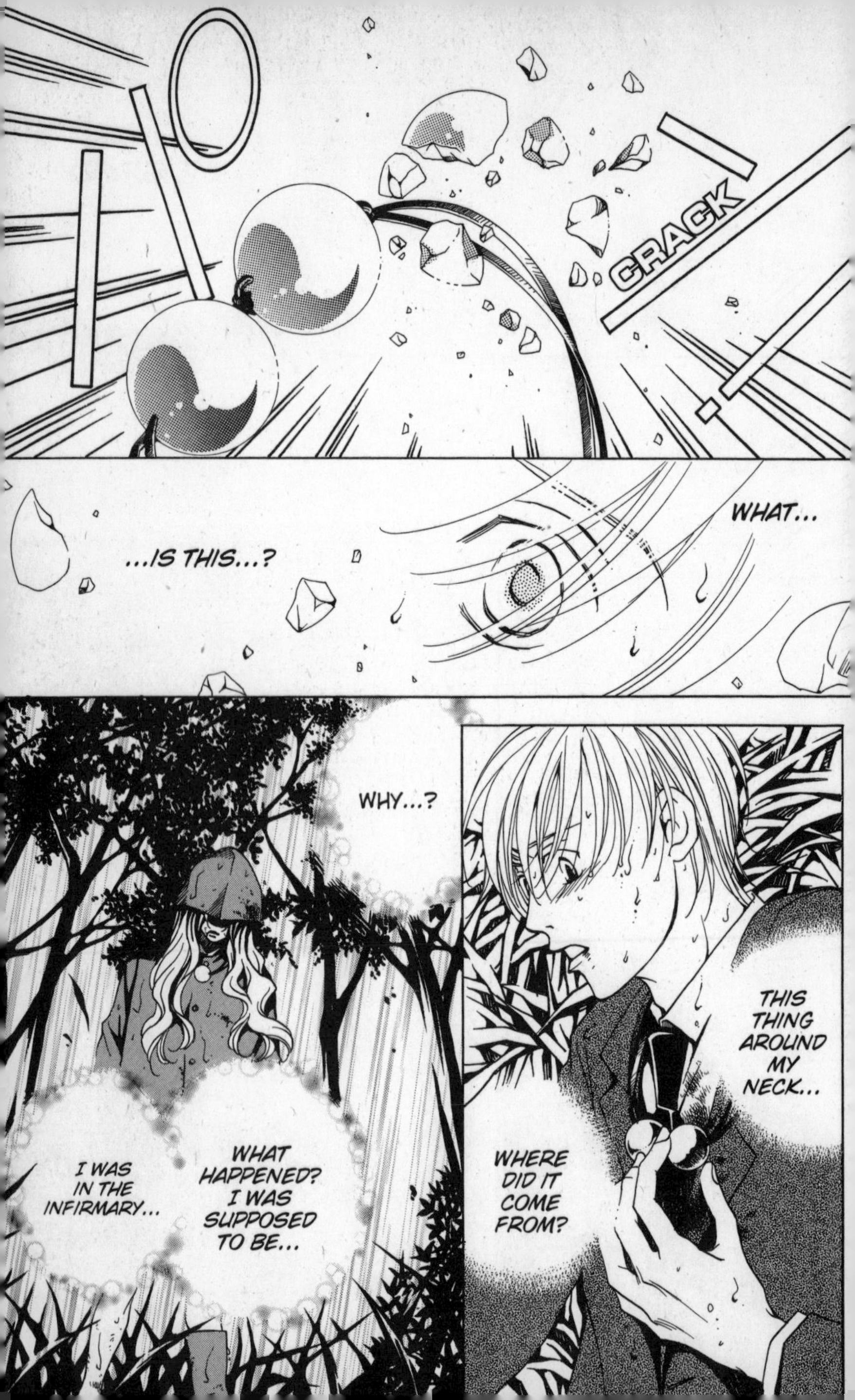
CRACK
WHAT...
...IS THIS...?
THIS THING AROUND MY NECK...
WHERE DID IT COME FROM?
WHY...?
WHAT HAPPENED? I WAS SUPPOSED TO BE...
I WAS IN THE INFIRMARY...

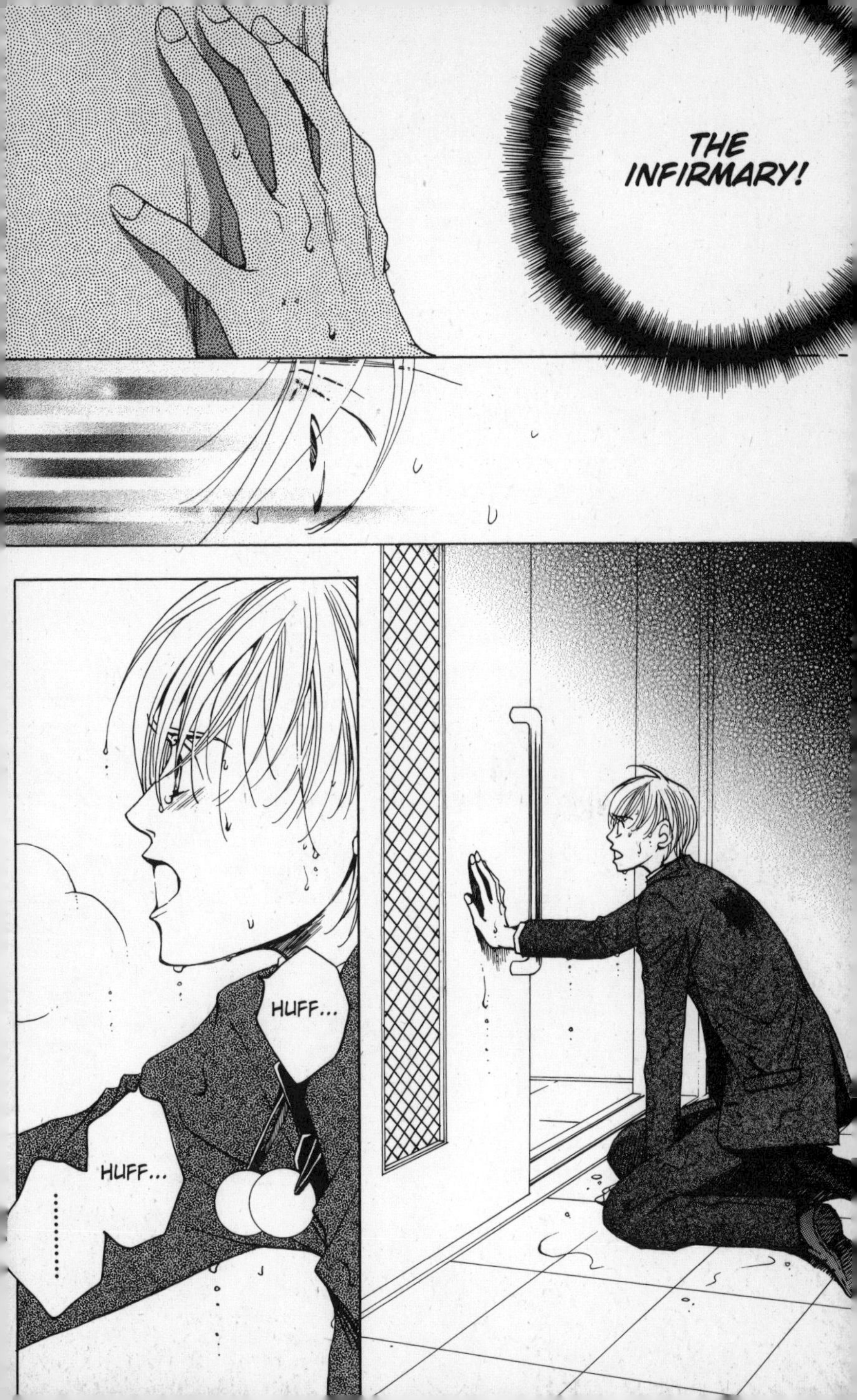
THE INFIRMARY!
HUFF...
HUFF...

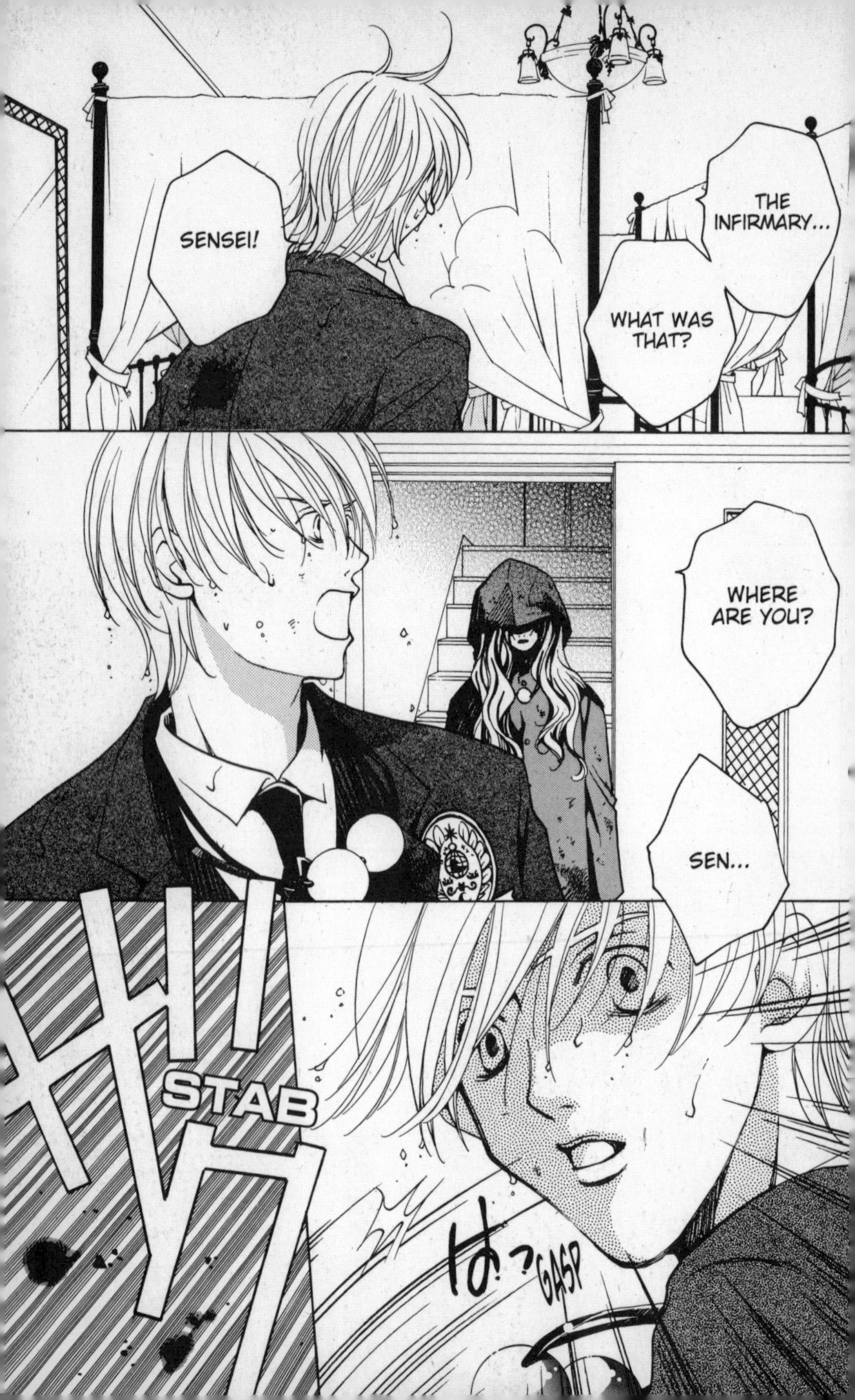
THE INFIRMARY...
WHAT WAS THAT?
SENSEI!
WHERE ARE YOU?
SEN...
GASP
STAB

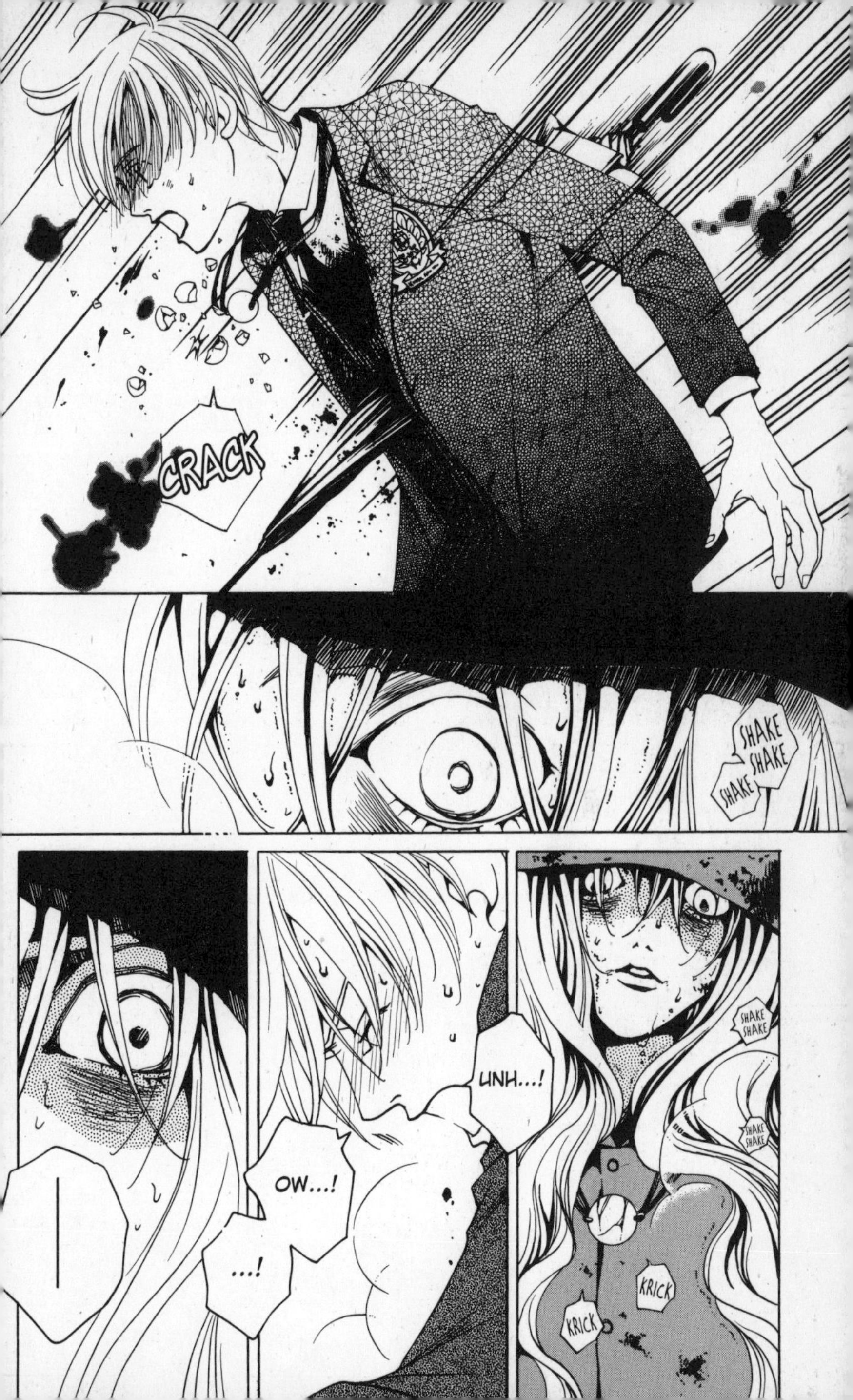
CRACK
SHAKE SHAKE SHAKE
SHAKE SHAKE
SHAKE SHAKE
KRICK
KRICK
UNH...!
OW...!
...!
—

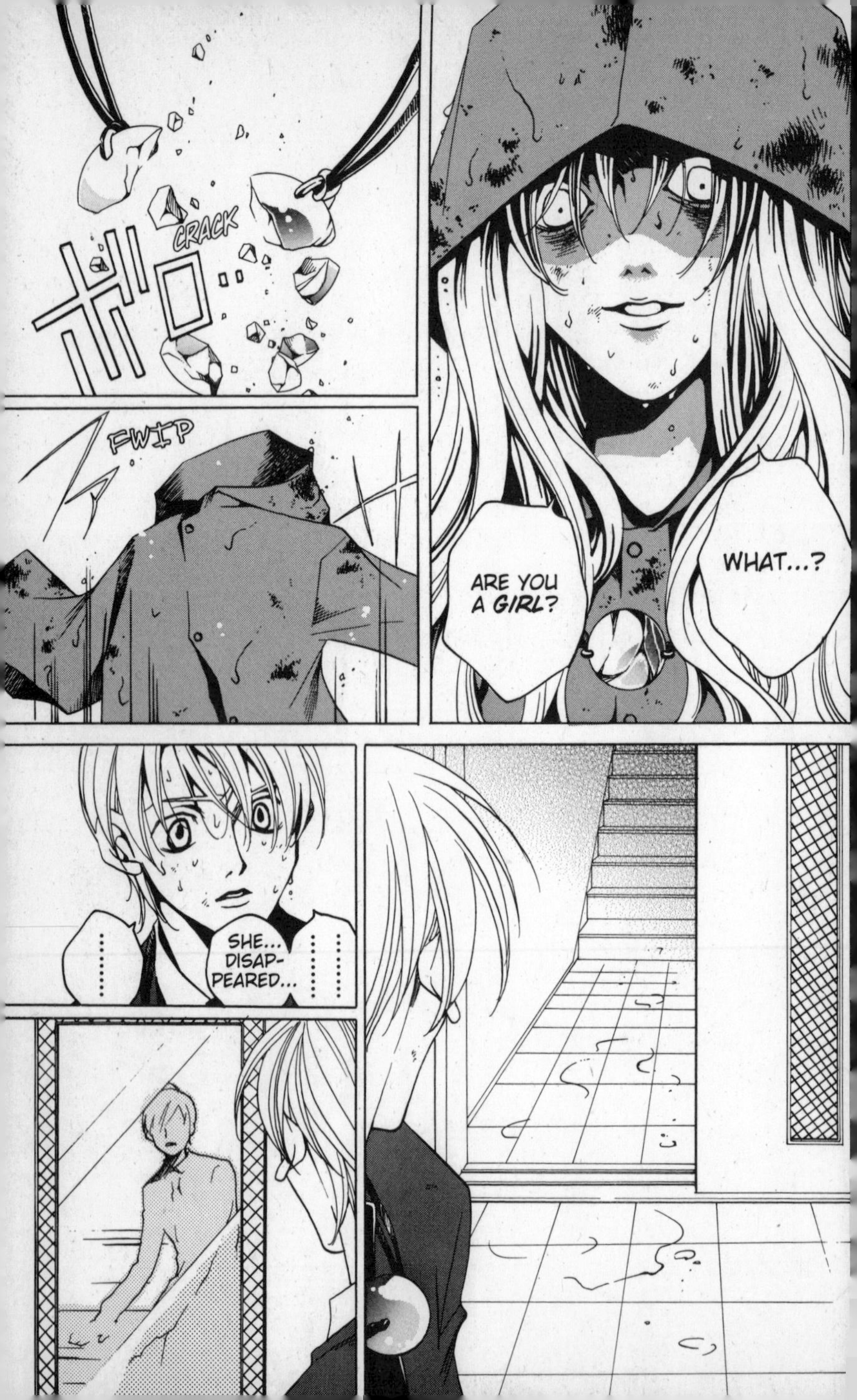
WHAT...?
ARE YOU A GIRL?
CRACK
FWIP
......
SHE... DISAP-PEARED...
......

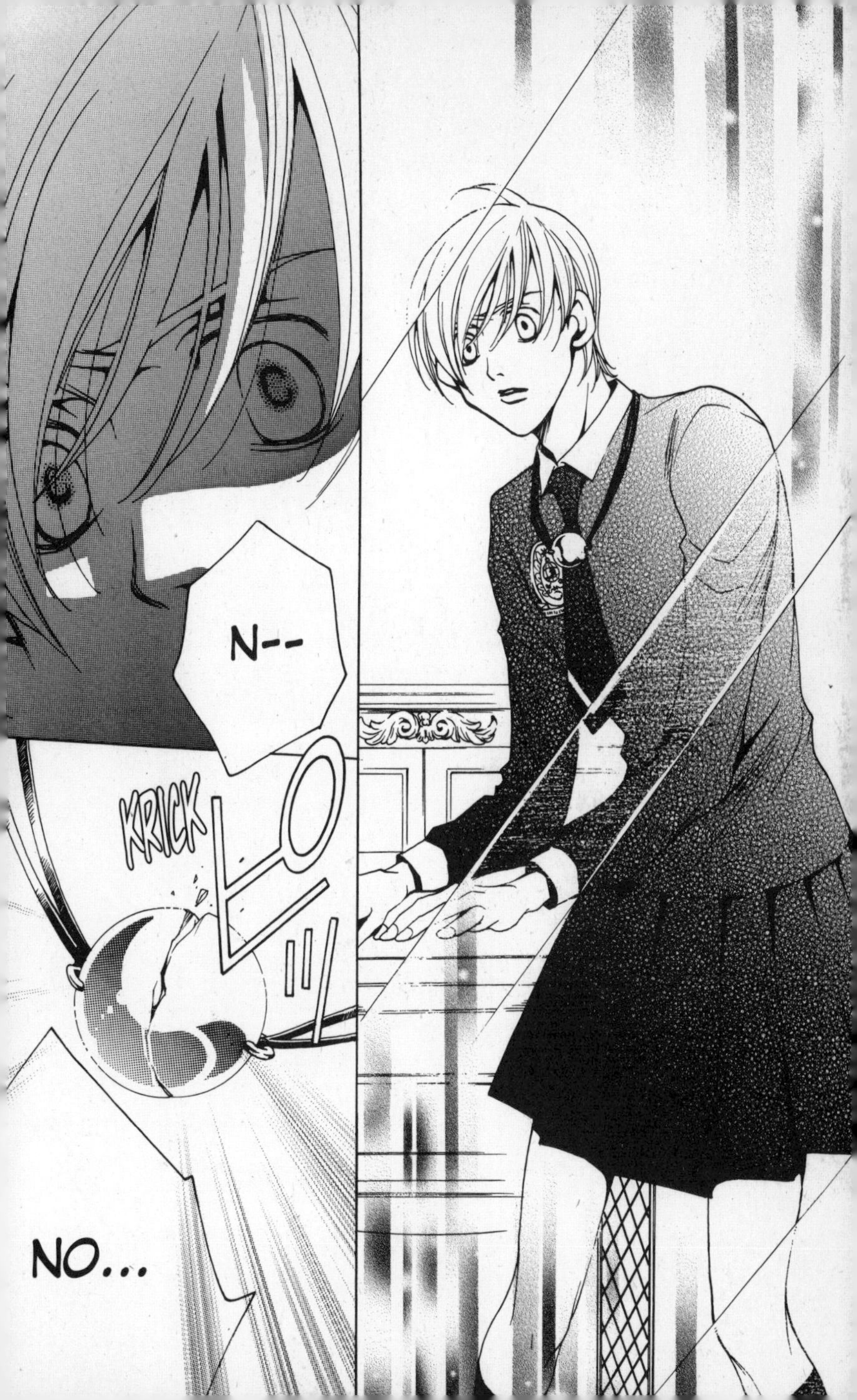
N--
KRICK
NO...

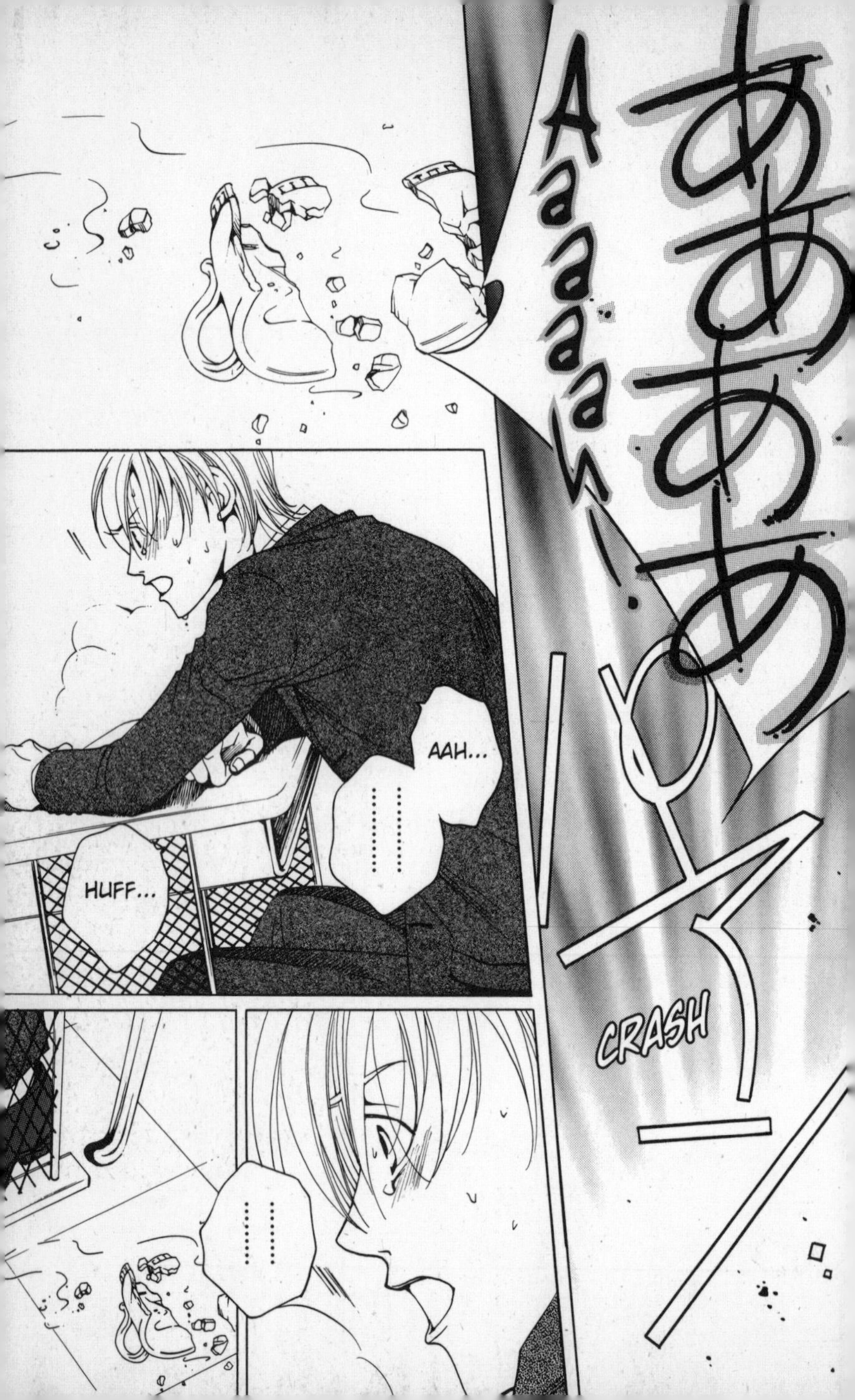
ああああ
Aaaaaaah!
CRASH
AAH...
......
HUFF...
......

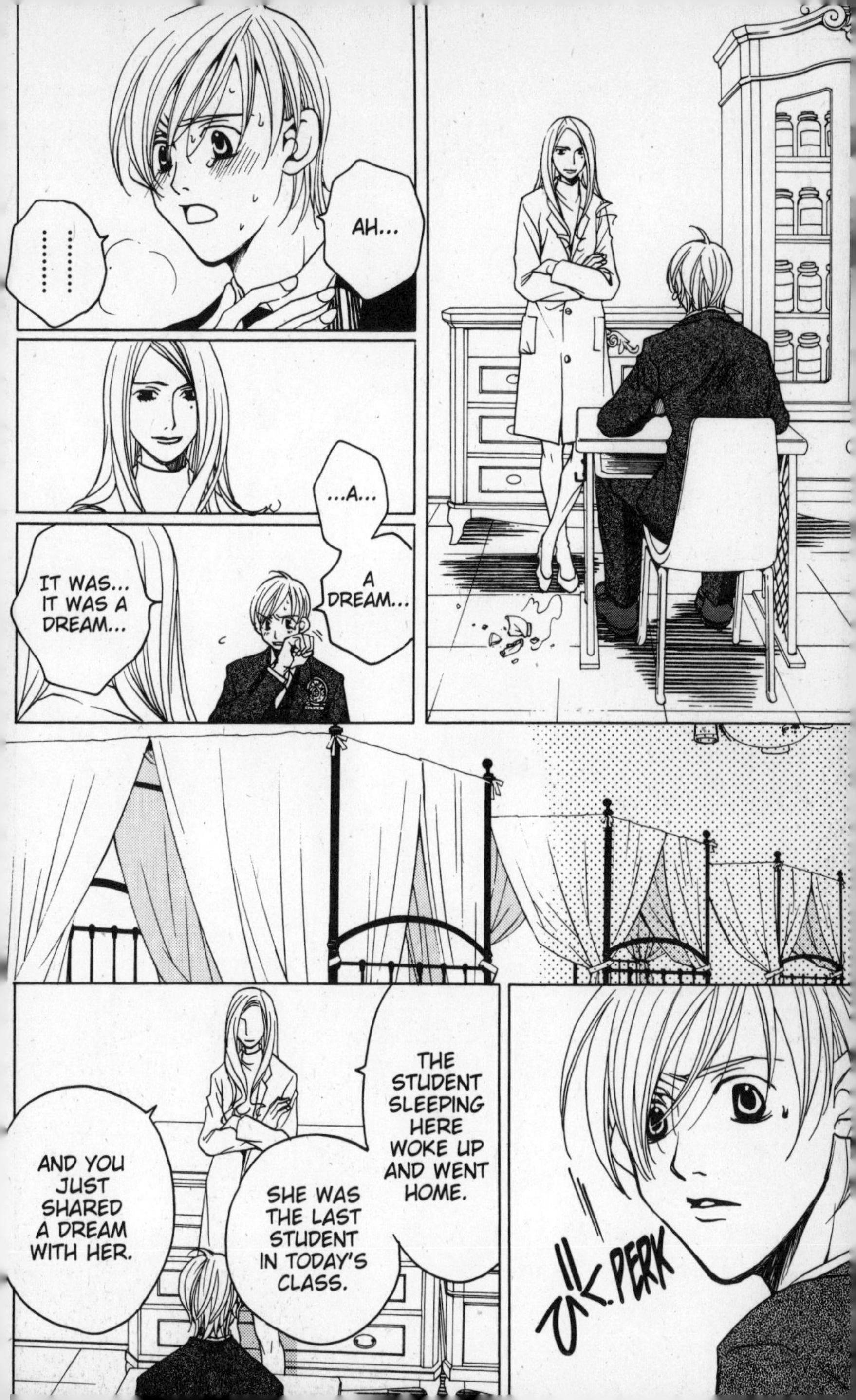
AH...
......
...A...
A DREAM...
IT WAS... IT WAS A DREAM...
PERK
THE STUDENT SLEEPING HERE WOKE UP AND WENT HOME.
SHE WAS THE LAST STUDENT IN TODAY'S CLASS.
AND YOU JUST SHARED A DREAM WITH HER.

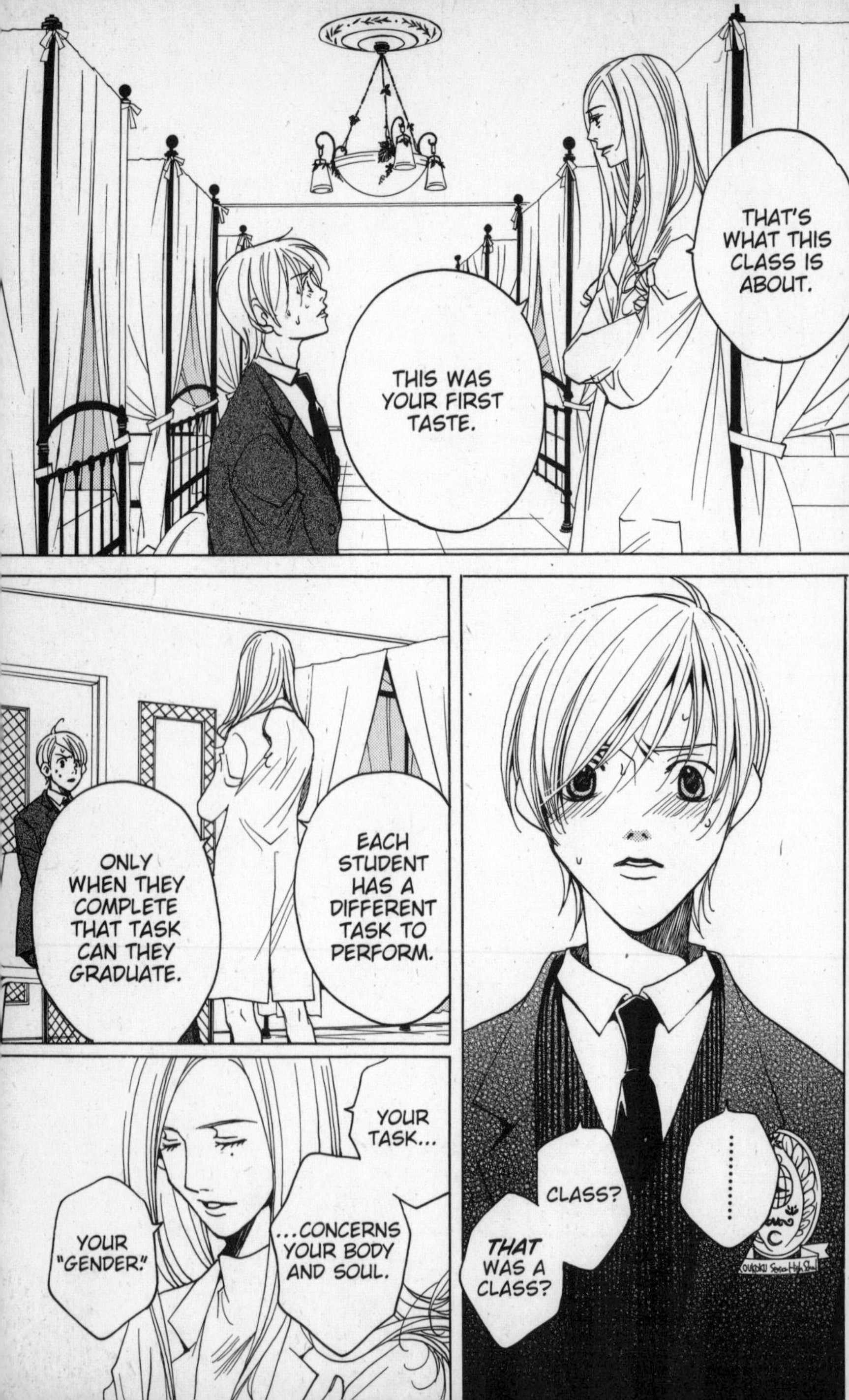
THAT'S WHAT THIS CLASS IS ABOUT.
THIS WAS YOUR FIRST TASTE.
......
CLASS?
THAT WAS A CLASS?
EACH STUDENT HAS A DIFFERENT TASK TO PERFORM.
ONLY WHEN THEY COMPLETE THAT TASK CAN THEY GRADUATE.
YOUR TASK...
...CONCERNS YOUR BODY AND SOUL.
YOUR "GENDER."

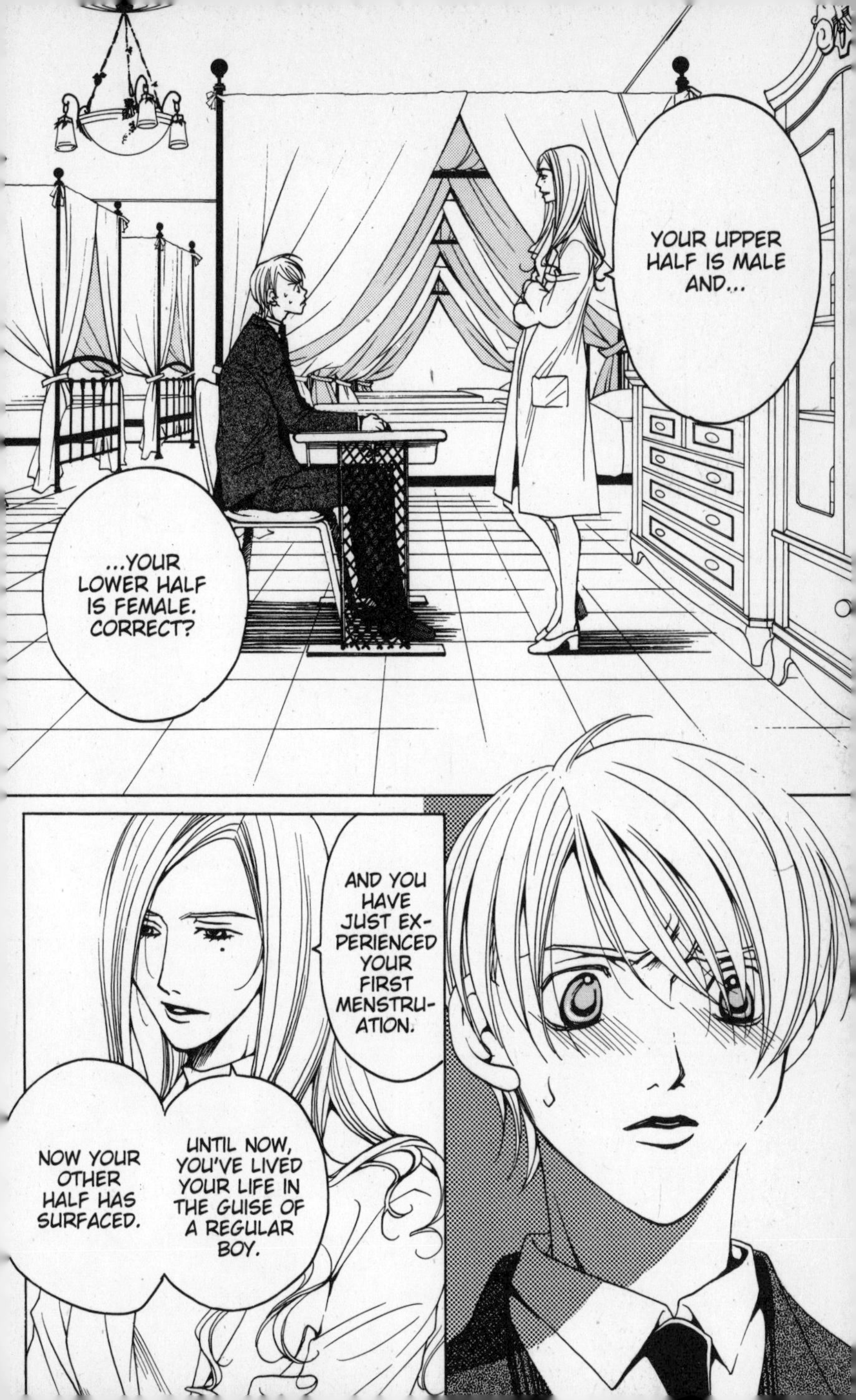
YOUR UPPER HALF IS MALE AND...
...YOUR LOWER HALF IS FEMALE. CORRECT?
AND YOU HAVE JUST EXPERIENCED YOUR FIRST MENSTRUATION.
UNTIL NOW, YOU'VE LIVED YOUR LIFE IN THE GUISE OF A REGULAR BOY.
NOW YOUR OTHER HALF HAS SURFACED.

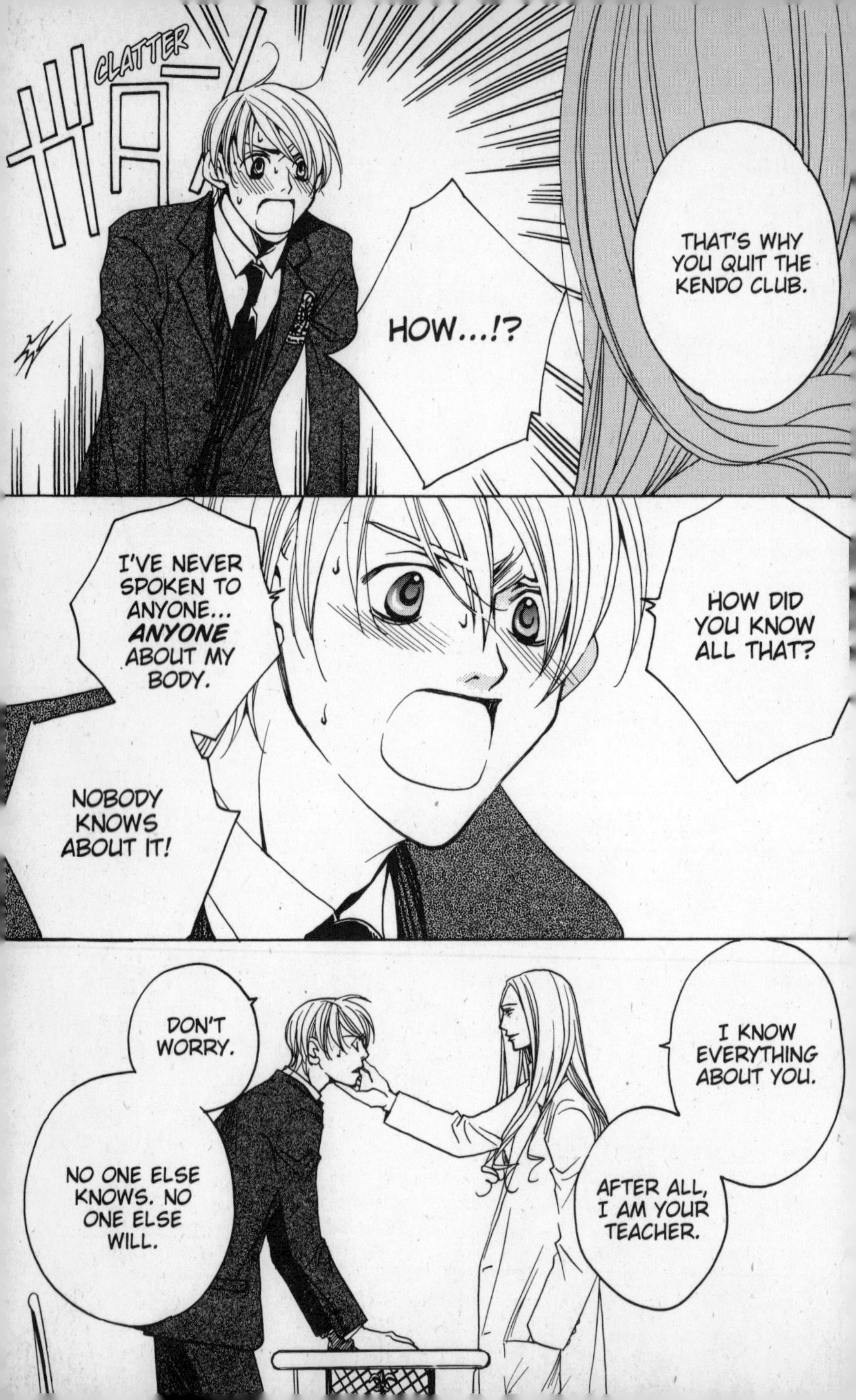
THAT'S WHY YOU QUIT THE KENDO CLUB.
CLATTER
HOW...!?
HOW DID YOU KNOW ALL THAT?
I'VE NEVER SPOKEN TO ANYONE... ***ANYONE*** ABOUT MY BODY.
NOBODY KNOWS ABOUT IT!
I KNOW EVERYTHING ABOUT YOU.
AFTER ALL, I AM YOUR TEACHER.
DON'T WORRY.
NO ONE ELSE KNOWS. NO ONE ELSE WILL.

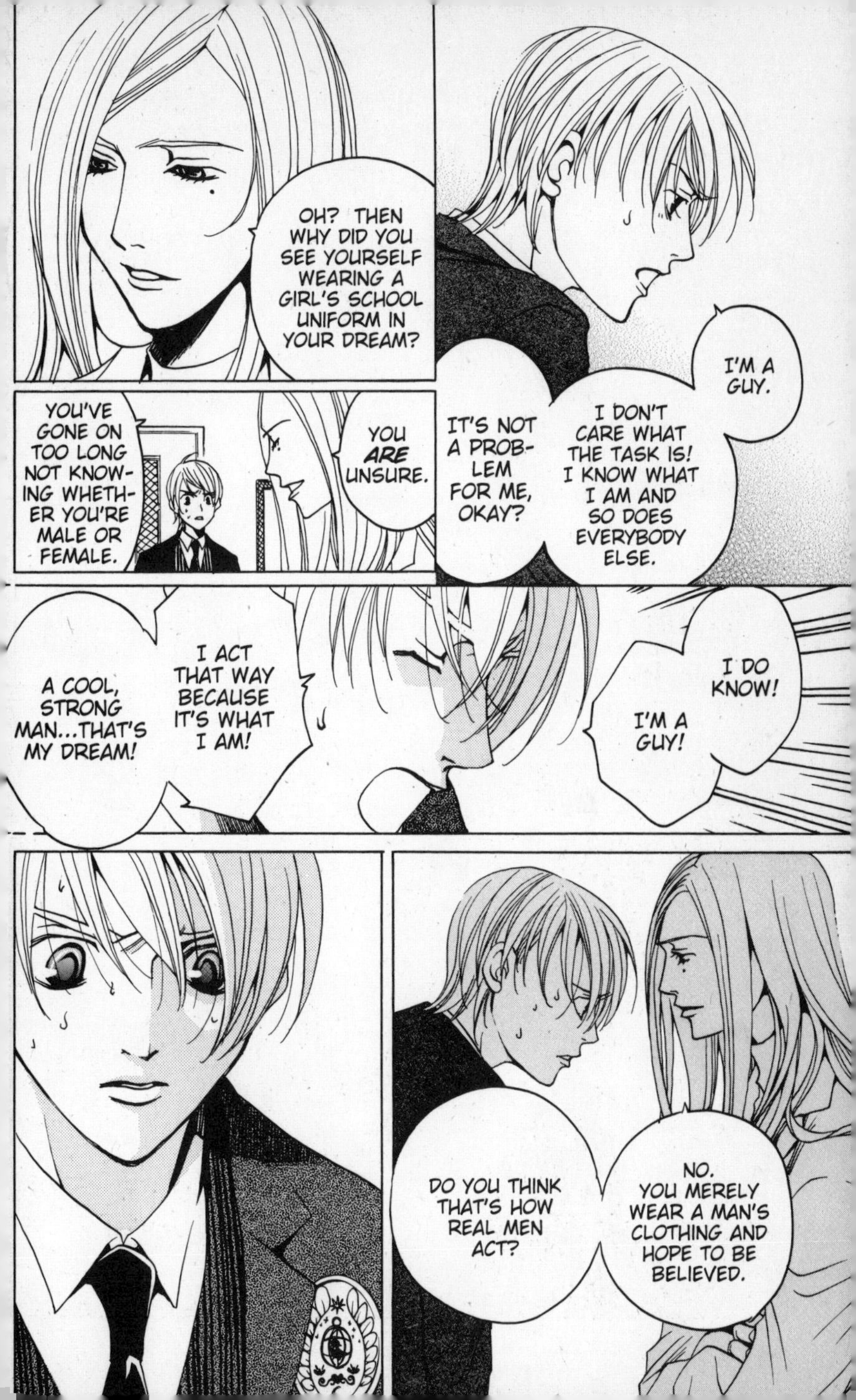
I'M A GUY.
I DON'T CARE WHAT THE TASK IS! I KNOW WHAT I AM AND SO DOES EVERYBODY ELSE.
IT'S NOT A PROB-LEM FOR ME, OKAY?
OH? THEN WHY DID YOU SEE YOURSELF WEARING A GIRL'S SCHOOL UNIFORM IN YOUR DREAM?
YOU **ARE** UNSURE.
YOU'VE GONE ON TOO LONG NOT KNOW-ING WHETH-ER YOU'RE MALE OR FEMALE.
I DO KNOW!
I'M A GUY!
I ACT THAT WAY BECAUSE IT'S WHAT I AM!
A COOL, STRONG MAN...THAT'S MY DREAM!
NO. YOU MERELY WEAR A MAN'S CLOTHING AND HOPE TO BE BELIEVED.
DO YOU THINK THAT'S HOW REAL MEN ACT?

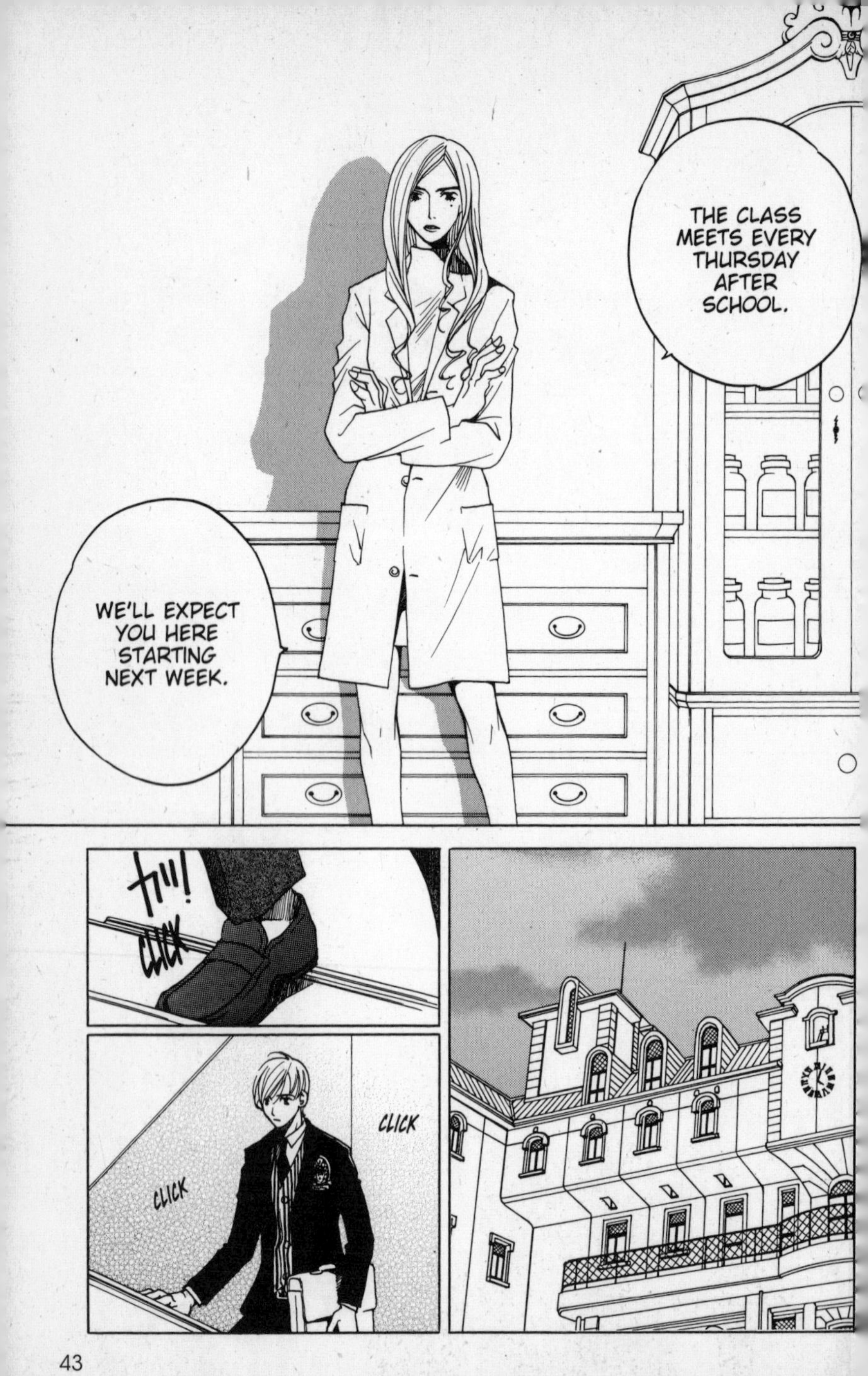
THE CLASS MEETS EVERY THURSDAY AFTER SCHOOL.
WE'LL EXPECT YOU HERE STARTING NEXT WEEK.
カツ!
CLICK
CLICK
CLICK

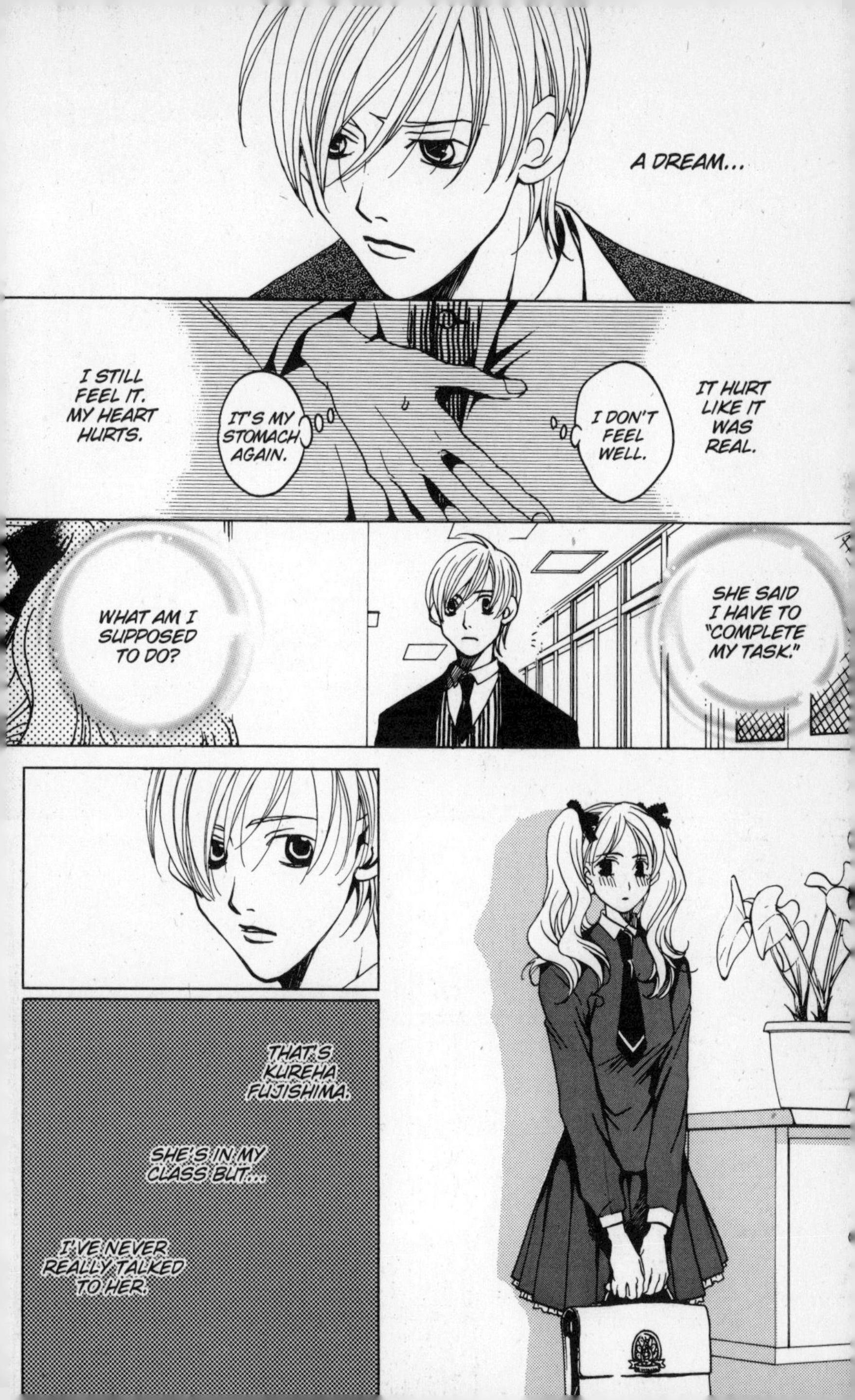
A DREAM...
IT HURT LIKE IT WAS REAL.
I DON'T FEEL WELL.
IT'S MY STOMACH AGAIN.
I STILL FEEL IT. MY HEART HURTS.
SHE SAID I HAVE TO "COMPLETE MY TASK."
WHAT AM I SUPPOSED TO DO?
THAT'S KUREHA FUJISHIMA.
SHE'S IN MY CLASS BUT...
I'VE NEVER REALLY TALKED TO HER.

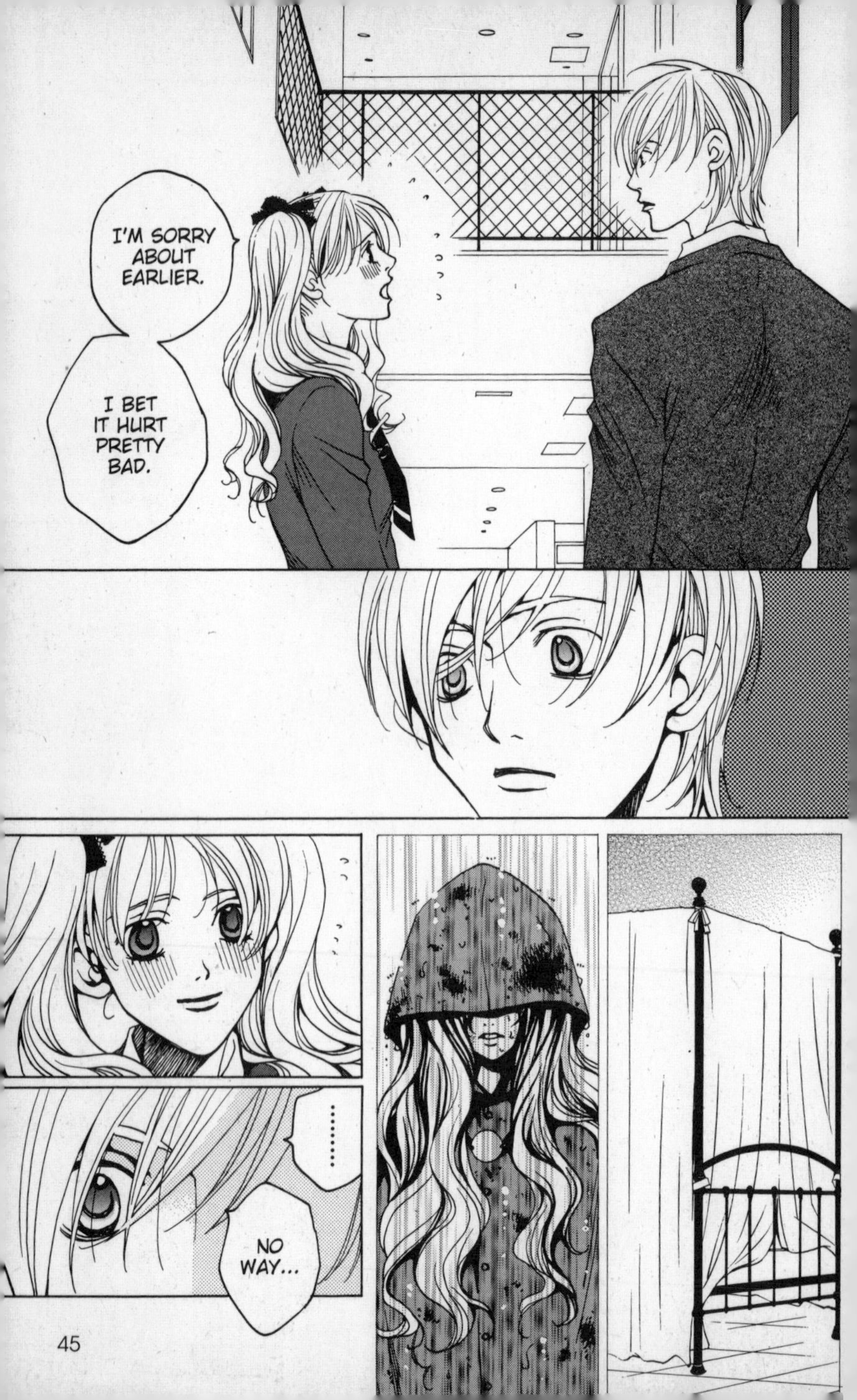
I'M SORRY ABOUT EARLIER.
I BET IT HURT PRETTY BAD.
......
NO WAY...

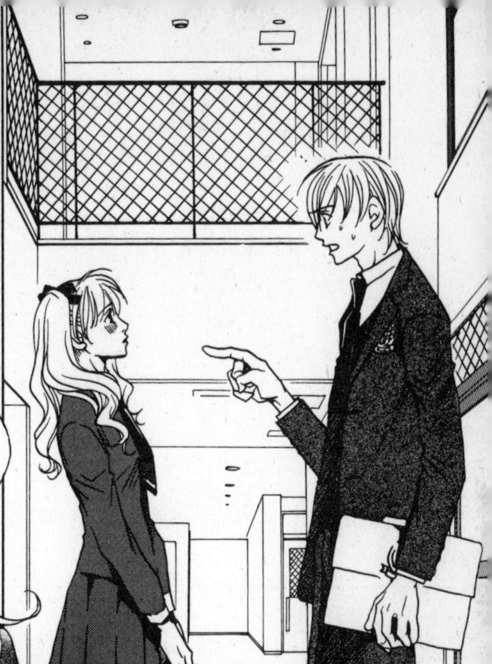
YOU MEAN...
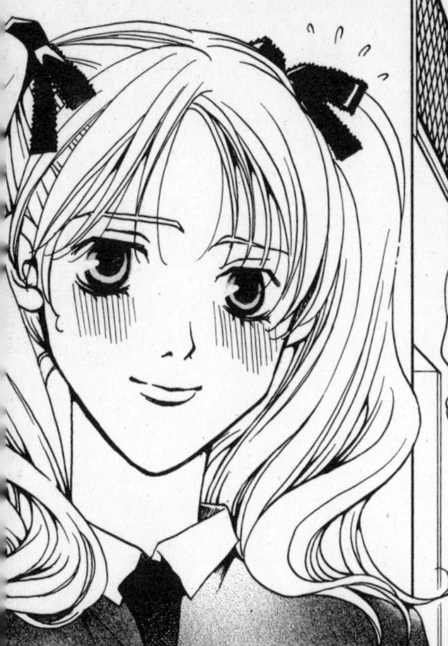
...THAT WAS YOU?
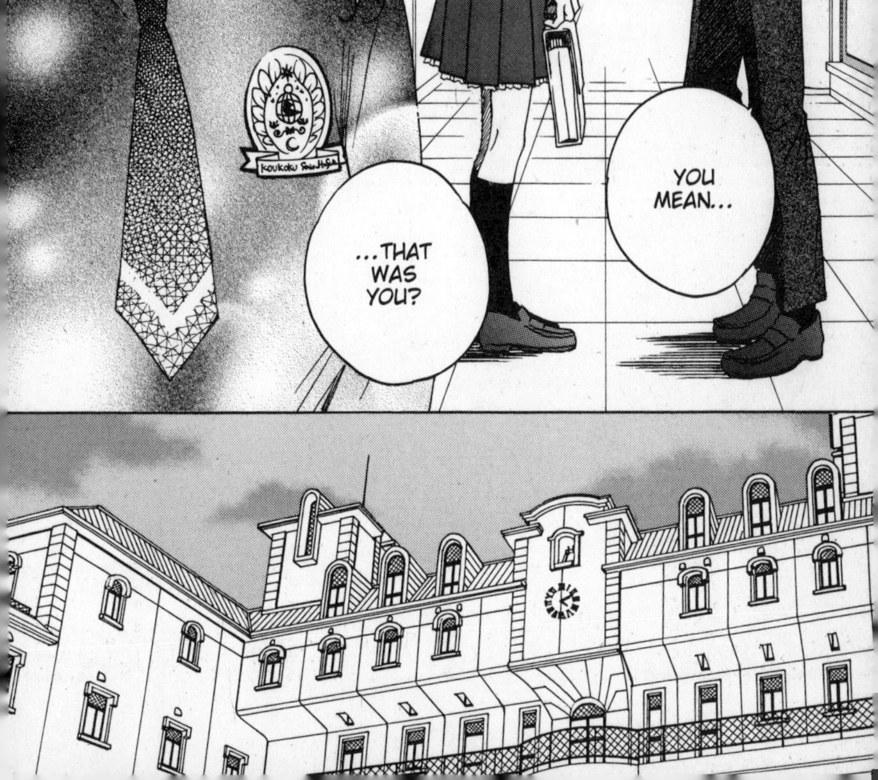

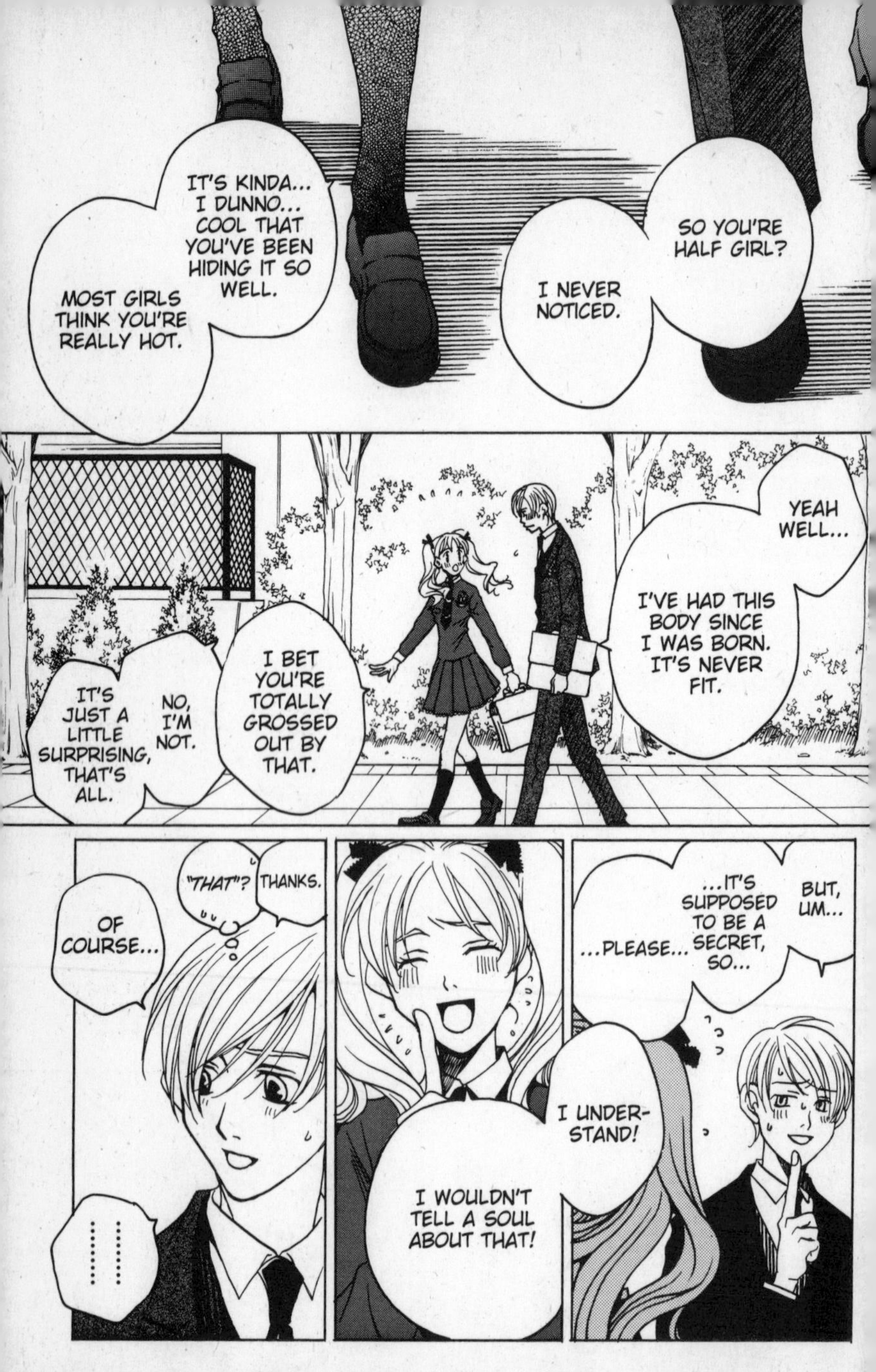
SO YOU'RE HALF GIRL?
I NEVER NOTICED.
IT'S KINDA... I DUNNO... COOL THAT YOU'VE BEEN HIDING IT SO WELL.
MOST GIRLS THINK YOU'RE REALLY HOT.
YEAH WELL...
I'VE HAD THIS BODY SINCE I WAS BORN. IT'S NEVER FIT.
I BET YOU'RE TOTALLY GROSSED OUT BY THAT.
NO, I'M NOT.
IT'S JUST A LITTLE SURPRISING, THAT'S ALL.
BUT, UM...
...IT'S SUPPOSED TO BE A SECRET, SO...
...PLEASE...
I UNDER-STAND!
I WOULDN'T TELL A SOUL ABOUT THAT!
THANKS.
"THAT"?
OF COURSE...
......

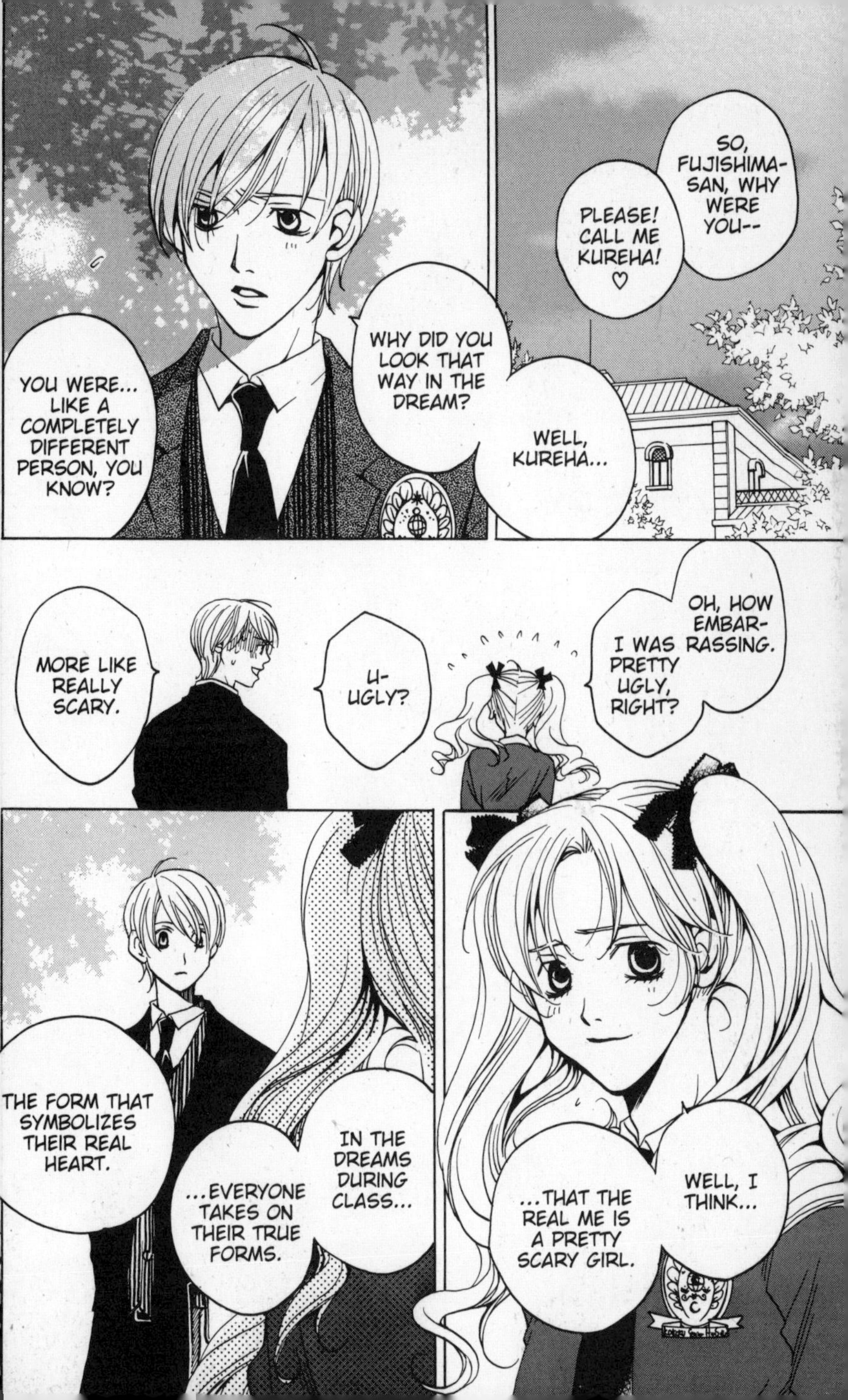
SO, FUJISHIMA-SAN, WHY WERE YOU--
PLEASE! CALL ME KUREHA! ♡
WELL, KUREHA...
WHY DID YOU LOOK THAT WAY IN THE DREAM?
YOU WERE... LIKE A COMPLETELY DIFFERENT PERSON, YOU KNOW?
OH, HOW EMBARRASSING. I WAS PRETTY UGLY, RIGHT?
U-UGLY?
MORE LIKE REALLY SCARY.
WELL, I THINK...
...THAT THE REAL ME IS A PRETTY SCARY GIRL.
IN THE DREAMS DURING CLASS...
...EVERYONE TAKES ON THEIR TRUE FORMS.
THE FORM THAT SYMBOLIZES THEIR REAL HEART.

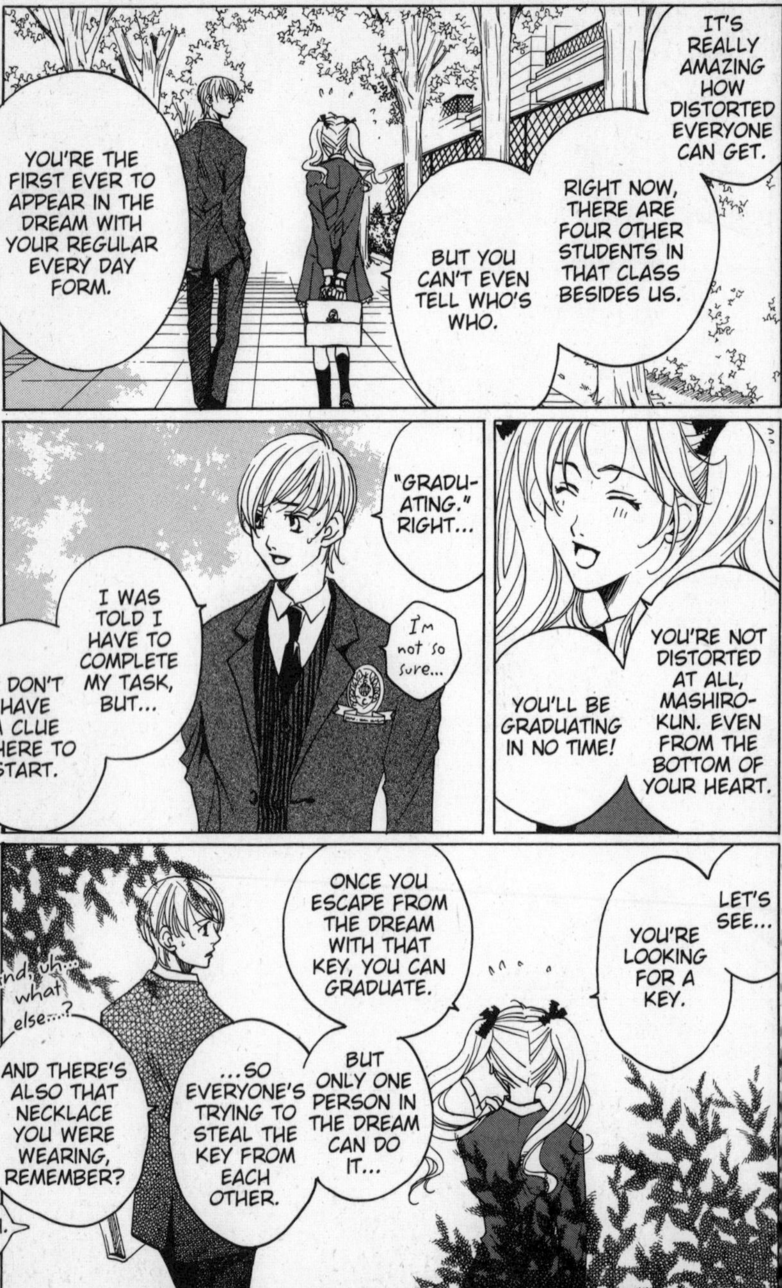
IT'S REALLY AMAZING HOW DISTORTED EVERYONE CAN GET.
RIGHT NOW, THERE ARE FOUR OTHER STUDENTS IN THAT CLASS BESIDES US.
BUT YOU CAN'T EVEN TELL WHO'S WHO.
YOU'RE THE FIRST EVER TO APPEAR IN THE DREAM WITH YOUR REGULAR EVERY DAY FORM.
YOU'RE NOT DISTORTED AT ALL, MASHIRO-KUN. EVEN FROM THE BOTTOM OF YOUR HEART.
YOU'LL BE GRADUATING IN NO TIME!
"GRADU-ATING." RIGHT...
I'm not so sure...
I WAS TOLD I HAVE TO COMPLETE MY TASK, BUT...
I DON'T HAVE A CLUE WHERE TO START.
LET'S SEE...
YOU'RE LOOKING FOR A KEY.
ONCE YOU ESCAPE FROM THE DREAM WITH THAT KEY, YOU CAN GRADUATE.
BUT ONLY ONE PERSON IN THE DREAM CAN DO IT...
...SO EVERYONE'S TRYING TO STEAL THE KEY FROM EACH OTHER.
And, uh... what else...?
AND THERE'S ALSO THAT NECKLACE YOU WERE WEARING, REMEMBER?
YEAH.

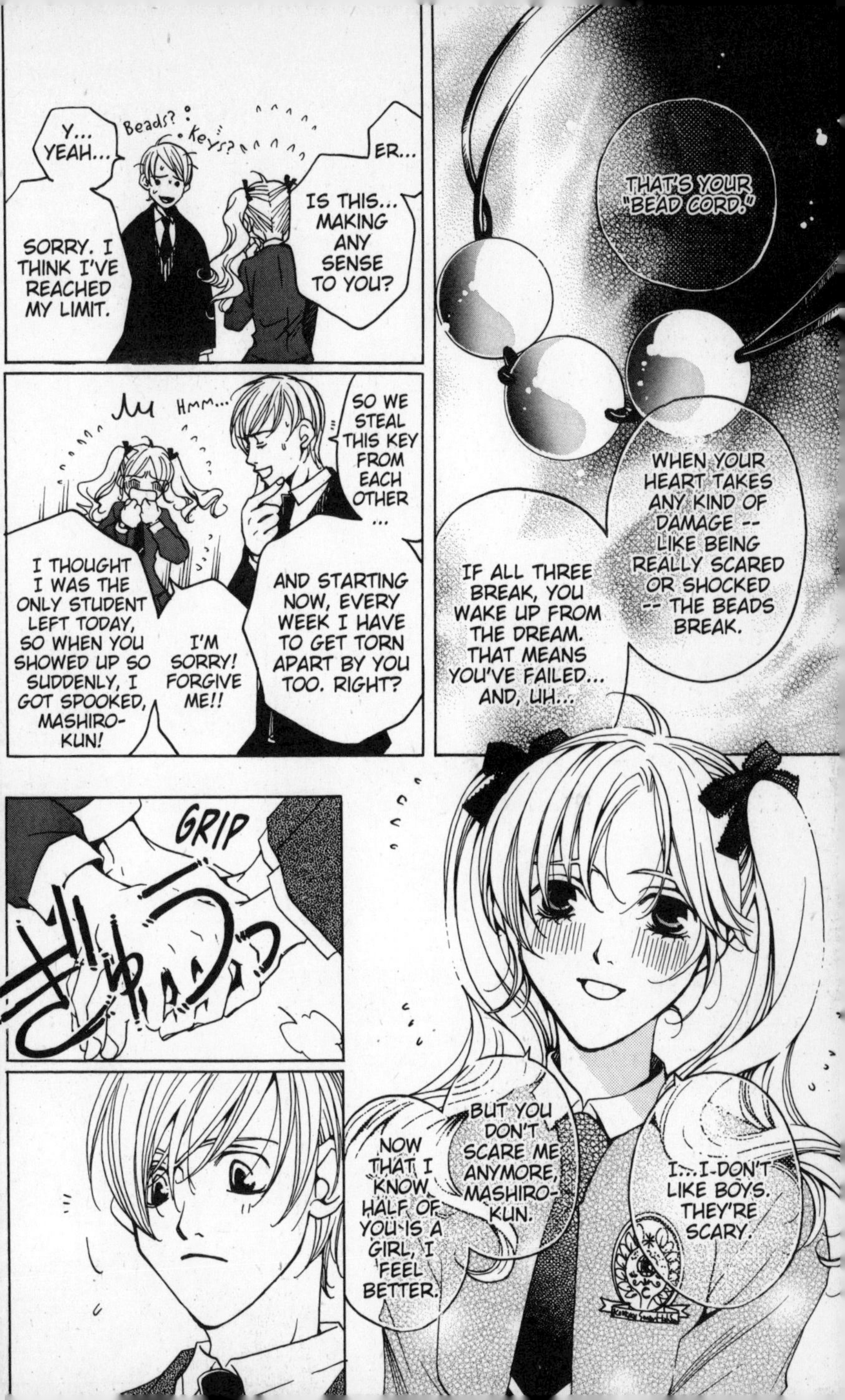
THAT'S YOUR "BEAD CORD."
WHEN YOUR HEART TAKES ANY KIND OF DAMAGE -- LIKE BEING REALLY SCARED OR SHOCKED -- THE BEADS BREAK.
IF ALL THREE BREAK, YOU WAKE UP FROM THE DREAM. THAT MEANS YOU'VE FAILED... AND, UH...
ER...
IS THIS... MAKING ANY SENSE TO YOU?
Beads? Keys?
Y... YEAH...
SORRY. I THINK I'VE REACHED MY LIMIT.
SO WE STEAL THIS KEY FROM EACH OTHER ...
AND STARTING NOW, EVERY WEEK I HAVE TO GET TORN APART BY YOU TOO. RIGHT?
HMM...
I'M SORRY! FORGIVE ME!!
I THOUGHT I WAS THE ONLY STUDENT LEFT TODAY, SO WHEN YOU SHOWED UP SO SUDDENLY, I GOT SPOOKED, MASHIRO-KUN!
I... I-DON'T LIKE BOYS. THEY'RE SCARY.
BUT YOU DON'T SCARE ME ANYMORE, MASHIRO-KUN.
NOW THAT I KNOW HALF OF YOU IS A GIRL, I FEEL BETTER.
GRIP
ぎゅっ

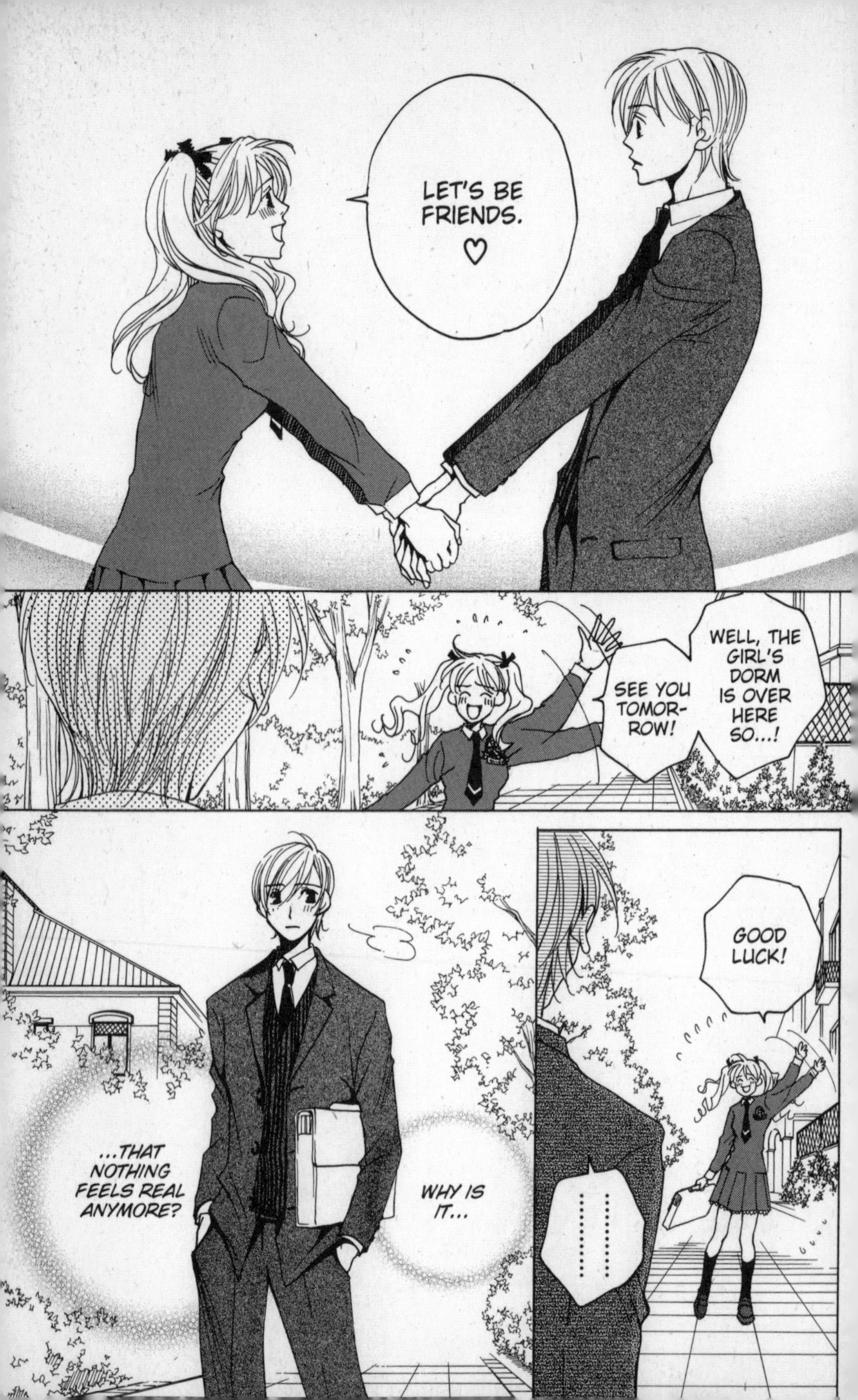
LET'S BE FRIENDS. ♡
WELL, THE GIRL'S DORM IS OVER HERE SO...!
SEE YOU TOMOR-ROW!
GOOD LUCK!
......
WHY IS IT...
...THAT NOTHING FEELS REAL ANYMORE?

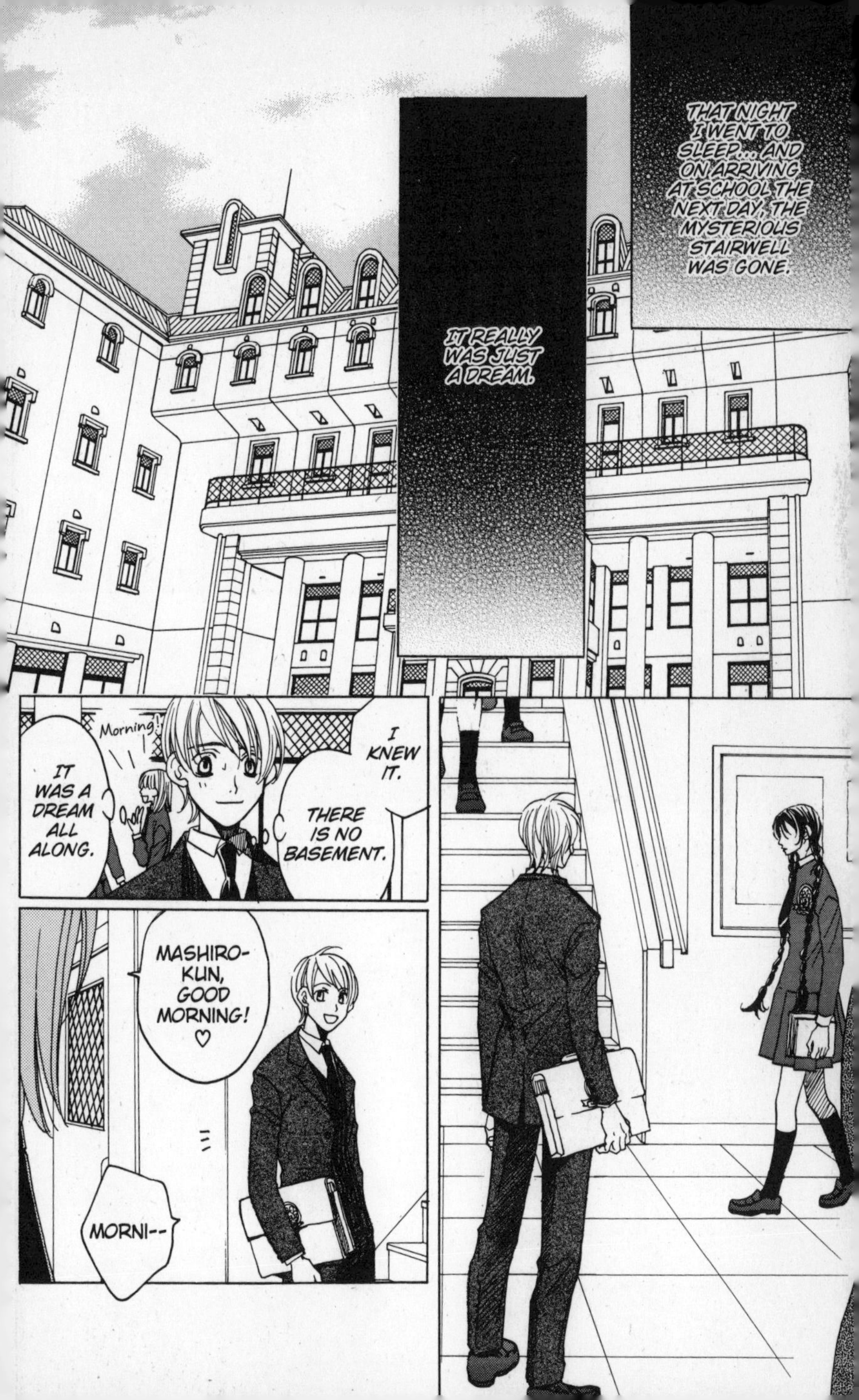
THAT NIGHT I WENT TO SLEEP... AND ON ARRIVING AT SCHOOL THE NEXT DAY, THE MYSTERIOUS STAIRWELL WAS GONE.
IT REALLY WAS JUST A DREAM.
I KNEW IT.
THERE IS NO BASEMENT.
Morning!
IT WAS A DREAM ALL ALONG.
MASHIRO-KUN, GOOD MORNING! ♡
MORNI--

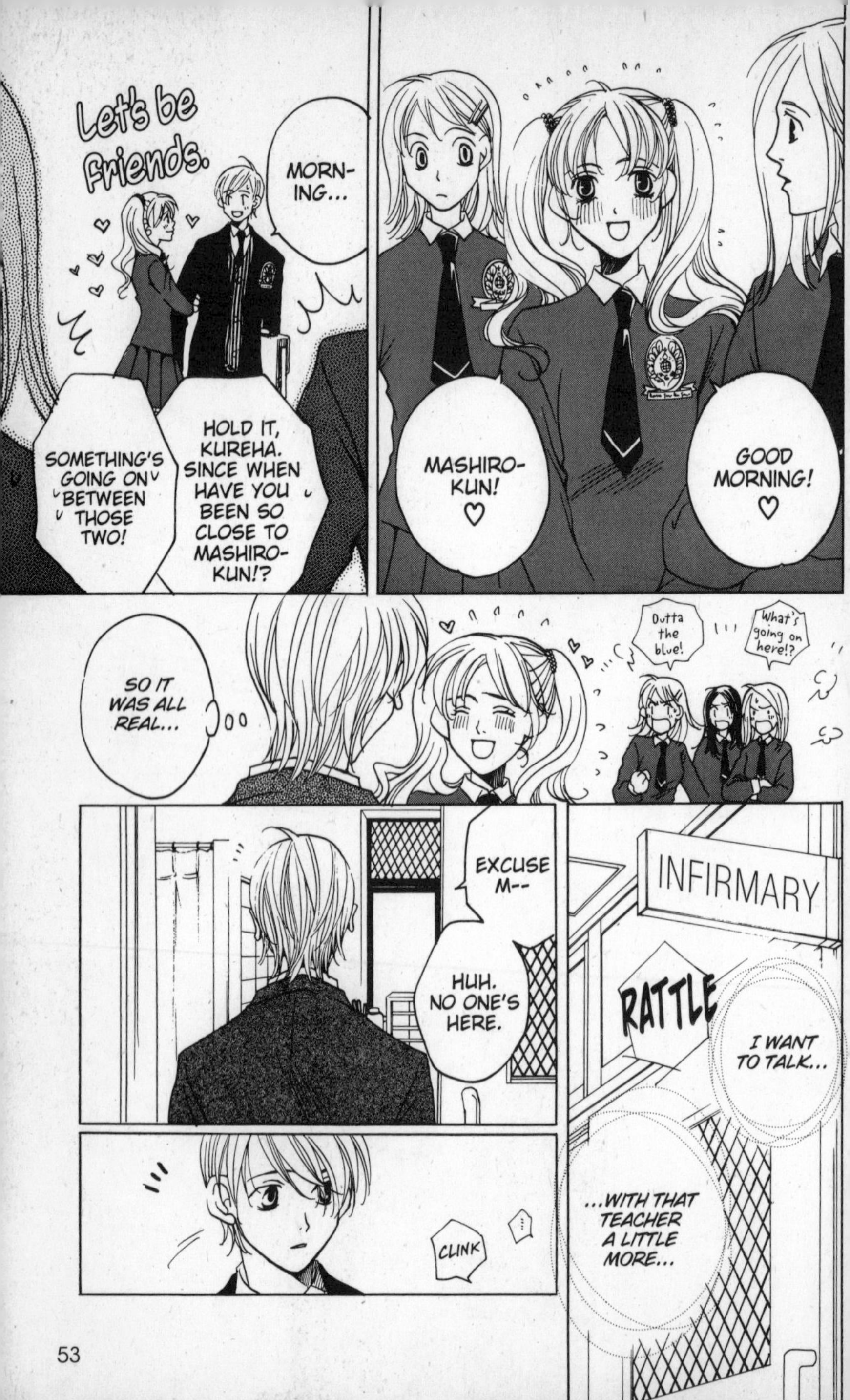
GOOD MORNING! ♡
MASHIRO-KUN! ♡
MORN-ING...
Let's be friends.
HOLD IT, KUREHA. SINCE WHEN HAVE YOU BEEN SO CLOSE TO MASHIRO-KUN!?
SOMETHING'S GOING ON BETWEEN THOSE TWO!
What's going on here!?
Outta the blue!
SO IT WAS ALL REAL...
INFIRMARY
RATTLE
I WANT TO TALK...
...WITH THAT TEACHER A LITTLE MORE...
EXCUSE M--
HUH. NO ONE'S HERE.
CLINK
...

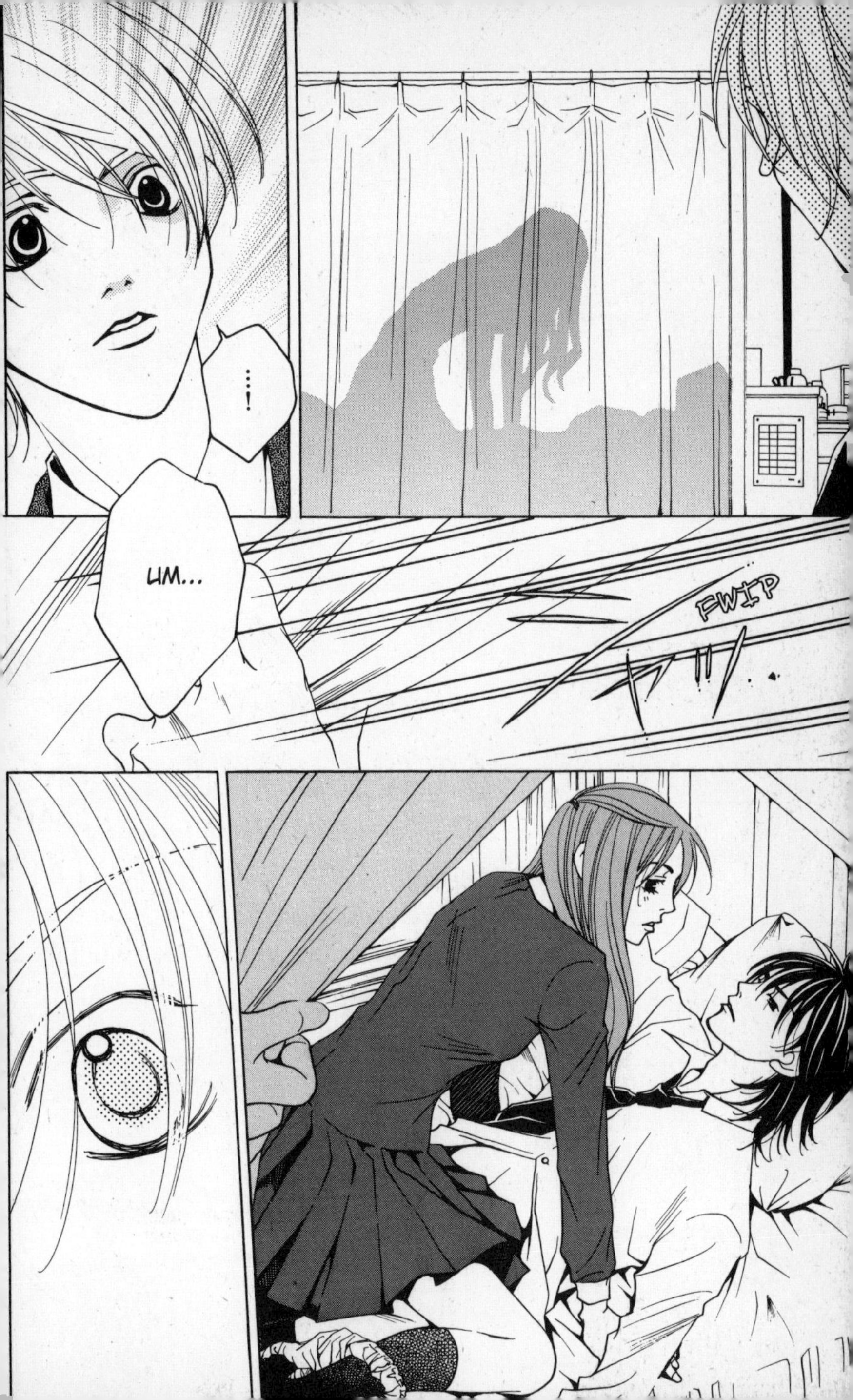
...!
UM...
FWIP

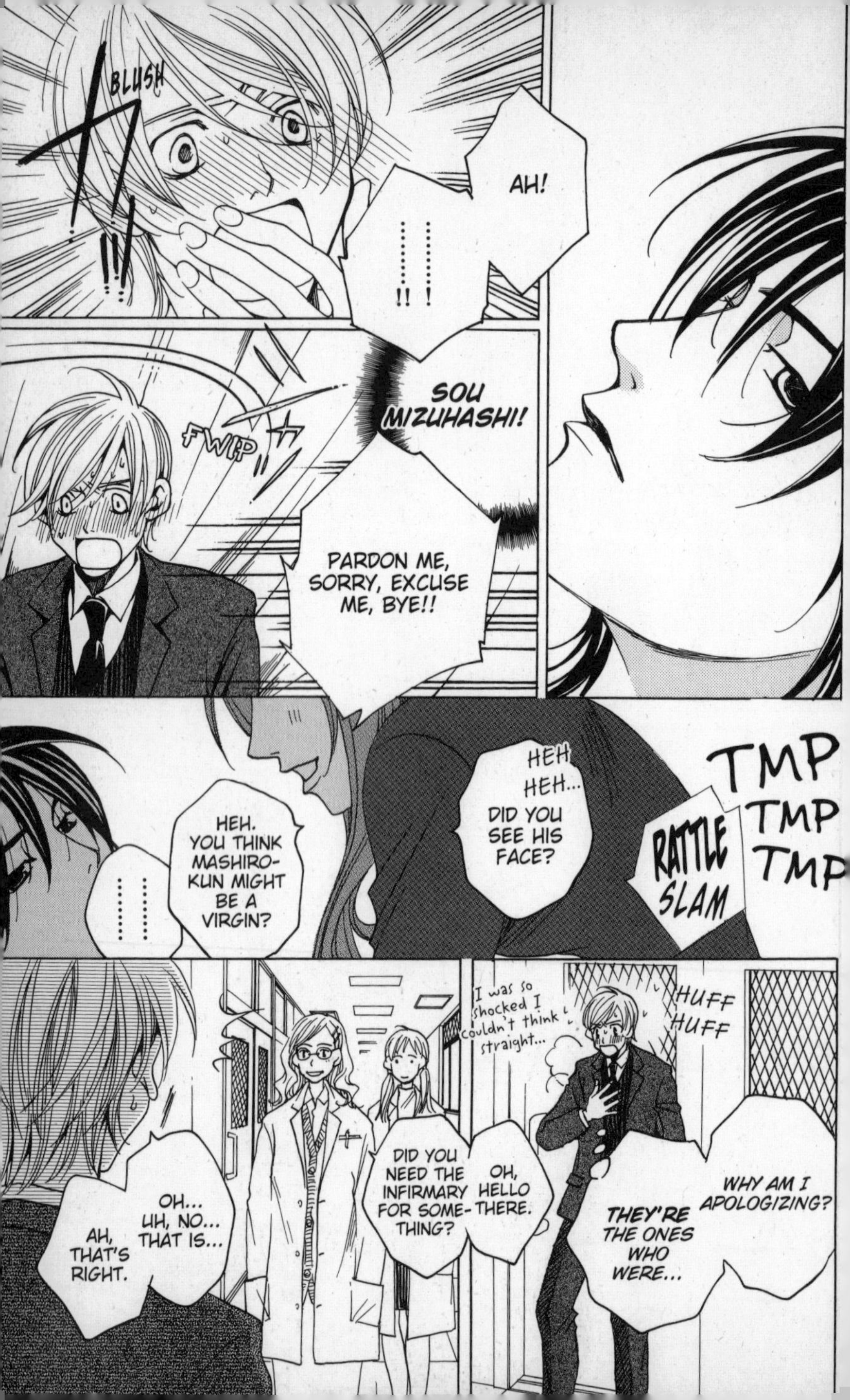
AH!
SOU MIZUHASHI!
……!!!
BLUSH
!!!
FWIP
PARDON ME, SORRY, EXCUSE ME, BYE!!
TMP TMP TMP
RATTLE SLAM
HEH HEH… DID YOU SEE HIS FACE?
HEH. YOU THINK MASHIRO-KUN MIGHT BE A VIRGIN?
……
HUFF HUFF
I was so shocked I couldn't think straight…
WHY AM I APOLOGIZING?
THEY'RE THE ONES WHO WERE…
OH, HELLO THERE.
DID YOU NEED THE INFIRMARY FOR SOME-THING?
OH… UH, NO… THAT IS…
AH, THAT'S RIGHT.

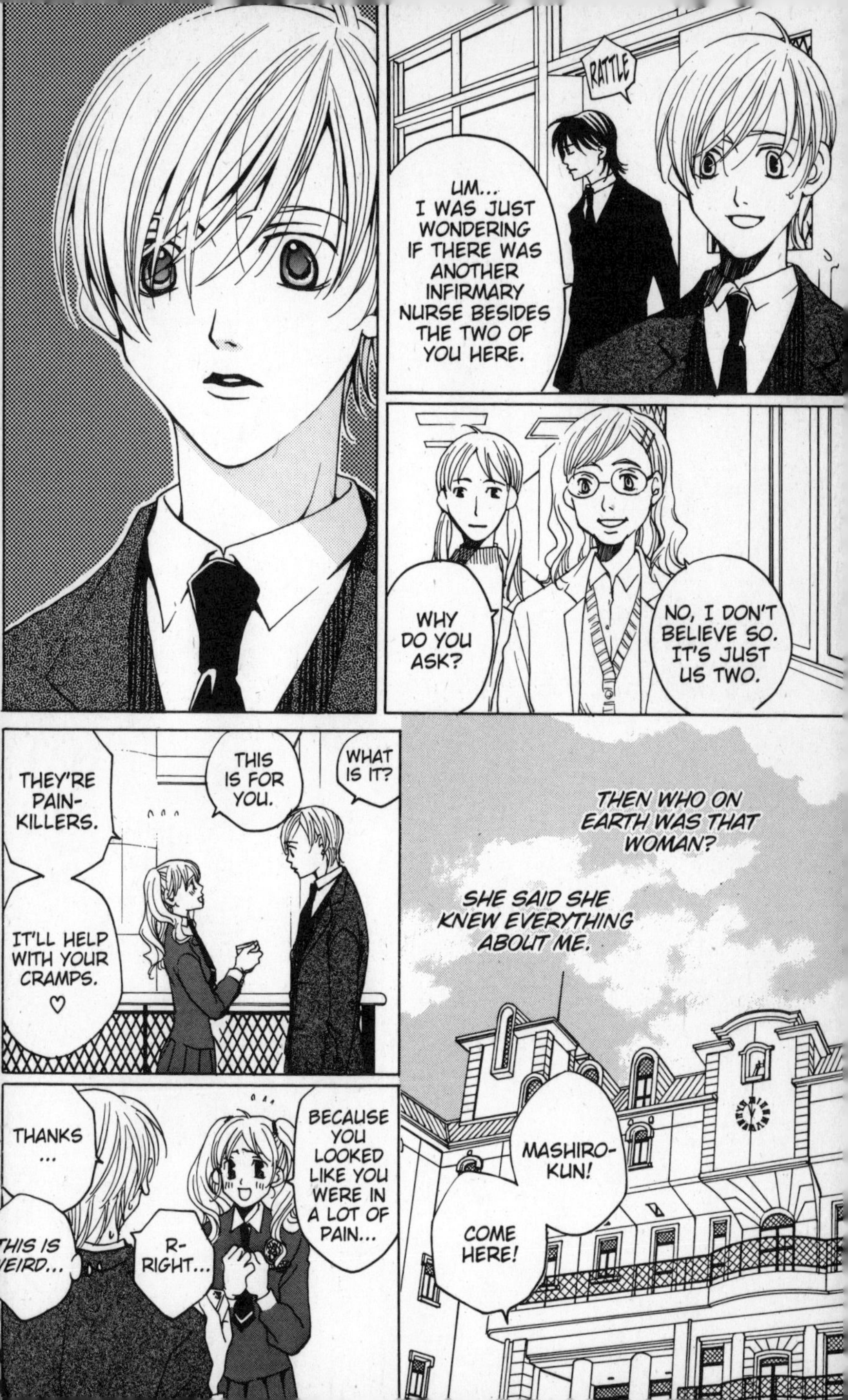
RATTLE
UM... I WAS JUST WONDERING IF THERE WAS ANOTHER INFIRMARY NURSE BESIDES THE TWO OF YOU HERE.
NO, I DON'T BELIEVE SO. IT'S JUST US TWO.
WHY DO YOU ASK?
THEN WHO ON EARTH WAS THAT WOMAN?
SHE SAID SHE KNEW EVERYTHING ABOUT ME.
MASHIRO-KUN!
COME HERE!
WHAT IS IT?
THIS IS FOR YOU.
THEY'RE PAIN-KILLERS.
IT'LL HELP WITH YOUR CRAMPS. ♡
BECAUSE YOU LOOKED LIKE YOU WERE IN A LOT OF PAIN...
THANKS ...
R-RIGHT...
THIS IS WEIRD...

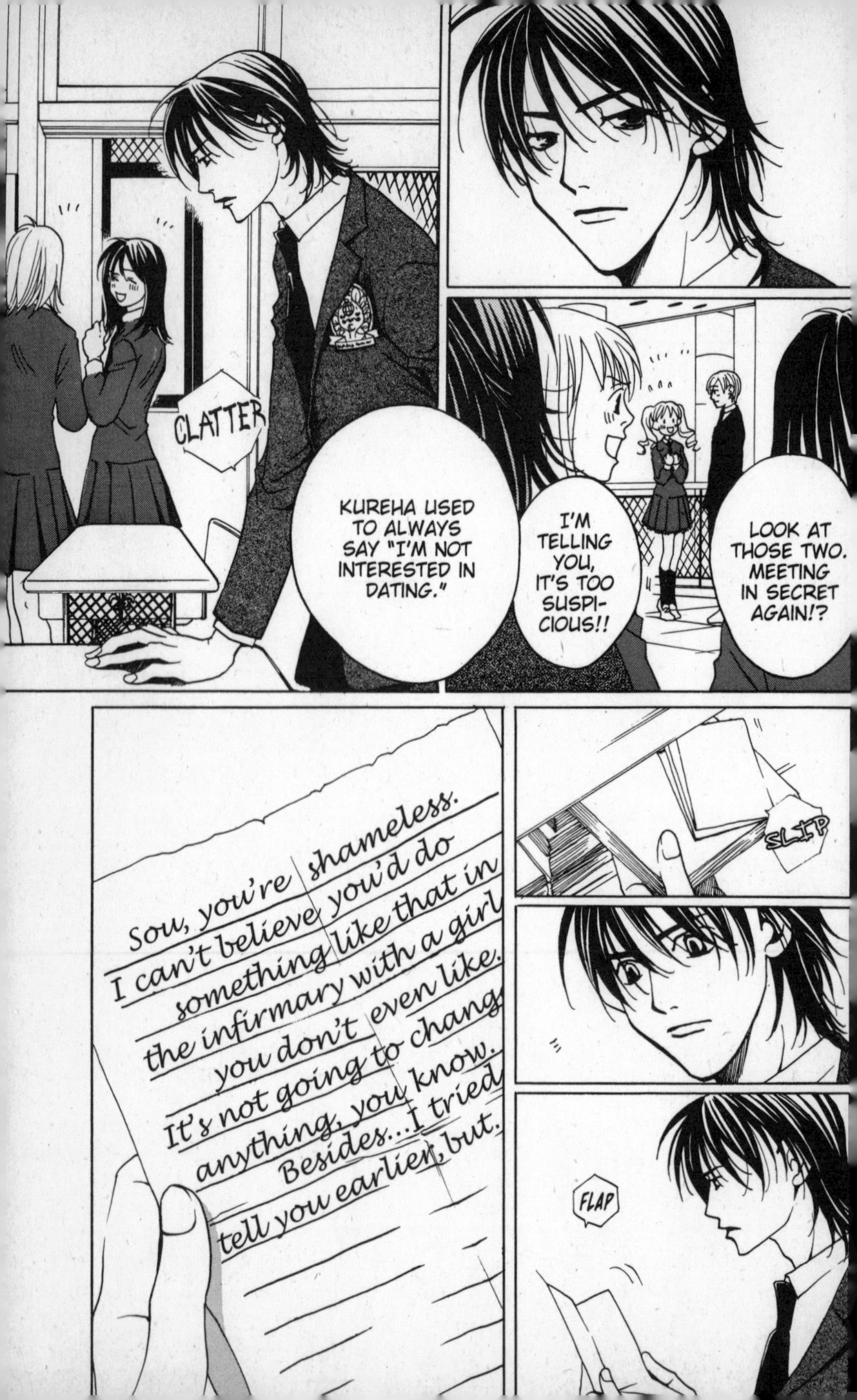
LOOK AT THOSE TWO. MEETING IN SECRET AGAIN!?
I'M TELLING YOU, IT'S TOO SUSPICIOUS!!
KUREHA USED TO ALWAYS SAY "I'M NOT INTERESTED IN DATING."
CLATTER
SLIP
FLAP
Sou, you're shameless.
I can't believe you'd do
something like that in
the infirmary with a girl
you don't even like.
It's not going to chang
anything, you know.
Besides...I tried
tell you earlier, but.

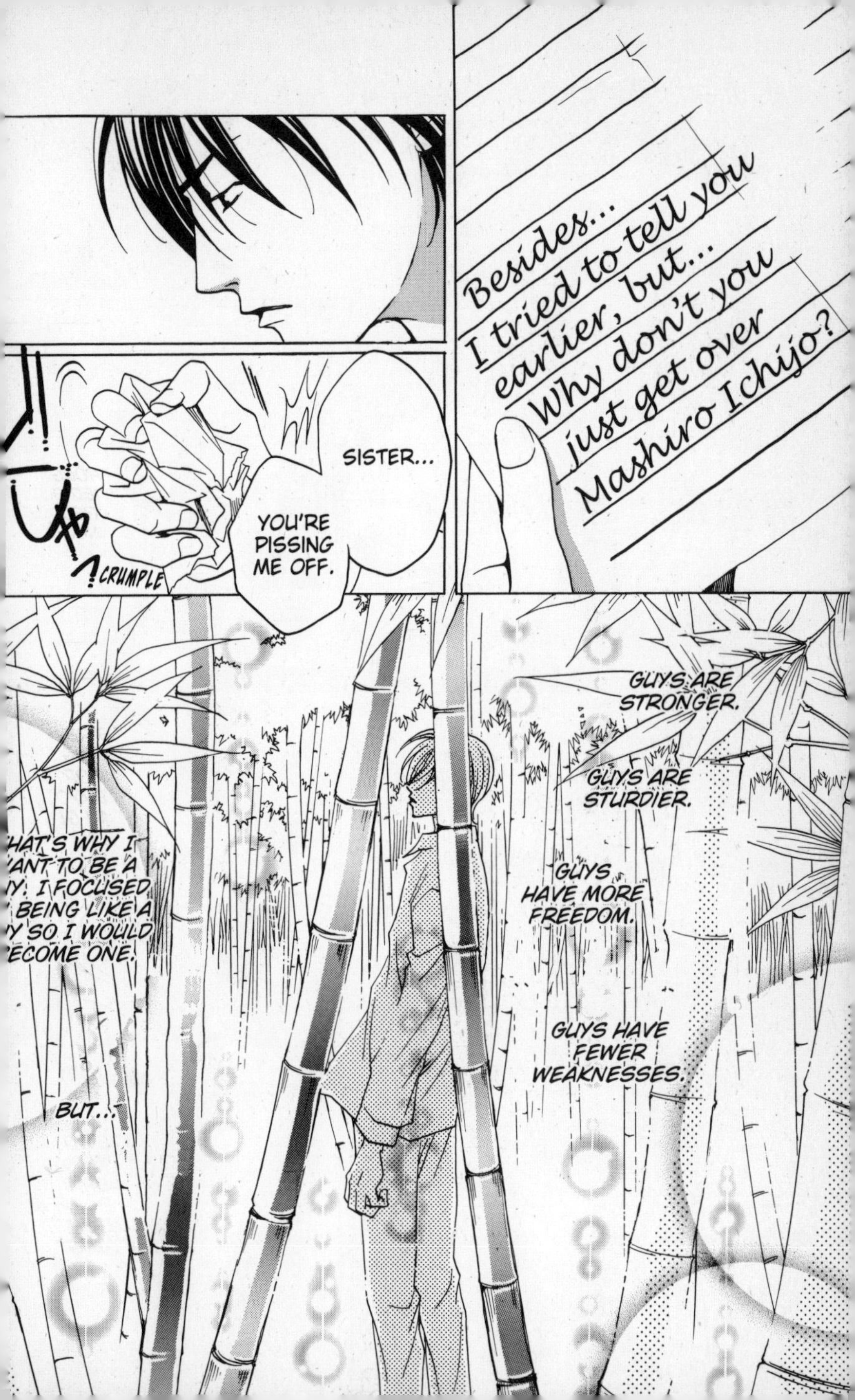
Besides...
I tried to tell you earlier, but...
Why don't you just get over Mashiro Ichijo?
SISTER...
YOU'RE PISSING ME OFF.
CRUMPLE
GUYS ARE STRONGER.
GUYS ARE STURDIER.
GUYS HAVE MORE FREEDOM.
GUYS HAVE FEWER WEAKNESSES.
HAT'S WHY I ANT TO BE A Y. I FOCUSED BEING LIKE A Y SO I WOULD ECOME ONE.
BUT...

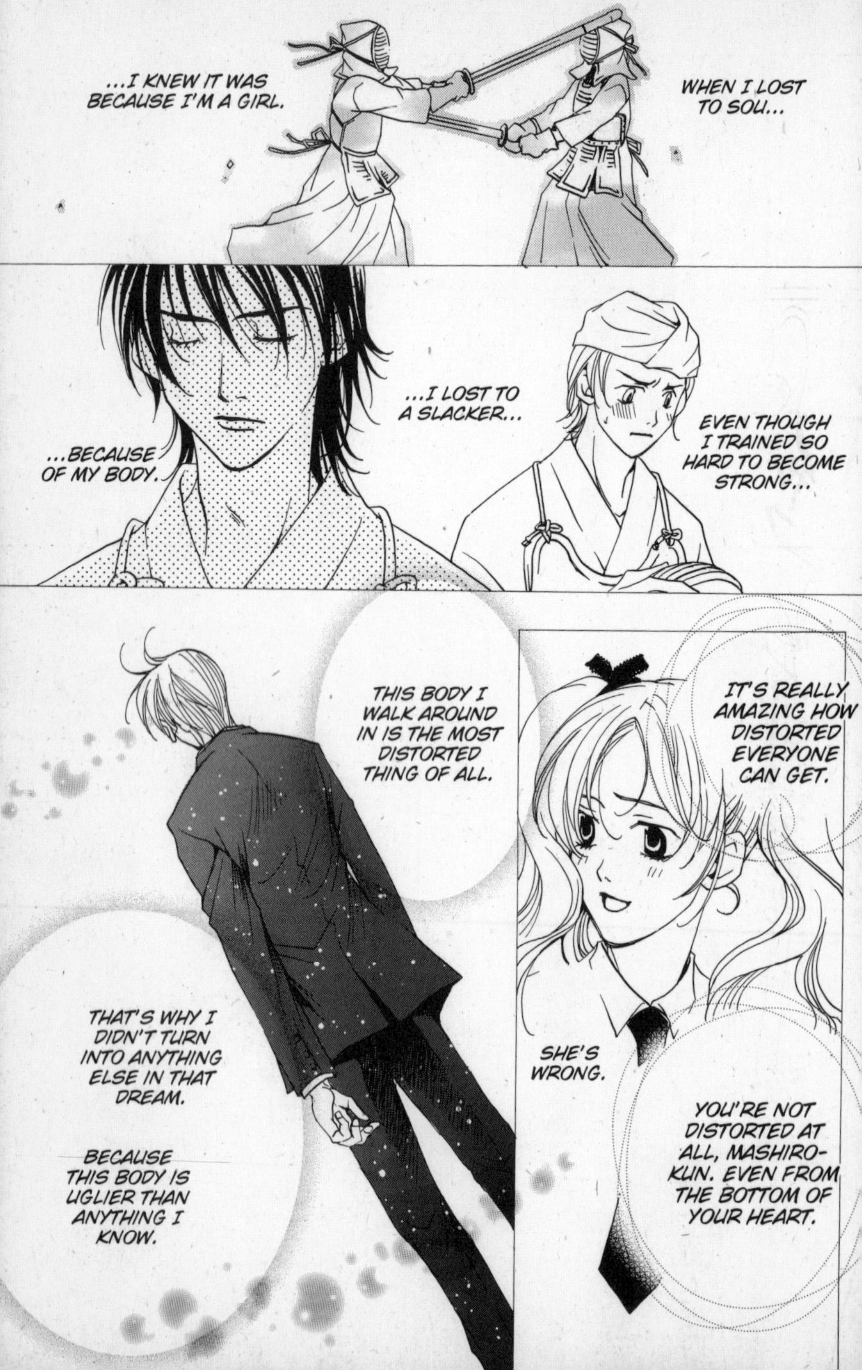
WHEN I LOST TO SOU...
...I KNEW IT WAS BECAUSE I'M A GIRL.
EVEN THOUGH I TRAINED SO HARD TO BECOME STRONG...
...I LOST TO A SLACKER...
...BECAUSE OF MY BODY.
IT'S REALLY AMAZING HOW DISTORTED EVERYONE CAN GET.
YOU'RE NOT DISTORTED AT ALL, MASHIRO-KUN. EVEN FROM THE BOTTOM OF YOUR HEART.
SHE'S WRONG.
THIS BODY I WALK AROUND IN IS THE MOST DISTORTED THING OF ALL.
THAT'S WHY I DIDN'T TURN INTO ANYTHING ELSE IN THAT DREAM.
BECAUSE THIS BODY IS UGLIER THAN ANYTHING I KNOW.

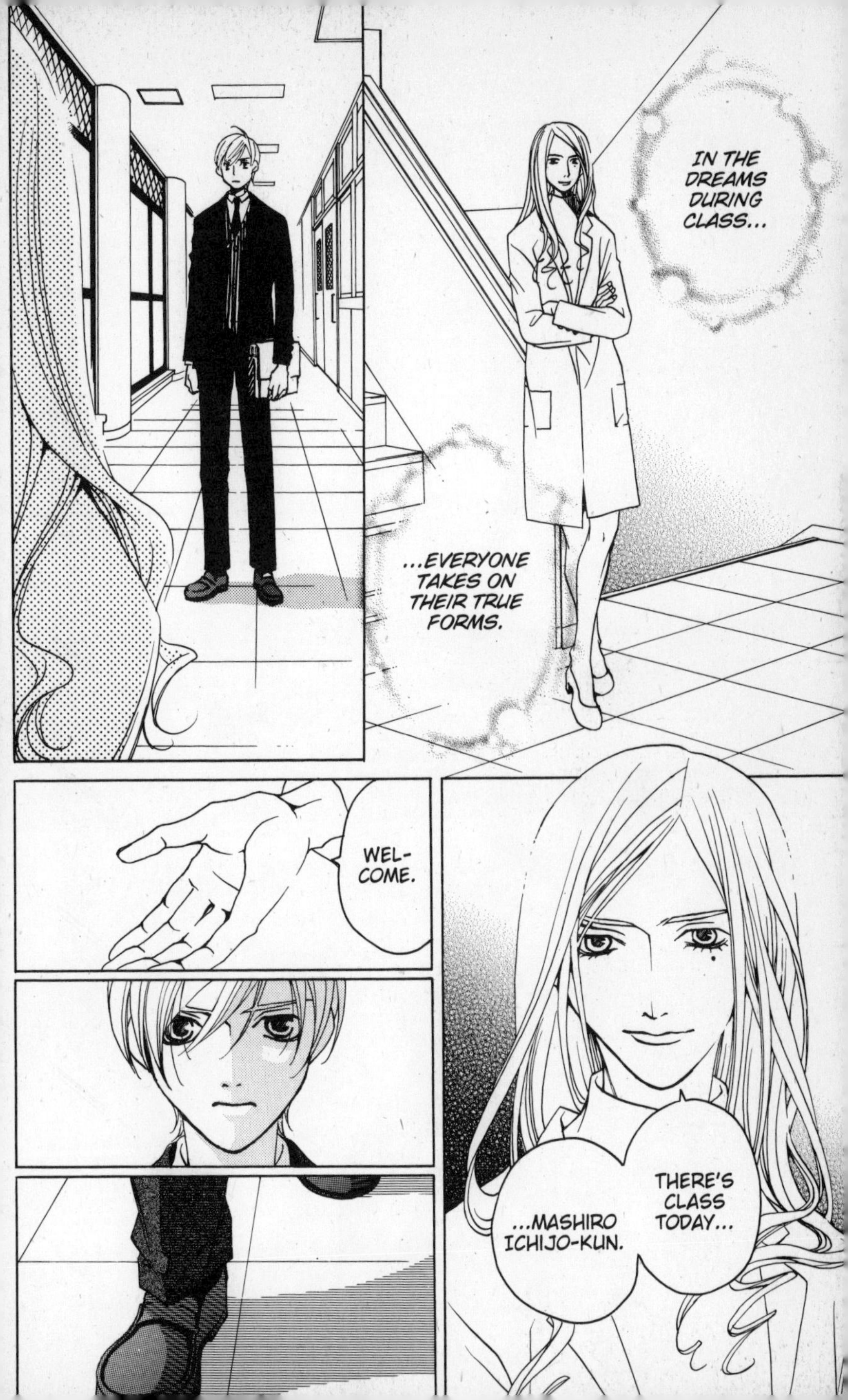
IN THE DREAMS DURING CLASS...
...EVERYONE TAKES ON THEIR TRUE FORMS.
THERE'S CLASS TODAY...
...MASHIRO ICHIJO-KUN.
WEL-COME.

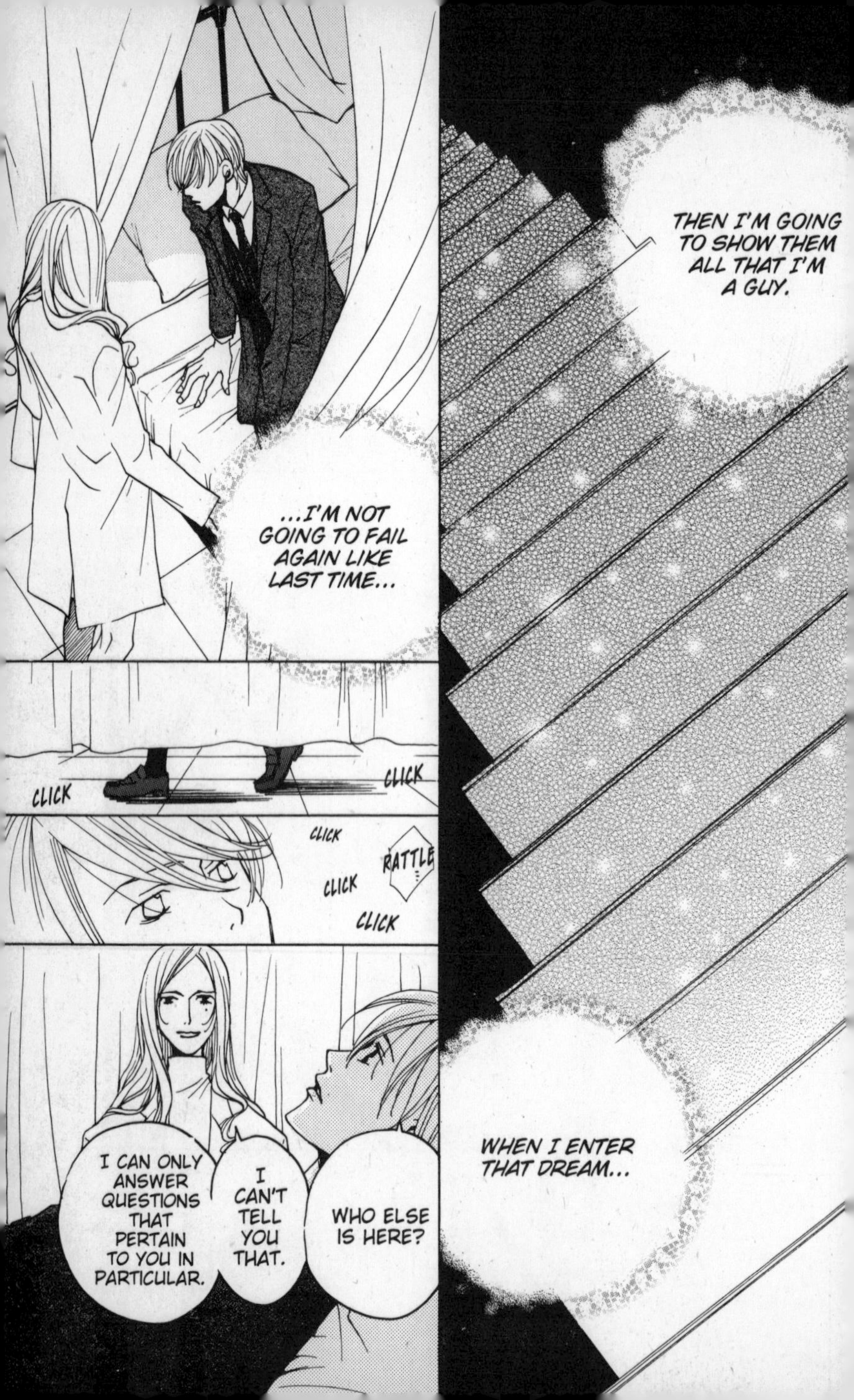
THEN I'M GOING TO SHOW THEM ALL THAT I'M A GUY.
WHEN I ENTER THAT DREAM...
...I'M NOT GOING TO FAIL AGAIN LIKE LAST TIME...
CLICK
CLICK
RATTLE
CLICK
CLICK
CLICK
WHO ELSE IS HERE?
I CAN'T TELL YOU THAT.
I CAN ONLY ANSWER QUESTIONS THAT PERTAIN TO YOU IN PARTICULAR.

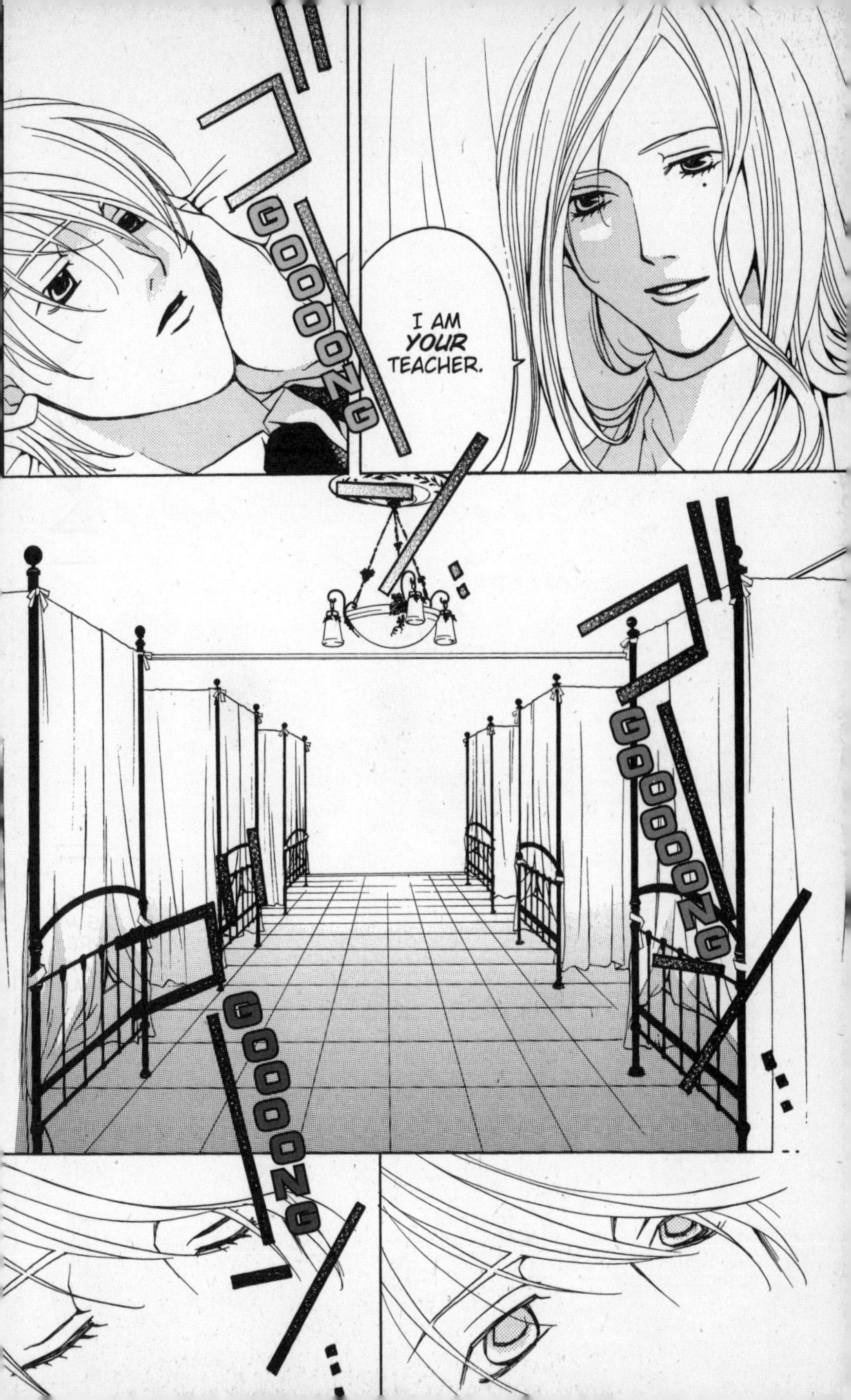
I AM *YOUR* TEACHER.
GOOOONG
GOOOOONG
GOOOONG

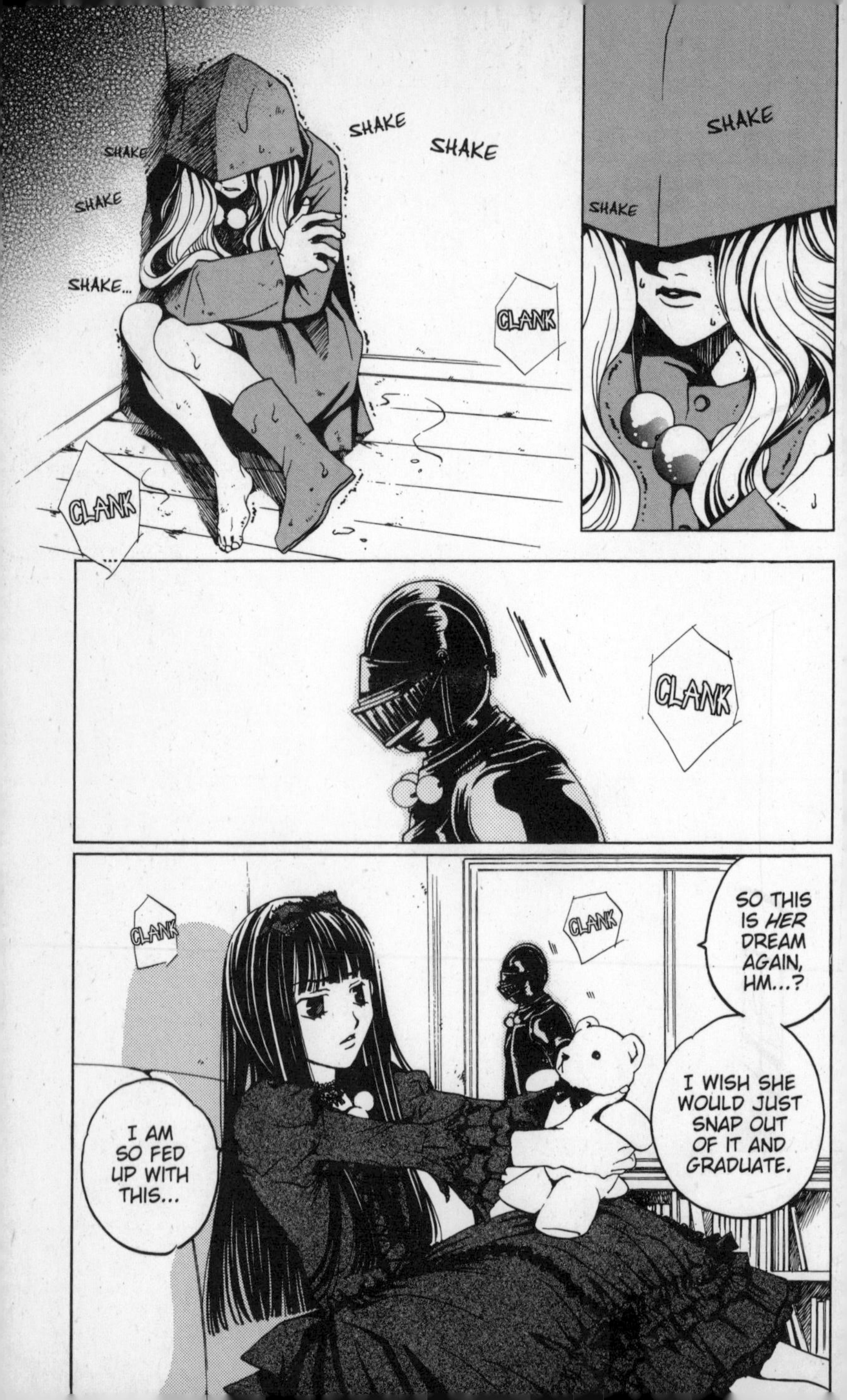
SHAKE
SHAKE
CLANK
SHAKE
SHAKE
SHAKE
SHAKE
SHAKE...
CLANK
CLANK
SO THIS IS *HER* DREAM AGAIN, HM...?
I WISH SHE WOULD JUST SNAP OUT OF IT AND GRADUATE.
CLANK
CLANK
I AM SO FED UP WITH THIS...

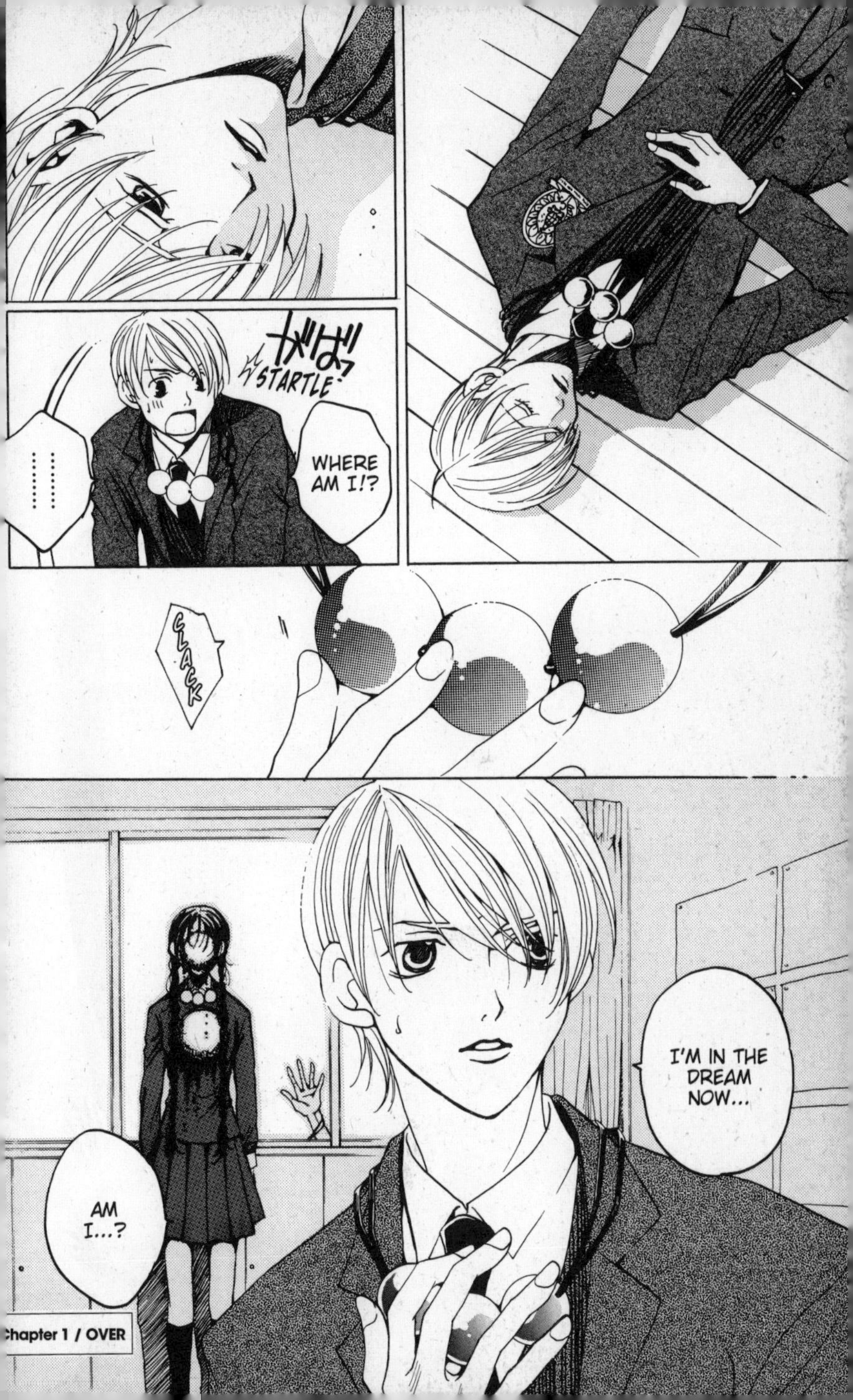
STARTLE
WHERE AM I!?
......
CLACK
I'M IN THE DREAM NOW...
AM I...?
Chapter 1 / OVER

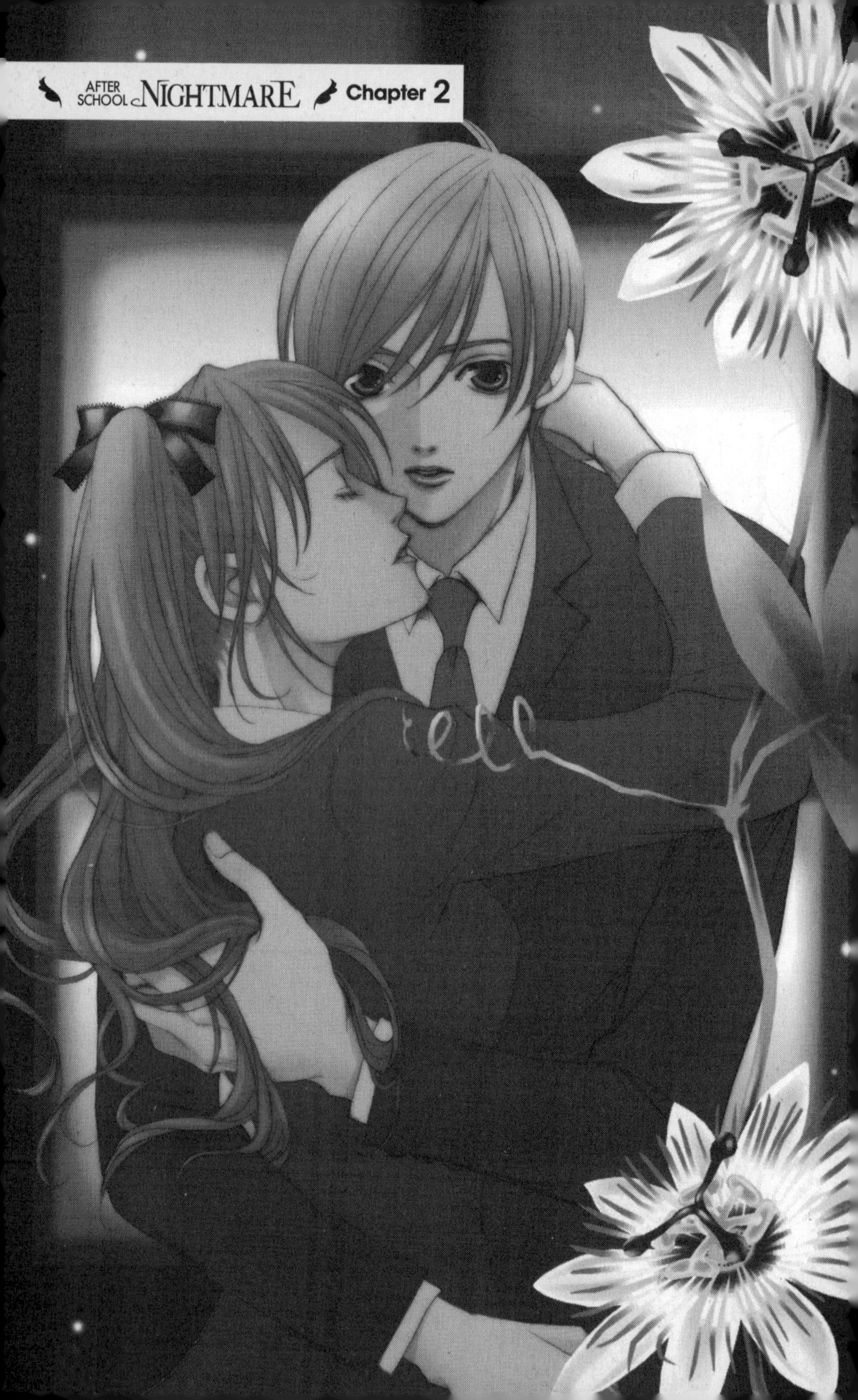
AFTER SCHOOL NIGHTMARE
Chapter 2

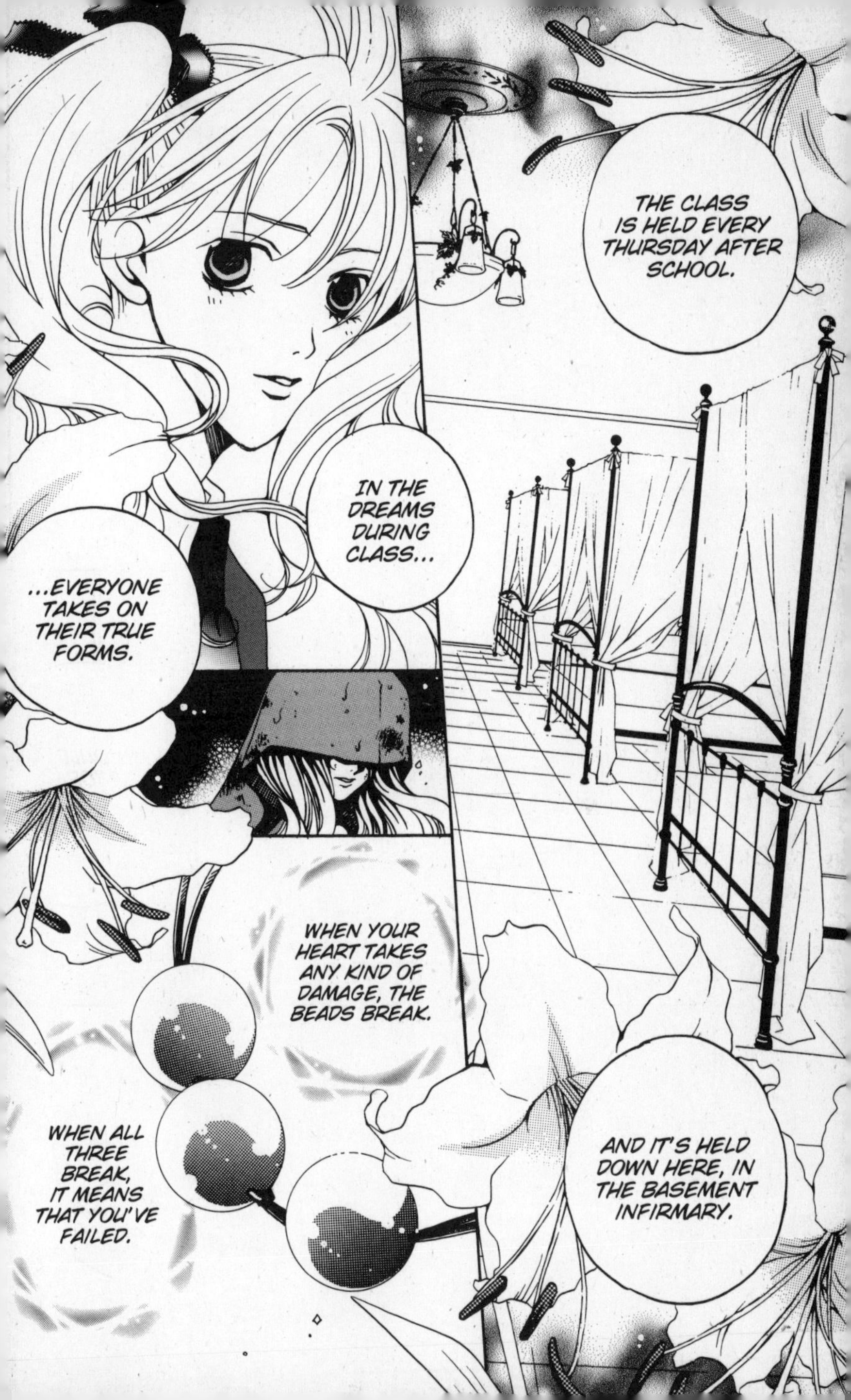
THE CLASS IS HELD EVERY THURSDAY AFTER SCHOOL.
AND IT'S HELD DOWN HERE, IN THE BASEMENT INFIRMARY.
IN THE DREAMS DURING CLASS...
...EVERYONE TAKES ON THEIR TRUE FORMS.
WHEN YOUR HEART TAKES ANY KIND OF DAMAGE, THE BEADS BREAK.
WHEN ALL THREE BREAK, IT MEANS THAT YOU'VE FAILED.

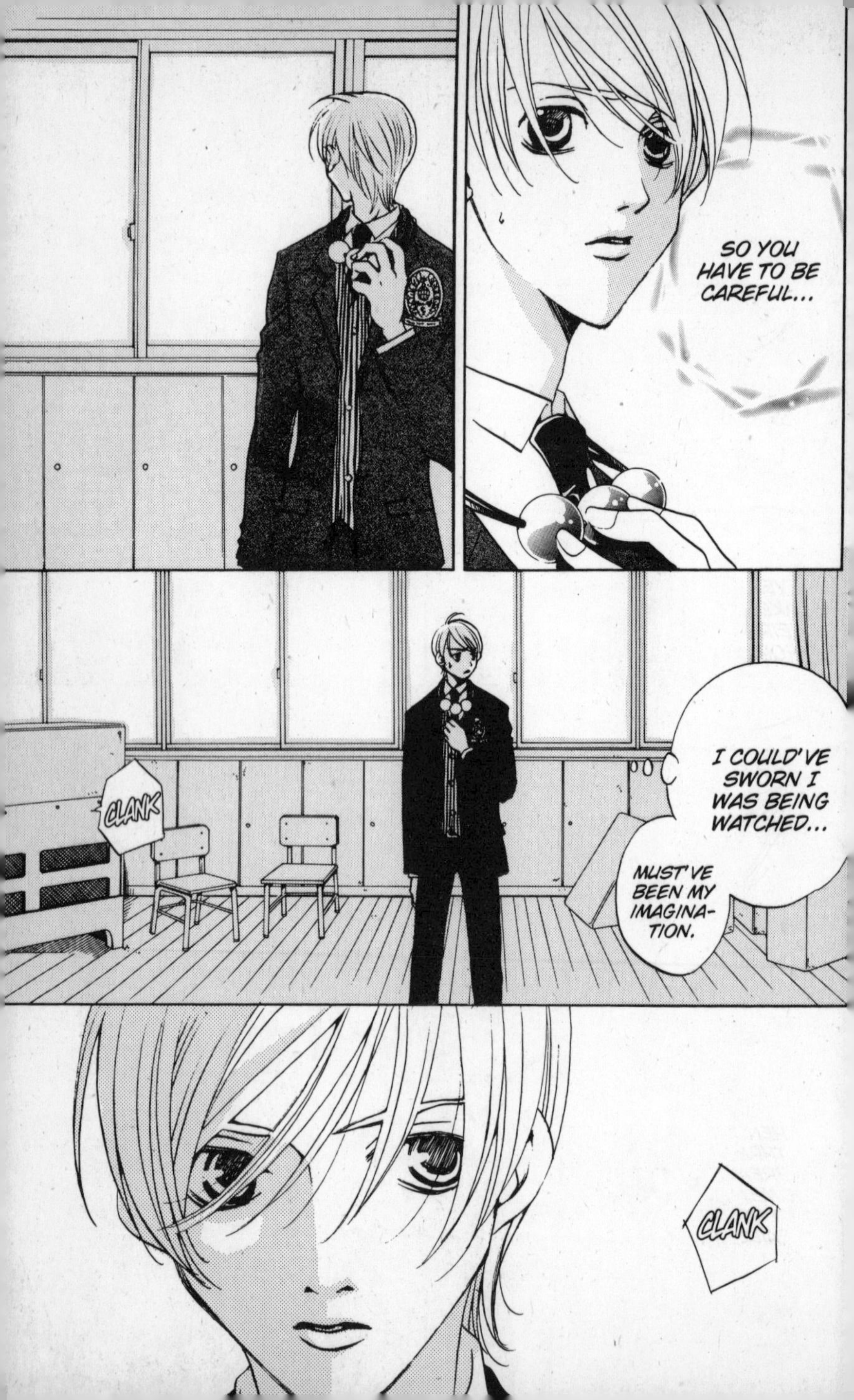
SO YOU HAVE TO BE CAREFUL...
I COULD'VE SWORN I WAS BEING WATCHED...
MUST'VE BEEN MY IMAGINATION.
CLANK
CLANK

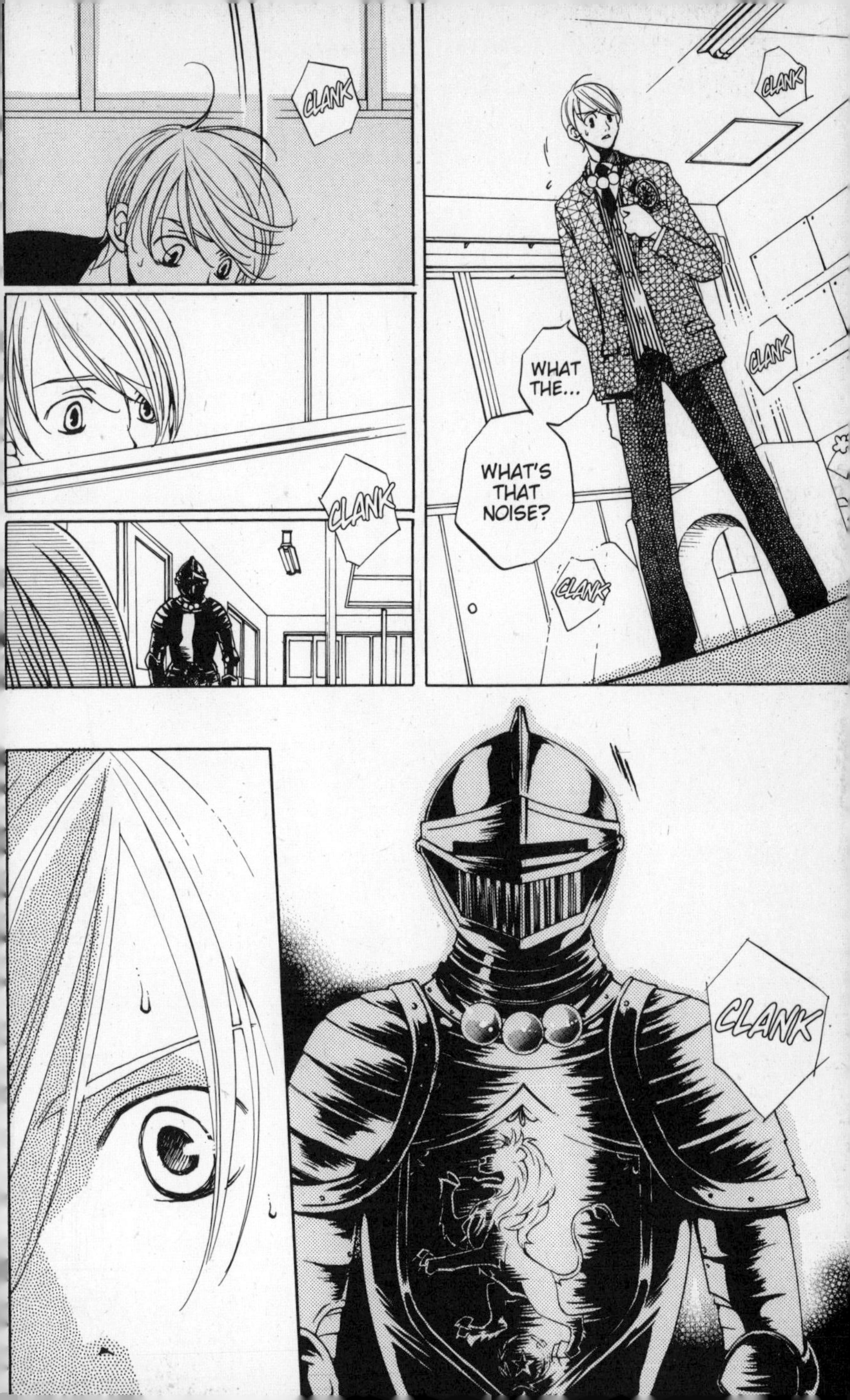
CLANK
CLANK
WHAT THE...
WHAT'S THAT NOISE?
CLANK
CLANK
CLANK
CLANK

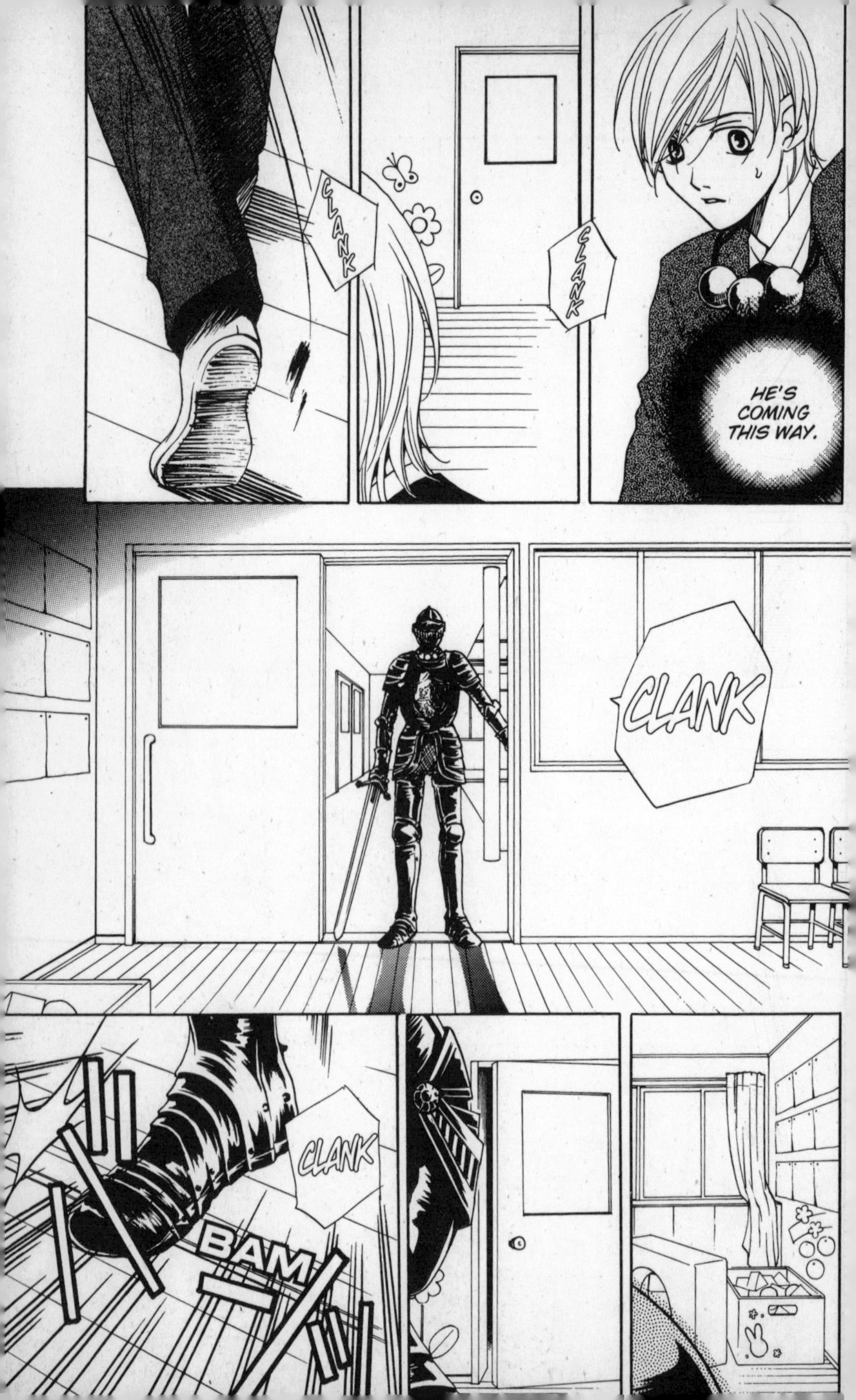
HE'S COMING THIS WAY.
CLANK
CLANK
CLANK
CLANK
BAM

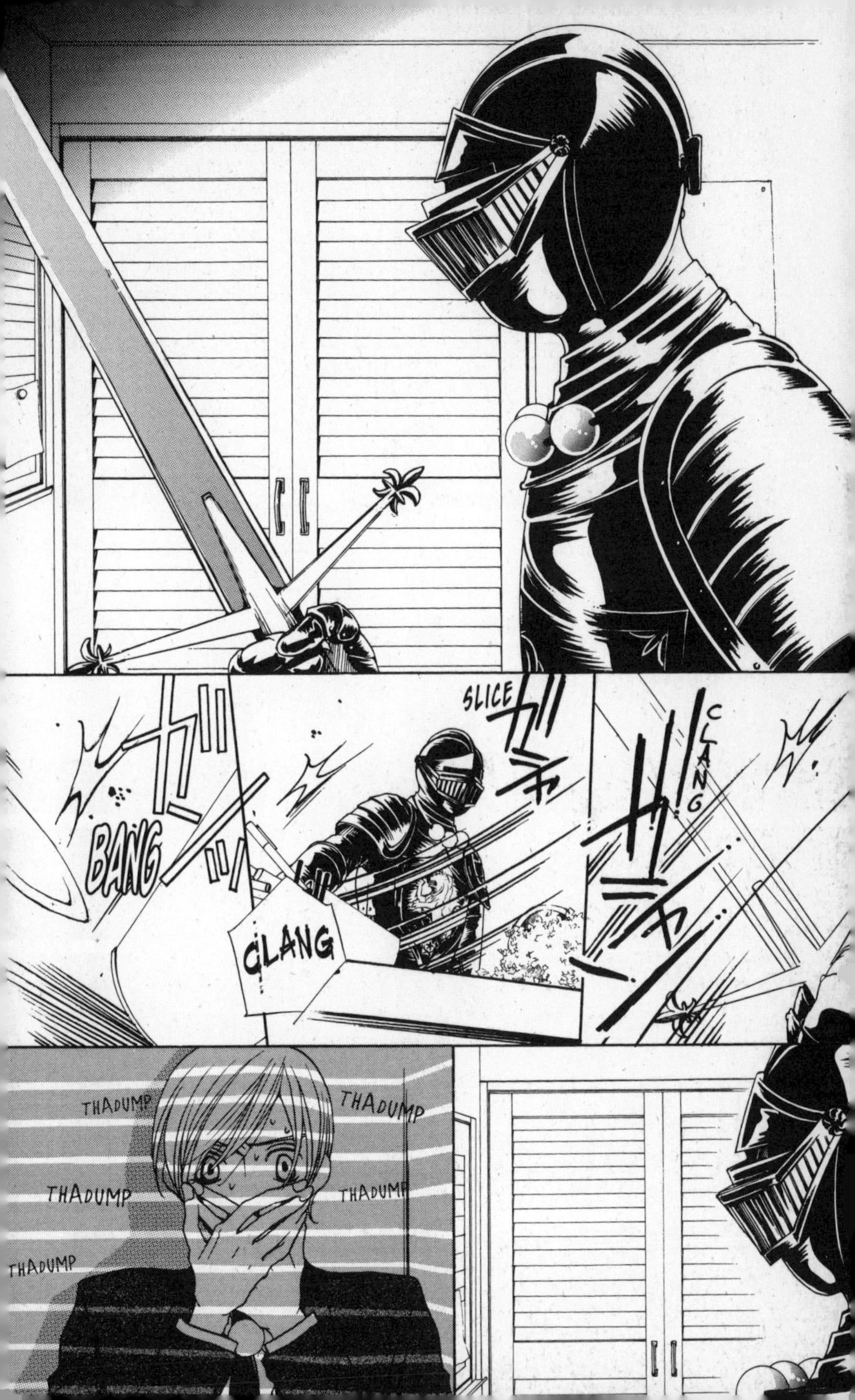
CLANG
SLICE
CLANG
BANG
THADUMP
THADUMP
THADUMP
THADUMP
THADUMP

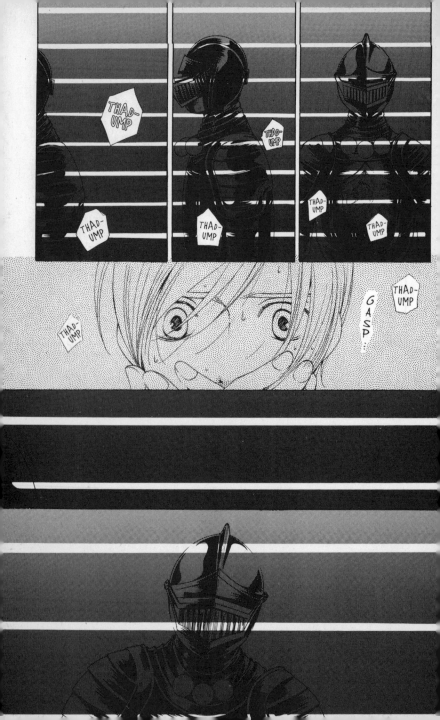

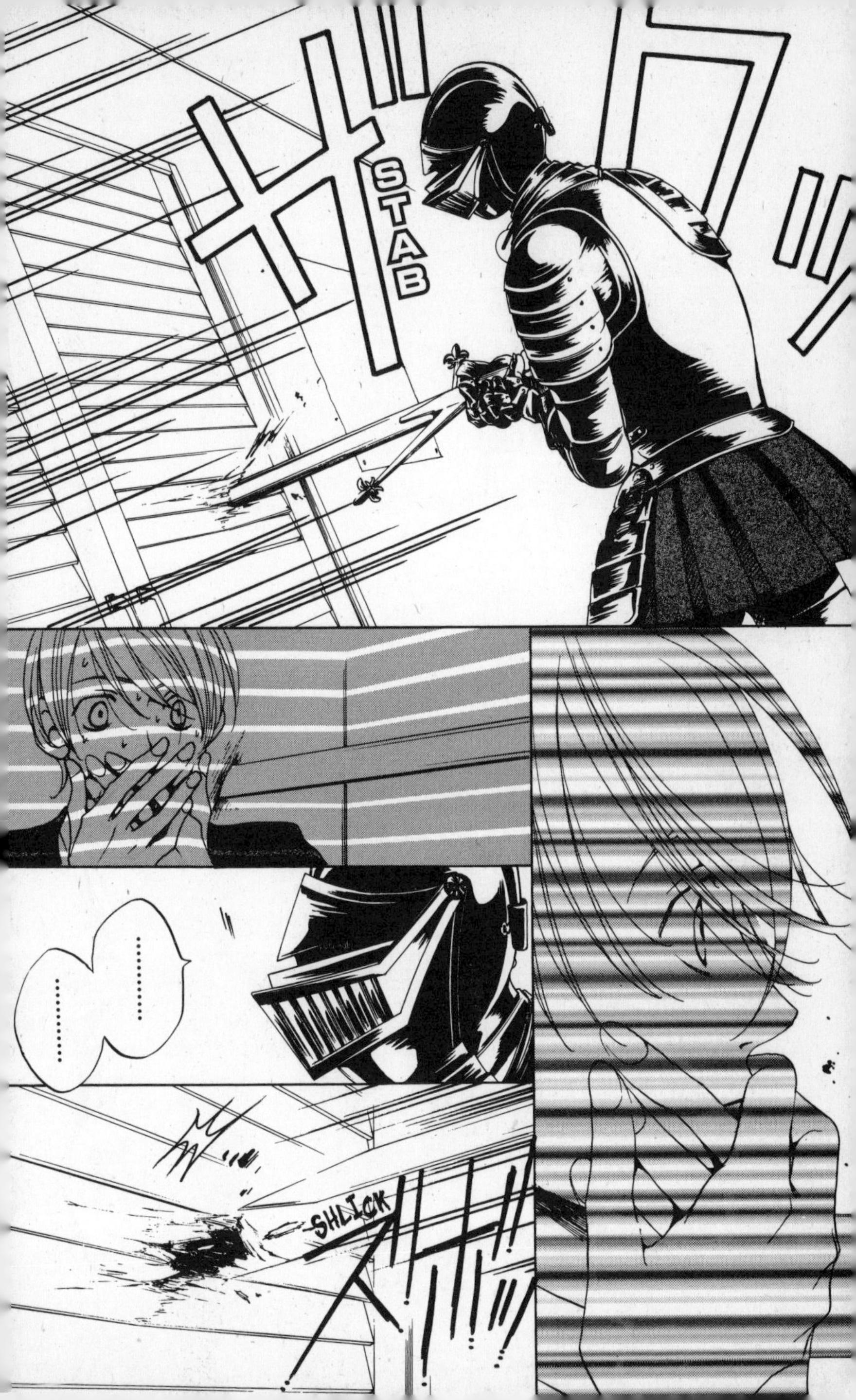
STAB
......
SHLICK

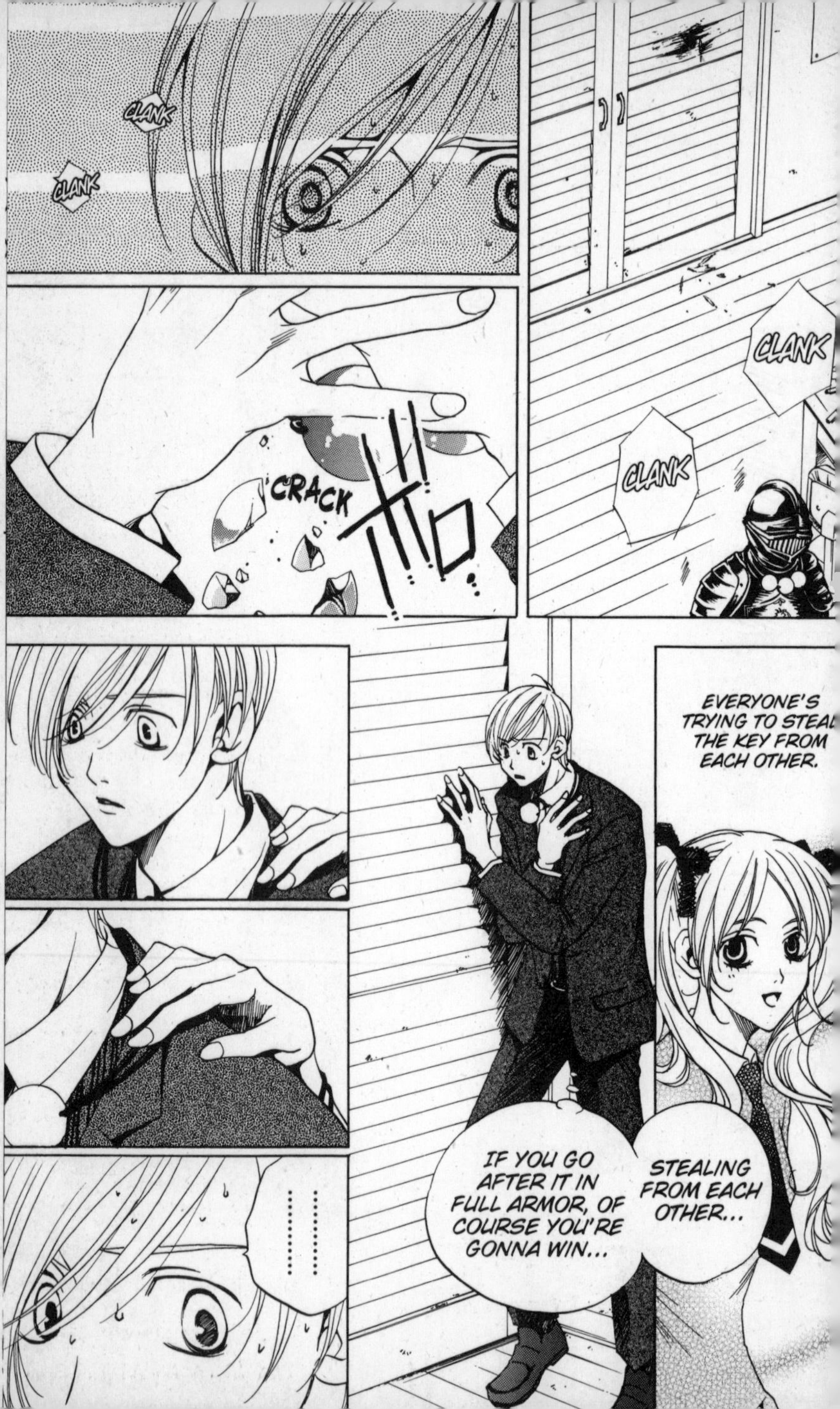
CLANK
CLANK
CLANK
CLANK
CRACK
EVERYONE'S TRYING TO STEAL THE KEY FROM EACH OTHER.
STEALING FROM EACH OTHER...
IF YOU GO AFTER IT IN FULL ARMOR, OF COURSE YOU'RE GONNA WIN...
......

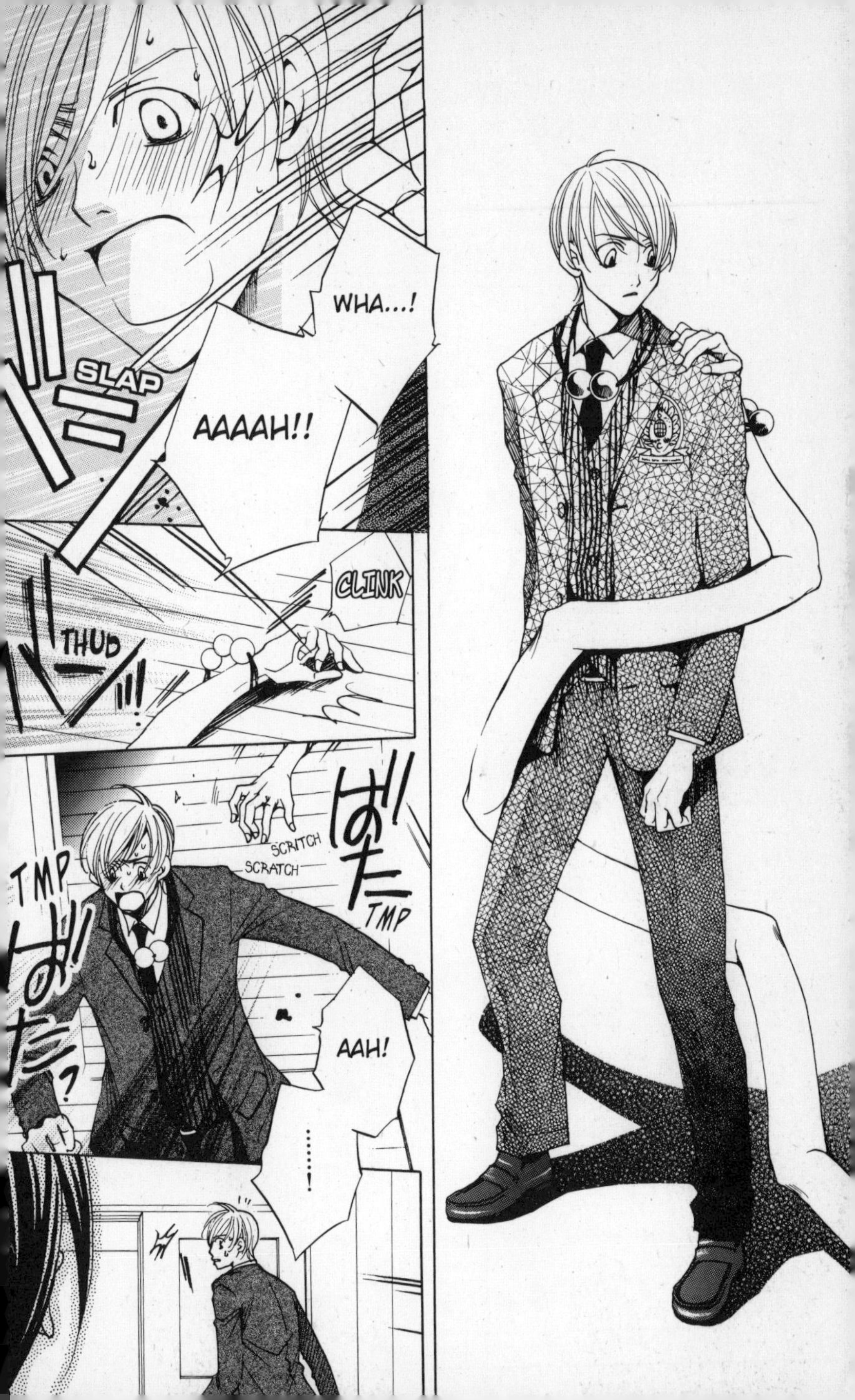
WHA...!
SLAP
AAAAH!!
CLINK
THUD
SCRITCH
SCRATCH
TMP
AAH!
TMP
......!

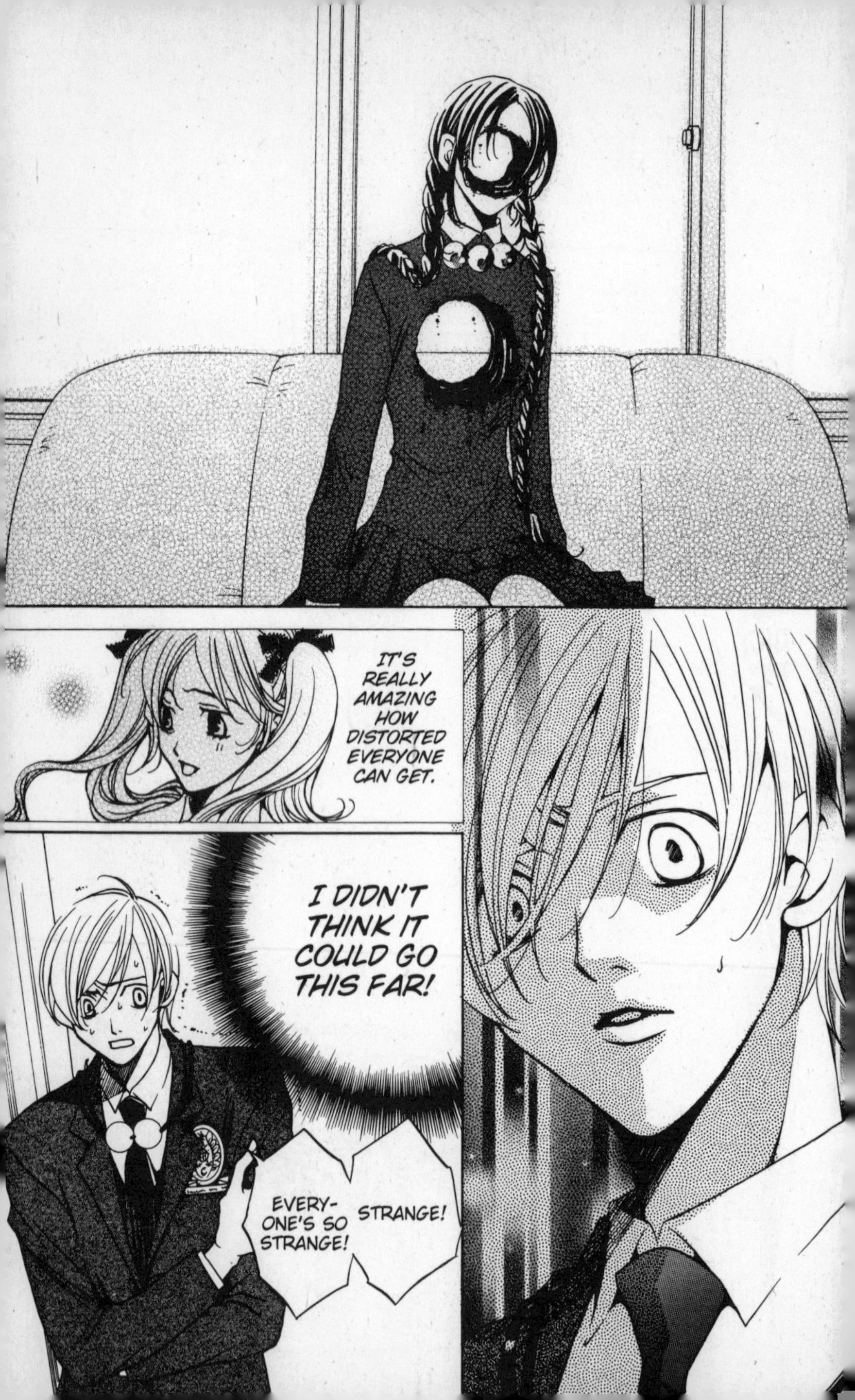
IT'S REALLY AMAZING HOW DISTORTED EVERYONE CAN GET.
I DIDN'T THINK IT COULD GO THIS FAR!
EVERY-ONE'S SO STRANGE!
STRANGE!

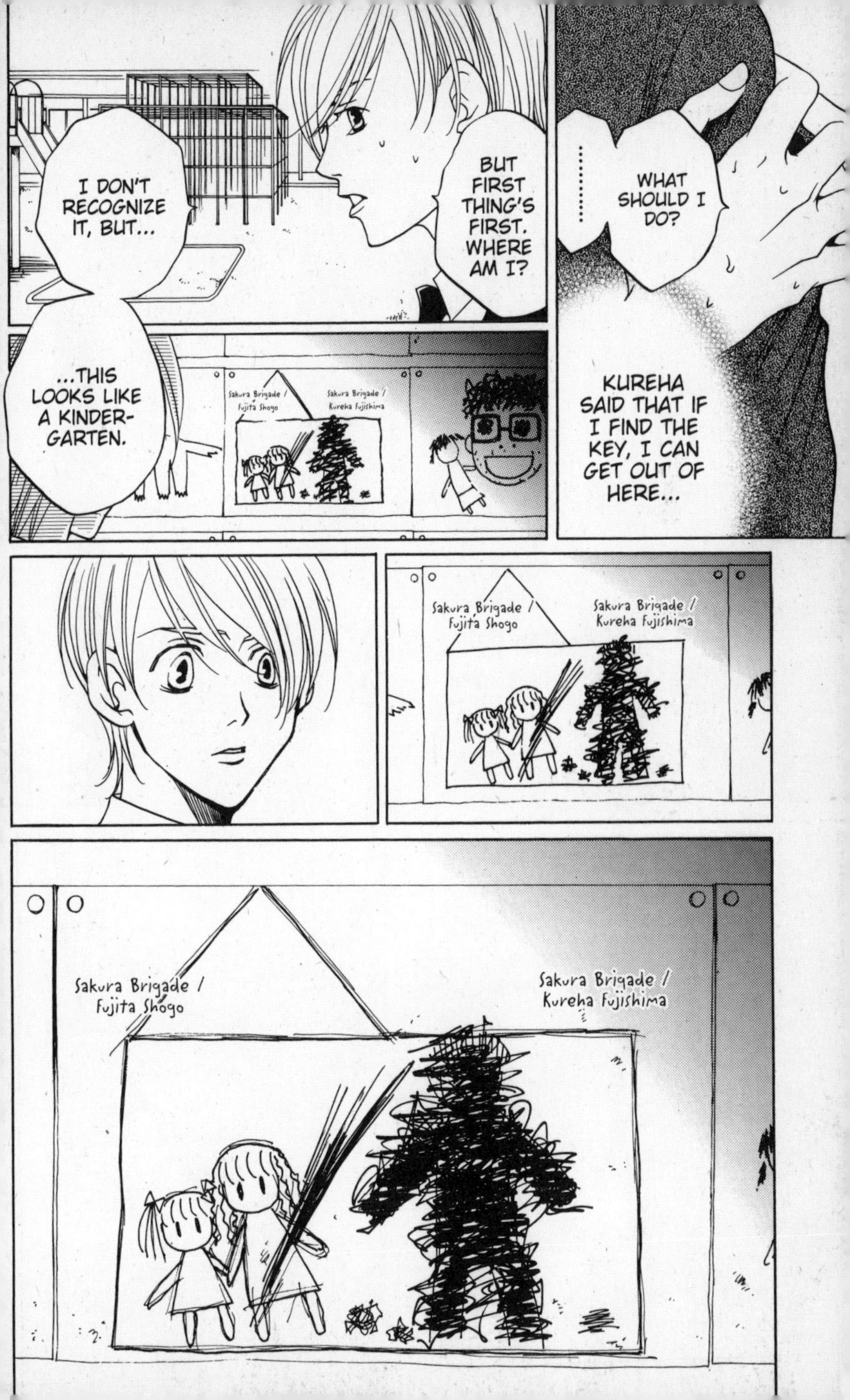
......
WHAT SHOULD I DO?
KUREHA SAID THAT IF I FIND THE KEY, I CAN GET OUT OF HERE...
BUT FIRST THING'S FIRST. WHERE AM I?
I DON'T RECOGNIZE IT, BUT...
...THIS LOOKS LIKE A KINDERGARTEN.
Sakura Brigade / Kureha Fujishima
Sakura Brigade / Fujita Shogo
Sakura Brigade / Kureha Fujishima
Sakura Brigade / Fujita Shogo
Sakura Brigade / Kureha Fujishima
Sakura Brigade / Fujita Shogo

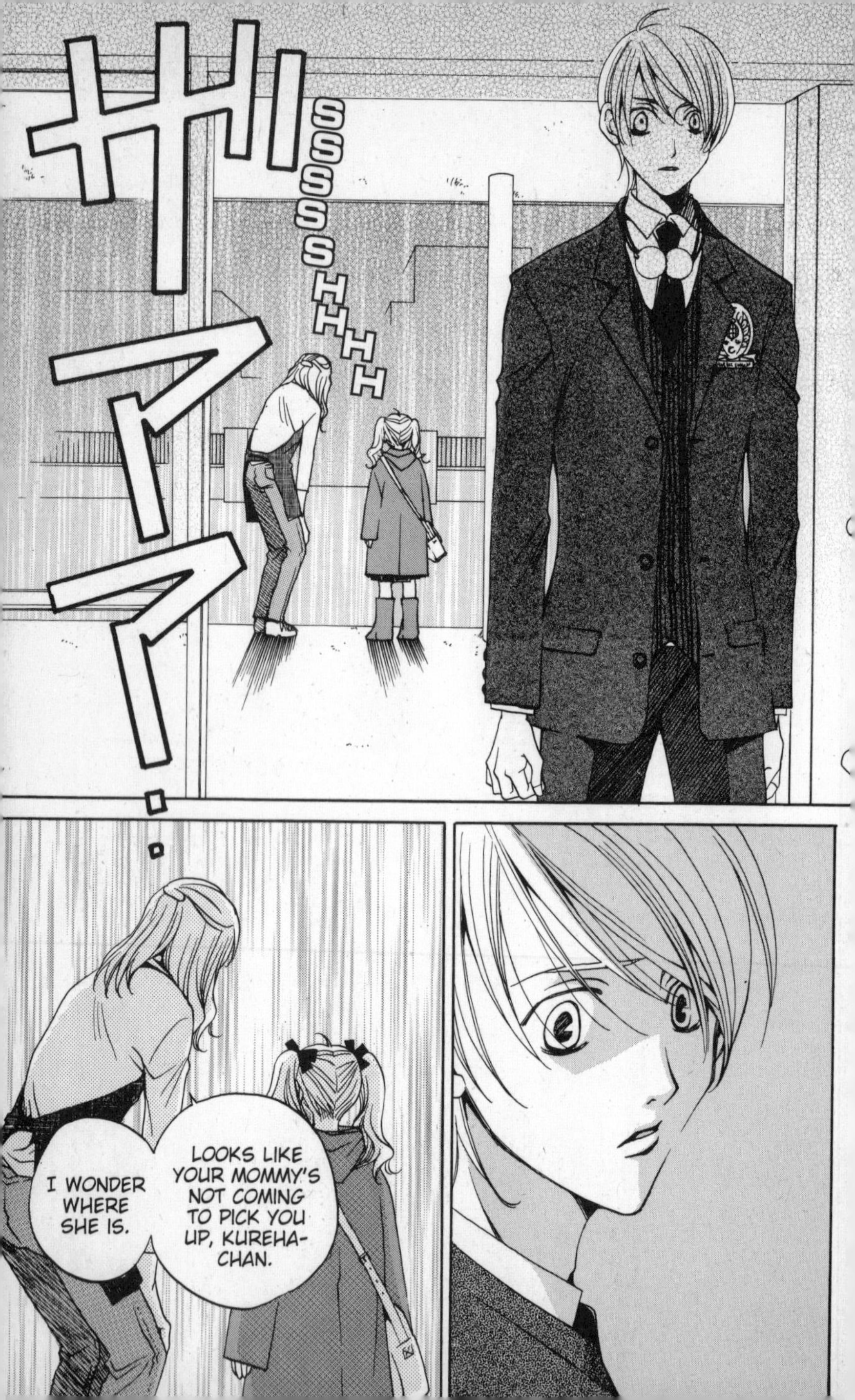
SSSSSHHHH
LOOKS LIKE YOUR MOMMY'S NOT COMING TO PICK YOU UP, KUREHA-CHAN.
I WONDER WHERE SHE IS.

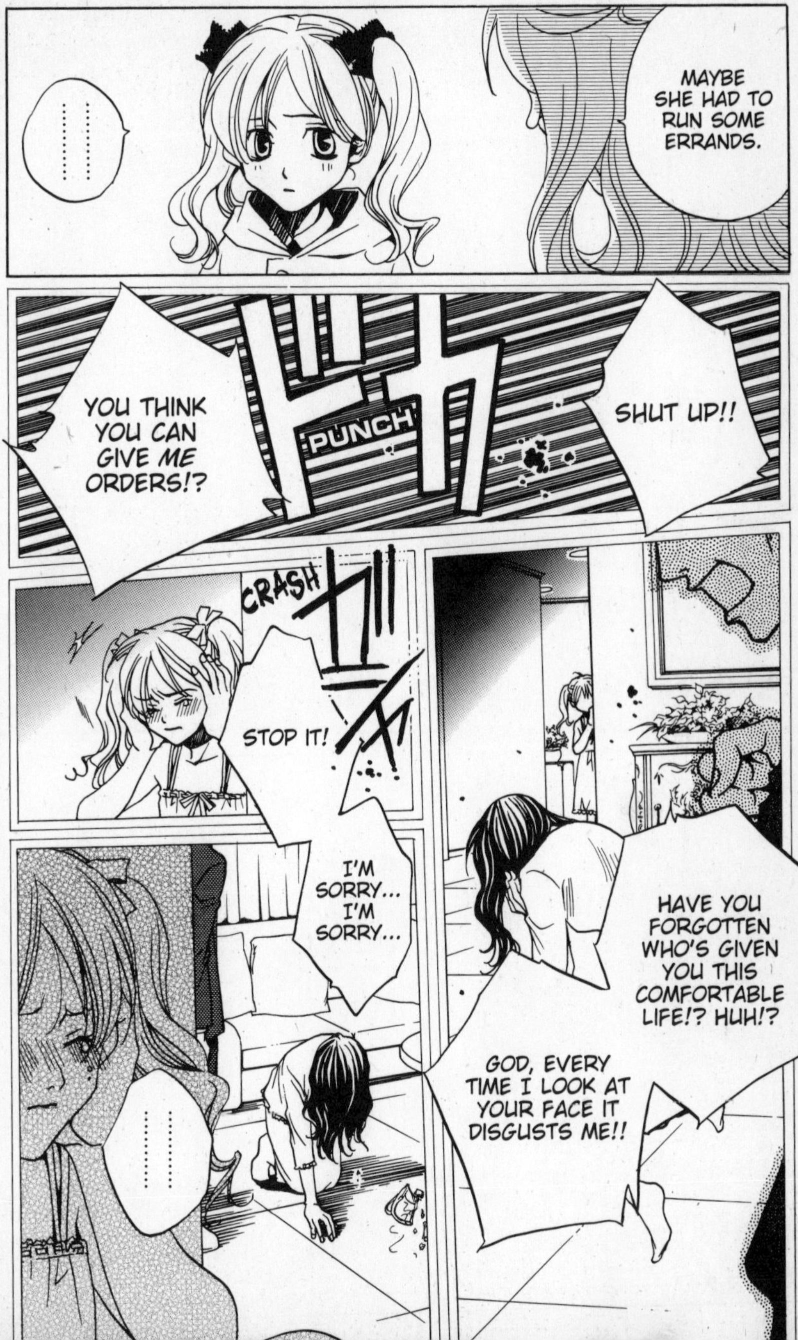
MAYBE SHE HAD TO RUN SOME ERRANDS.
……
SHUT UP!!
PUNCH
YOU THINK YOU CAN GIVE ME ORDERS!?
HAVE YOU FORGOTTEN WHO'S GIVEN YOU THIS COMFORTABLE LIFE!? HUH!?
GOD, EVERY TIME I LOOK AT YOUR FACE IT DISGUSTS ME!!
CRASH
STOP IT!
I'M SORRY... I'M SORRY...
……

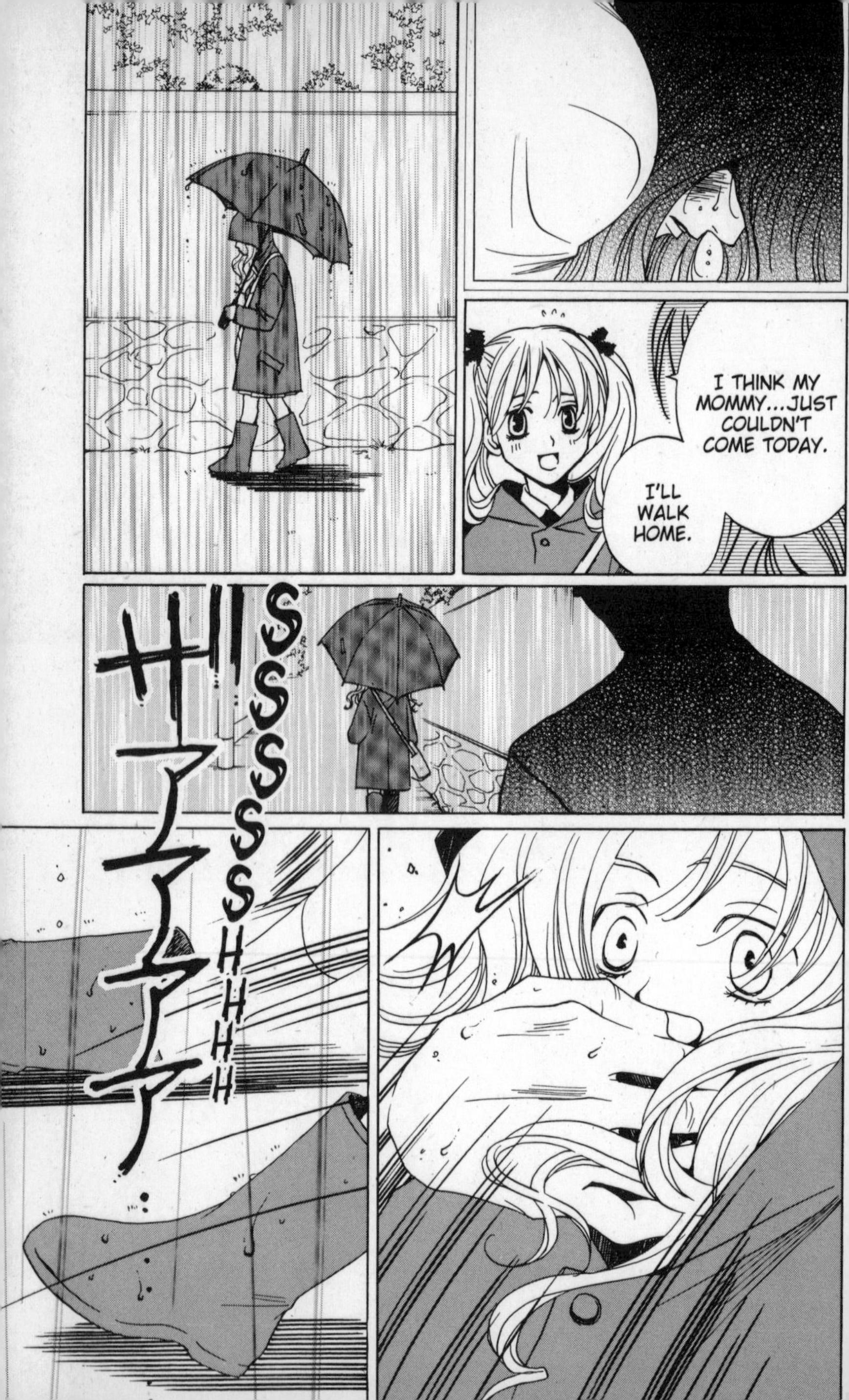
I THINK MY MOMMY...JUST COULDN'T COME TODAY.
I'LL WALK HOME.
SSSSSSHHHH

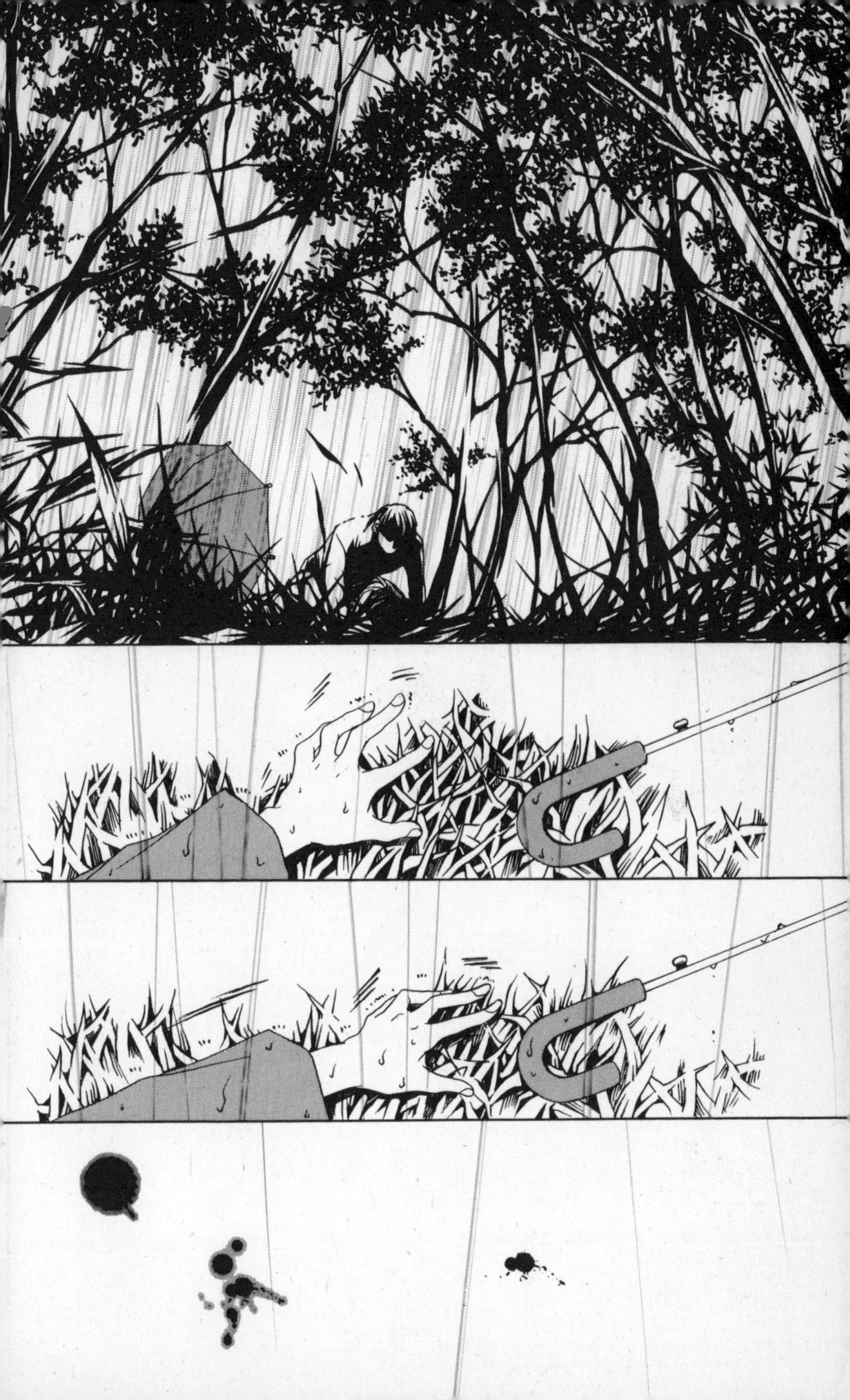

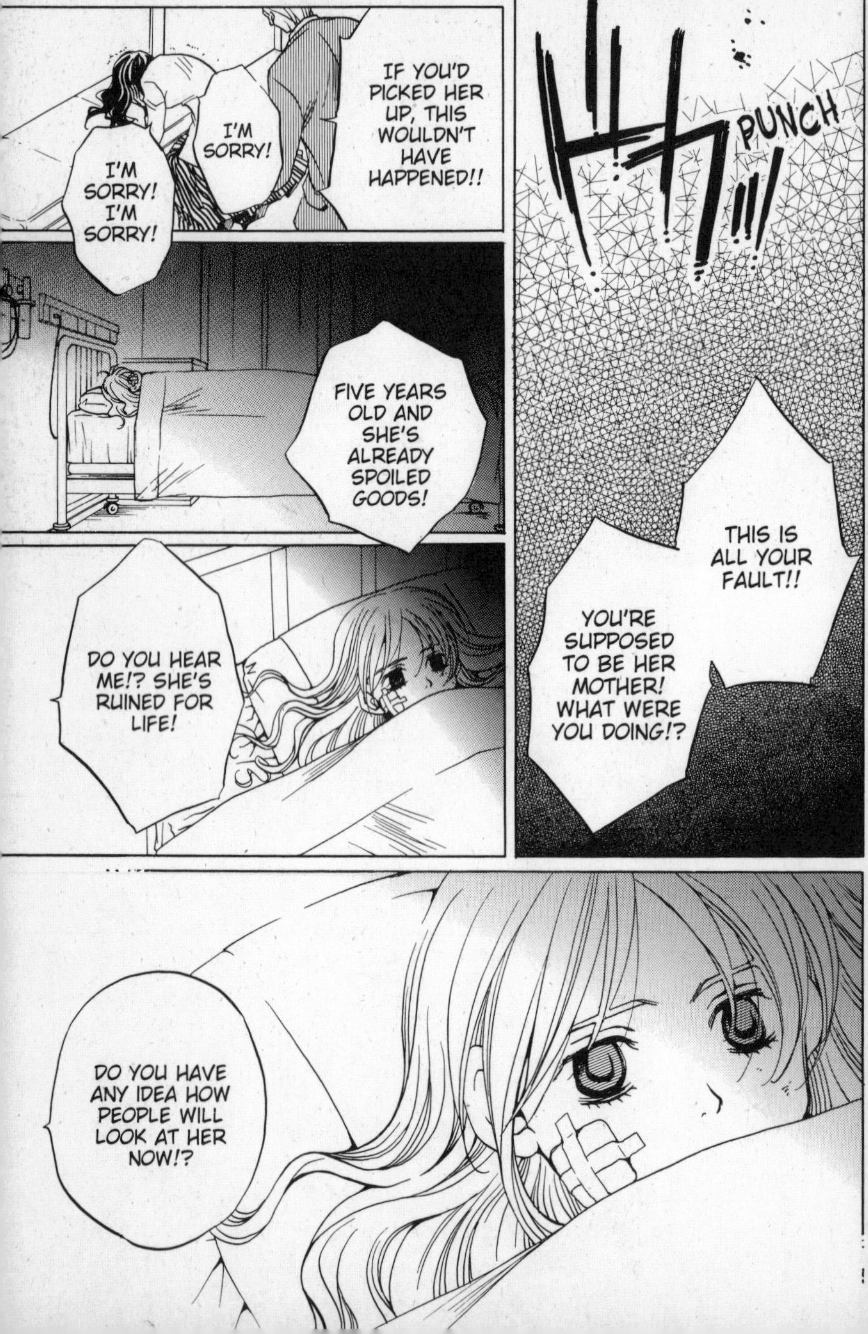
PUNCH
THIS IS ALL YOUR FAULT!!
YOU'RE SUPPOSED TO BE HER MOTHER! WHAT WERE YOU DOING!?
IF YOU'D PICKED HER UP, THIS WOULDN'T HAVE HAPPENED!!
I'M SORRY!
I'M SORRY! I'M SORRY!
FIVE YEARS OLD AND SHE'S ALREADY SPOILED GOODS!
DO YOU HEAR ME!? SHE'S RUINED FOR LIFE!
DO YOU HAVE ANY IDEA HOW PEOPLE WILL LOOK AT HER NOW!?

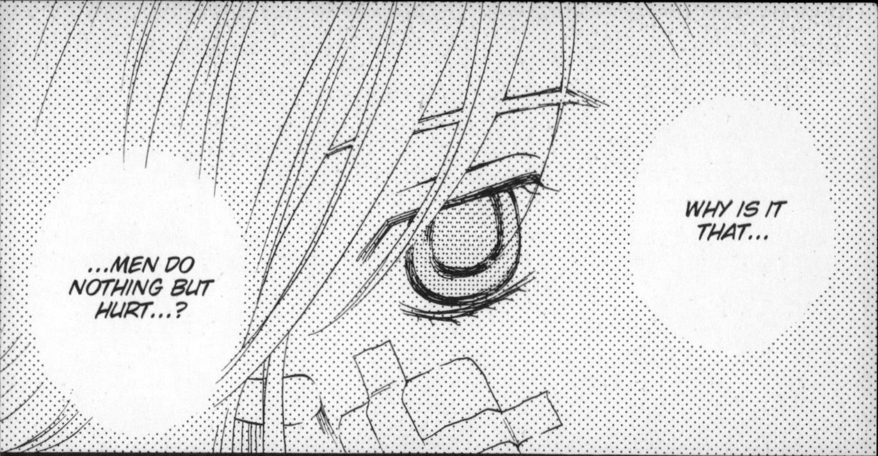
WHY IS IT THAT...
...MEN DO NOTHING BUT HURT...?
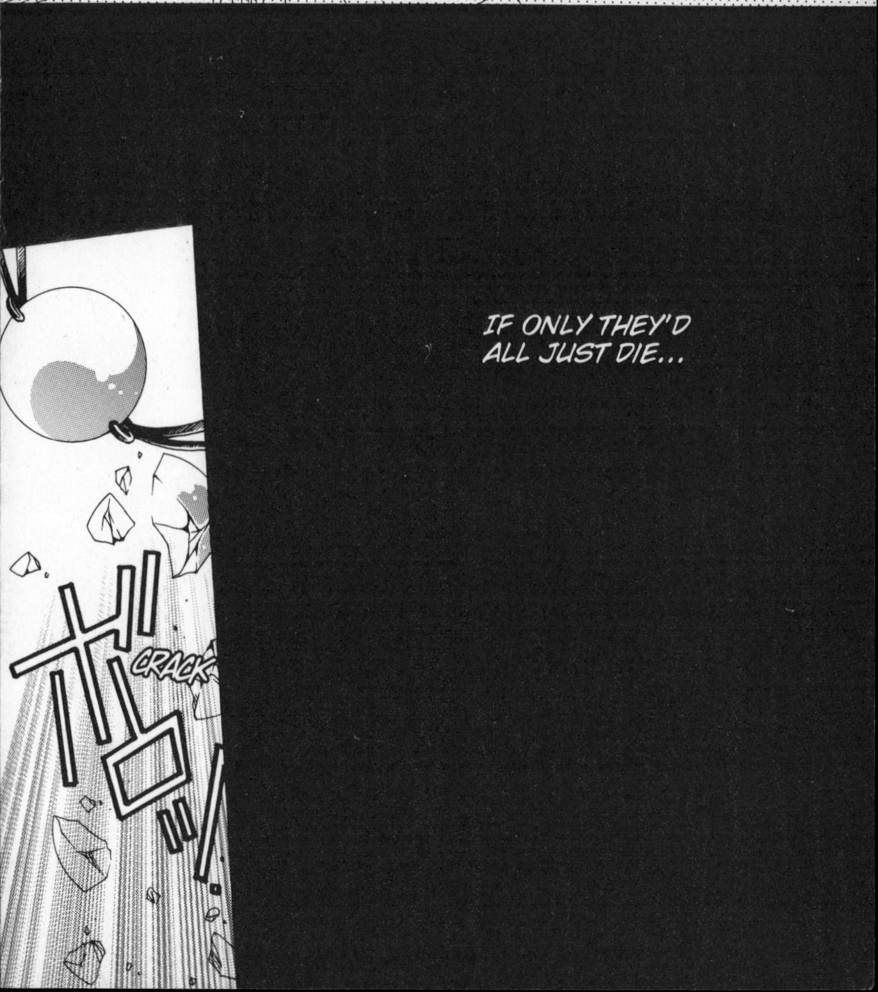
IF ONLY THEY'D ALL JUST DIE...
CRACK

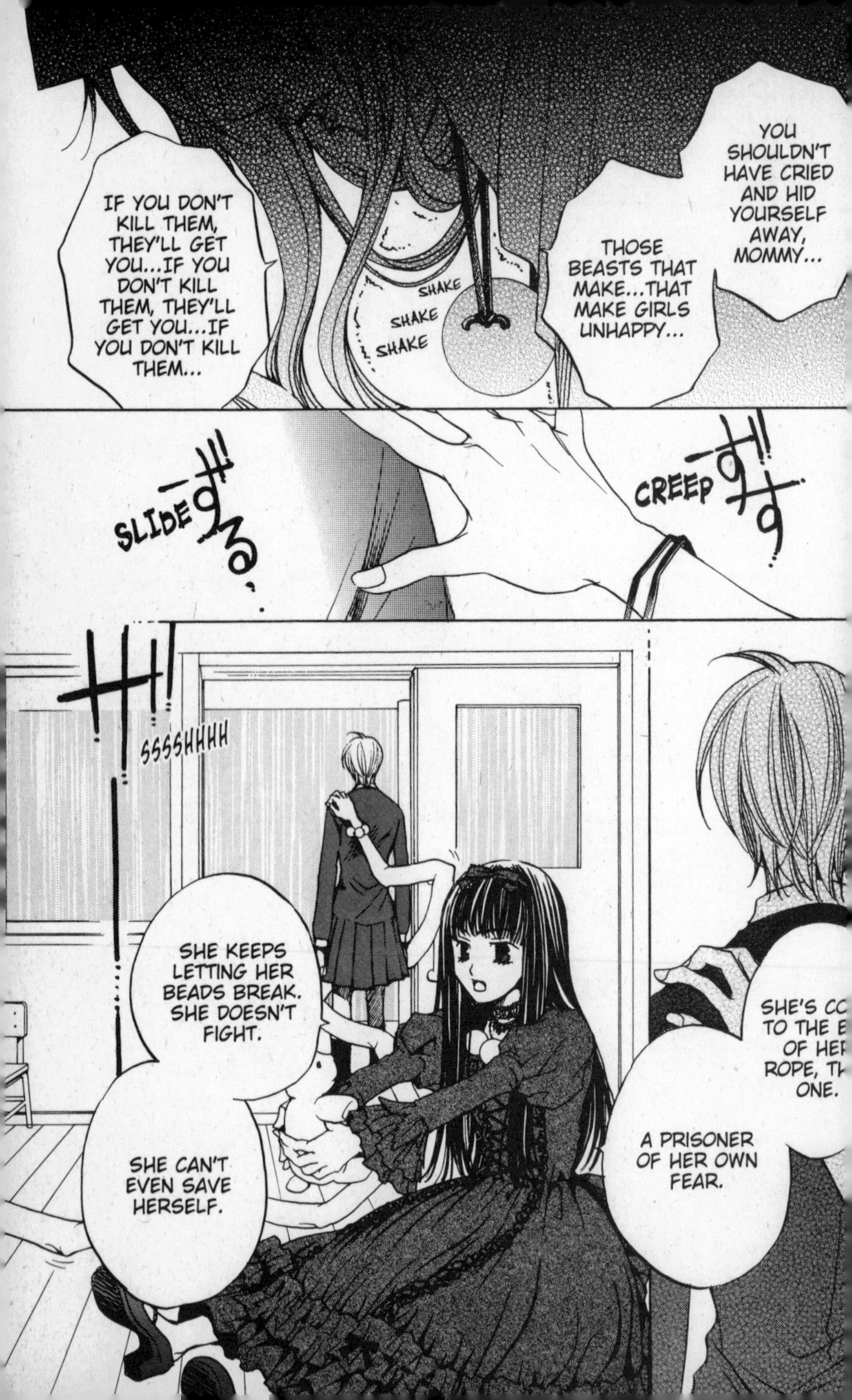
YOU SHOULDN'T HAVE CRIED AND HID YOURSELF AWAY, MOMMY...
THOSE BEASTS THAT MAKE...THAT MAKE GIRLS UNHAPPY...
SHAKE
SHAKE
SHAKE
IF YOU DON'T KILL THEM, THEY'LL GET YOU...IF YOU DON'T KILL THEM, THEY'LL GET YOU...IF YOU DON'T KILL THEM...
CREEP
SLIDE
SSSSHHHH
SHE'S CO TO THE E OF HEF ROPE, TH ONE.
A PRISONER OF HER OWN FEAR.
SHE KEEPS LETTING HER BEADS BREAK. SHE DOESN'T FIGHT.
SHE CAN'T EVEN SAVE HERSELF.

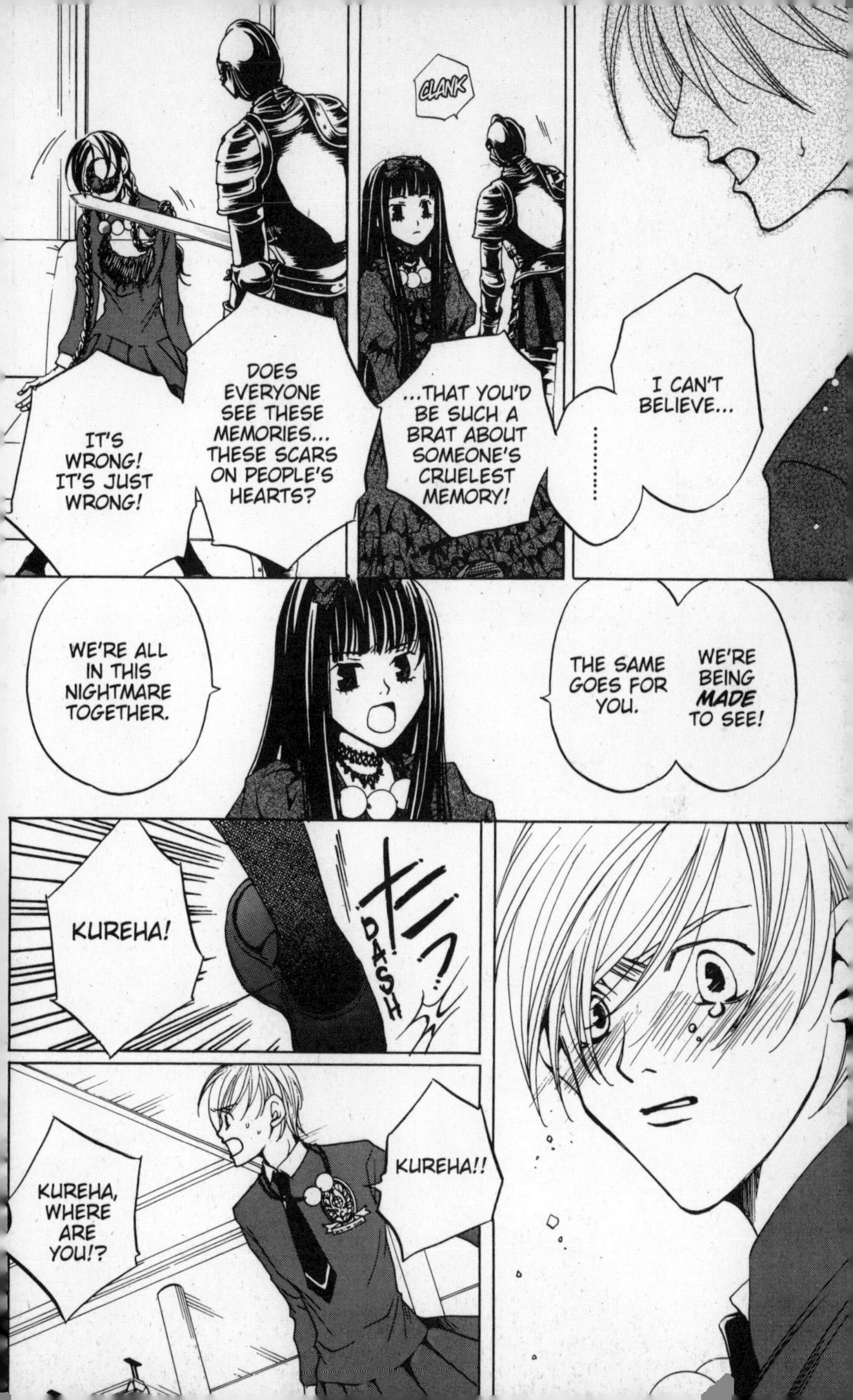

I CAN'T BELIEVE...
......
...THAT YOU'D BE SUCH A BRAT ABOUT SOMEONE'S CRUELEST MEMORY!
CLANK
DOES EVERYONE SEE THESE MEMORIES... THESE SCARS ON PEOPLE'S HEARTS?
IT'S WRONG! IT'S JUST WRONG!
THE SAME GOES FOR YOU. WE'RE BEING *MADE* TO SEE!
WE'RE ALL IN THIS NIGHTMARE TOGETHER.
DASH
KUREHA!
KUREHA!!
KUREHA, WHERE ARE YOU!?

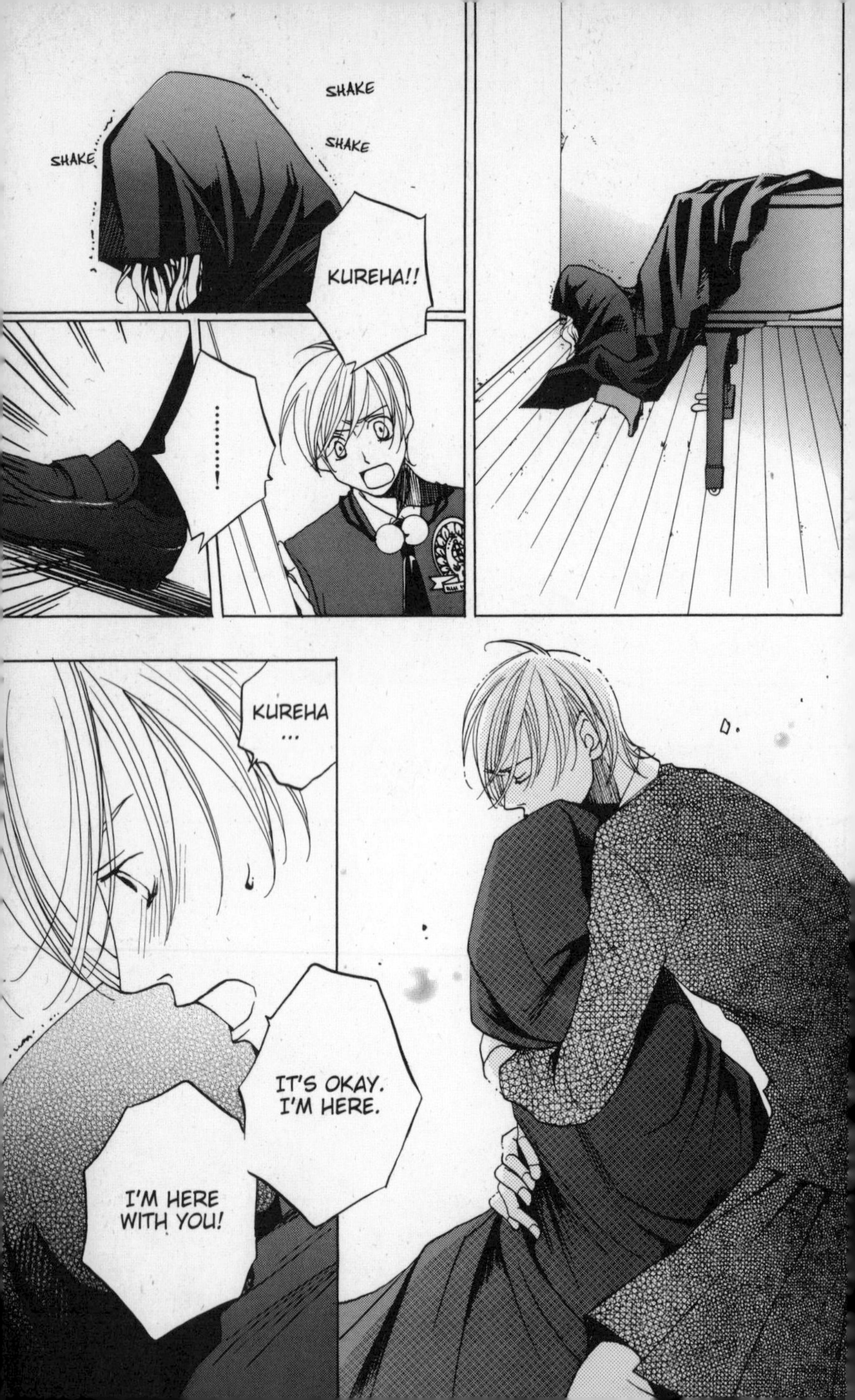
SHAKE
SHAKE
SHAKE
KUREHA!!
......!
KUREHA ...
IT'S OKAY. I'M HERE.
I'M HERE WITH YOU!

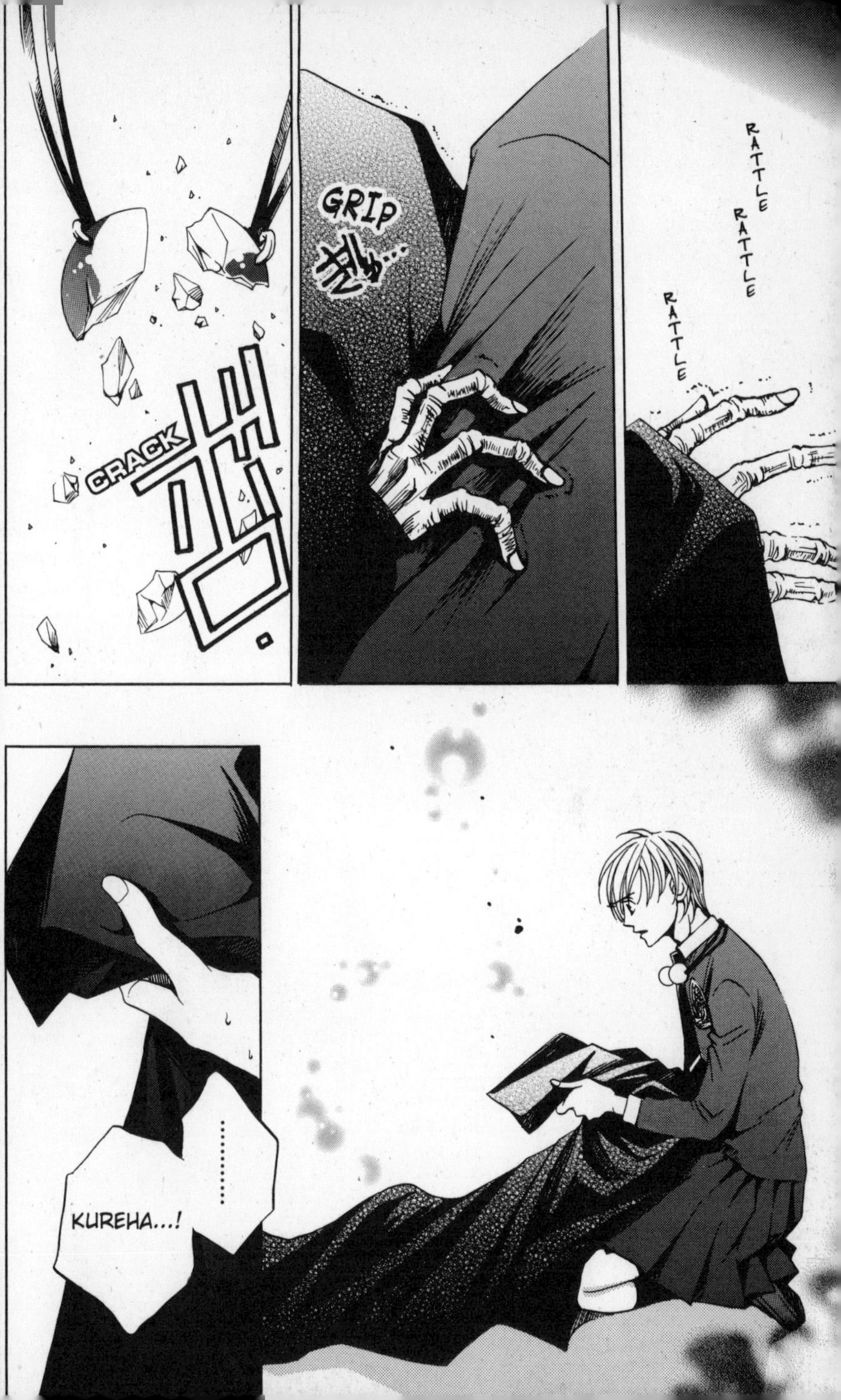
RATTLE
RATTLE
RATTLE
GRIP
CRACK
......
KUREHA...!

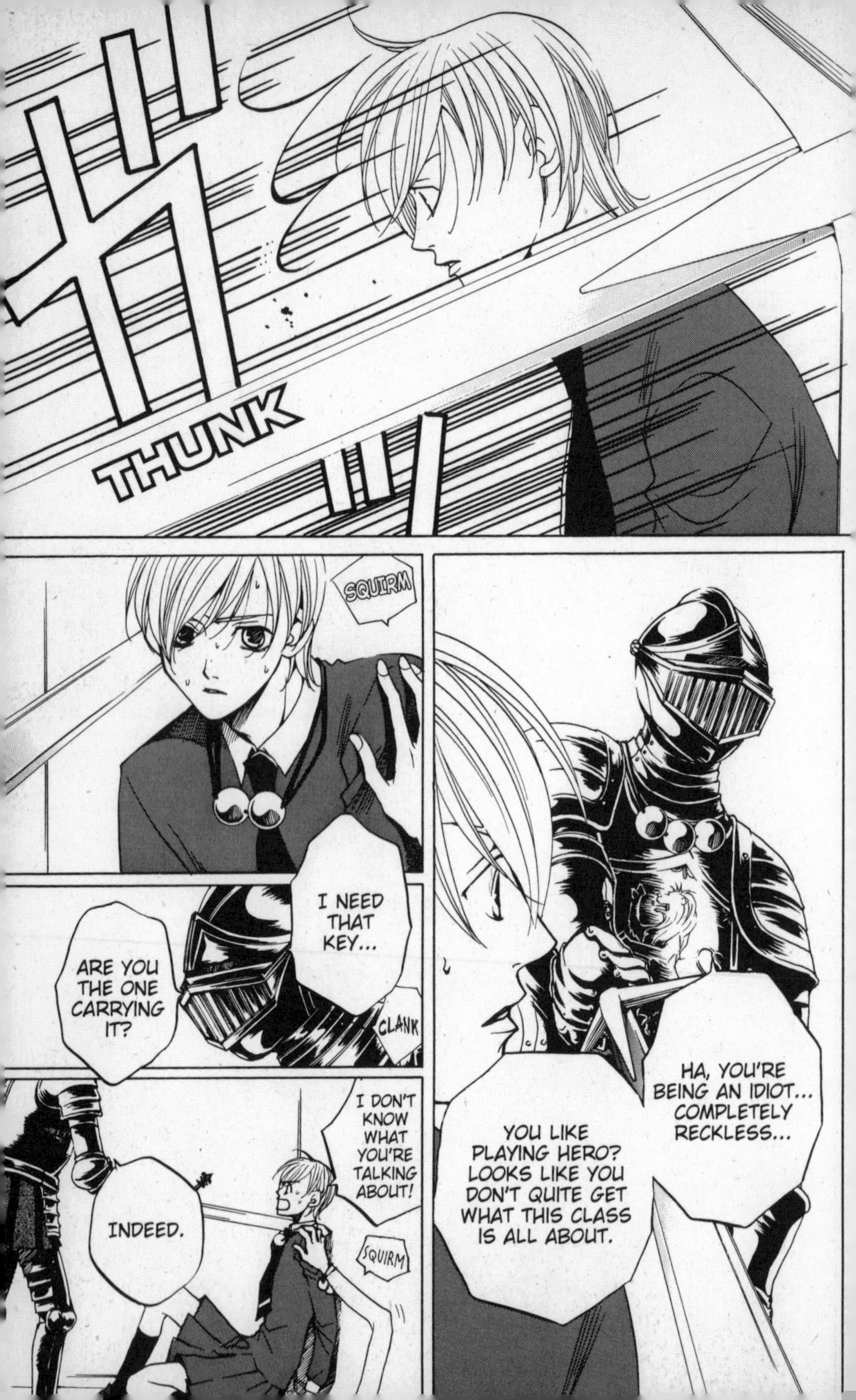
THUNK
HA, YOU'RE BEING AN IDIOT... COMPLETELY RECKLESS...
YOU LIKE PLAYING HERO? LOOKS LIKE YOU DON'T QUITE GET WHAT THIS CLASS IS ALL ABOUT.
SQUIRM
I NEED THAT KEY...
ARE YOU THE ONE CARRYING IT?
CLANK
I DON'T KNOW WHAT YOU'RE TALKING ABOUT!
SQUIRM
INDEED.

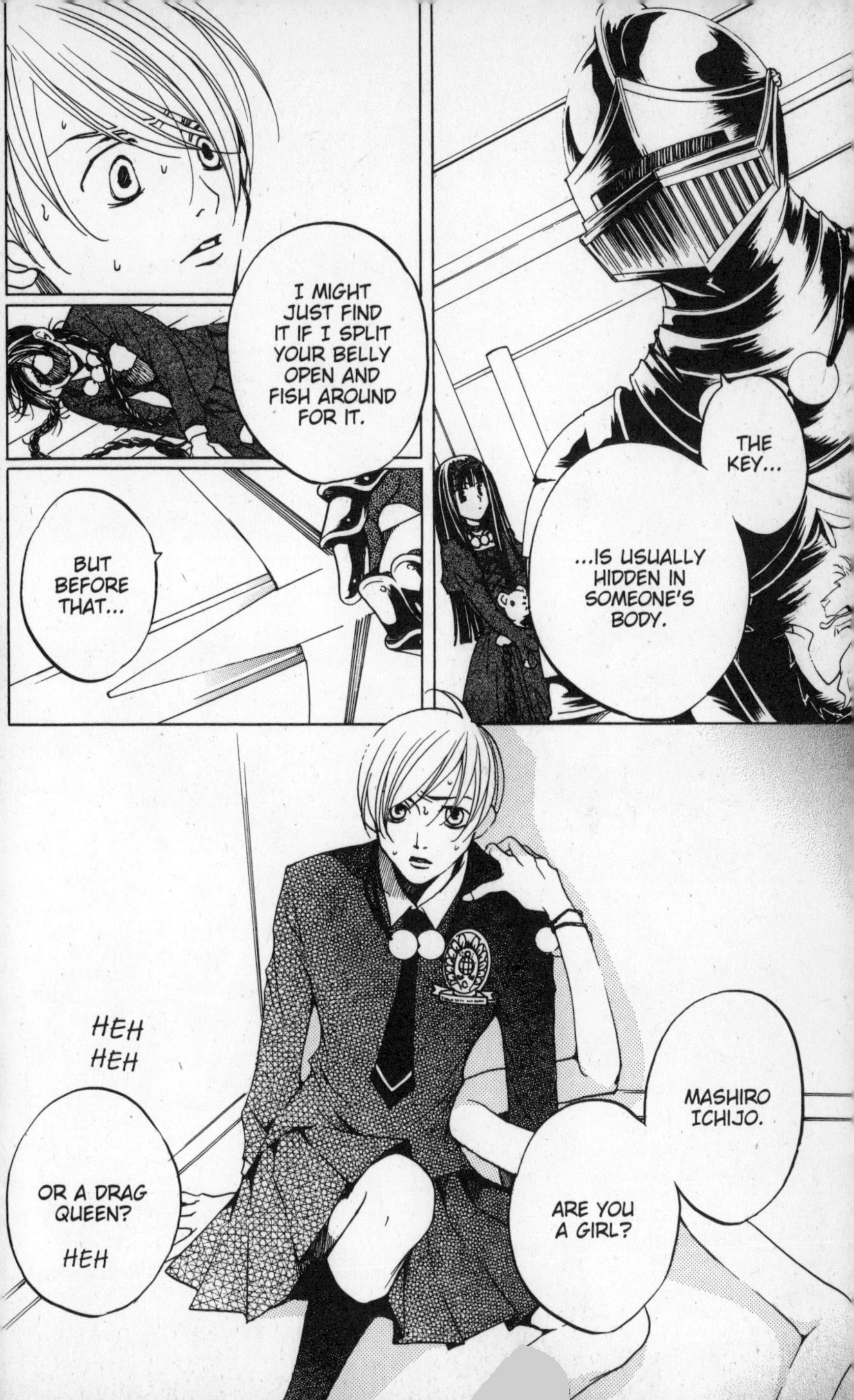
THE KEY...
...IS USUALLY HIDDEN IN SOMEONE'S BODY.
I MIGHT JUST FIND IT IF I SPLIT YOUR BELLY OPEN AND FISH AROUND FOR IT.
BUT BEFORE THAT...
MASHIRO ICHIJO.
ARE YOU A GIRL?
HEH HEH
OR A DRAG QUEEN?
HEH

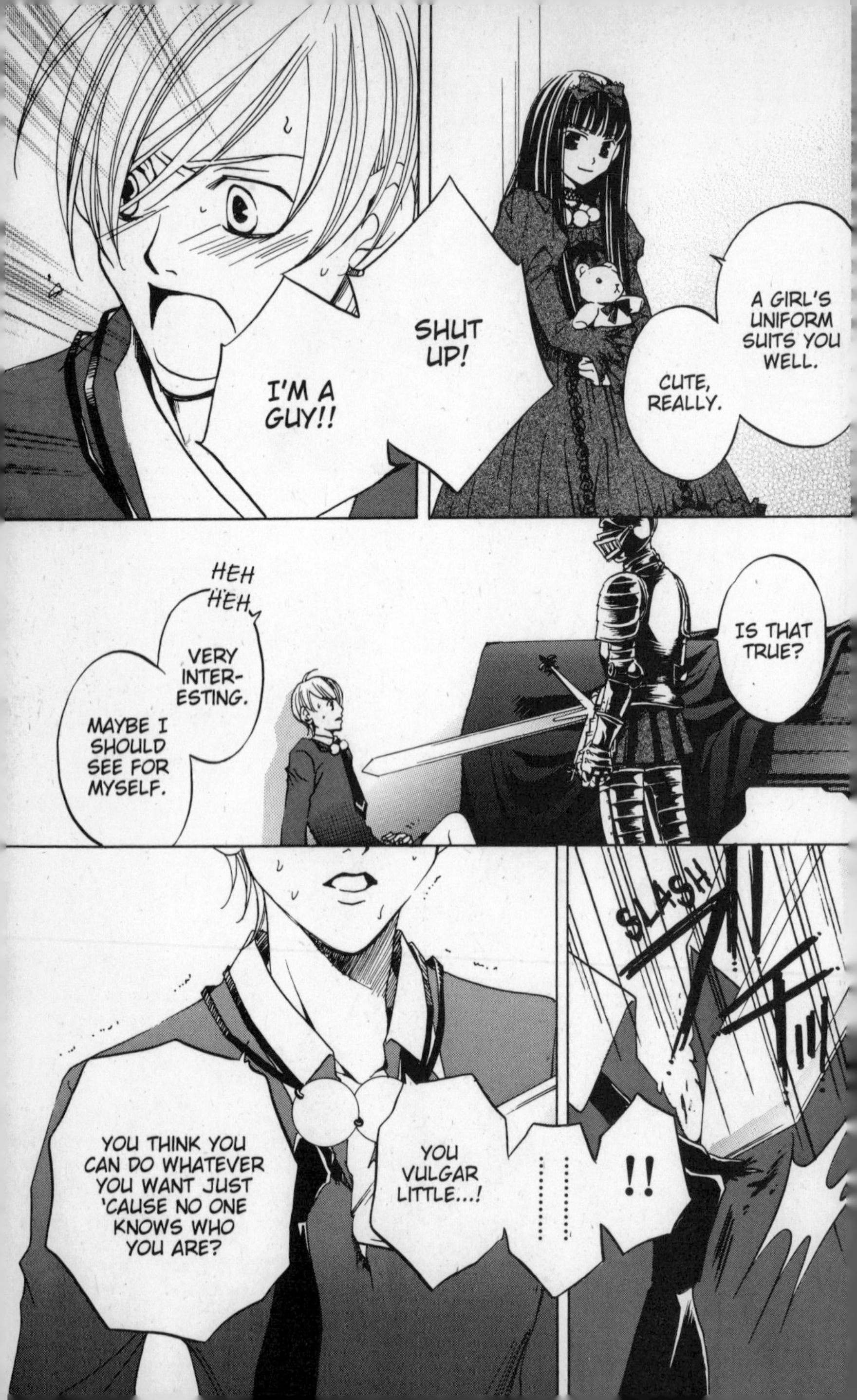
A GIRL'S UNIFORM SUITS YOU WELL.
CUTE, REALLY.
SHUT UP!
I'M A GUY!!
IS THAT TRUE?
HEH HEH
VERY INTER-ESTING.
MAYBE I SHOULD SEE FOR MYSELF.
SLASH
!!
......
YOU VULGAR LITTLE...!
YOU THINK YOU CAN DO WHATEVER YOU WANT JUST 'CAUSE NO ONE KNOWS WHO YOU ARE?

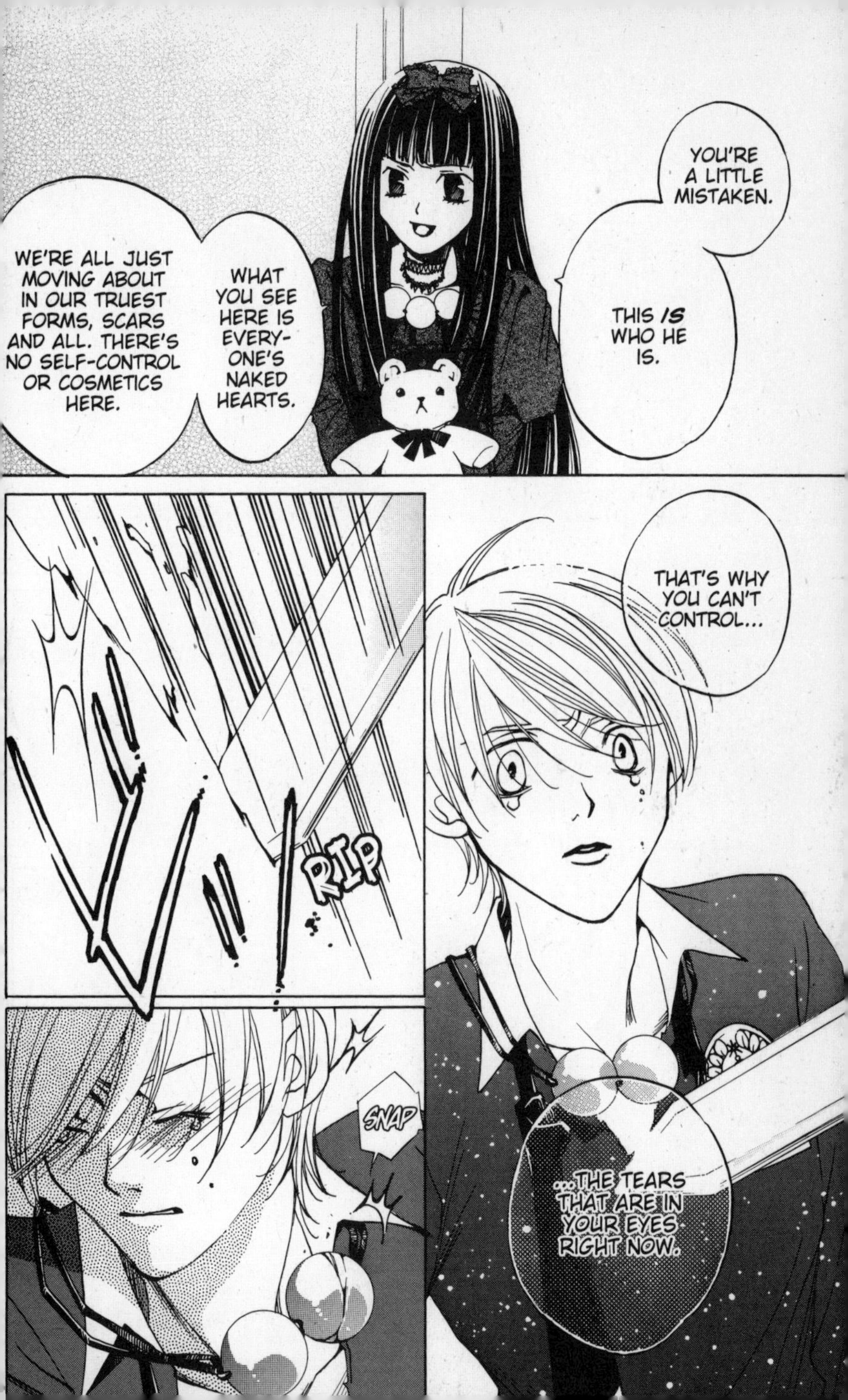
YOU'RE A LITTLE MISTAKEN.
THIS *IS* WHO HE IS.
WHAT YOU SEE HERE IS EVERY-ONE'S NAKED HEARTS.
WE'RE ALL JUST MOVING ABOUT IN OUR TRUEST FORMS, SCARS AND ALL. THERE'S NO SELF-CONTROL OR COSMETICS HERE.
THAT'S WHY YOU CAN'T CONTROL...
...THE TEARS THAT ARE IN YOUR EYES RIGHT NOW.
RIP
SNAP

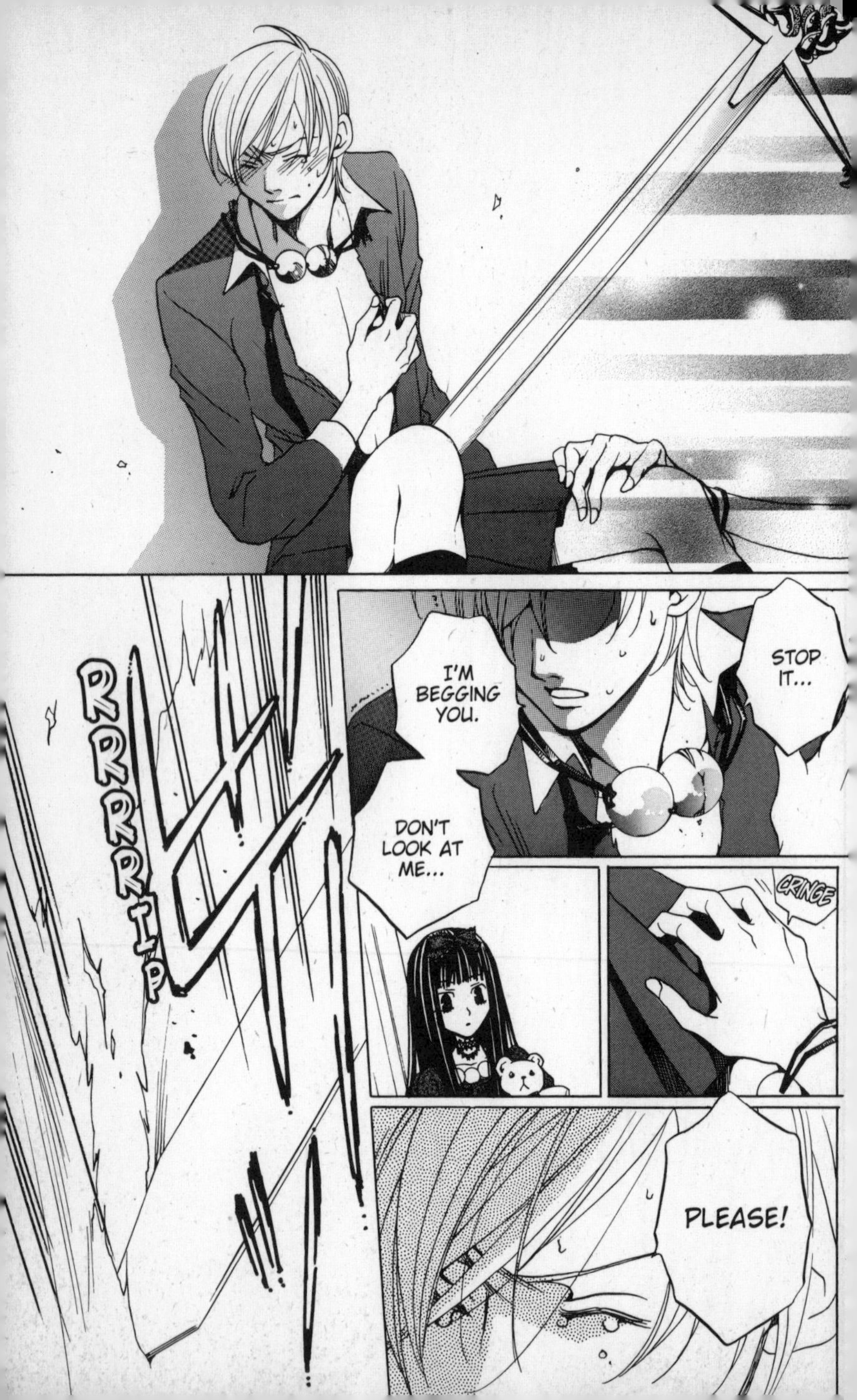
STOP IT...
I'M BEGGING YOU.
DON'T LOOK AT ME...
CRINGE
PLEASE!
RRRRRIP

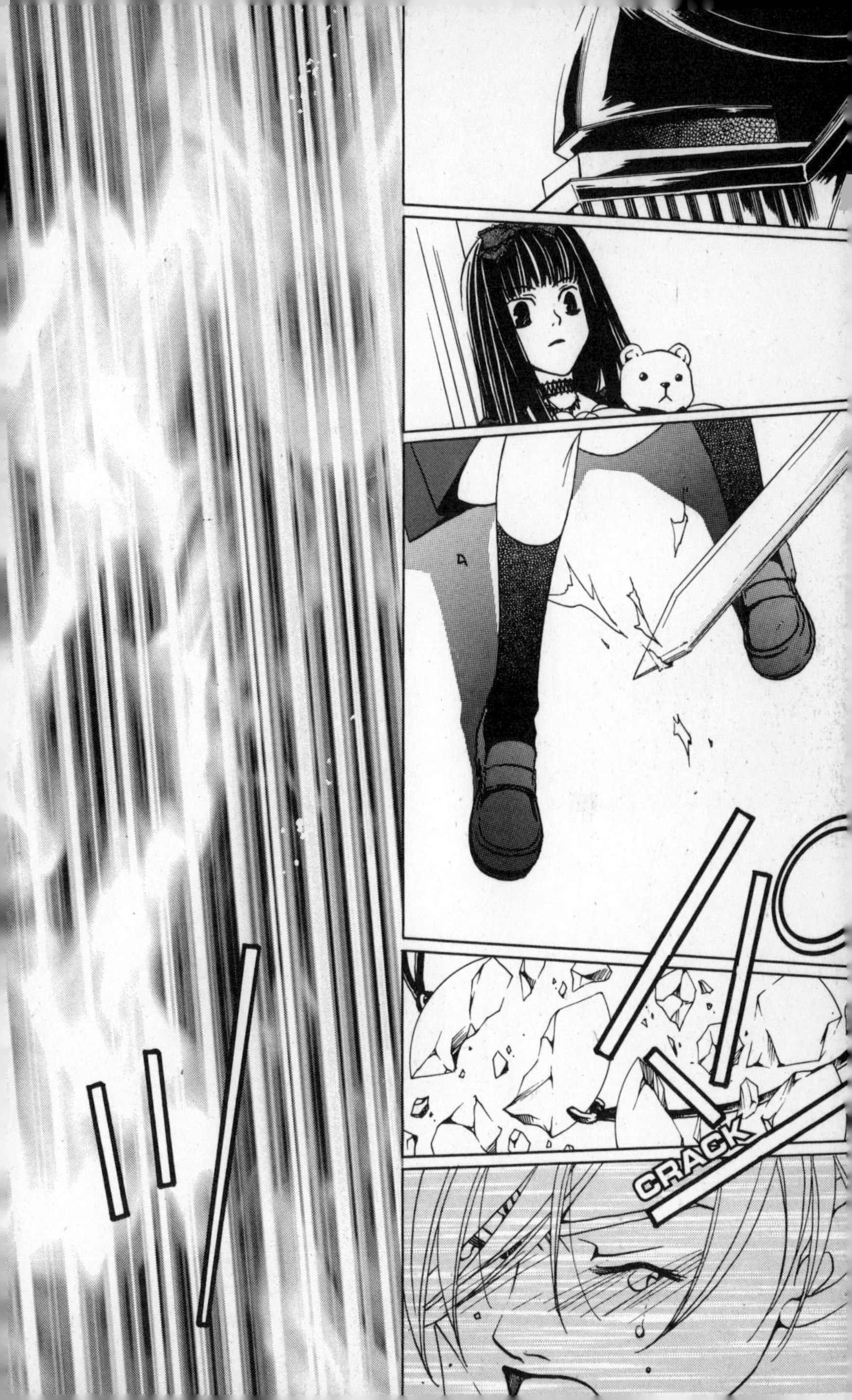
CRACK

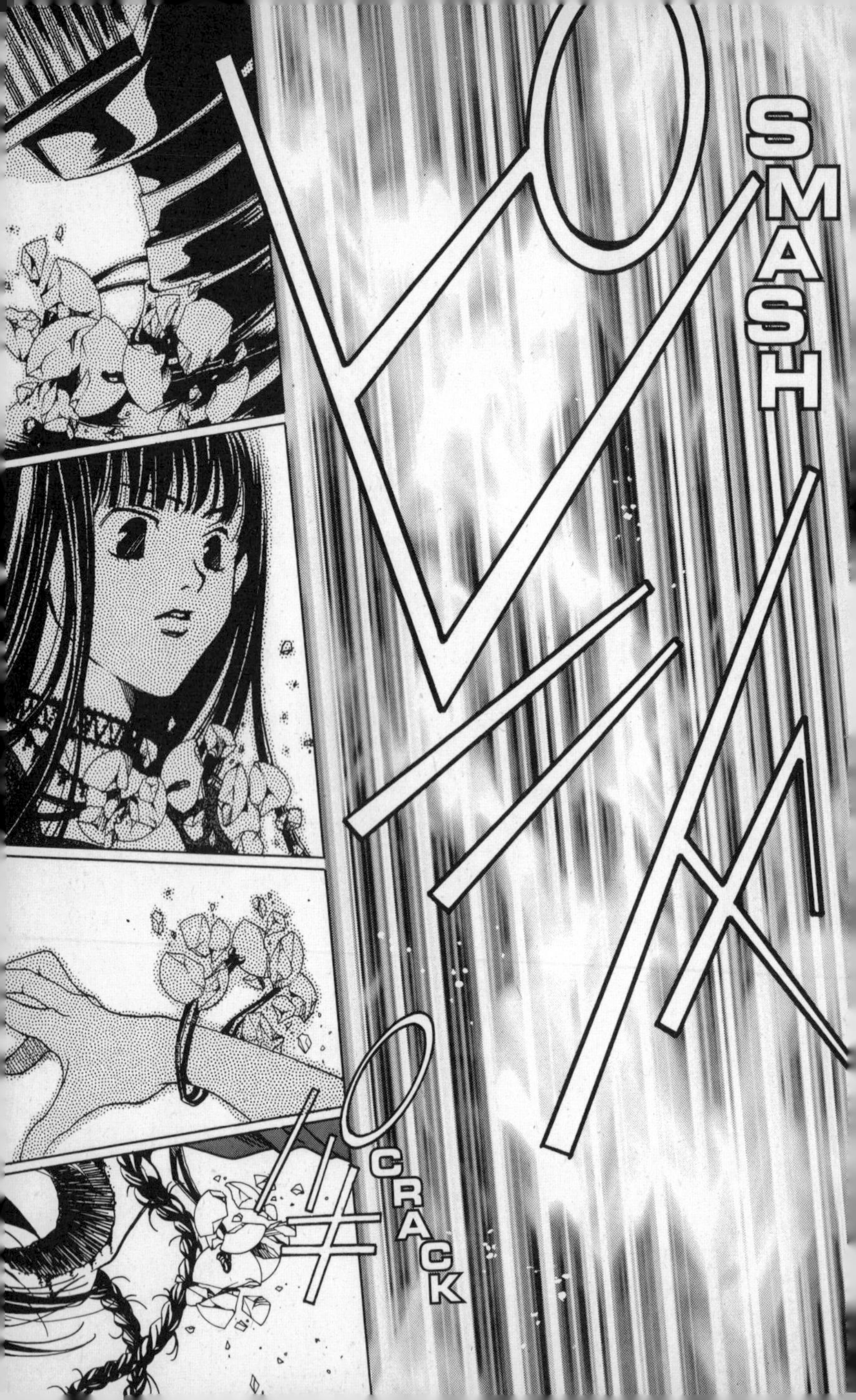
SMASH
CRACK

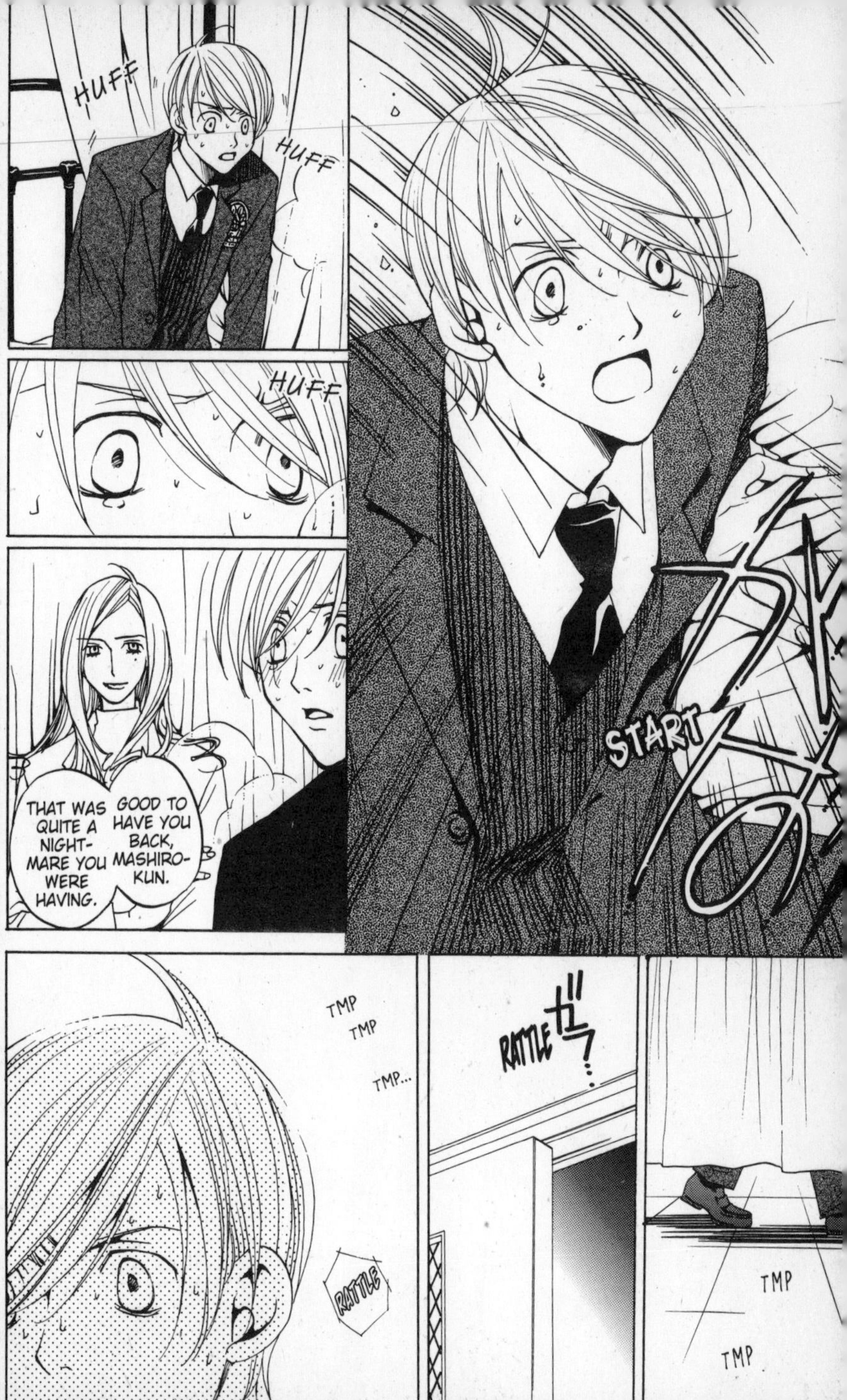
START
HUFF
HUFF
HUFF
GOOD TO HAVE YOU BACK, MASHIRO-KUN.
THAT WAS QUITE A NIGHT-MARE YOU WERE HAVING.
TMP
TMP
RATTLE
TMP
TMP
TMP...
RATTLE

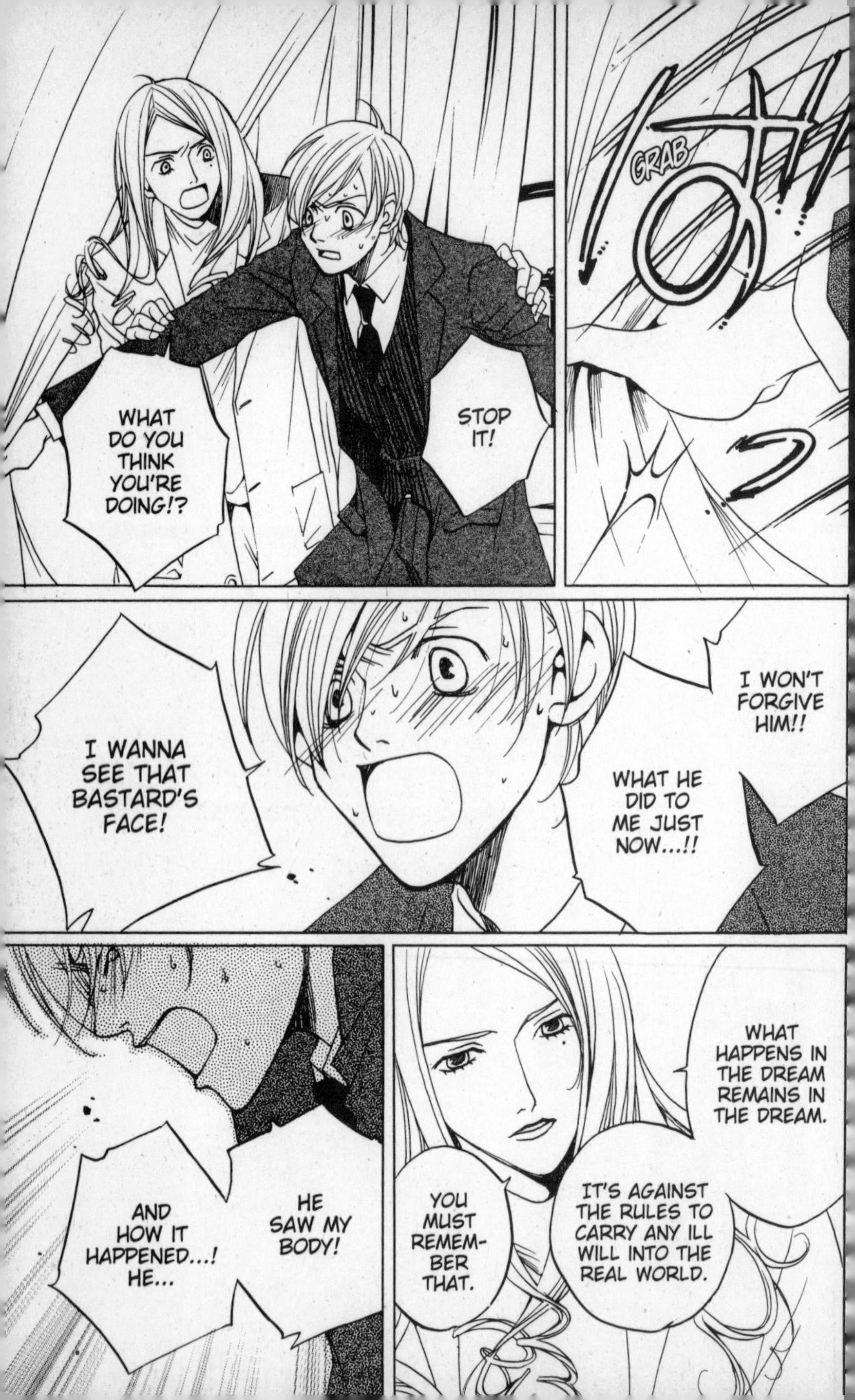
GRAB
STOP IT!
WHAT DO YOU THINK YOU'RE DOING!?
I WON'T FORGIVE HIM!!
WHAT HE DID TO ME JUST NOW...!!
I WANNA SEE THAT BASTARD'S FACE!
WHAT HAPPENS IN THE DREAM REMAINS IN THE DREAM.
IT'S AGAINST THE RULES TO CARRY ANY ILL WILL INTO THE REAL WORLD.
YOU MUST REMEM-BER THAT.
HE SAW MY BODY!
AND HOW IT HAPPENED...! HE...

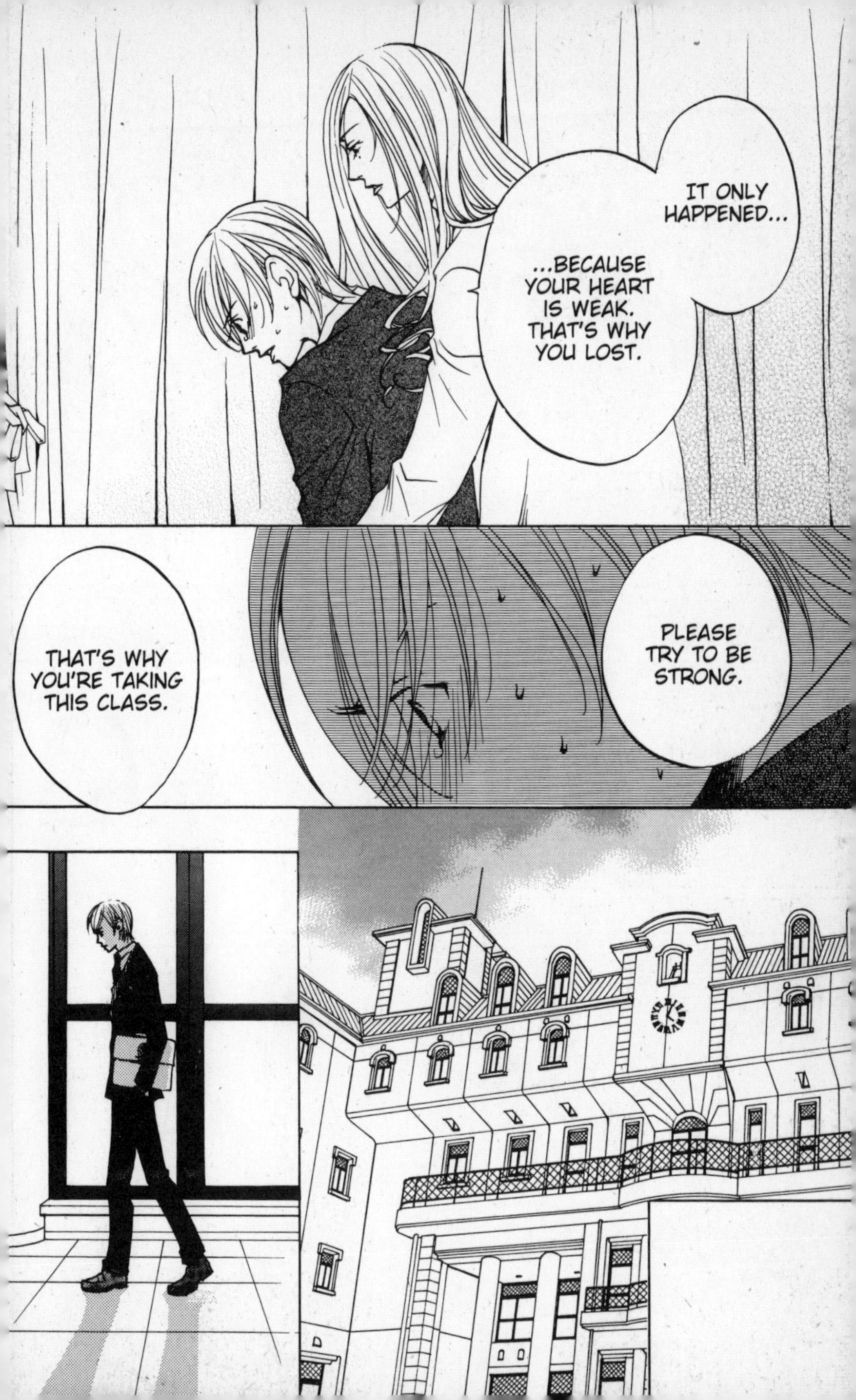
IT ONLY HAPPENED...
...BECAUSE YOUR HEART IS WEAK. THAT'S WHY YOU LOST.
PLEASE TRY TO BE STRONG.
THAT'S WHY YOU'RE TAKING THIS CLASS.

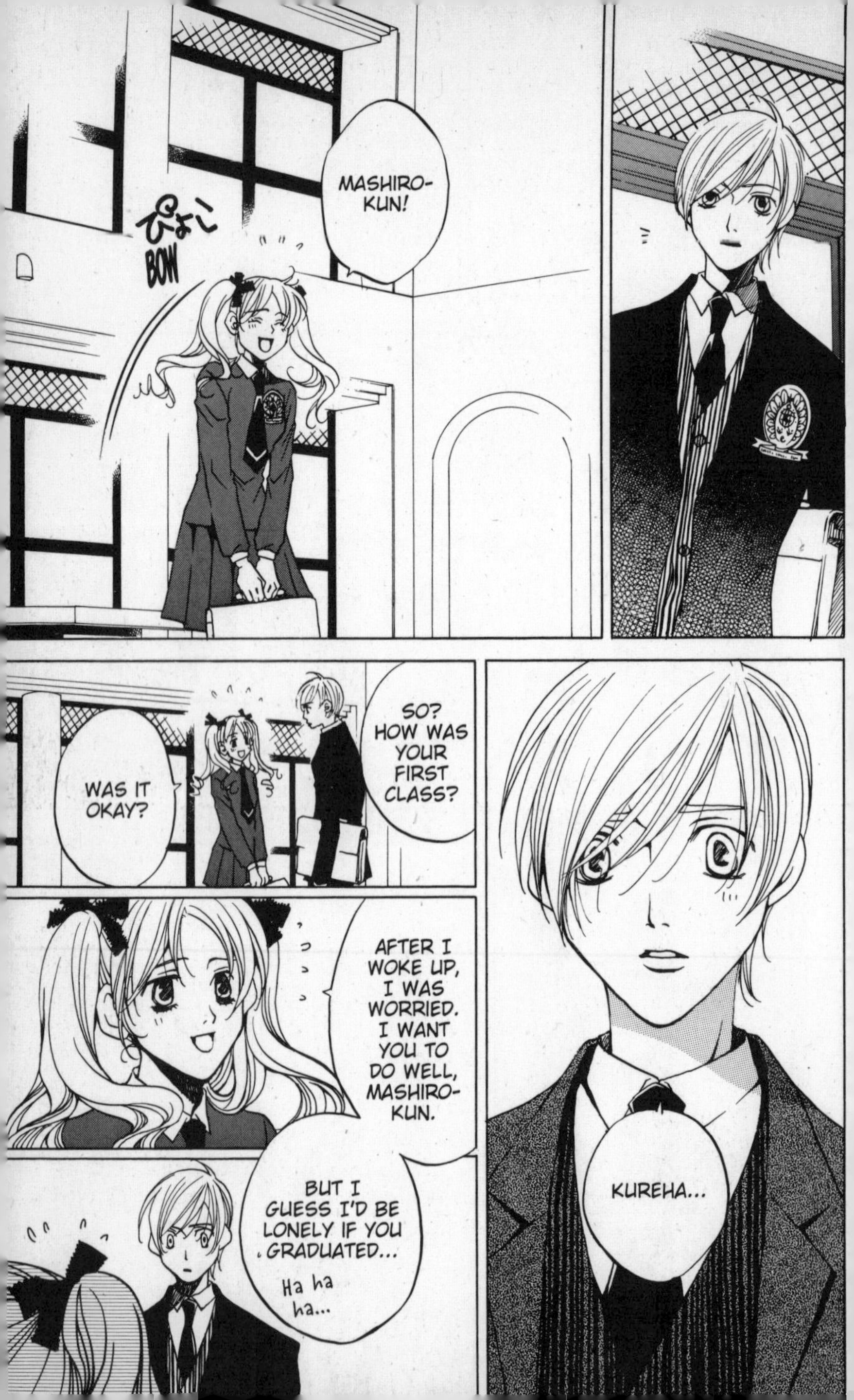
MASHIRO-KUN!
ぴょこ
BOW
KUREHA...
SO? HOW WAS YOUR FIRST CLASS?
WAS IT OKAY?
AFTER I WOKE UP, I WAS WORRIED. I WANT YOU TO DO WELL, MASHIRO-KUN.
BUT I GUESS I'D BE LONELY IF YOU GRADUATED...
Ha ha ha...

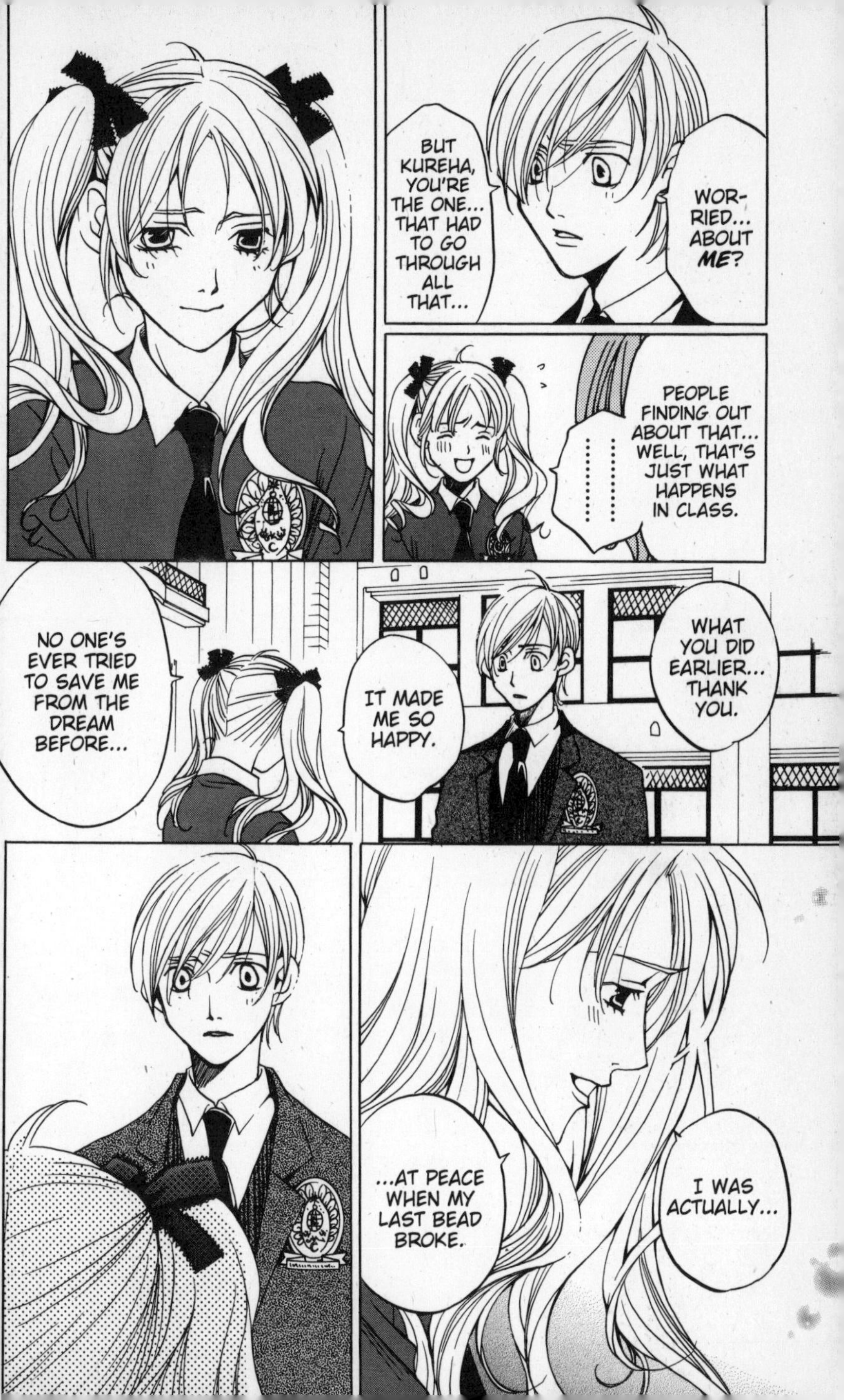
WOR-RIED... ABOUT *ME*?
BUT KUREHA, YOU'RE THE ONE... THAT HAD TO GO THROUGH ALL THAT...
PEOPLE FINDING OUT ABOUT THAT... WELL, THAT'S JUST WHAT HAPPENS IN CLASS.
......
WHAT YOU DID EARLIER... THANK YOU.
IT MADE ME SO HAPPY.
NO ONE'S EVER TRIED TO SAVE ME FROM THE DREAM BEFORE...
I WAS ACTUALLY...
...AT PEACE WHEN MY LAST BEAD BROKE.

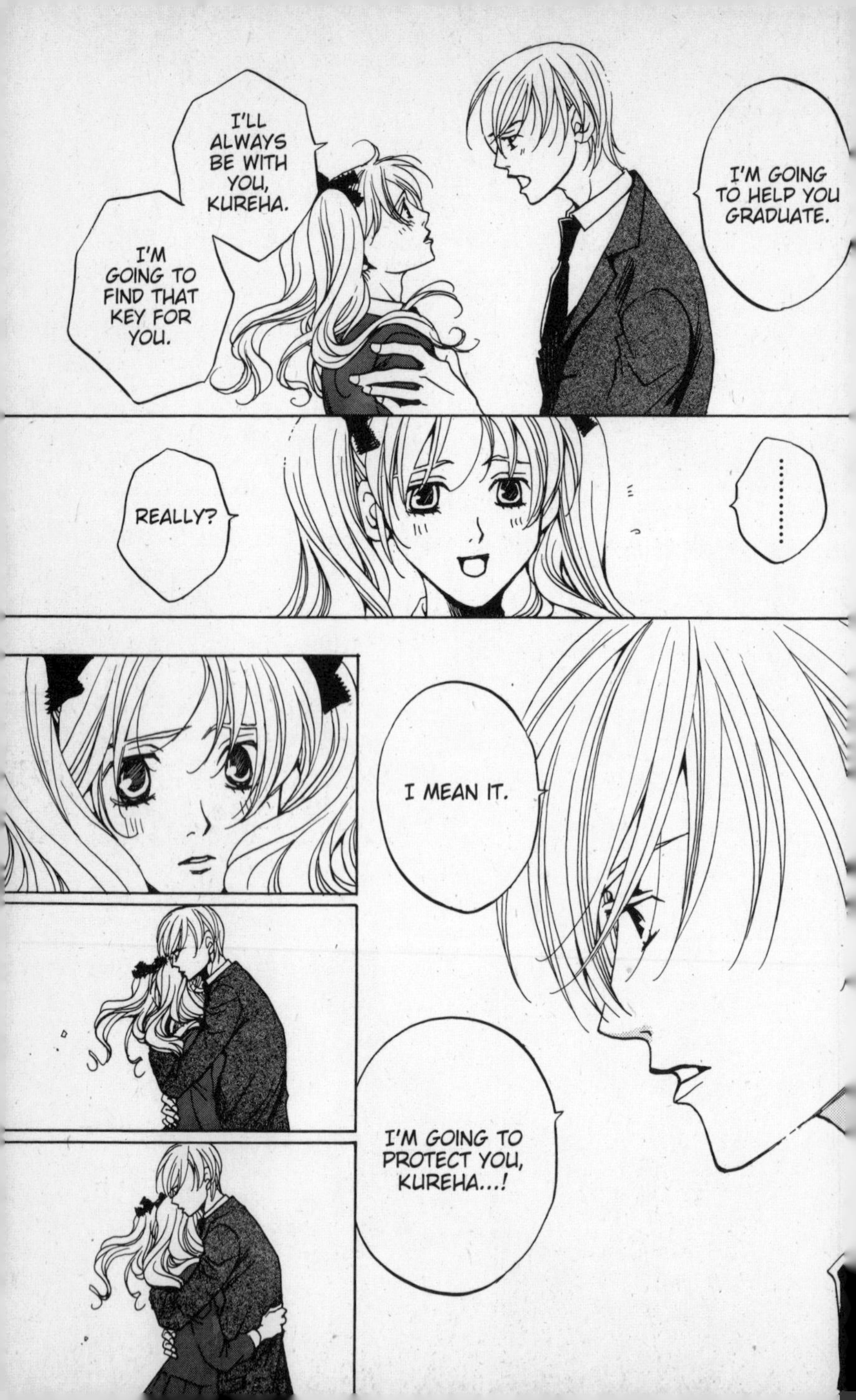
I'M GOING TO HELP YOU GRADUATE.
I'LL ALWAYS BE WITH YOU, KUREHA.
I'M GOING TO FIND THAT KEY FOR YOU.
....
REALLY?
I MEAN IT.
I'M GOING TO PROTECT YOU, KUREHA...!

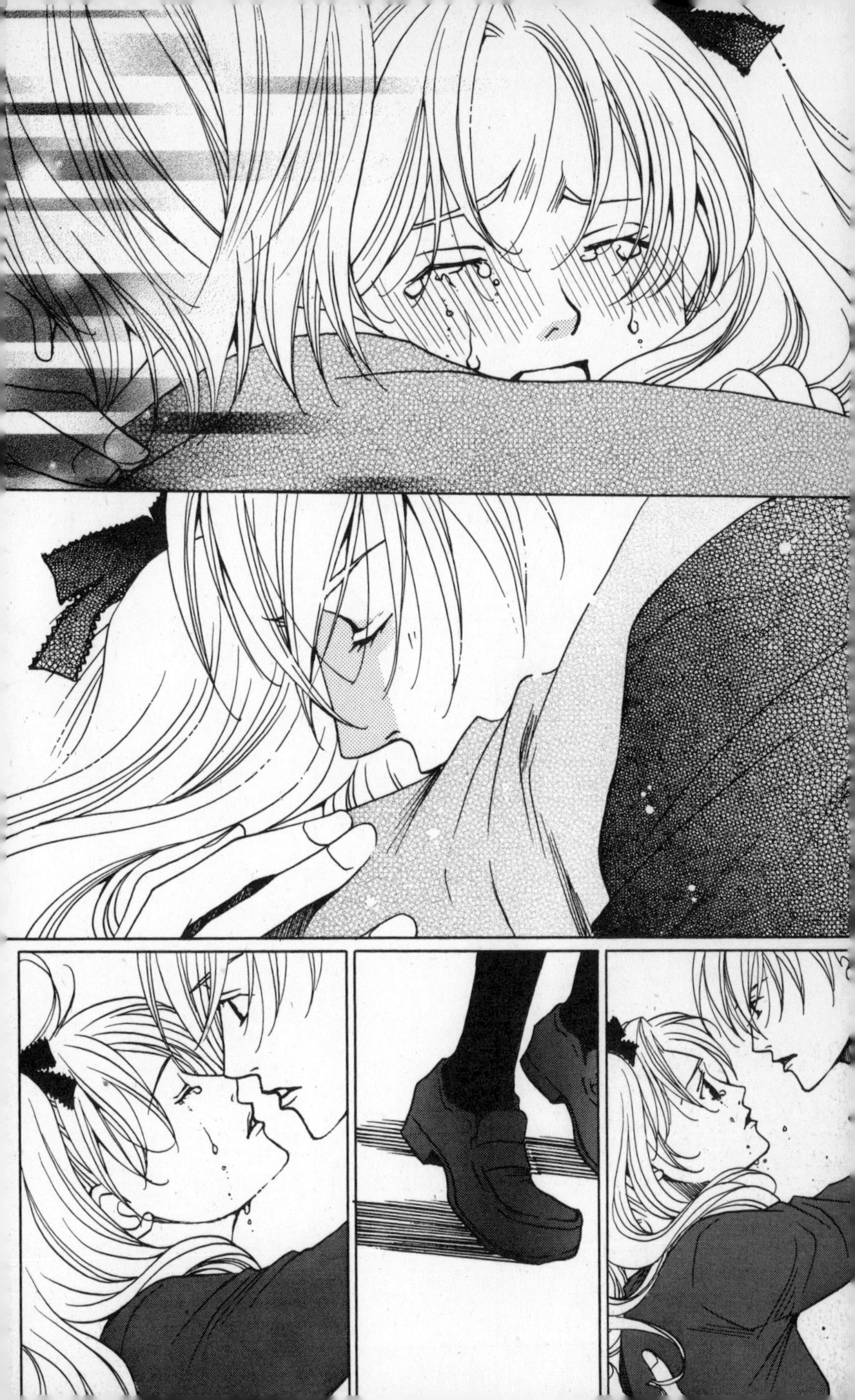

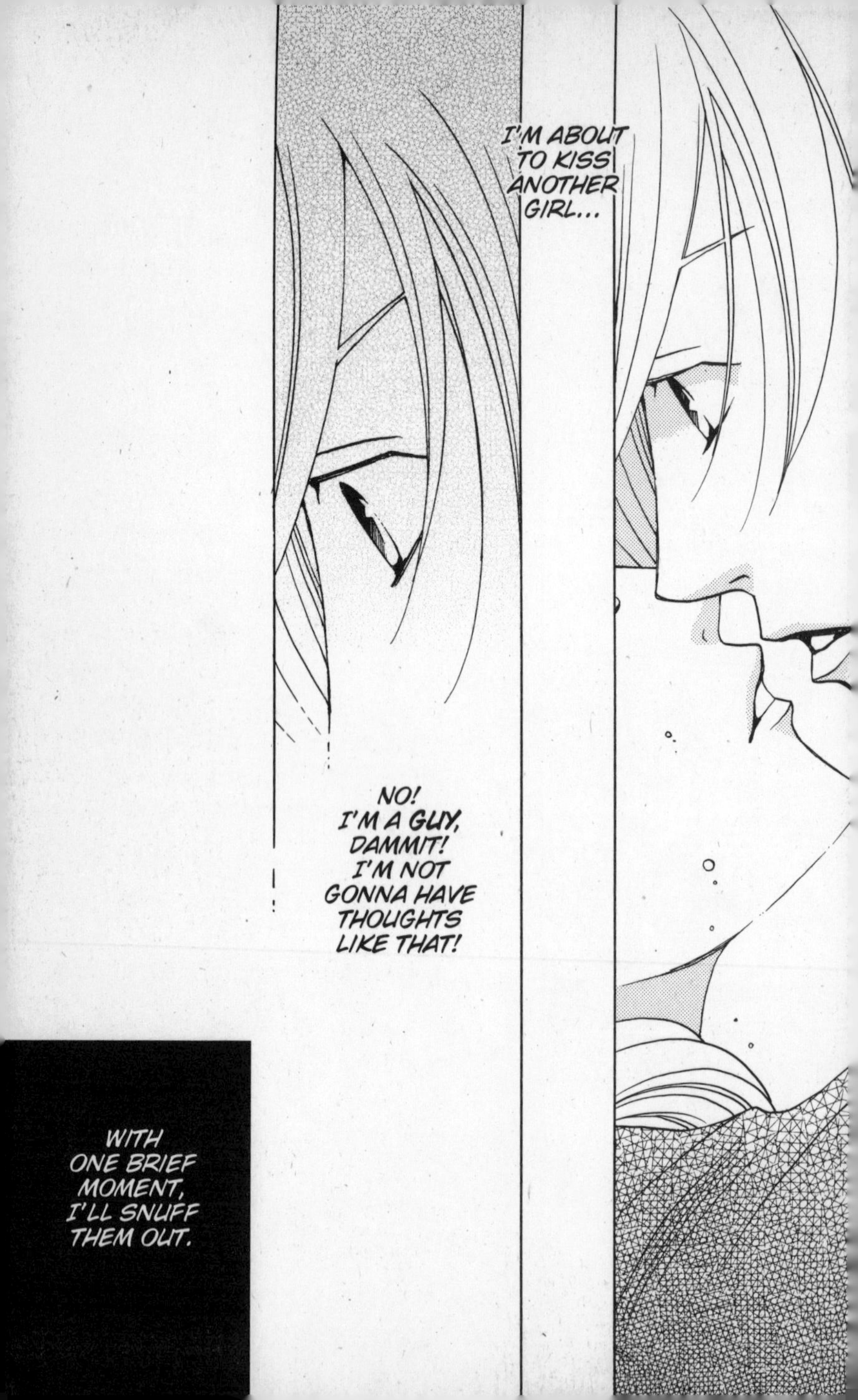
I'M ABOUT TO KISS ANOTHER GIRL...
NO! I'M A GUY, DAMMIT! I'M NOT GONNA HAVE THOUGHTS LIKE THAT!
WITH ONE BRIEF MOMENT, I'LL SNUFF THEM OUT.

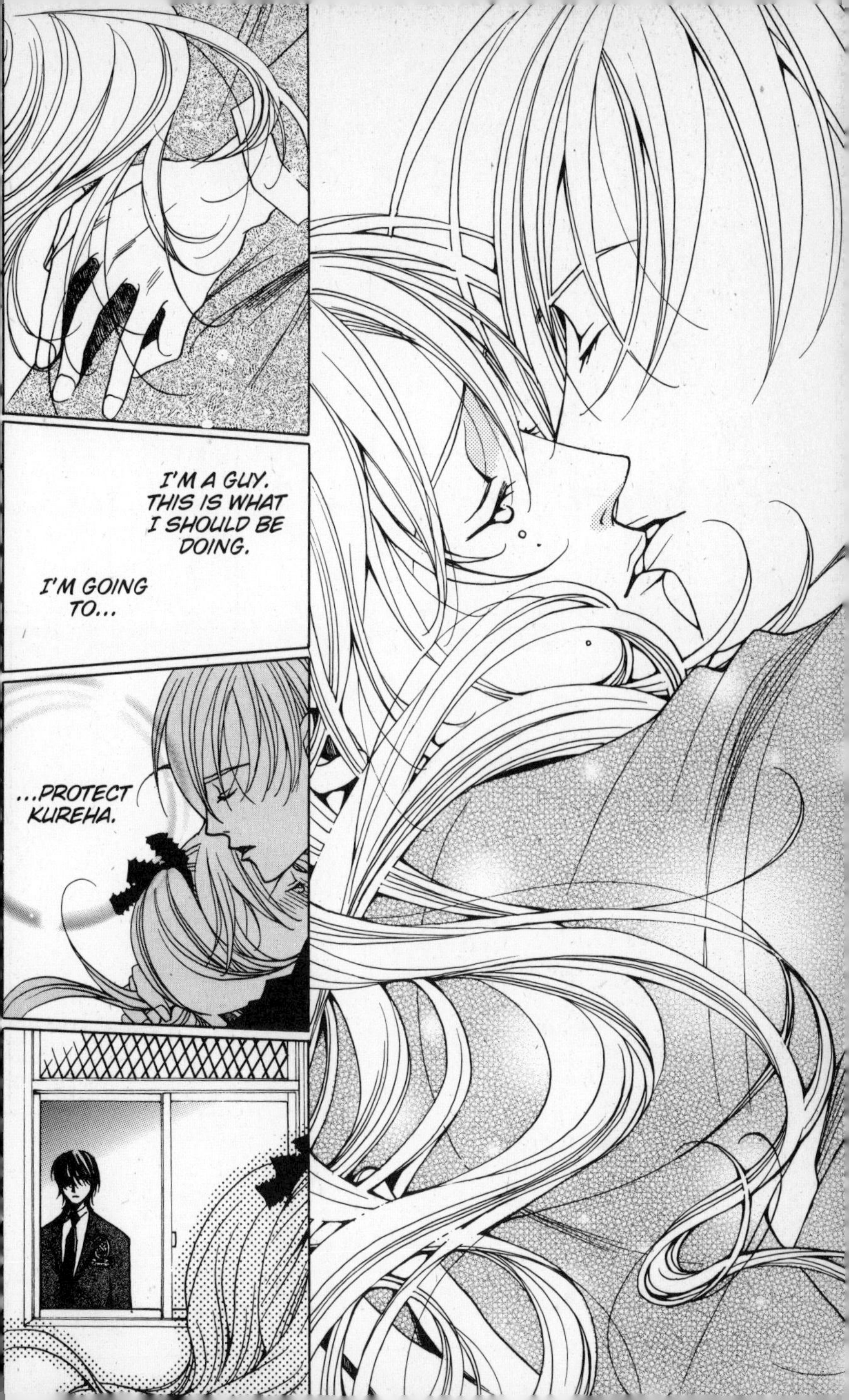
I'M A GUY. THIS IS WHAT I SHOULD BE DOING.
I'M GOING TO...
...PROTECT KUREHA.

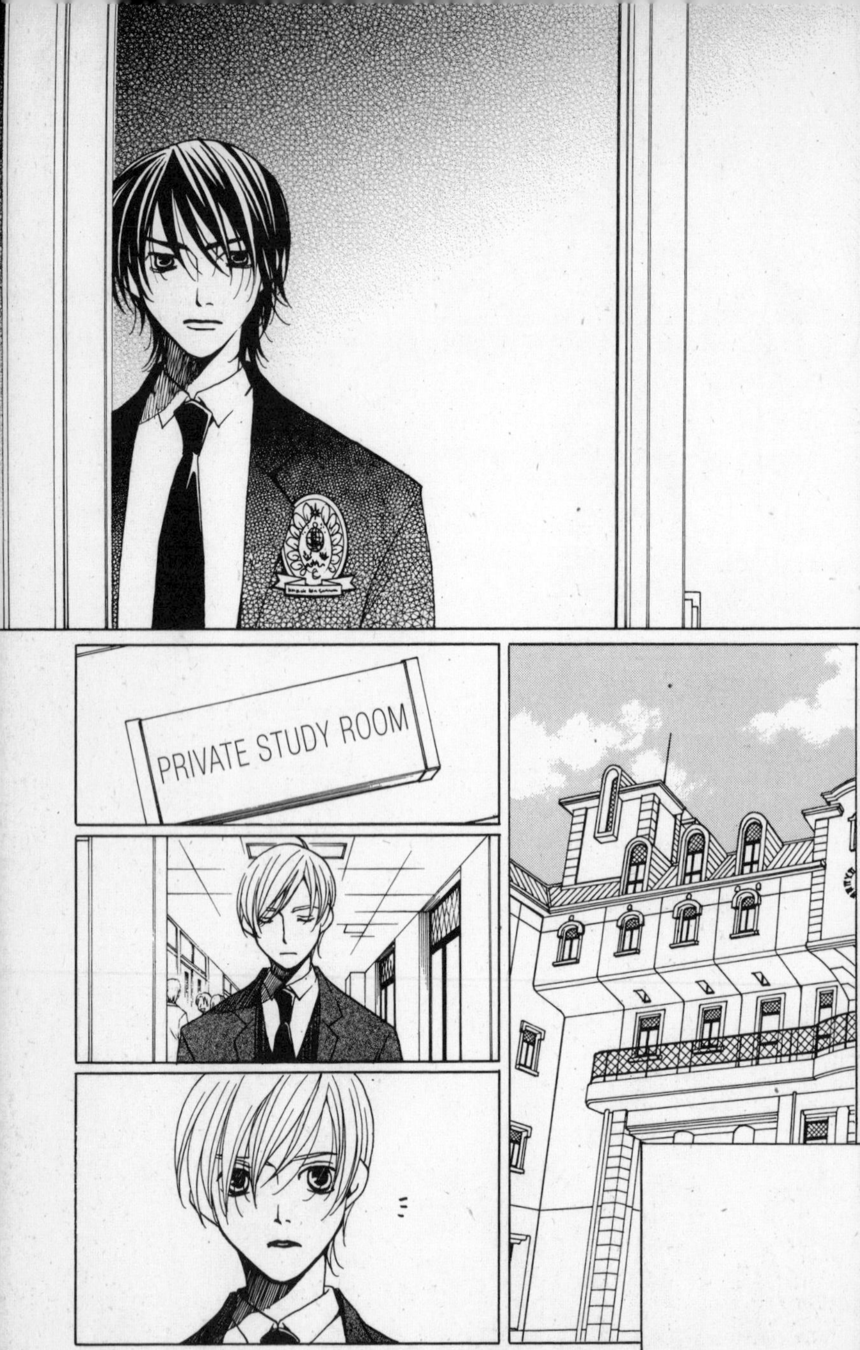
PRIVATE STUDY ROOM

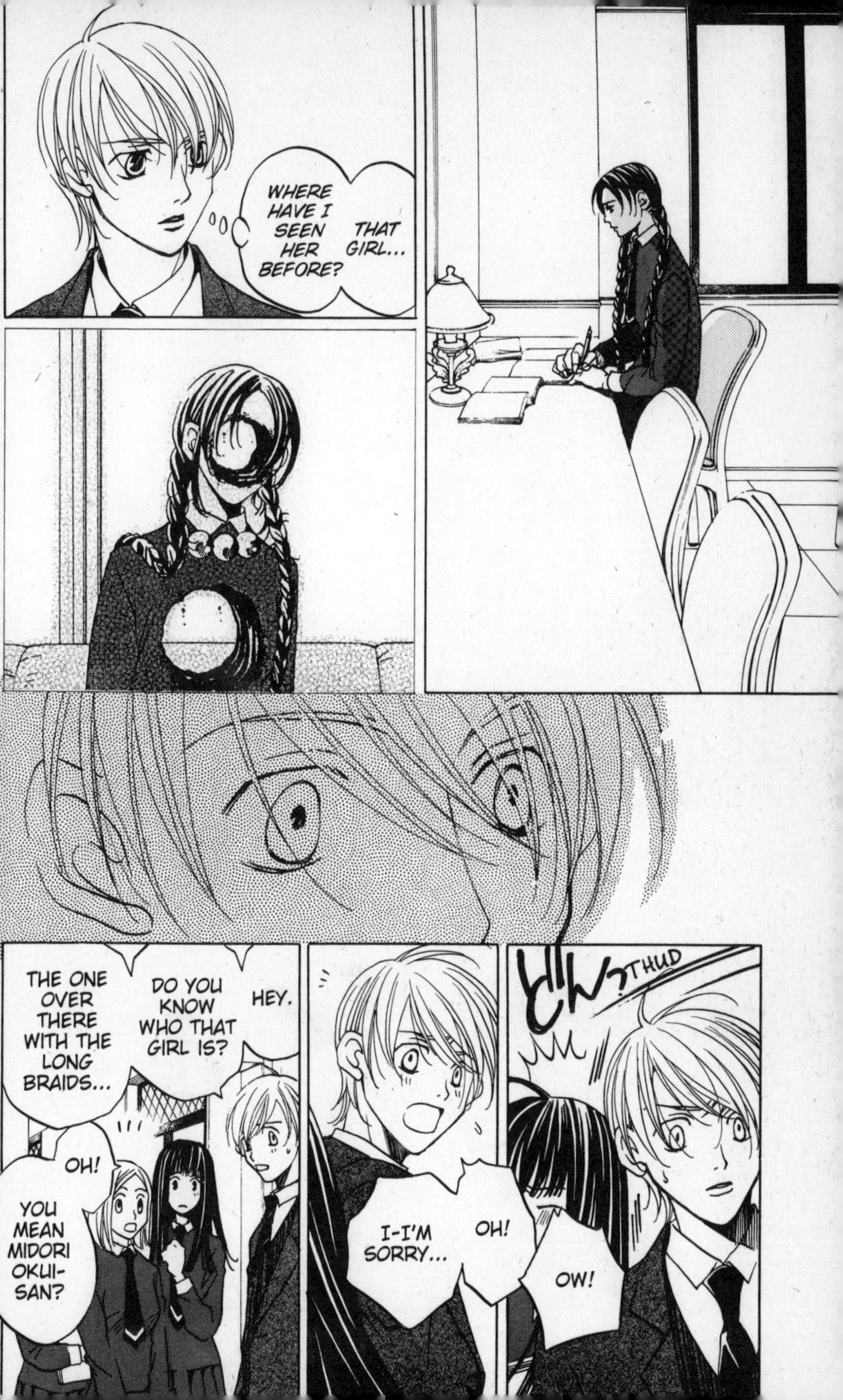
THAT GIRL...
WHERE HAVE I SEEN HER BEFORE?
THUD
OW!
OH!
I-I'M SORRY...
HEY.
DO YOU KNOW WHO THAT GIRL IS?
THE ONE OVER THERE WITH THE LONG BRAIDS...
OH!
YOU MEAN MIDORI OKUI-SAN?

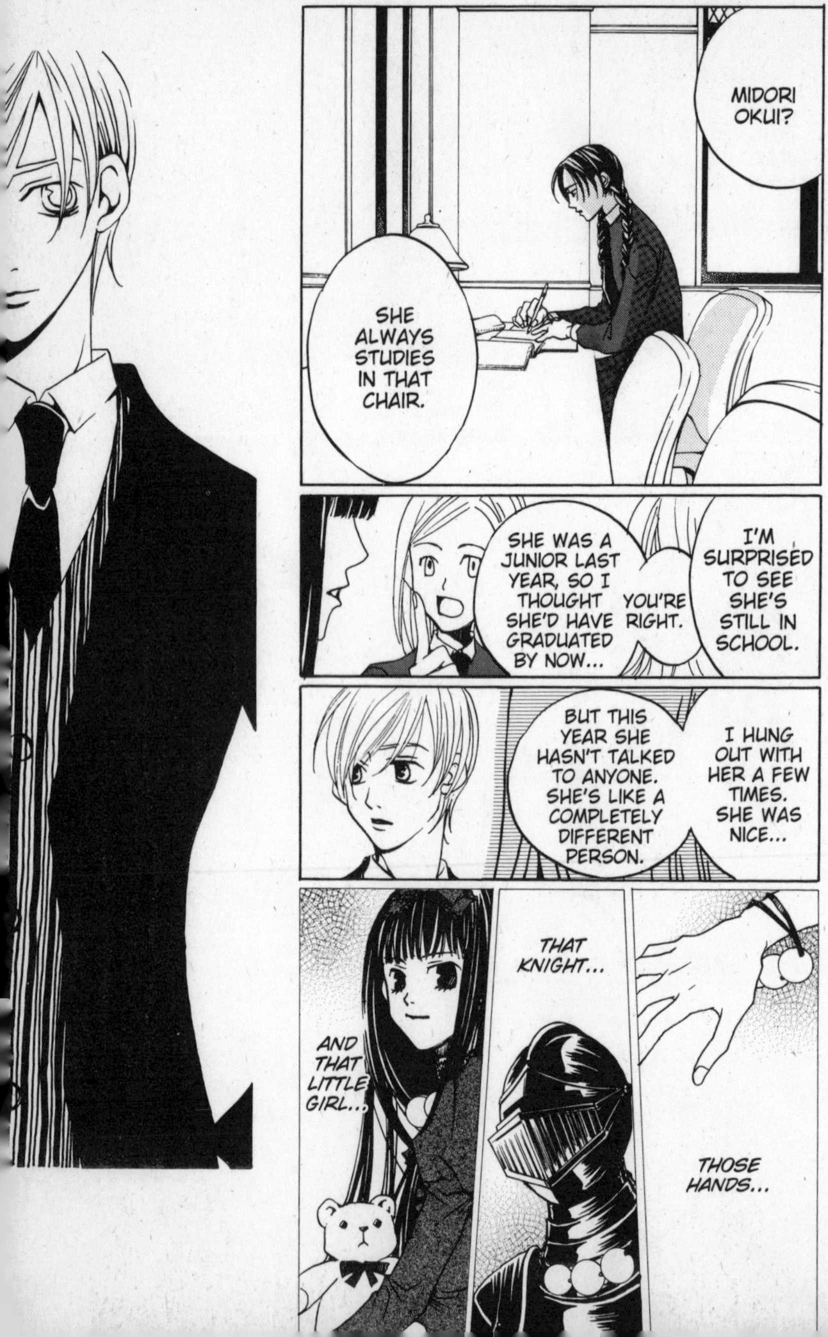
MIDORI OKUI?
SHE ALWAYS STUDIES IN THAT CHAIR.
I'M SURPRISED TO SEE SHE'S STILL IN SCHOOL.
YOU'RE RIGHT.
SHE WAS A JUNIOR LAST YEAR, SO I THOUGHT SHE'D HAVE GRADUATED BY NOW...
I HUNG OUT WITH HER A FEW TIMES. SHE WAS NICE...
BUT THIS YEAR SHE HASN'T TALKED TO ANYONE. SHE'S LIKE A COMPLETELY DIFFERENT PERSON.
THOSE HANDS...
THAT KNIGHT...
AND THAT LITTLE GIRL...

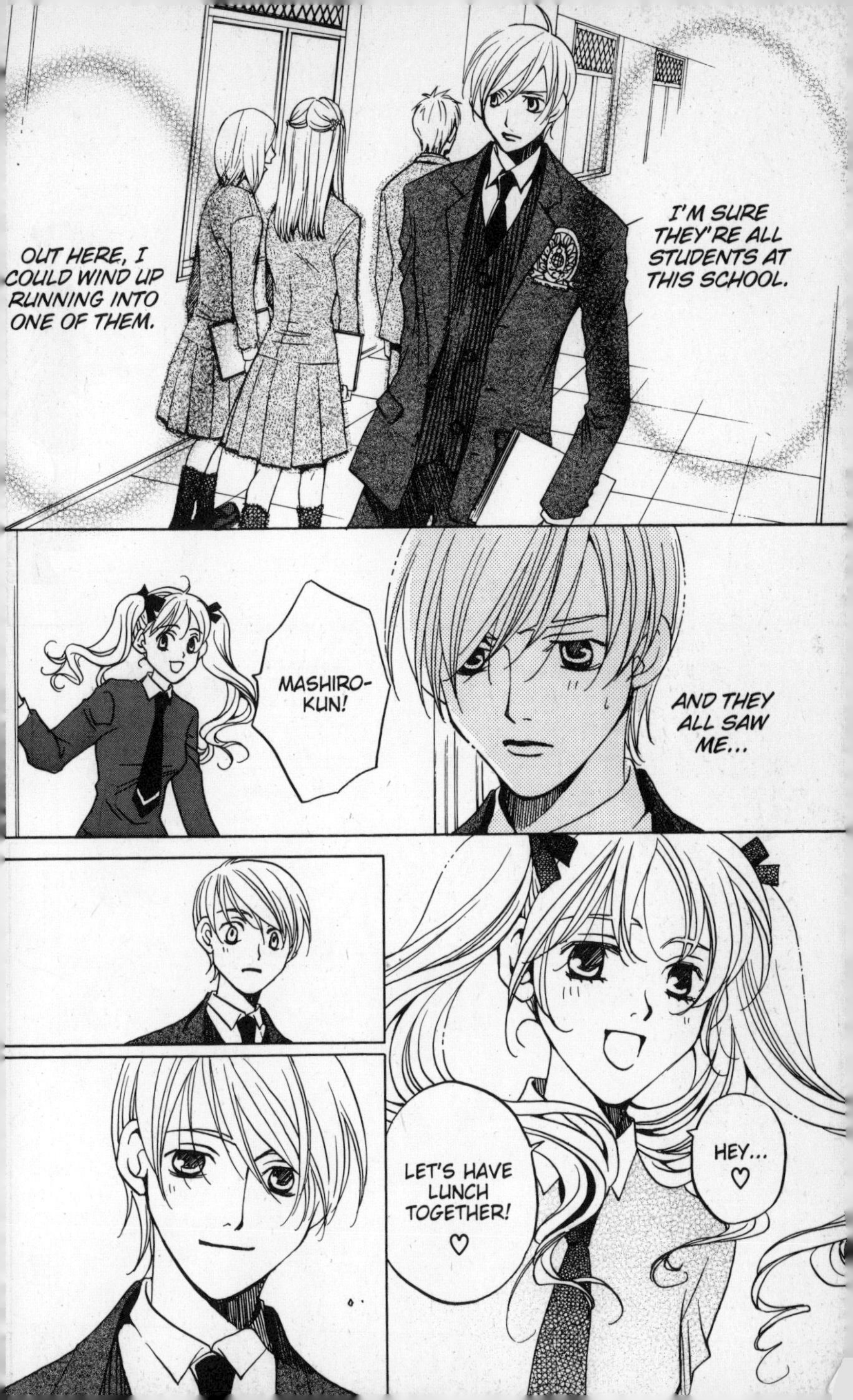
I'M SURE THEY'RE ALL STUDENTS AT THIS SCHOOL.
OUT HERE, I COULD WIND UP RUNNING INTO ONE OF THEM.
AND THEY ALL SAW ME...
MASHIRO-KUN!
HEY... ♡
LET'S HAVE LUNCH TOGETHER! ♡

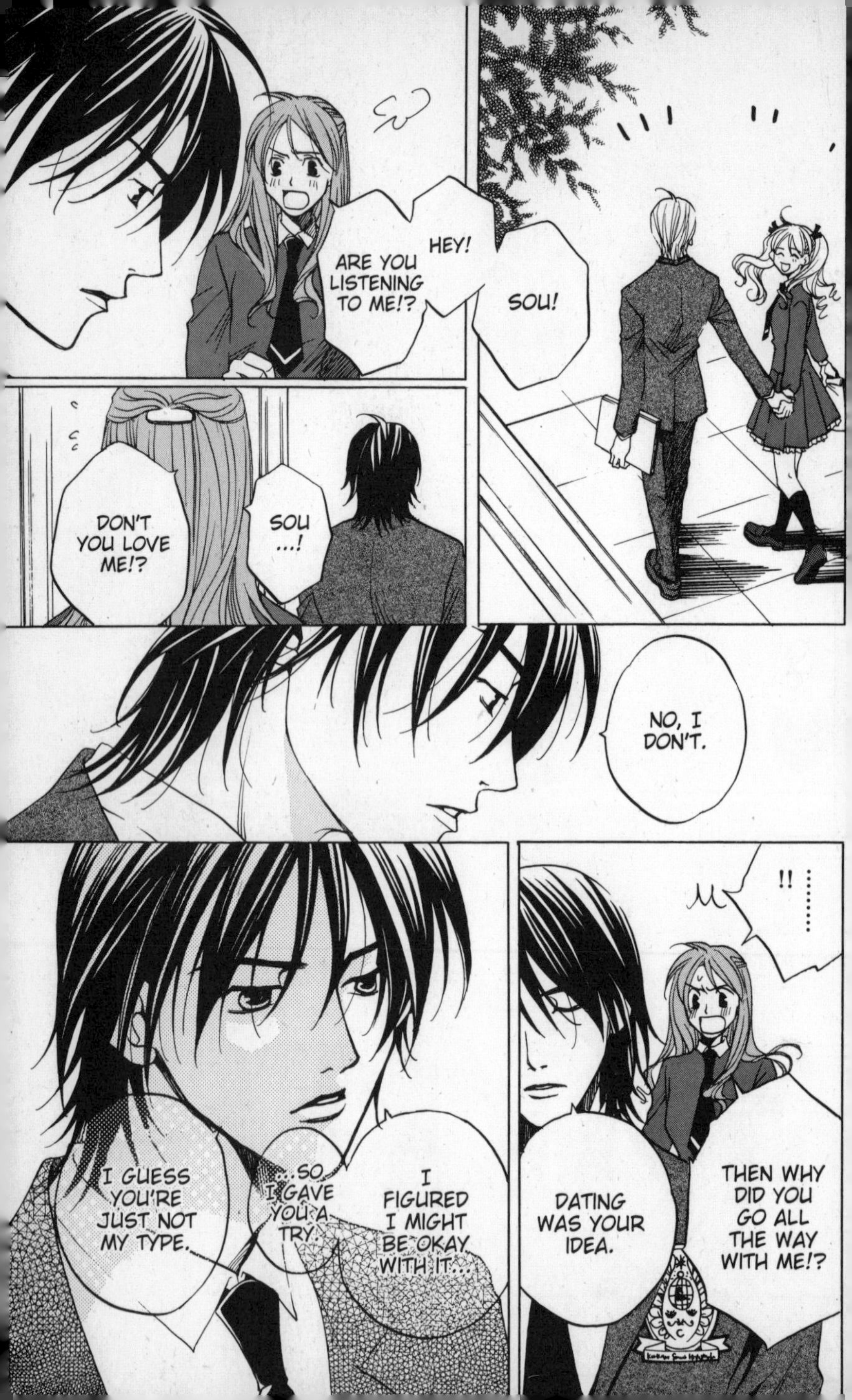
SOU!
HEY!
ARE YOU LISTENING TO ME!?
SOU ...!
DON'T YOU LOVE ME!?
NO, I DON'T.
!! ......
THEN WHY DID YOU GO ALL THE WAY WITH ME!?
DATING WAS YOUR IDEA.
I FIGURED I MIGHT BE OKAY WITH IT...
...SO I GAVE YOU A TRY.
I GUESS YOU'RE JUST NOT MY TYPE.

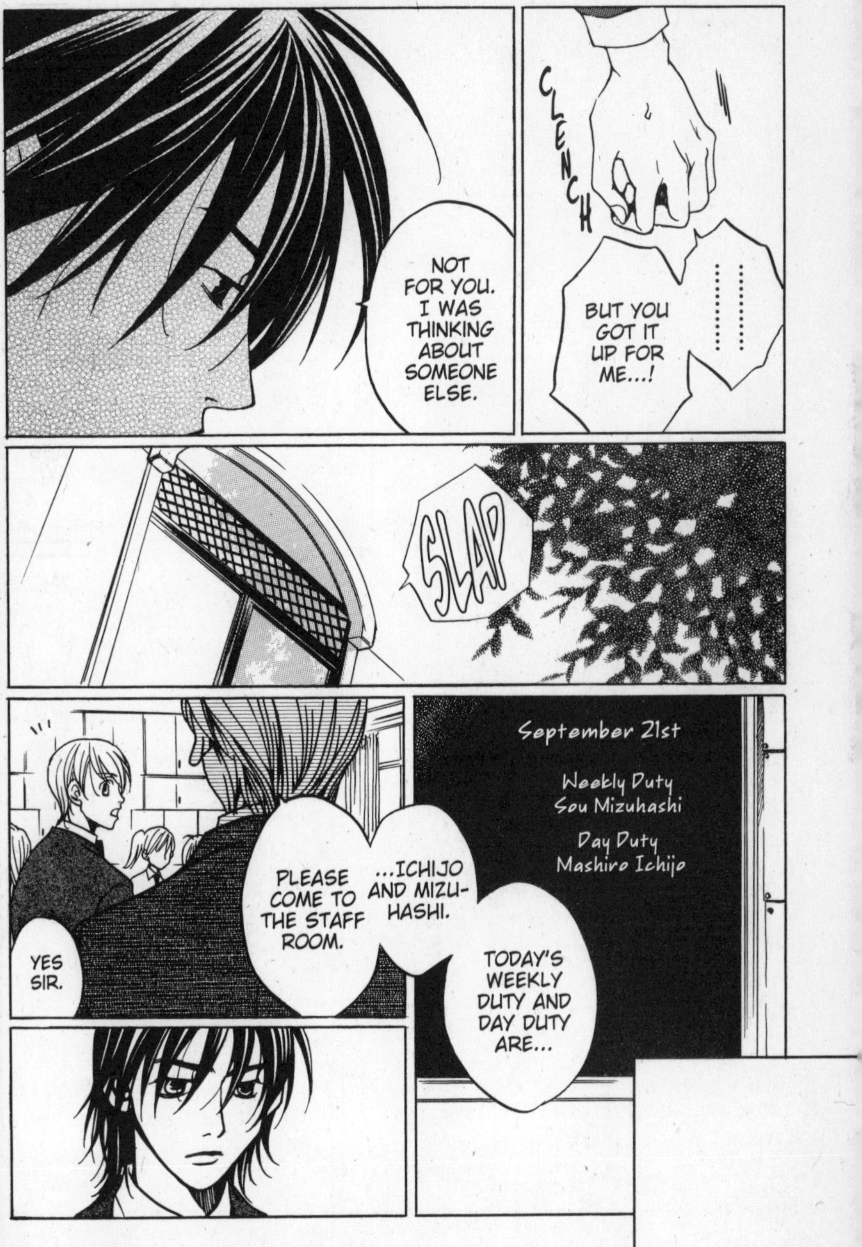
CLENCH
......
BUT YOU GOT IT UP FOR ME...!
NOT FOR YOU. I WAS THINKING ABOUT SOMEONE ELSE.
SLAP
September 21st
Weekly Duty Sou Mizuhashi
Day Duty Mashiro Ichijo
TODAY'S WEEKLY DUTY AND DAY DUTY ARE...
...ICHIJO AND MIZUHASHI.
PLEASE COME TO THE STAFF ROOM.
YES SIR.

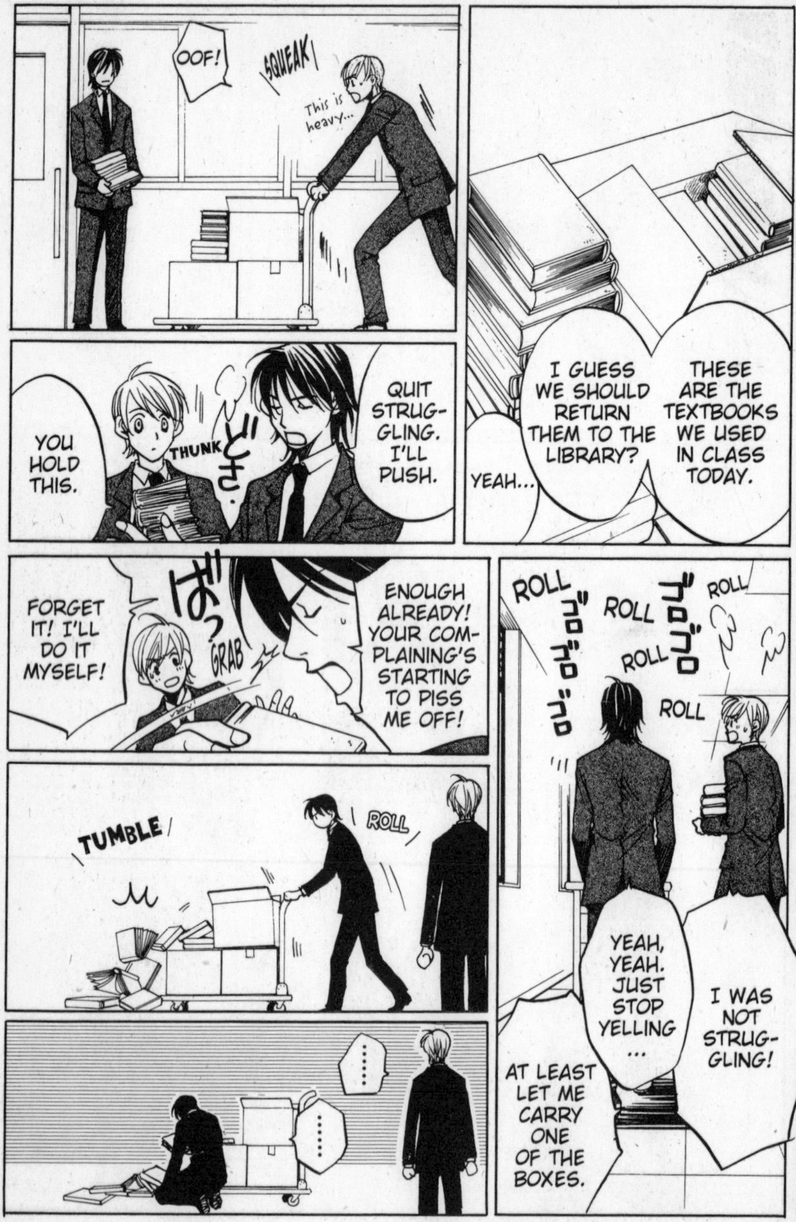
THESE ARE THE TEXTBOOKS WE USED IN CLASS TODAY.
I GUESS WE SHOULD RETURN THEM TO THE LIBRARY?
YEAH...
SQUEAK
OOF!
This is heavy...
QUIT STRUG-GLING. I'LL PUSH.
THUNK
どさ
YOU HOLD THIS.
ROLL
ゴロゴロ
ROLL
ROLL
ゴロゴロ
ROLL
ROLL
I WAS NOT STRUG-GLING!
YEAH, YEAH. JUST STOP YELLING...
AT LEAST LET ME CARRY ONE OF THE BOXES.
ENOUGH ALREADY! YOUR COM-PLAINING'S STARTING TO PISS ME OFF!
GRAB
ぱっ
FORGET IT! I'LL DO IT MYSELF!
ROLL
TUMBLE
......
......

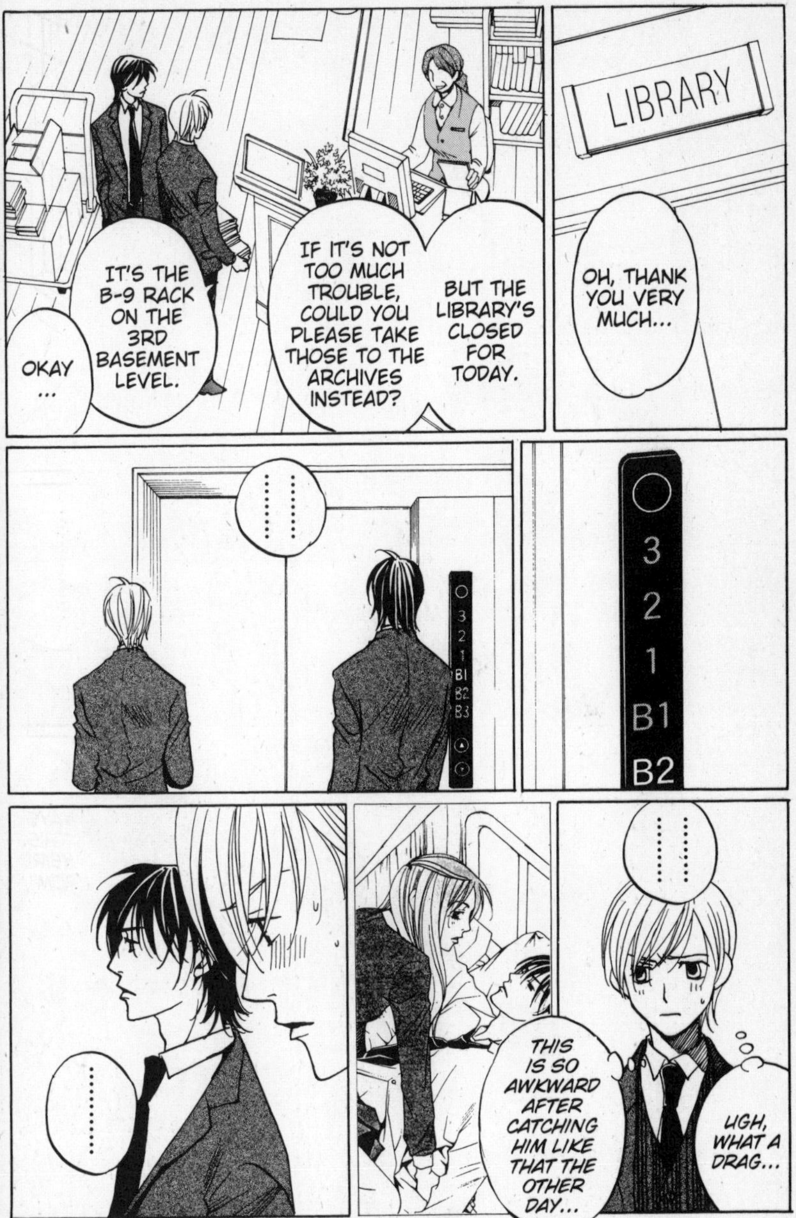
LIBRARY
OH, THANK YOU VERY MUCH...
BUT THE LIBRARY'S CLOSED FOR TODAY.
IF IT'S NOT TOO MUCH TROUBLE, COULD YOU PLEASE TAKE THOSE TO THE ARCHIVES INSTEAD?
IT'S THE B-9 RACK ON THE 3RD BASEMENT LEVEL.
OKAY ...
3
2
1
B1
B2
......
......
UGH, WHAT A DRAG...
THIS IS SO AWKWARD AFTER CATCHING HIM LIKE THAT THE OTHER DAY...
......

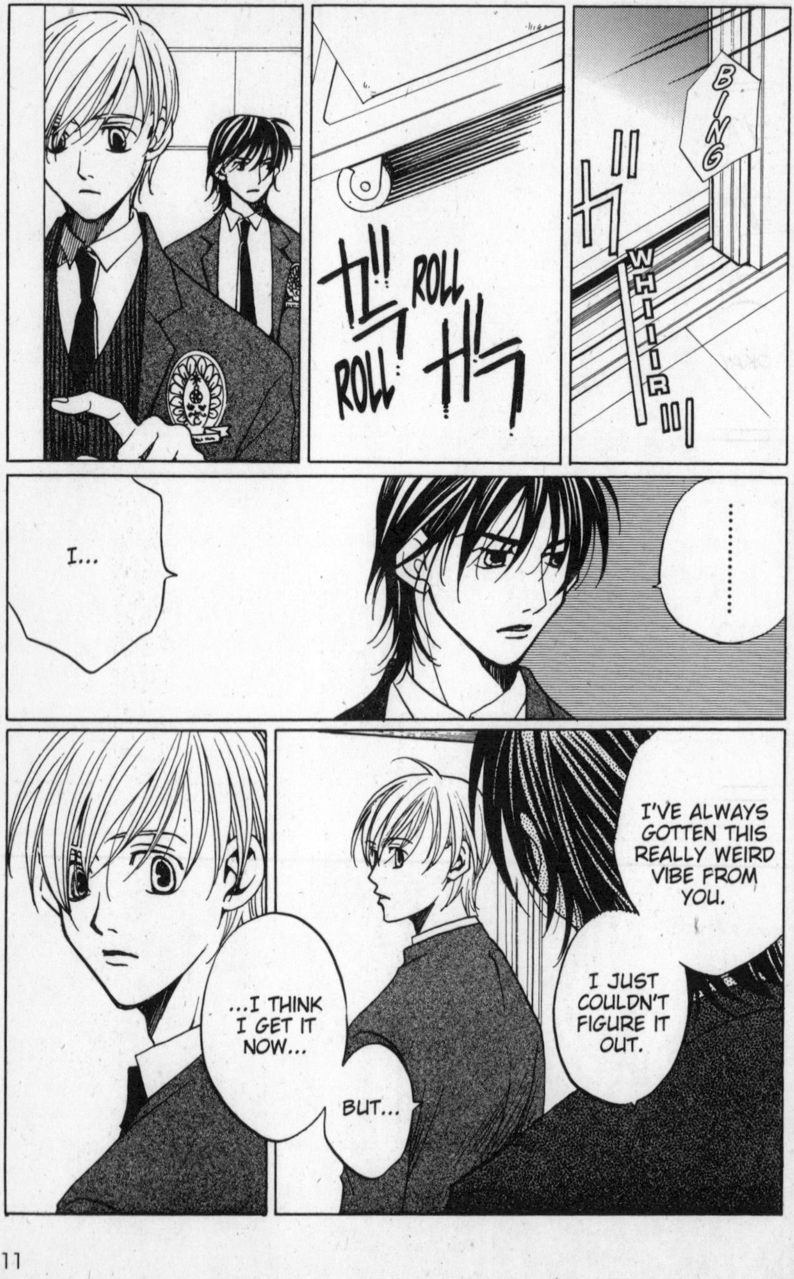
BING
ガ
WHIIIR
ガラ
ROLL
ROLL
ガラ
......
I...
I'VE ALWAYS GOTTEN THIS REALLY WEIRD VIBE FROM YOU.
I JUST COULDN'T FIGURE IT OUT.
...I THINK I GET IT NOW...
BUT...

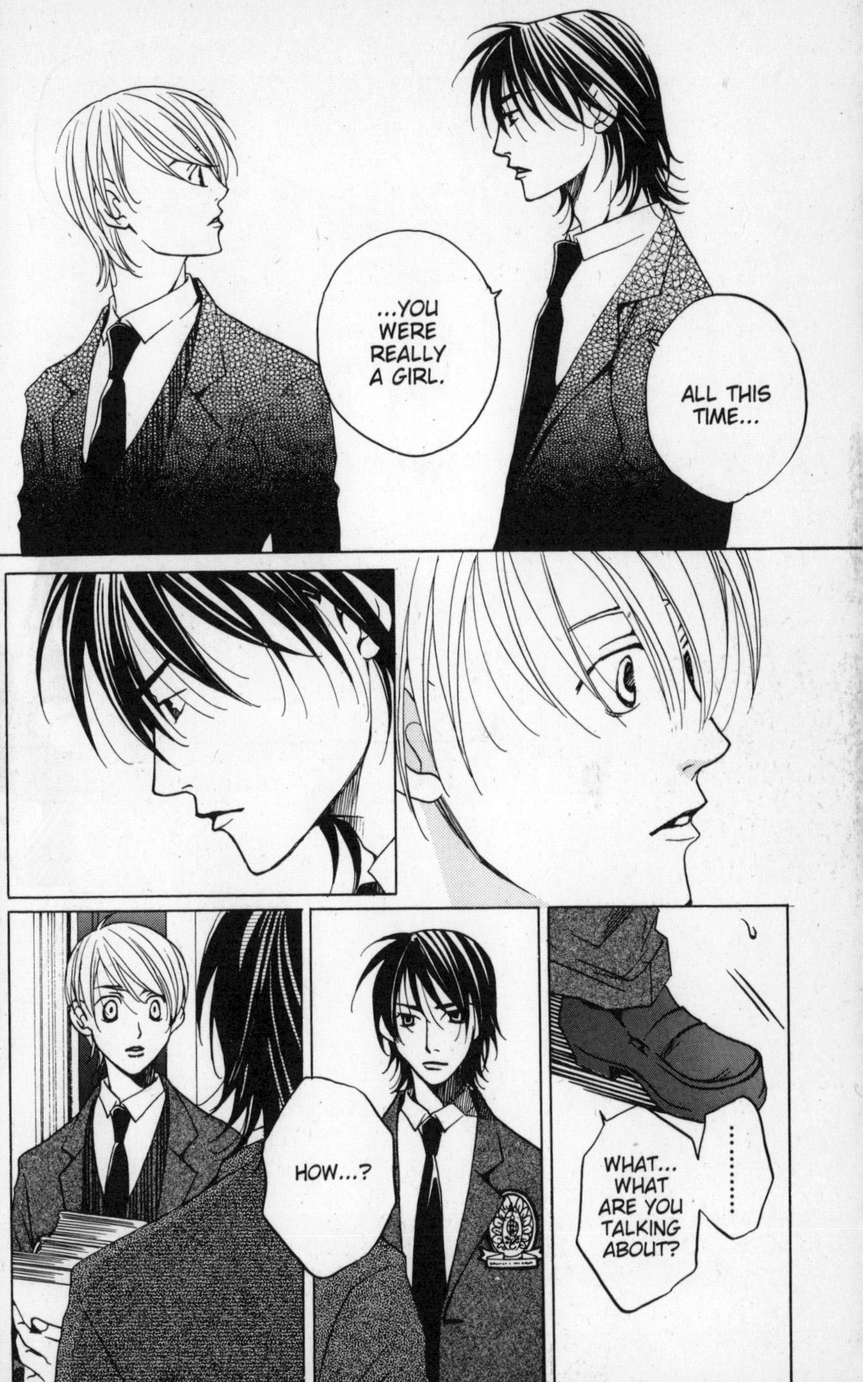
ALL THIS TIME...
...YOU WERE REALLY A GIRL.
......
WHAT... WHAT ARE YOU TALKING ABOUT?
HOW...?

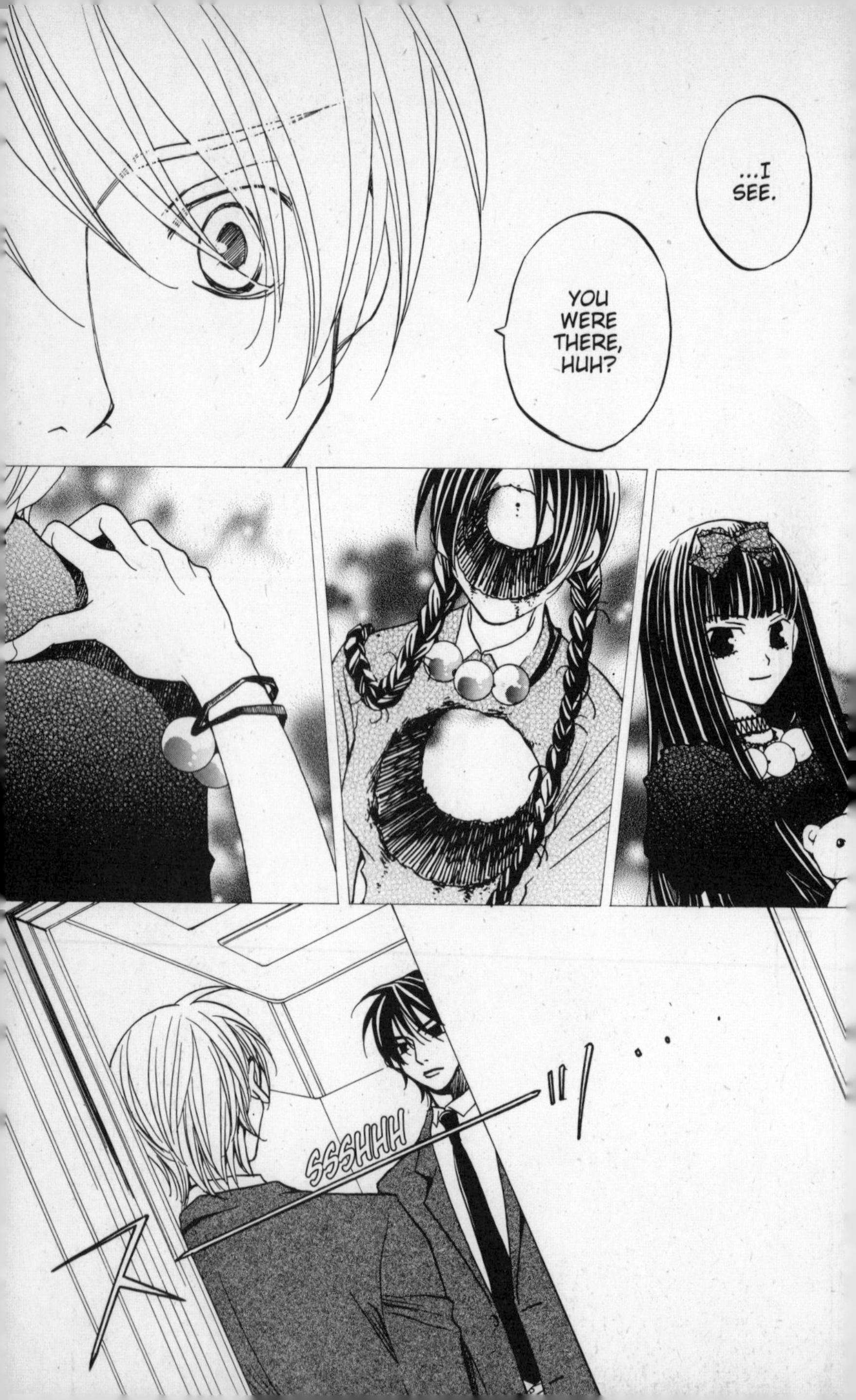
...I SEE.
YOU WERE THERE, HUH?
...
SSSHHH

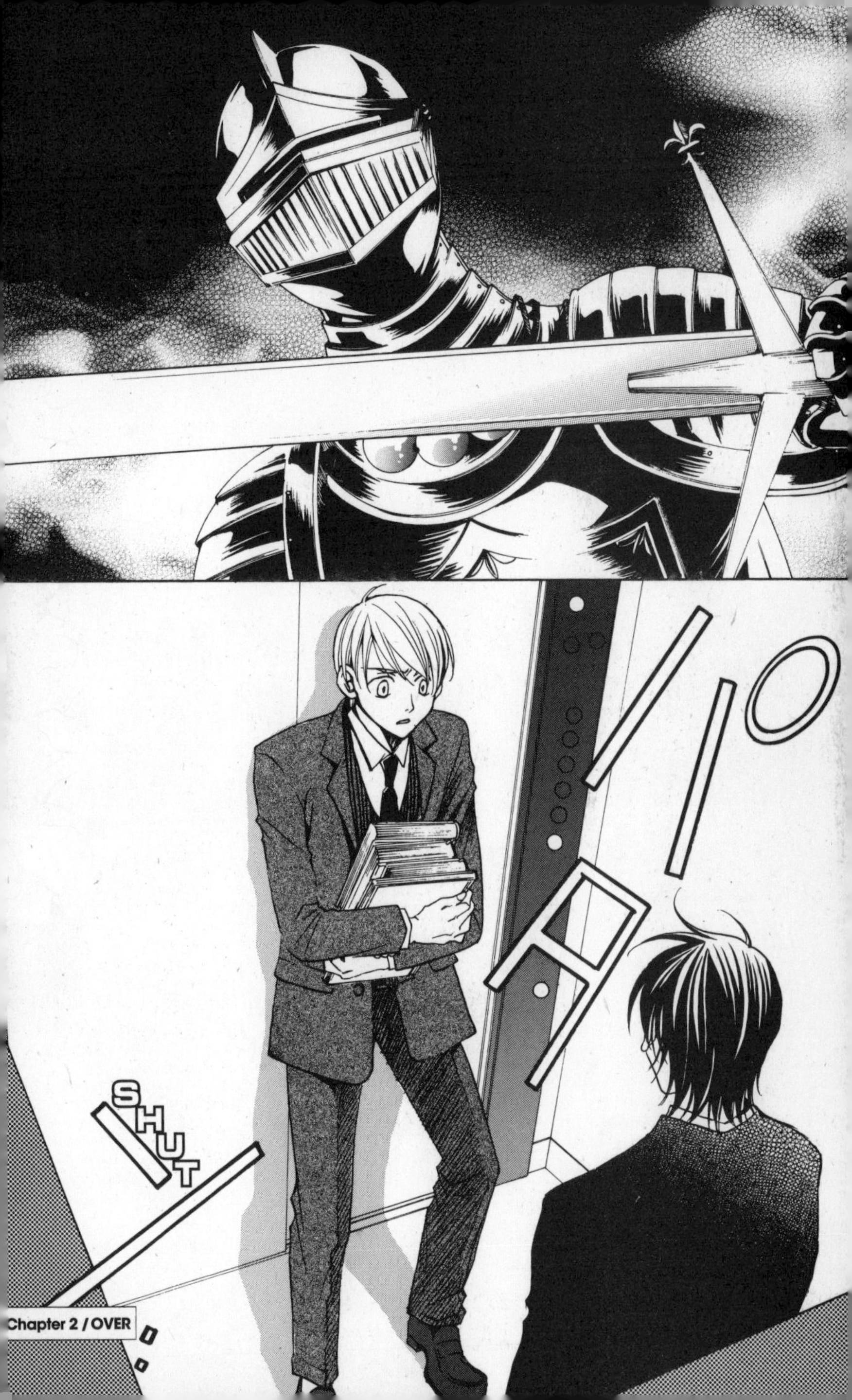
SHUT
Chapter 2 / OVER

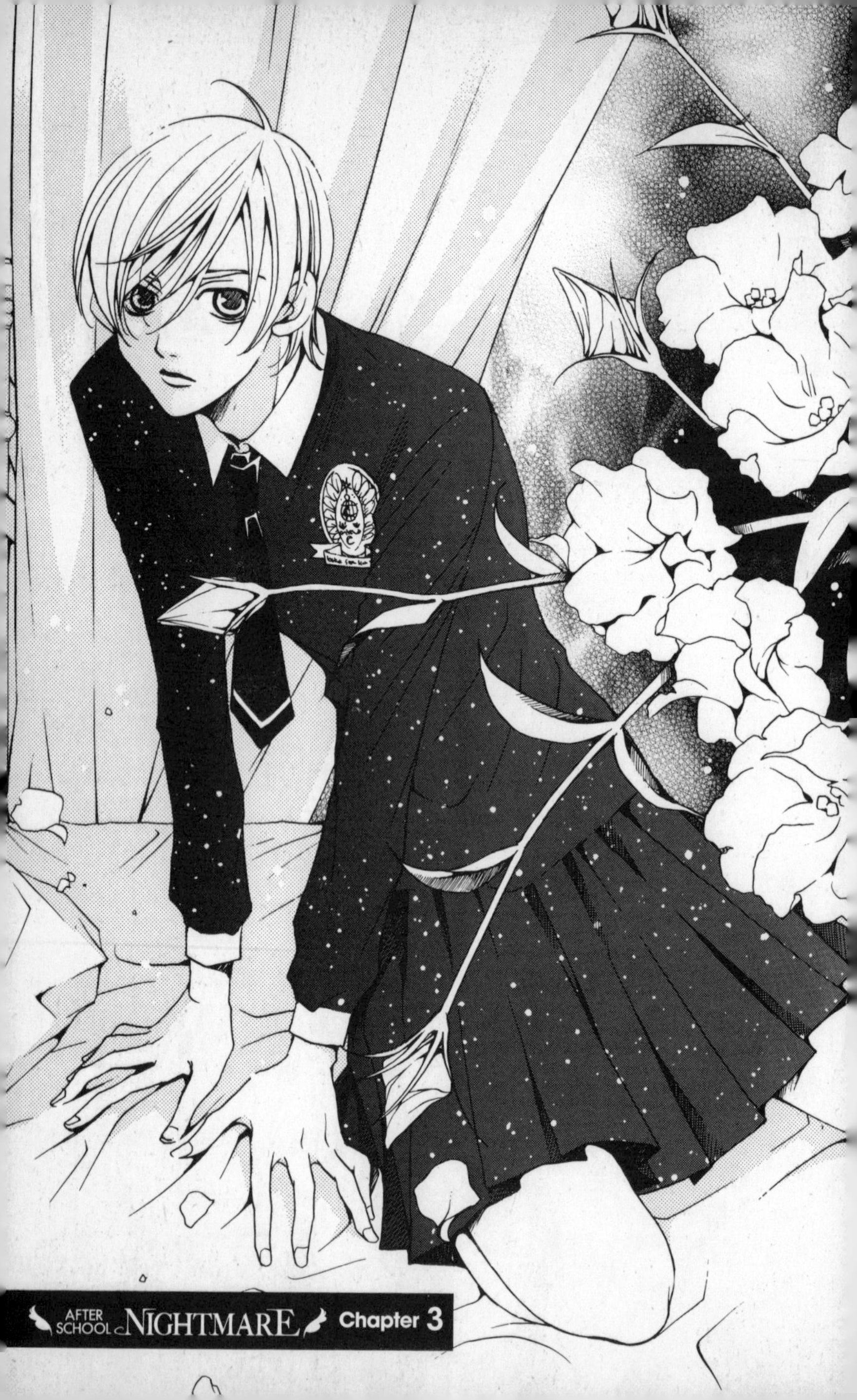

AFTER SCHOOL NIGHTMARE Chapter 3

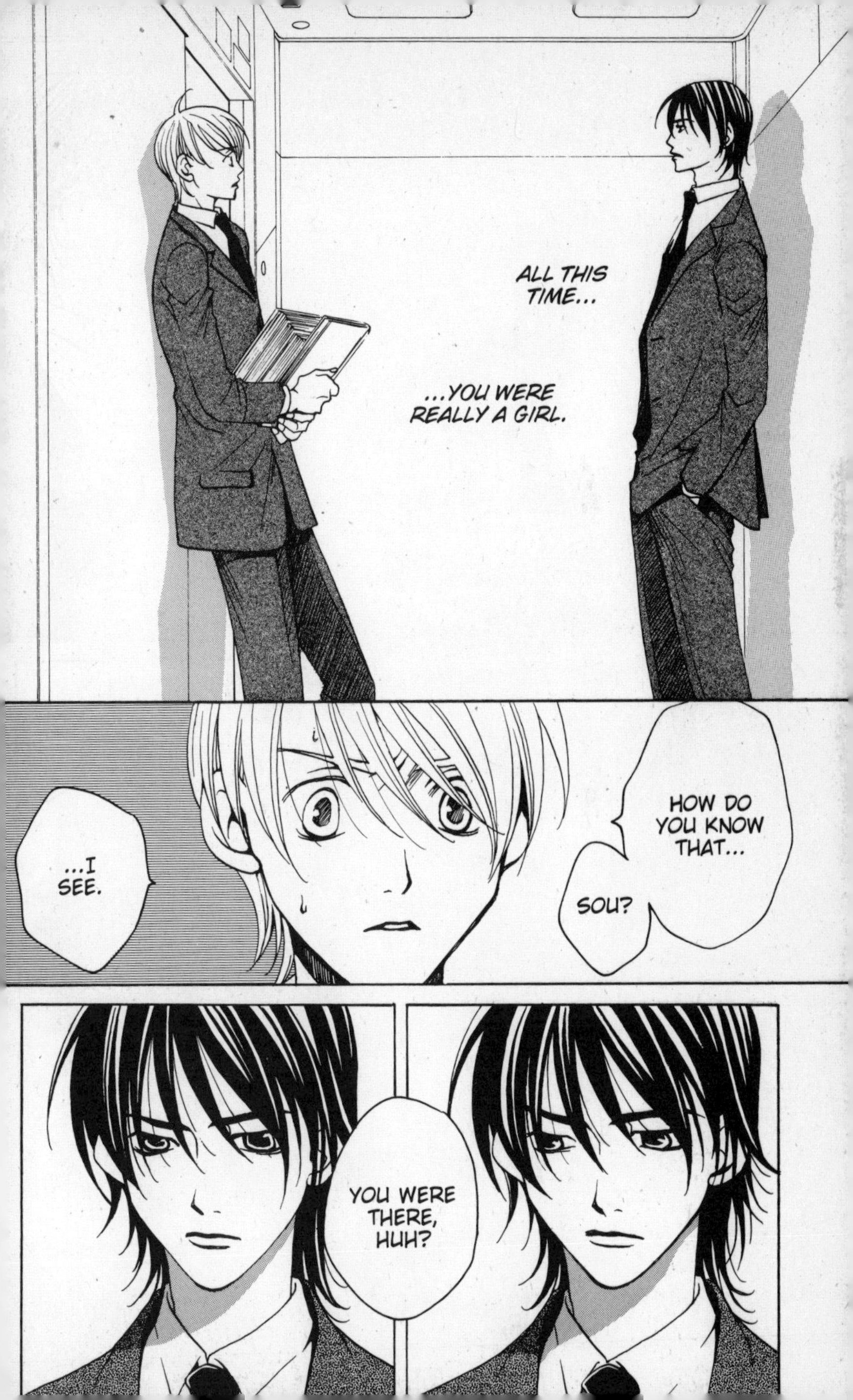
ALL THIS TIME...
...YOU WERE REALLY A GIRL.
HOW DO YOU KNOW THAT...
SOU?
...I SEE.
YOU WERE THERE, HUH?

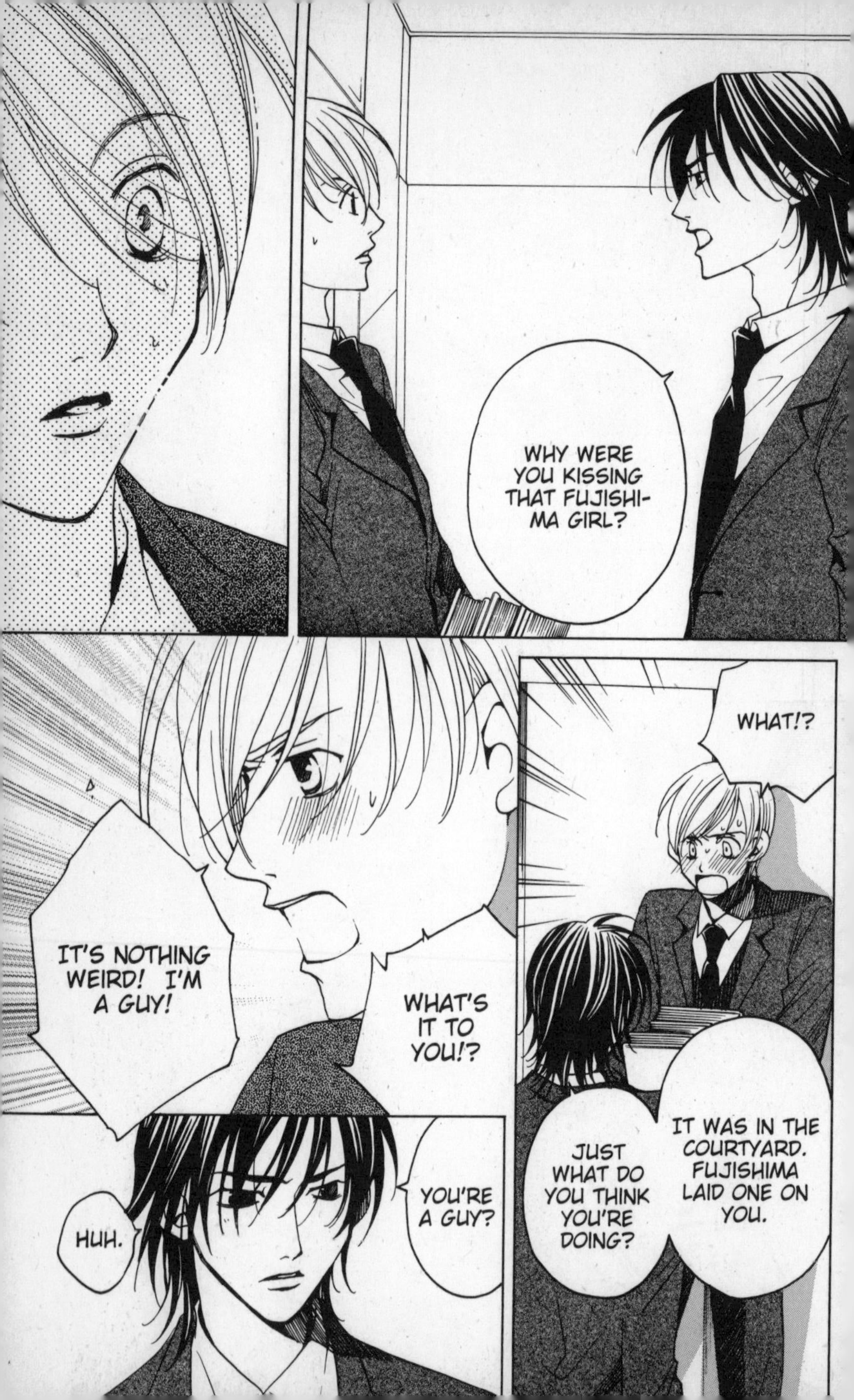
WHY WERE YOU KISSING THAT FUJISHI-MA GIRL?
WHAT!?
IT WAS IN THE COURTYARD. FUJISHIMA LAID ONE ON YOU.
JUST WHAT DO YOU THINK YOU'RE DOING?
WHAT'S IT TO YOU!?
IT'S NOTHING WEIRD! I'M A GUY!
YOU'RE A GUY?
HUH.

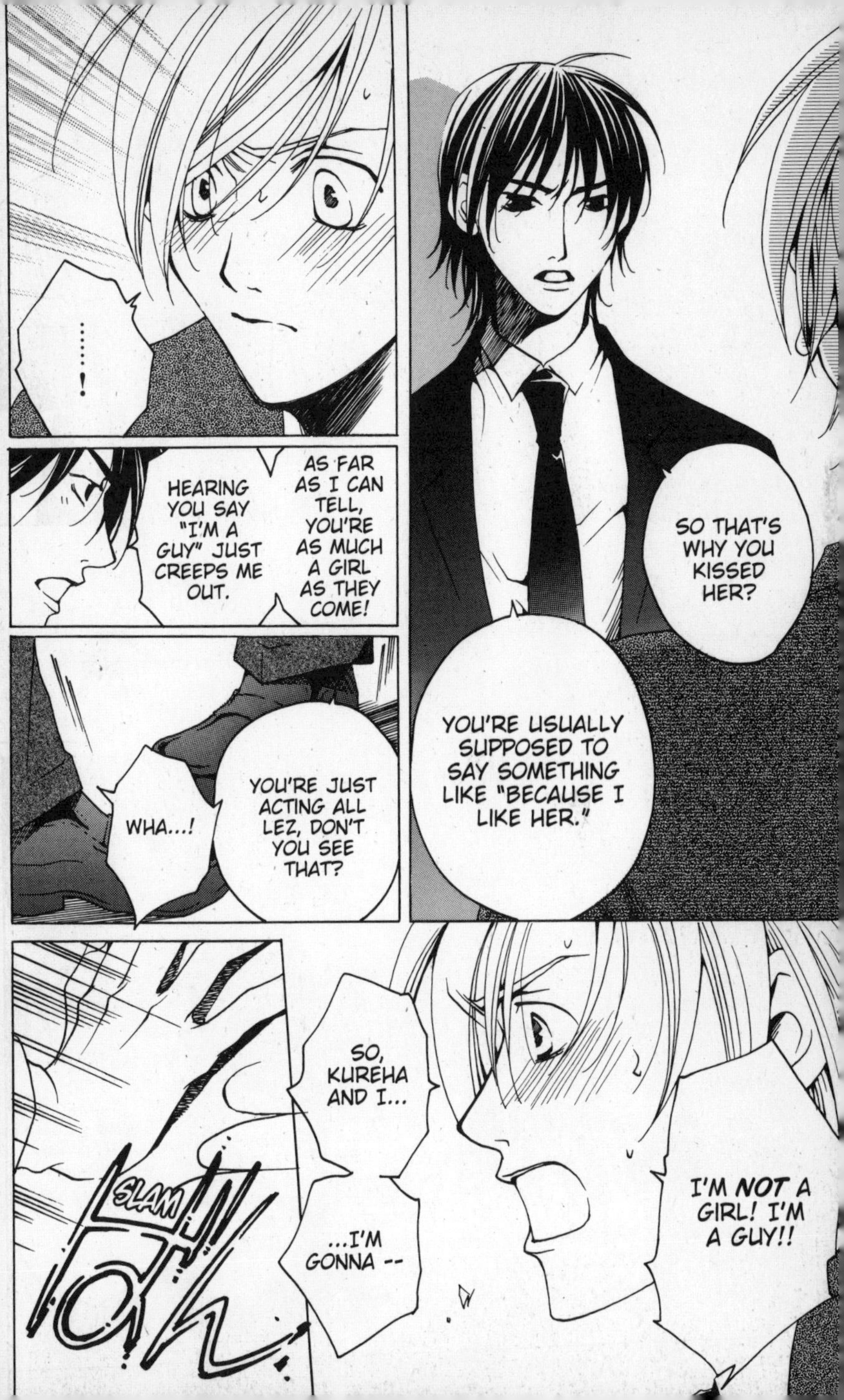
SO THAT'S WHY YOU KISSED HER?
YOU'RE USUALLY SUPPOSED TO SAY SOMETHING LIKE "BECAUSE I LIKE HER."
......!
AS FAR AS I CAN TELL, YOU'RE AS MUCH A GIRL AS THEY COME!
HEARING YOU SAY "I'M A GUY" JUST CREEPS ME OUT.
YOU'RE JUST ACTING ALL LEZ, DON'T YOU SEE THAT?
WHA...!
I'M NOT A GIRL! I'M A GUY!!
SO, KUREHA AND I...
...I'M GONNA --
SLAM

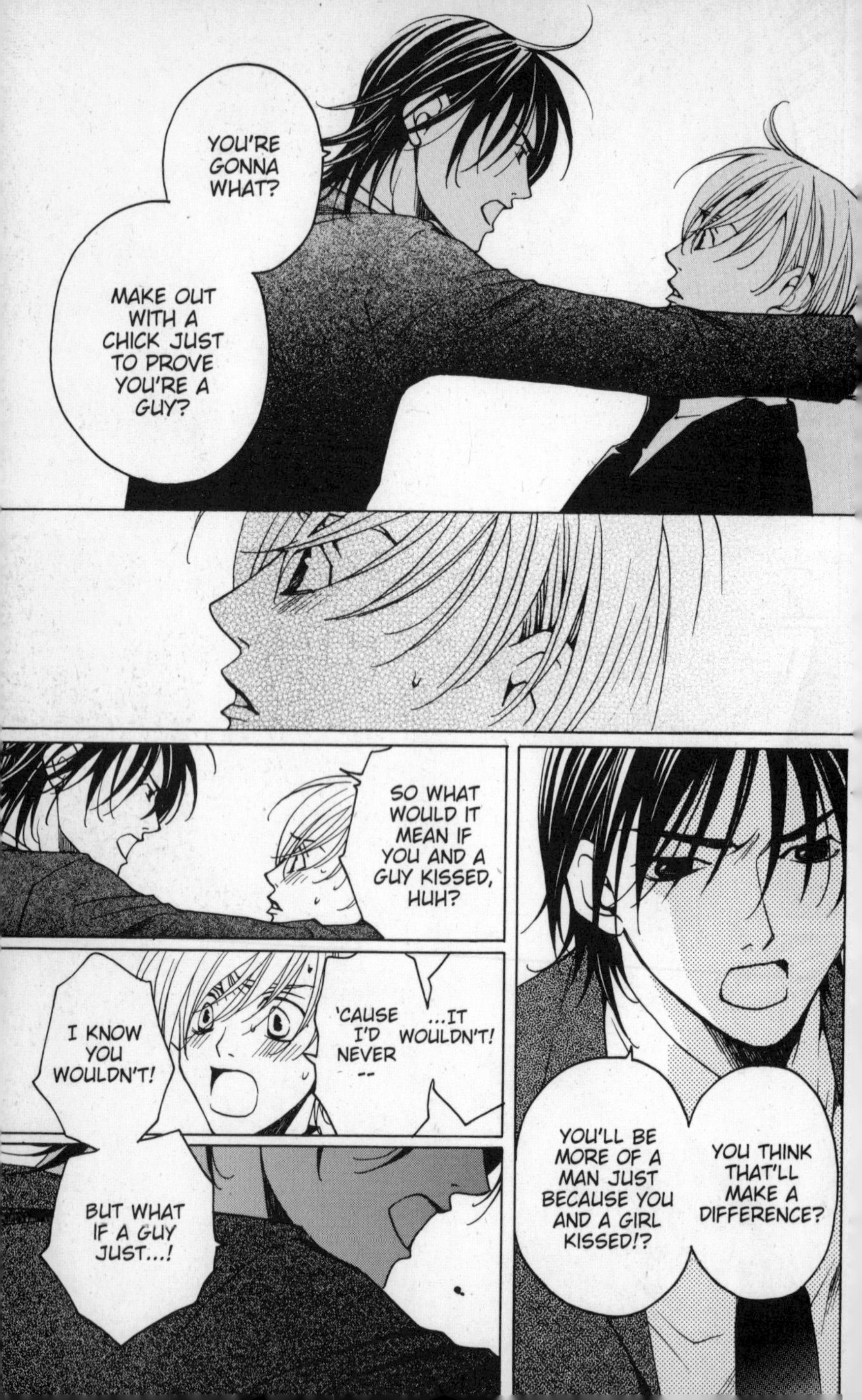
YOU'RE GONNA WHAT?
MAKE OUT WITH A CHICK JUST TO PROVE YOU'RE A GUY?
YOU THINK THAT'LL MAKE A DIFFERENCE?
YOU'LL BE MORE OF A MAN JUST BECAUSE YOU AND A GIRL KISSED!?
SO WHAT WOULD IT MEAN IF YOU AND A GUY KISSED, HUH?
...IT WOULDN'T!
'CAUSE I'D NEVER --
I KNOW YOU WOULDN'T!
BUT WHAT IF A GUY JUST...!

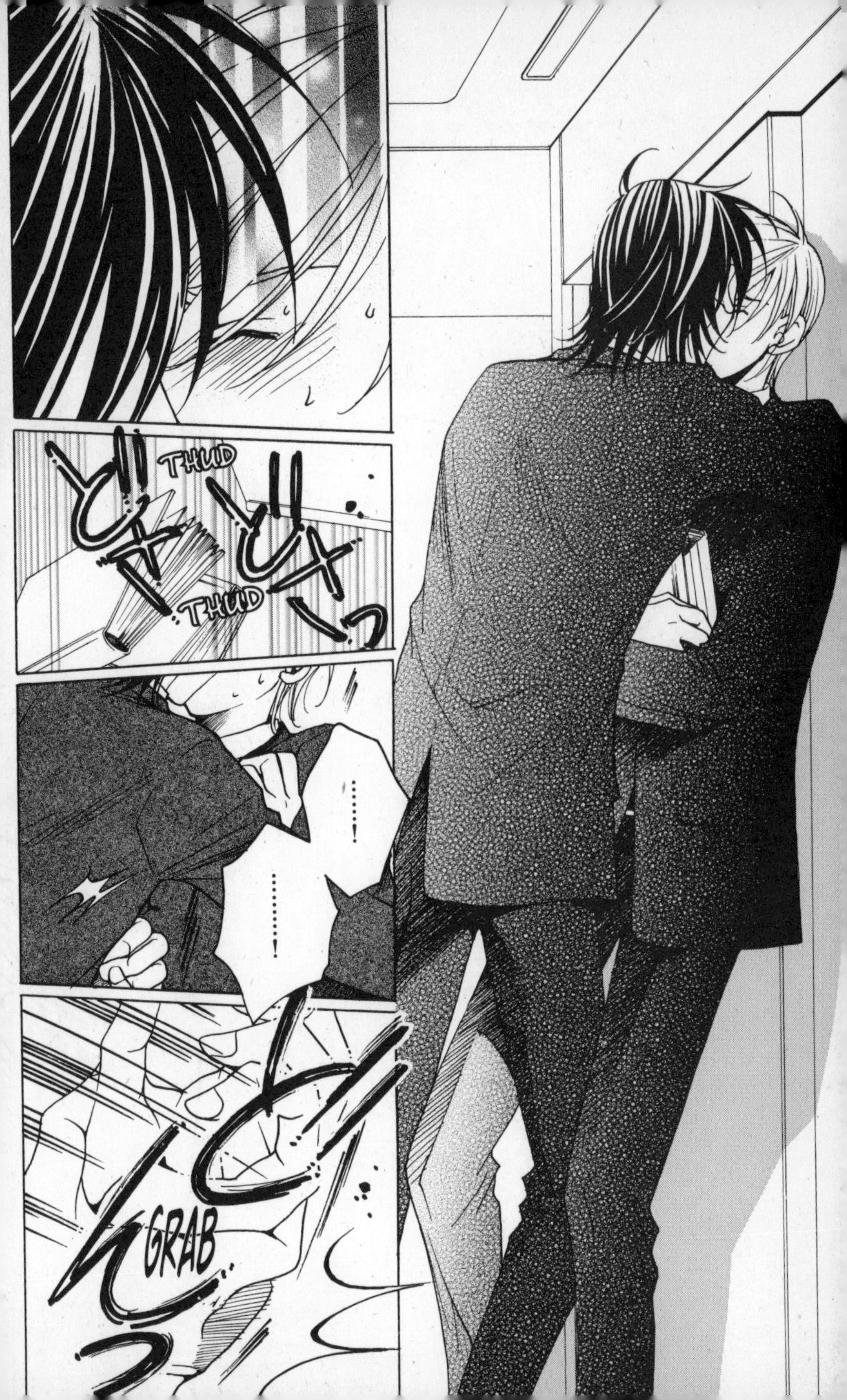
THUD
THUD
......!
......!
GRAB

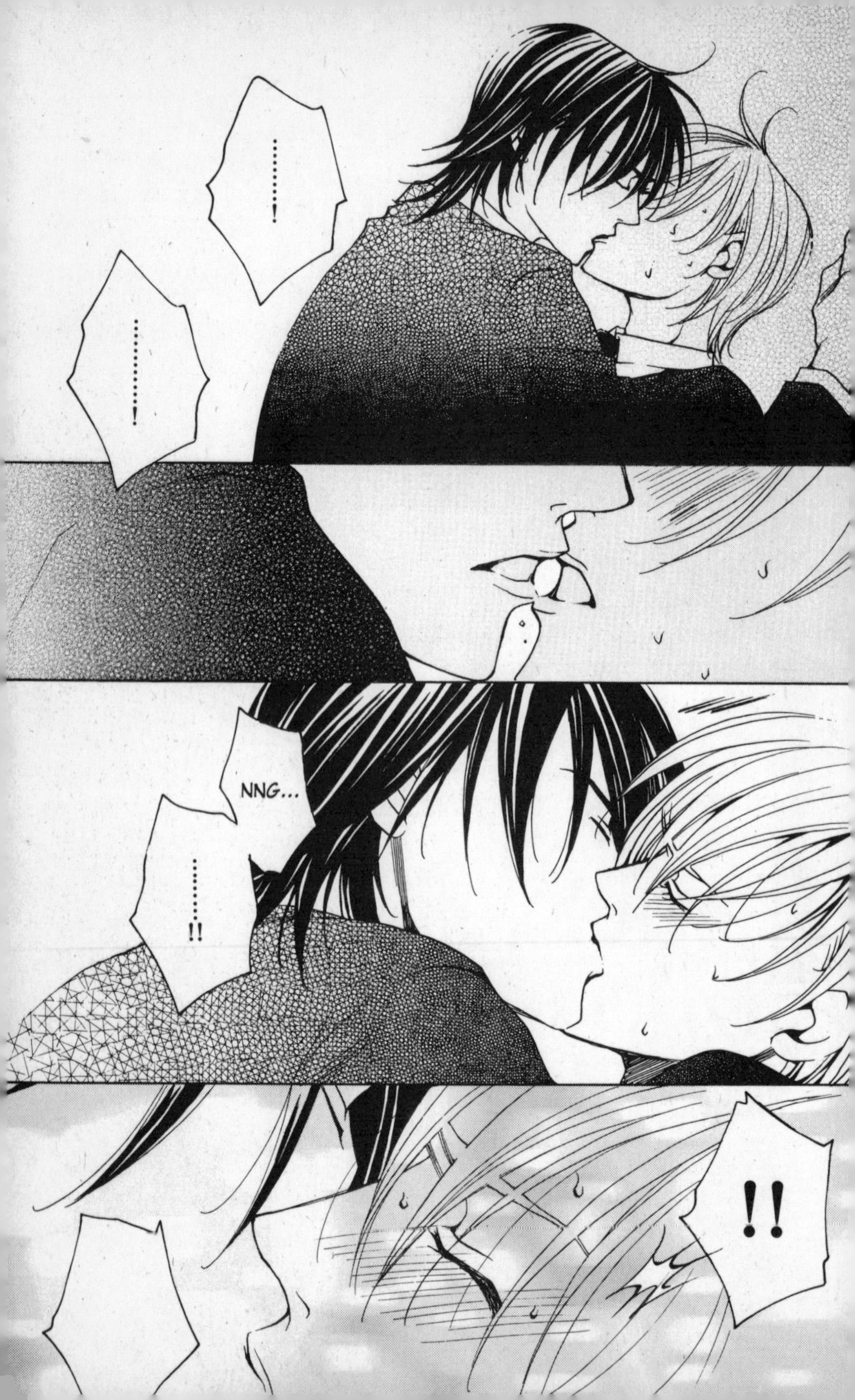
......!
......!
NNG...
......!!
!!

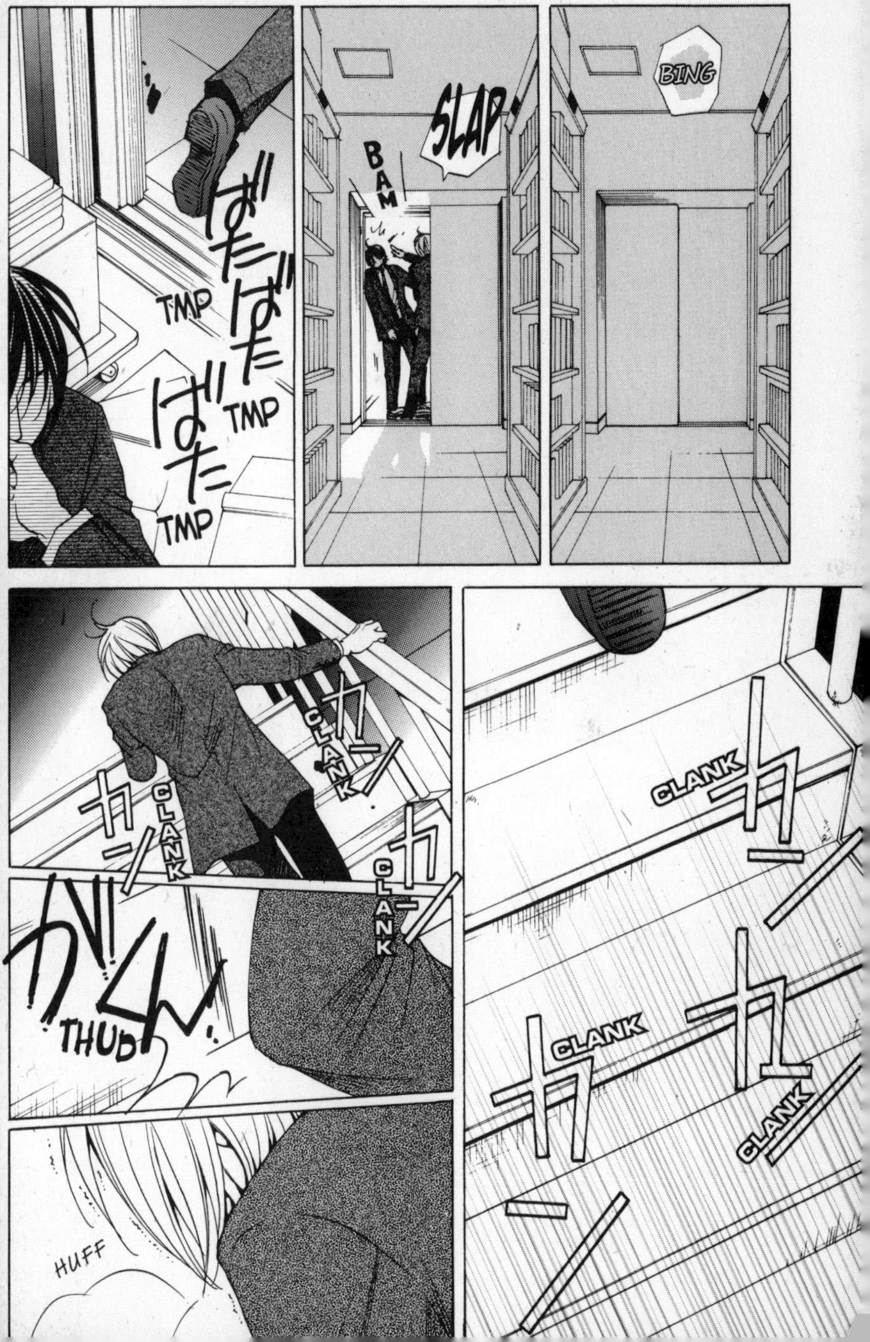
BING
SLAP
BAM
ばたばた
TMP
ばた
TMP
TMP
CLANK
CLANK
CLANK
CLANK
CLANK
CLANK
CLANK
THUD
HUFF

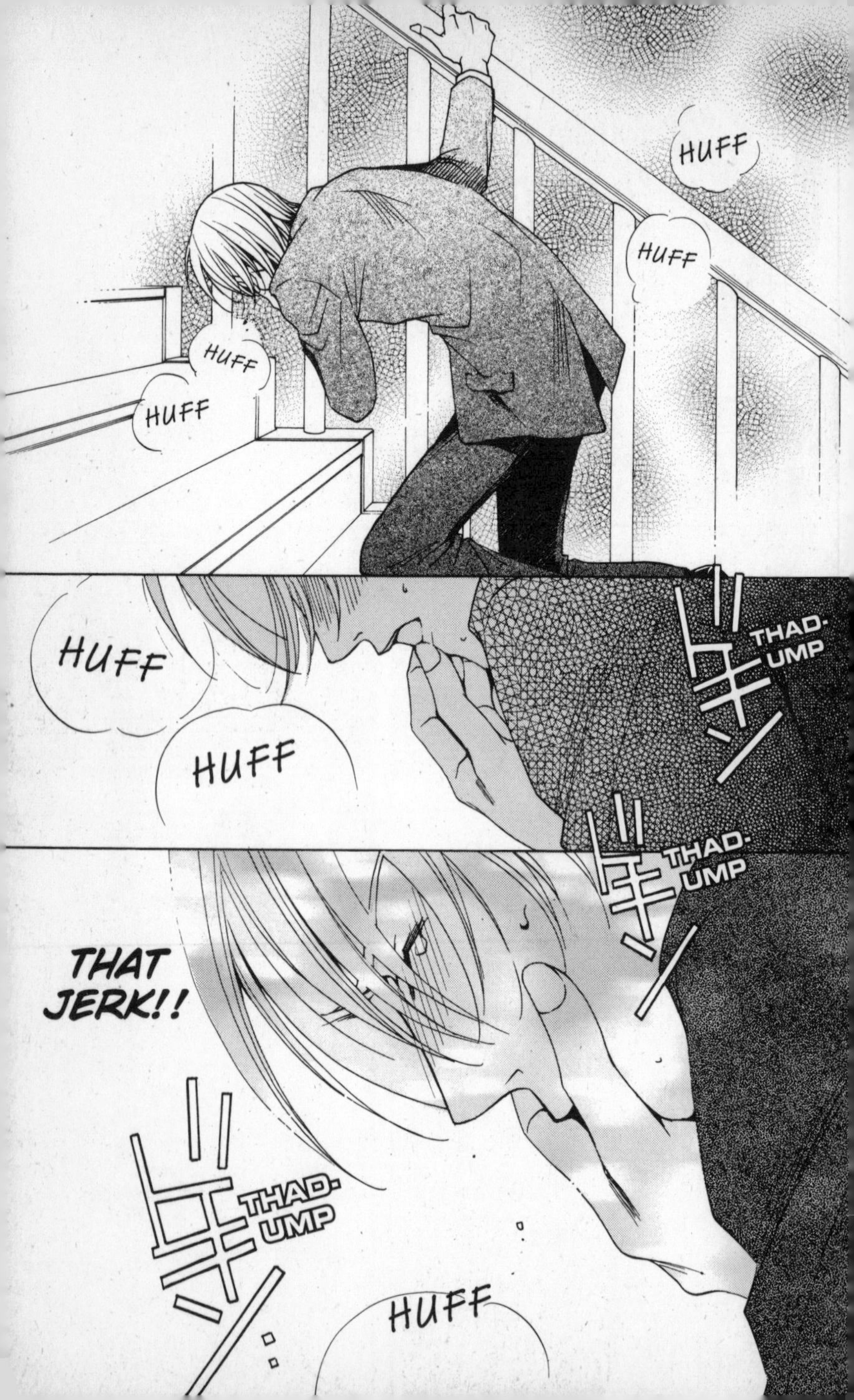
HUFF
HUFF
HUFF
HUFF
THAD-UMP
HUFF
HUFF
THAD-UMP
THAT JERK!!
THAD-UMP
HUFF

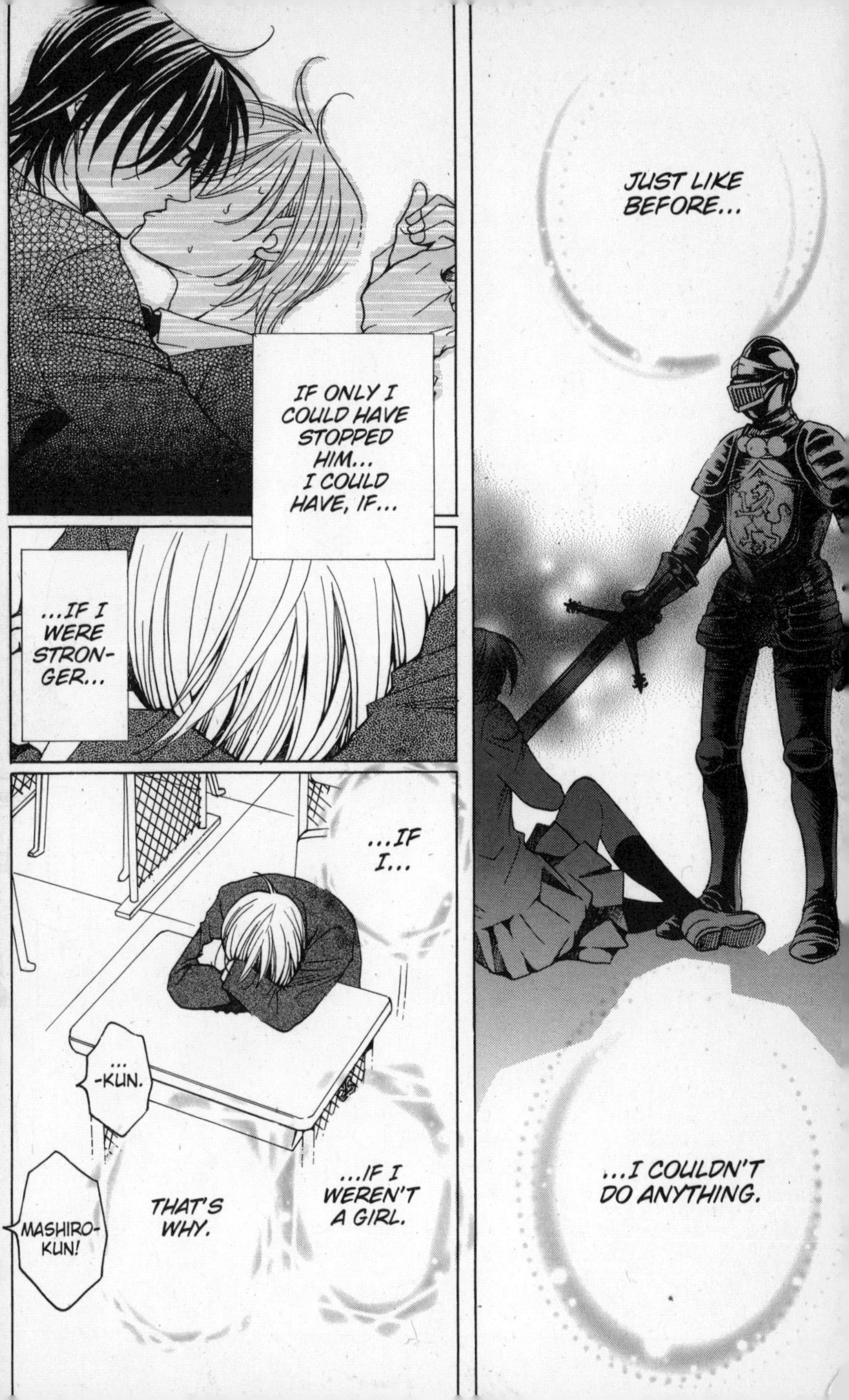
IF ONLY I COULD HAVE STOPPED HIM... I COULD HAVE, IF...
...IF I WERE STRONGER...
...IF I...
...IF I WEREN'T A GIRL.
THAT'S WHY.
... -KUN.
MASHIRO-KUN!
JUST LIKE BEFORE...
...I COULDN'T DO ANYTHING.

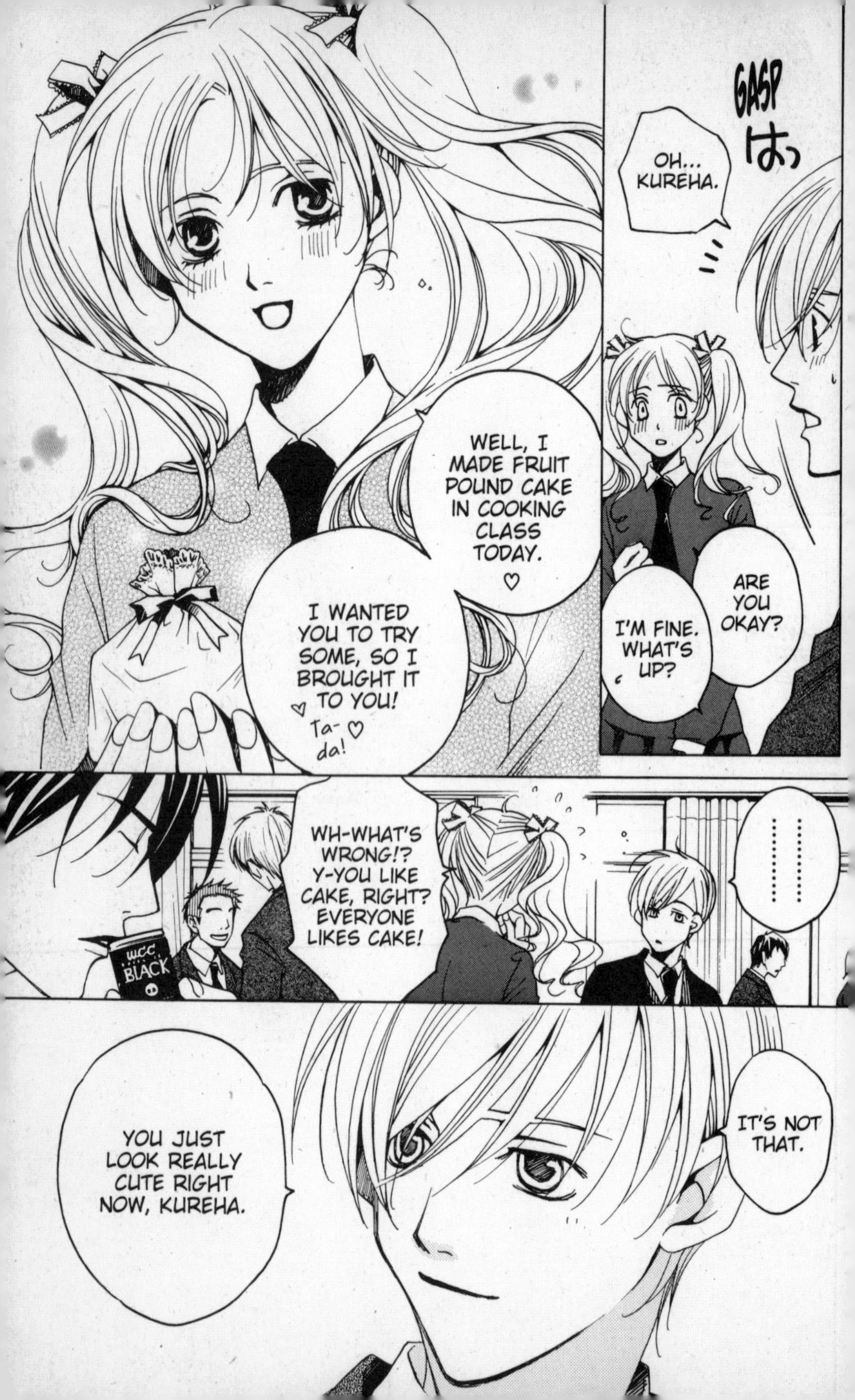
GASP
はっ
OH... KUREHA.
ARE YOU OKAY?
I'M FINE. WHAT'S UP?
WELL, I MADE FRUIT POUND CAKE IN COOKING CLASS TODAY. ♡
I WANTED YOU TO TRY SOME, SO I BROUGHT IT TO YOU! ♡
Ta-da! ♡
......
WH-WHAT'S WRONG!? Y-YOU LIKE CAKE, RIGHT? EVERYONE LIKES CAKE!
BLACK
IT'S NOT THAT.
YOU JUST LOOK REALLY CUTE RIGHT NOW, KUREHA.

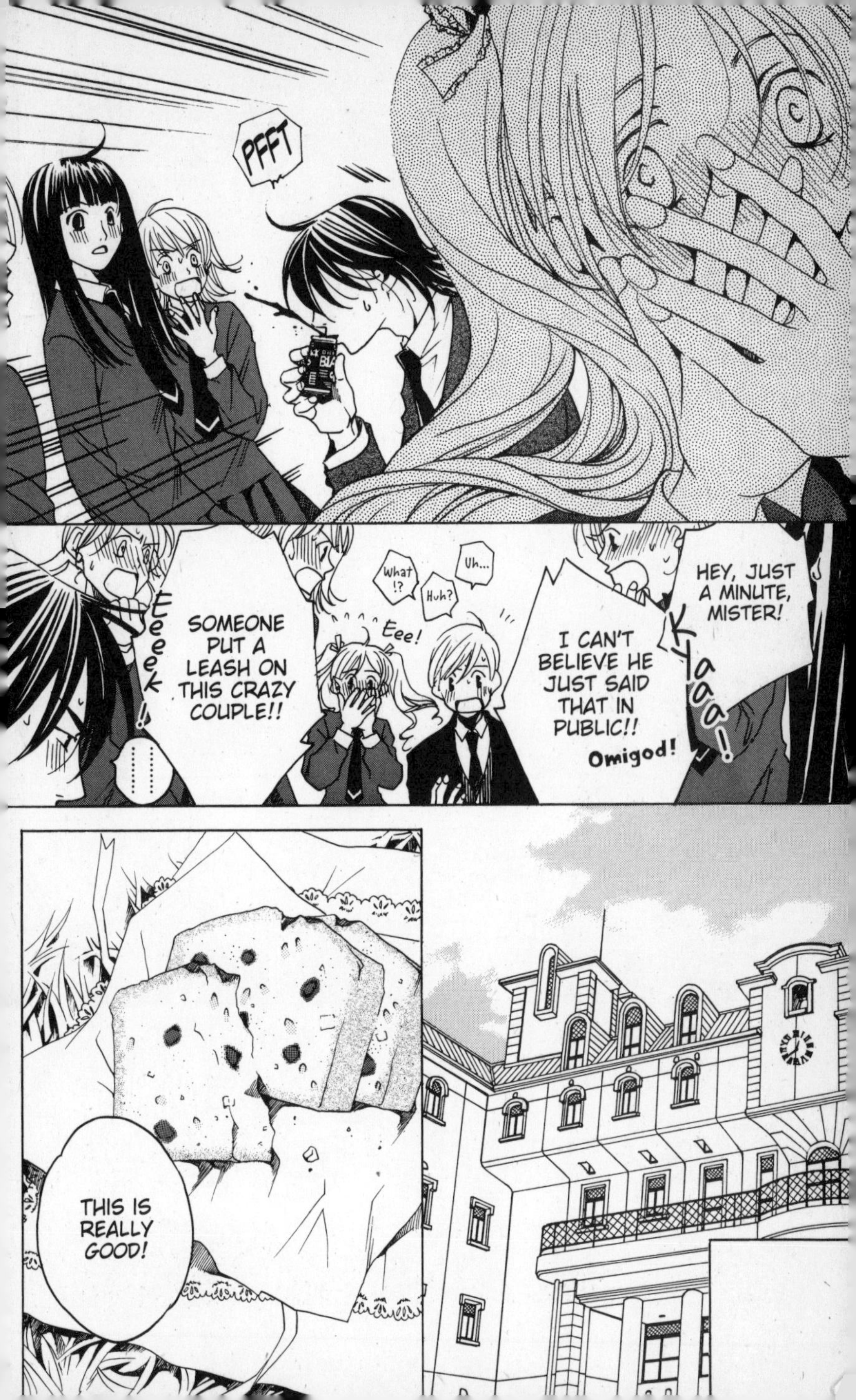
PFFT
HEY, JUST A MINUTE, MISTER!
Kyaaa!
I CAN'T BELIEVE HE JUST SAID THAT IN PUBLIC!!
Omigod!
Uh...
Huh?
What!?
Eee!
SOMEONE PUT A LEASH ON THIS CRAZY COUPLE!!
Eeeek!!
......
THIS IS REALLY GOOD!

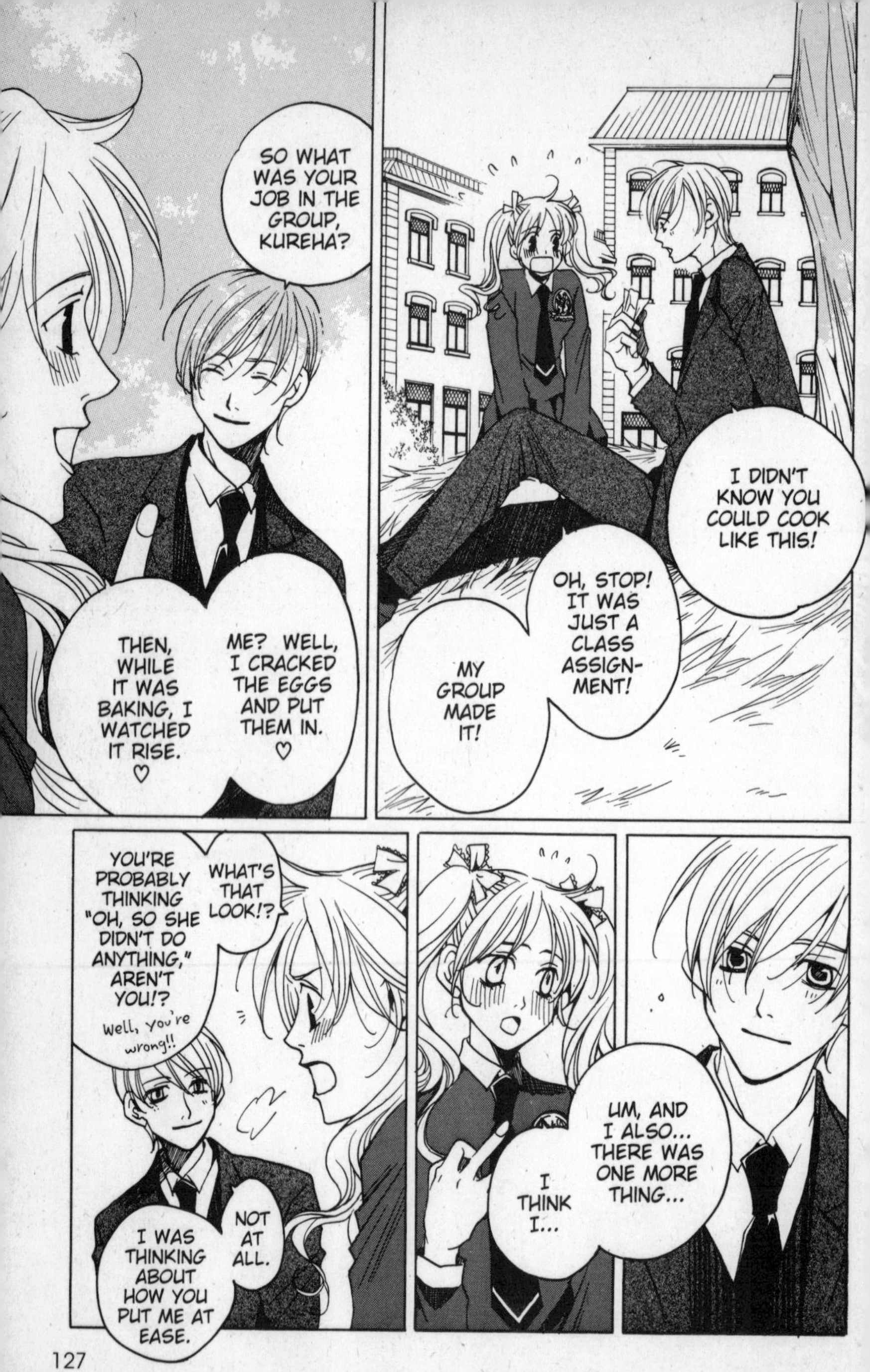
I DIDN'T KNOW YOU COULD COOK LIKE THIS!
OH, STOP! IT WAS JUST A CLASS ASSIGNMENT!
MY GROUP MADE IT!
SO WHAT WAS YOUR JOB IN THE GROUP, KUREHA?
ME? WELL, I CRACKED THE EGGS AND PUT THEM IN. ♡
THEN, WHILE IT WAS BAKING, I WATCHED IT RISE. ♡
UM, AND I ALSO... THERE WAS ONE MORE THING...
I THINK I...
WHAT'S THAT LOOK!?
YOU'RE PROBABLY THINKING "OH, SO SHE DIDN'T DO ANYTHING," AREN'T YOU!?
Well, you're wrong!!
NOT AT ALL.
I WAS THINKING ABOUT HOW YOU PUT ME AT EASE.

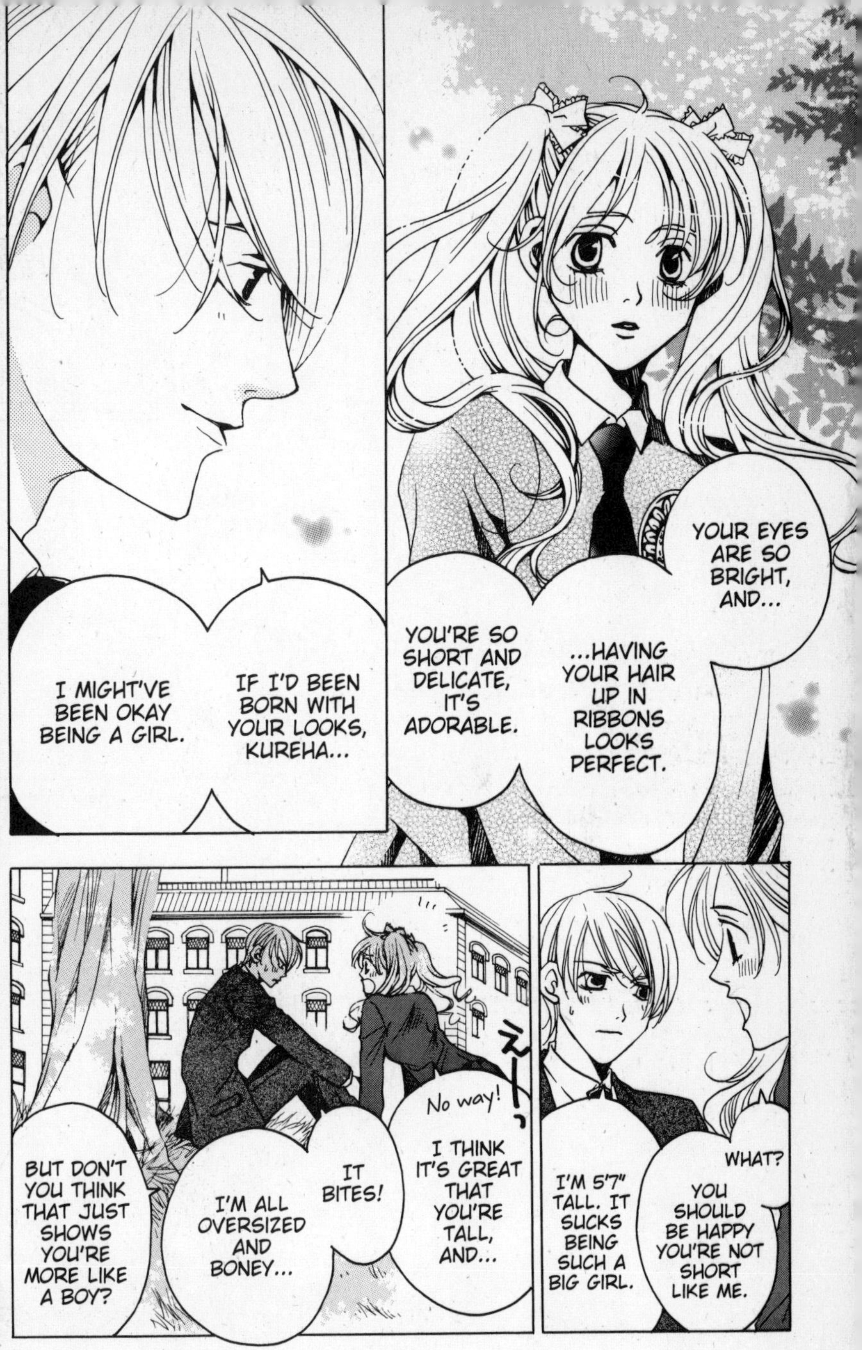
YOUR EYES ARE SO BRIGHT, AND...
...HAVING YOUR HAIR UP IN RIBBONS LOOKS PERFECT.
YOU'RE SO SHORT AND DELICATE, IT'S ADORABLE.
IF I'D BEEN BORN WITH YOUR LOOKS, KUREHA...
I MIGHT'VE BEEN OKAY BEING A GIRL.
WHAT?
YOU SHOULD BE HAPPY YOU'RE NOT SHORT LIKE ME.
I'M 5'7" TALL. IT SUCKS BEING SUCH A BIG GIRL.
えー!
No way!
I THINK IT'S GREAT THAT YOU'RE TALL, AND...
IT BITES!
I'M ALL OVERSIZED AND BONEY...
BUT DON'T YOU THINK THAT JUST SHOWS YOU'RE MORE LIKE A BOY?

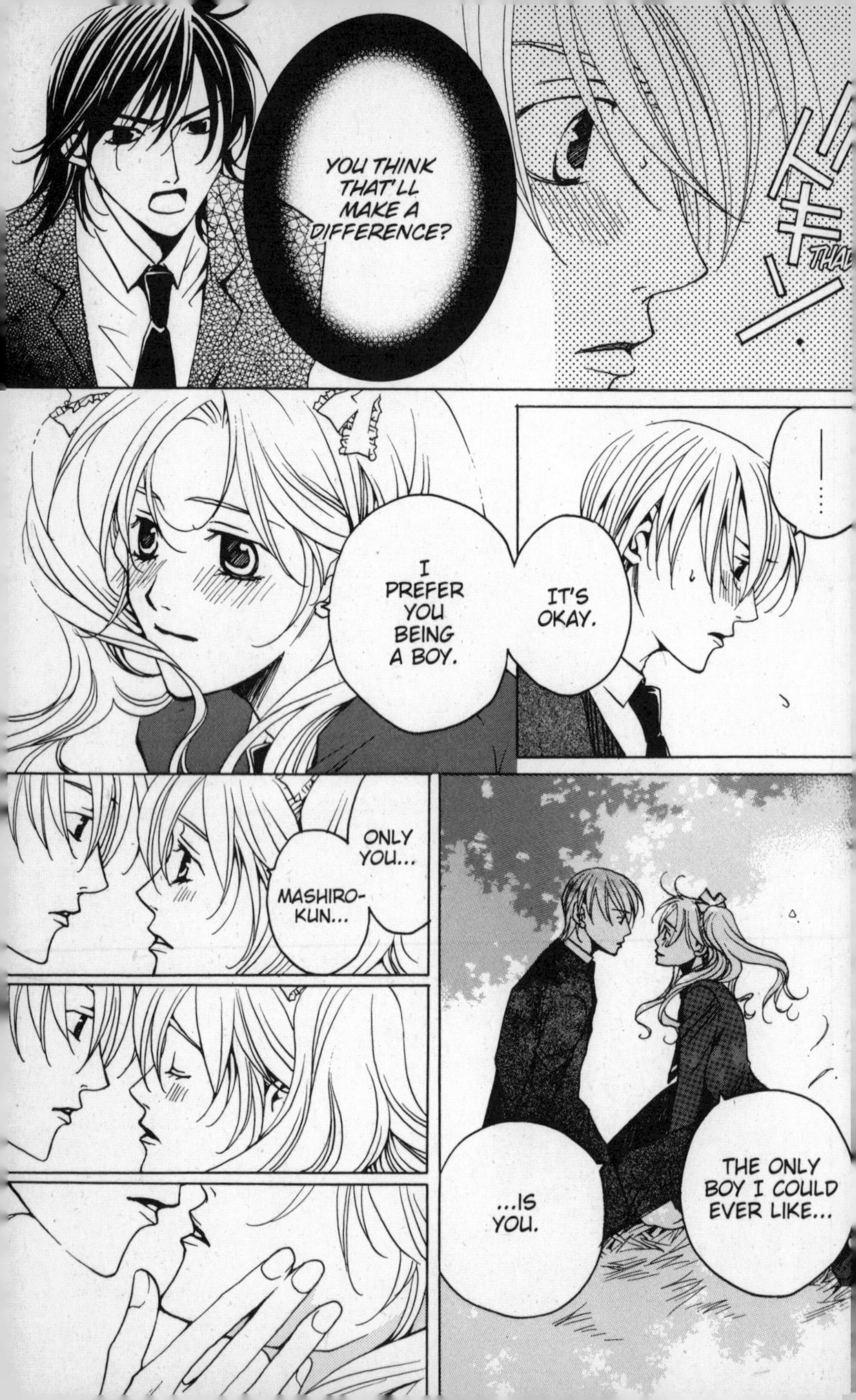
YOU THINK THAT'LL MAKE A DIFFERENCE?
......
IT'S OKAY.
I PREFER YOU BEING A BOY.
THE ONLY BOY I COULD EVER LIKE...
...IS YOU.
ONLY YOU...
MASHIRO-KUN...

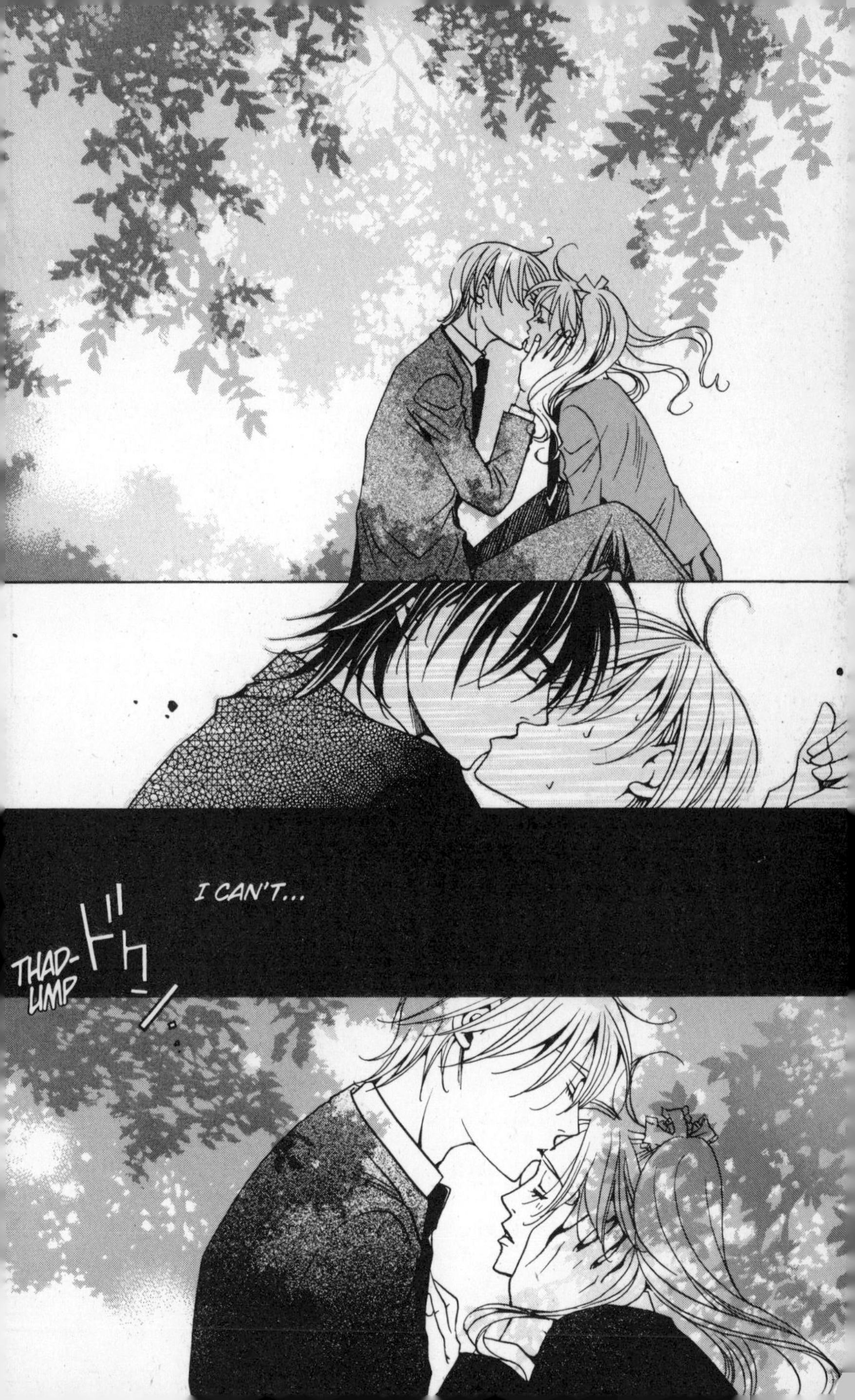
I CAN'T...
THAD-LUMP
ドクン

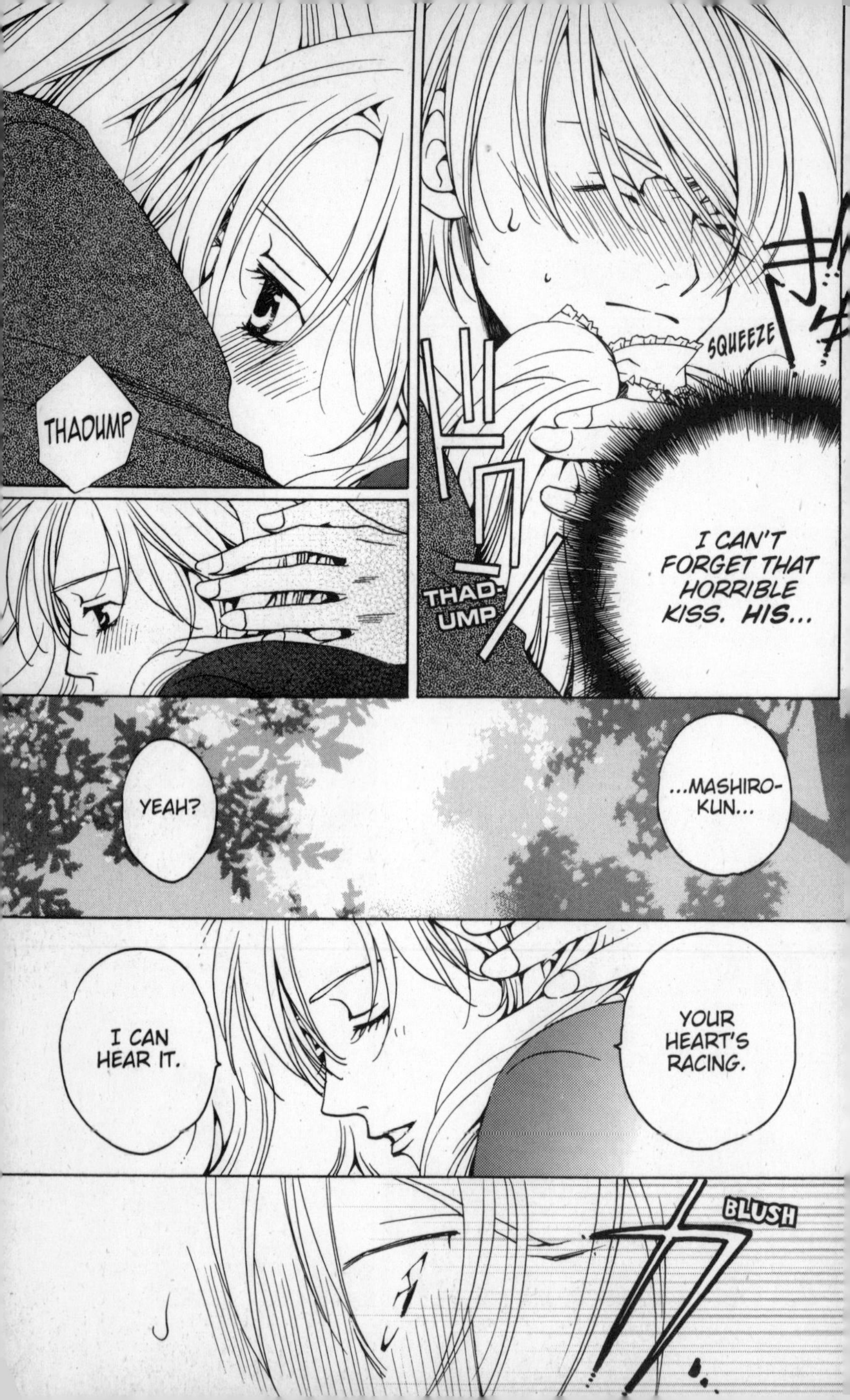
SQUEEZE
THAD-UMP
I CAN'T FORGET THAT HORRIBLE KISS. HIS...
THADUMP
...MASHIRO-KUN...
YEAH?
YOUR HEART'S RACING.
I CAN HEAR IT.
BLUSH

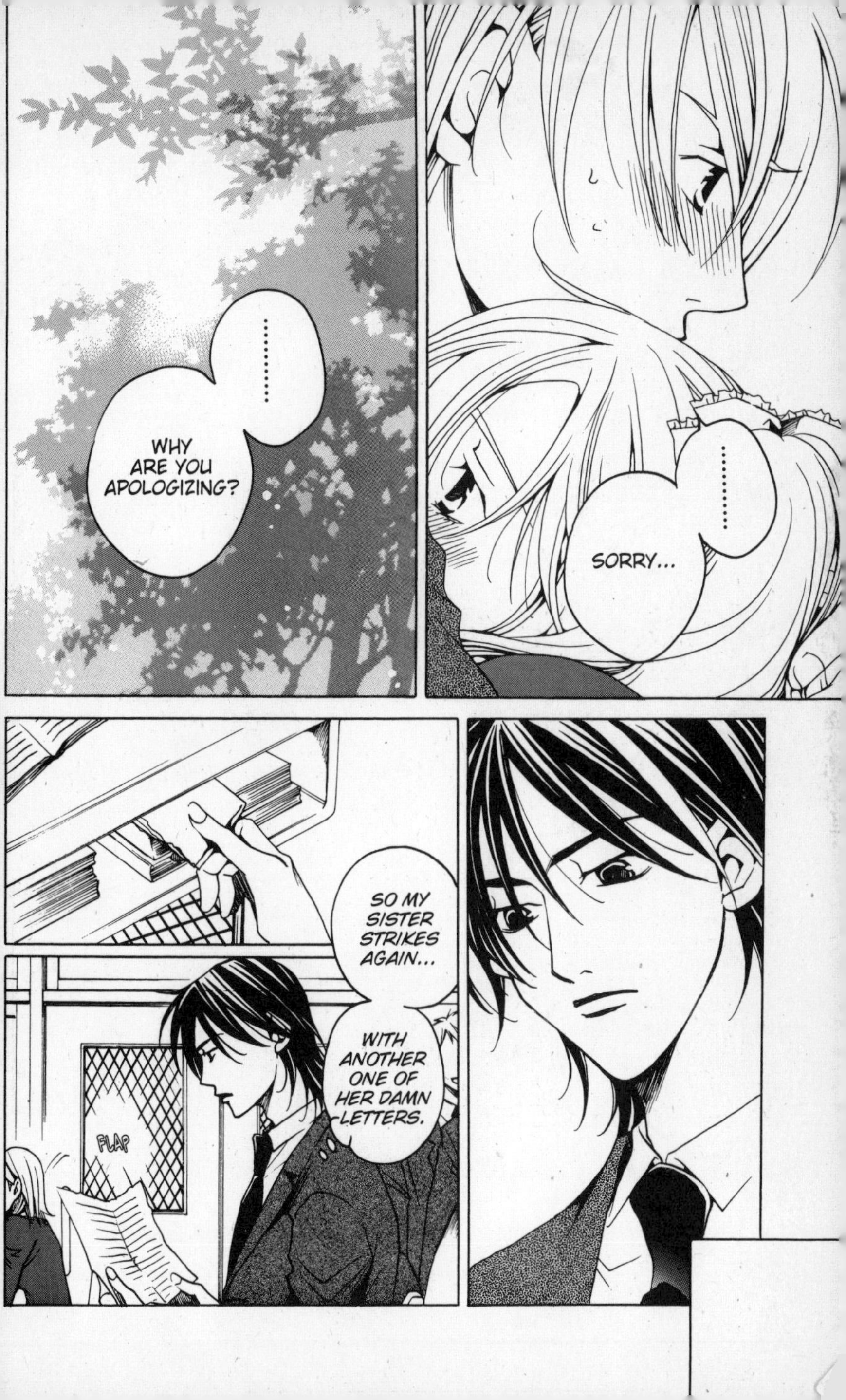
....
SORRY...
....
WHY ARE YOU APOLOGIZING?
SO MY SISTER STRIKES AGAIN...
WITH ANOTHER ONE OF HER DAMN LETTERS.
FLAP

Kissing him like that all of a sudden...

It's not like you, Sou.

And you got dumped.

Now Mashiro Ichijo will never go within ten feet of you.

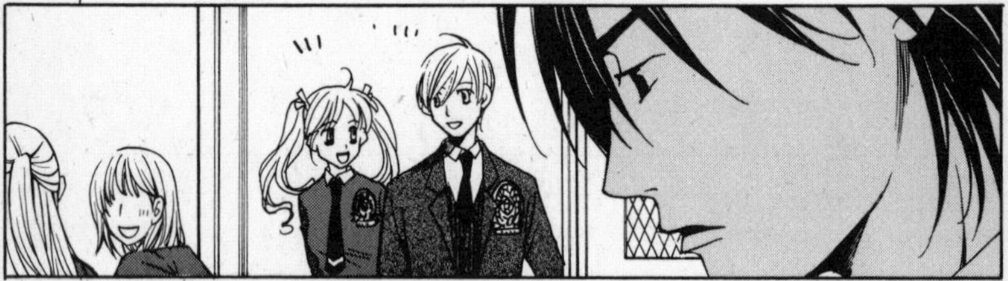

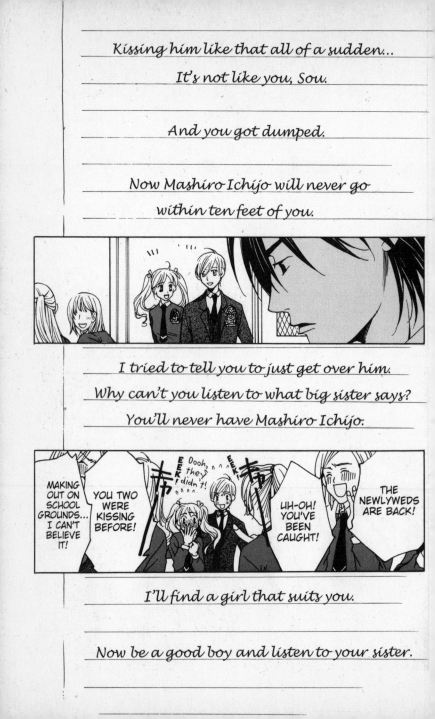

I tried to tell you to just get over him.

Why can't you listen to what big sister says?

You'll never have Mashiro Ichijo.

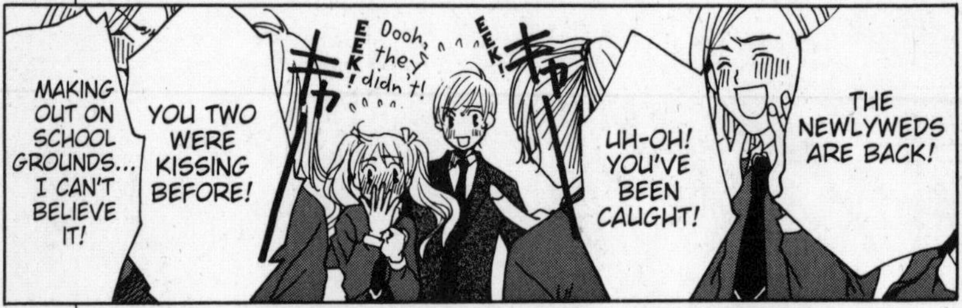
THE NEWLYWEDS ARE BACK!
UH-OH! YOU'VE BEEN CAUGHT!
EEK!
Oooh, they didn't!
EEK!
YOU TWO WERE KISSING BEFORE!
MAKING OUT ON SCHOOL GROUNDS... I CAN'T BELIEVE IT!

I'll find a girl that suits you.

Now be a good boy and listen to your sister.

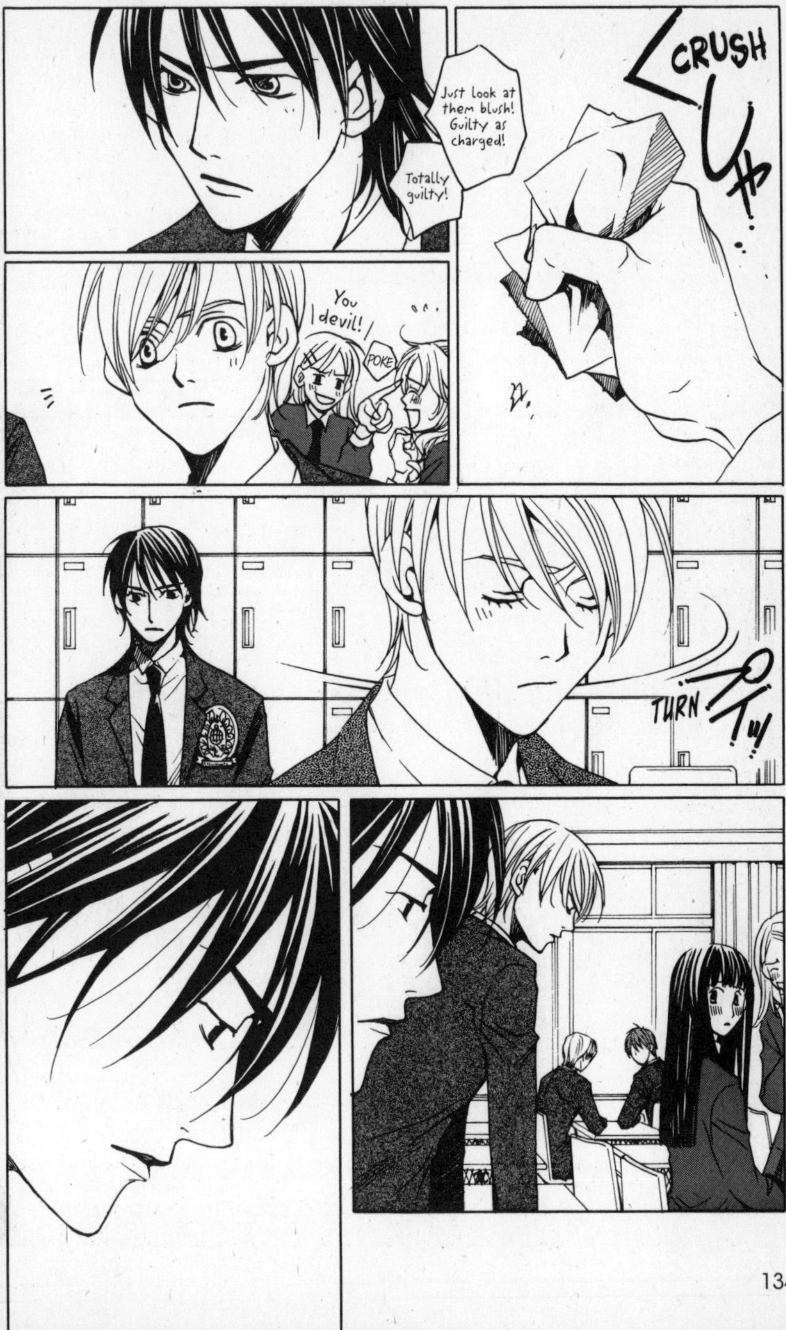
CRUSH
Just look at them blush! Guilty as charged!
Totally guilty!
You devil!
POKE
TURN

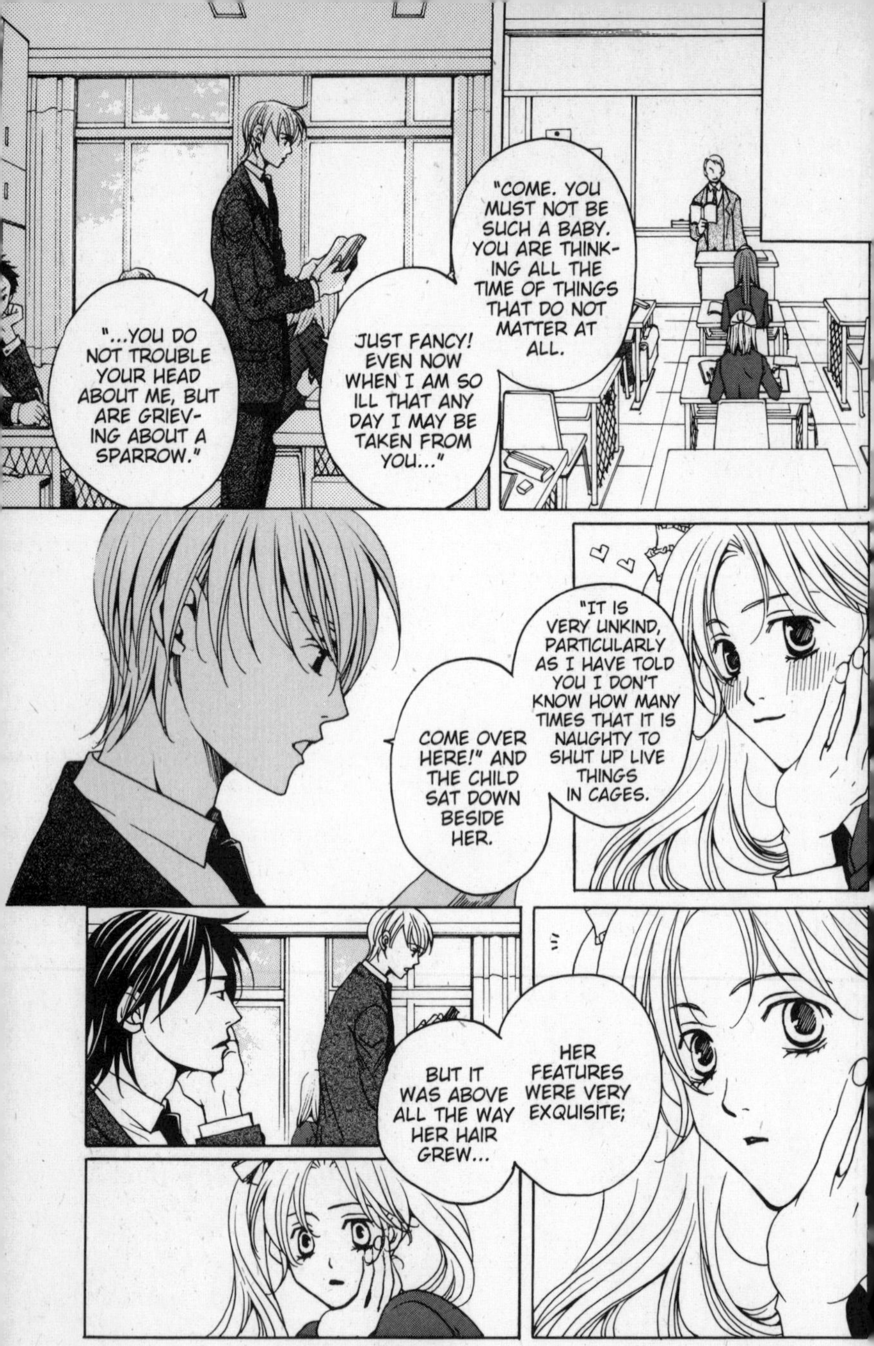
"COME. YOU MUST NOT BE SUCH A BABY. YOU ARE THINKING ALL THE TIME OF THINGS THAT DO NOT MATTER AT ALL.
JUST FANCY! EVEN NOW WHEN I AM SO ILL THAT ANY DAY I MAY BE TAKEN FROM YOU..."
"...YOU DO NOT TROUBLE YOUR HEAD ABOUT ME, BUT ARE GRIEVING ABOUT A SPARROW."
"IT IS VERY UNKIND, PARTICULARLY AS I HAVE TOLD YOU I DON'T KNOW HOW MANY TIMES THAT IT IS NAUGHTY TO SHUT UP LIVE THINGS IN CAGES.
COME OVER HERE!" AND THE CHILD SAT DOWN BESIDE HER.
HER FEATURES WERE VERY EXQUISITE;
BUT IT WAS ABOVE ALL THE WAY HER HAIR GREW...

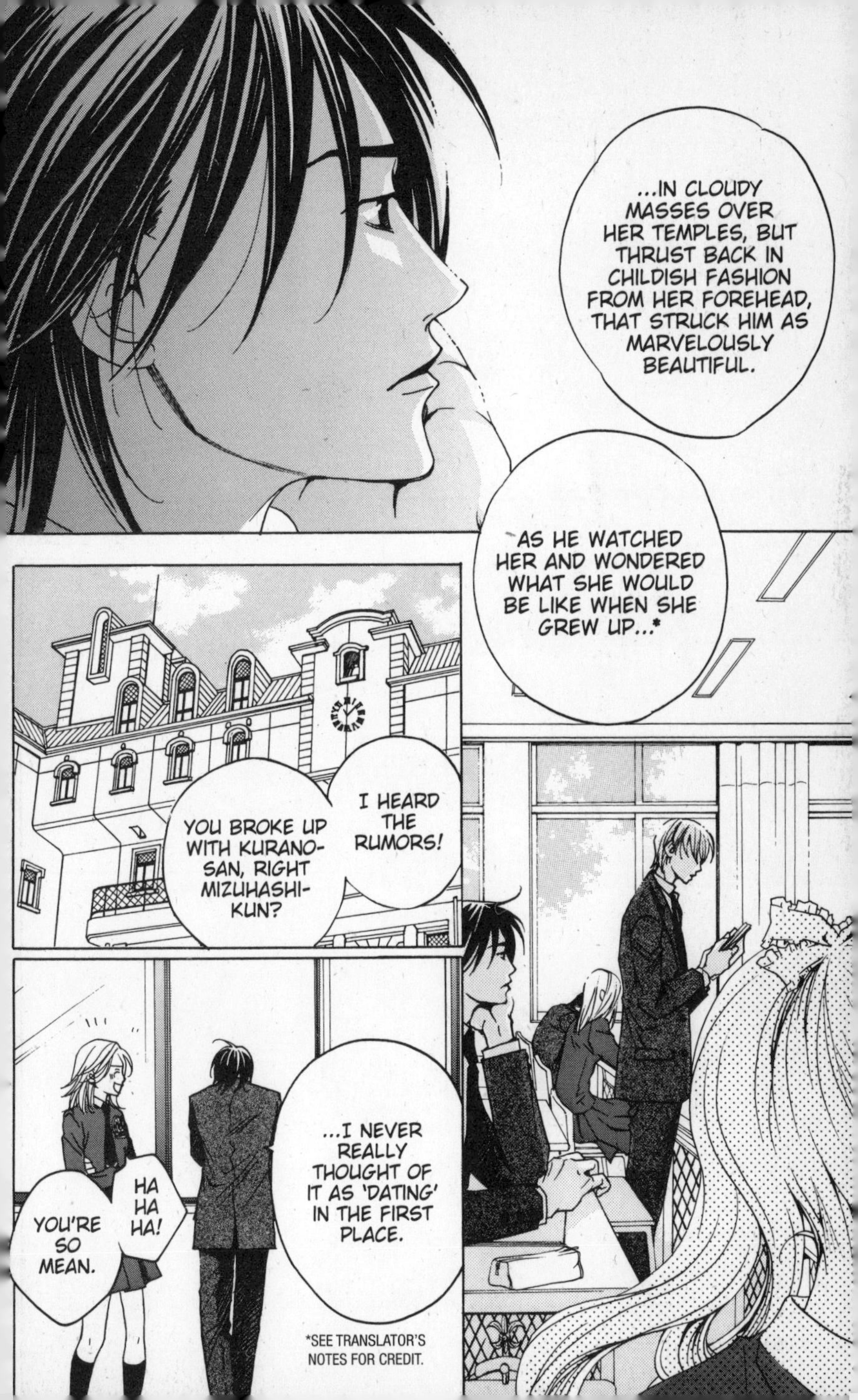
...IN CLOUDY MASSES OVER HER TEMPLES, BUT THRUST BACK IN CHILDISH FASHION FROM HER FOREHEAD, THAT STRUCK HIM AS MARVELOUSLY BEAUTIFUL.
AS HE WATCHED HER AND WONDERED WHAT SHE WOULD BE LIKE WHEN SHE GREW UP...*
I HEARD THE RUMORS!
YOU BROKE UP WITH KURANO-SAN, RIGHT MIZUHASHI-KUN?
...I NEVER REALLY THOUGHT OF IT AS 'DATING' IN THE FIRST PLACE.
HA HA HA!
YOU'RE SO MEAN.

*SEE TRANSLATOR'S NOTES FOR CREDIT.

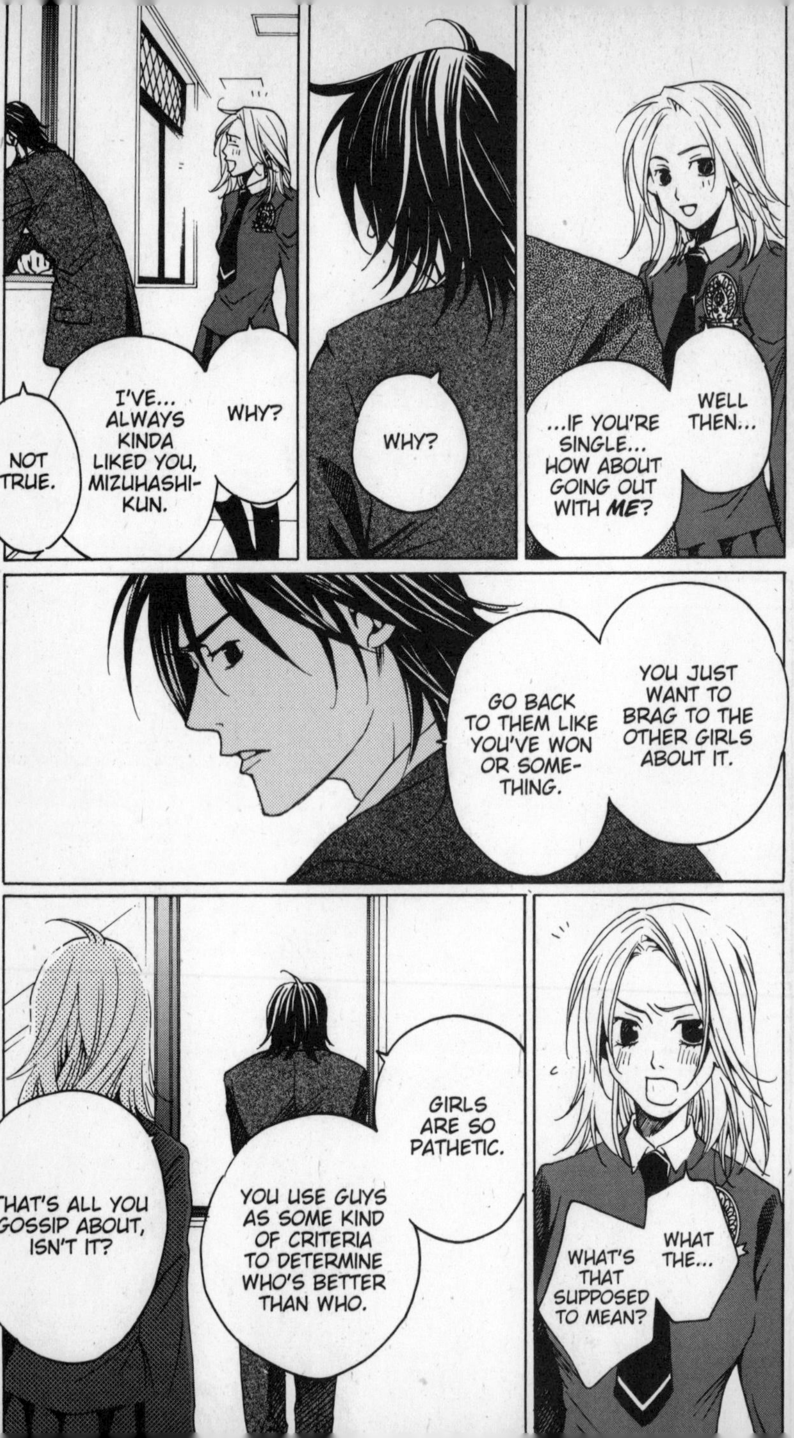
WELL THEN...
...IF YOU'RE SINGLE... HOW ABOUT GOING OUT WITH *ME*?
WHY?
WHY?
I'VE... ALWAYS KINDA LIKED YOU, MIZUHASHI-KUN.
NOT TRUE.
YOU JUST WANT TO BRAG TO THE OTHER GIRLS ABOUT IT.
GO BACK TO THEM LIKE YOU'VE WON OR SOME-THING.
WHAT THE...
WHAT'S THAT SUPPOSED TO MEAN?
GIRLS ARE SO PATHETIC.
YOU USE GUYS AS SOME KIND OF CRITERIA TO DETERMINE WHO'S BETTER THAN WHO.
THAT'S ALL YOU GOSSIP ABOUT, ISN'T IT?

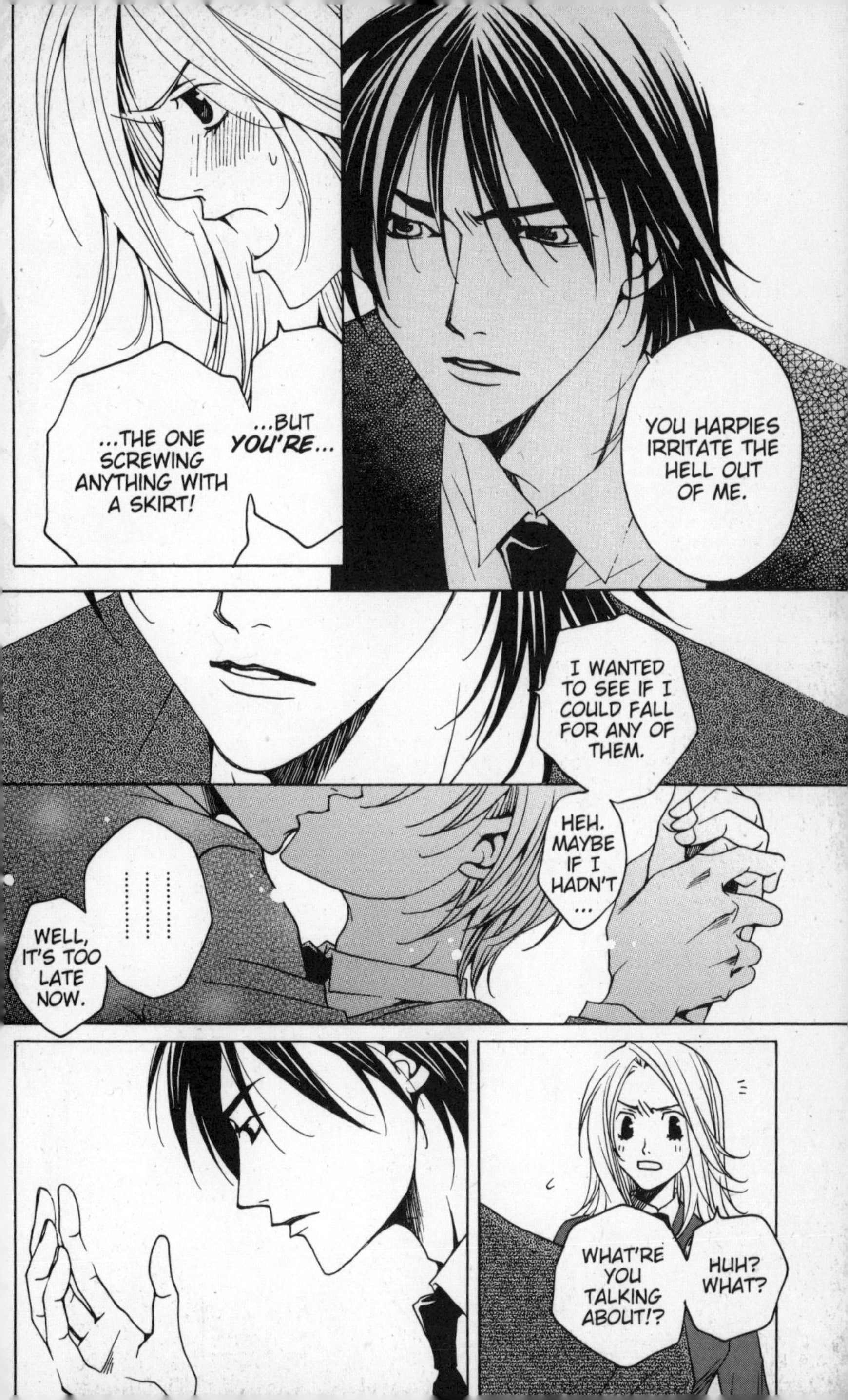
YOU HARPIES IRRITATE THE HELL OUT OF ME.
...BUT *YOU'RE*...
...THE ONE SCREWING ANYTHING WITH A SKIRT!
I WANTED TO SEE IF I COULD FALL FOR ANY OF THEM.
HEH. MAYBE IF I HADN'T...
......
WELL, IT'S TOO LATE NOW.
HUH? WHAT?
WHAT'RE YOU TALKING ABOUT!?

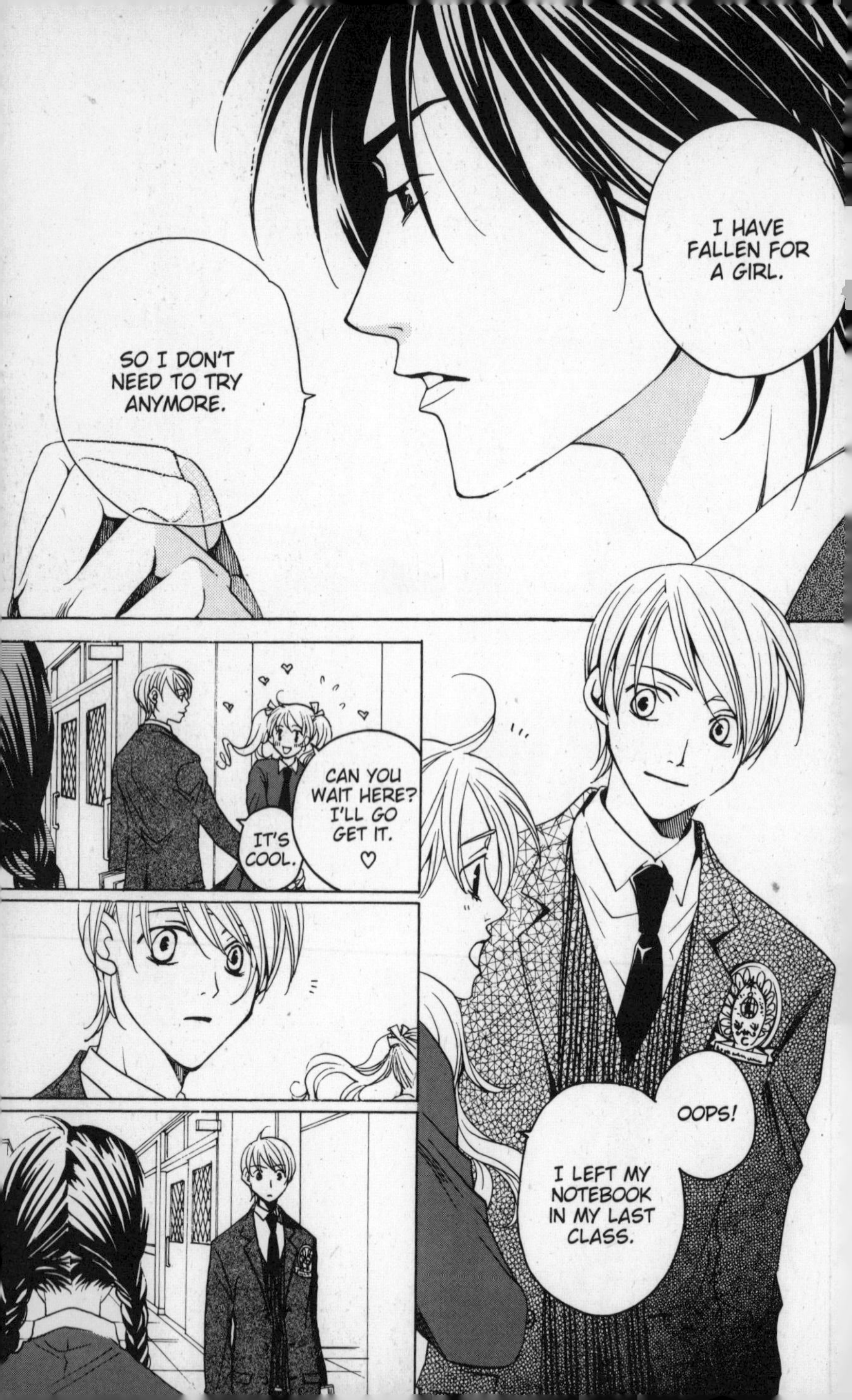
I HAVE FALLEN FOR A GIRL.
SO I DON'T NEED TO TRY ANYMORE.
OOPS!
I LEFT MY NOTEBOOK IN MY LAST CLASS.
CAN YOU WAIT HERE? I'LL GO GET IT. ♡
IT'S COOL.

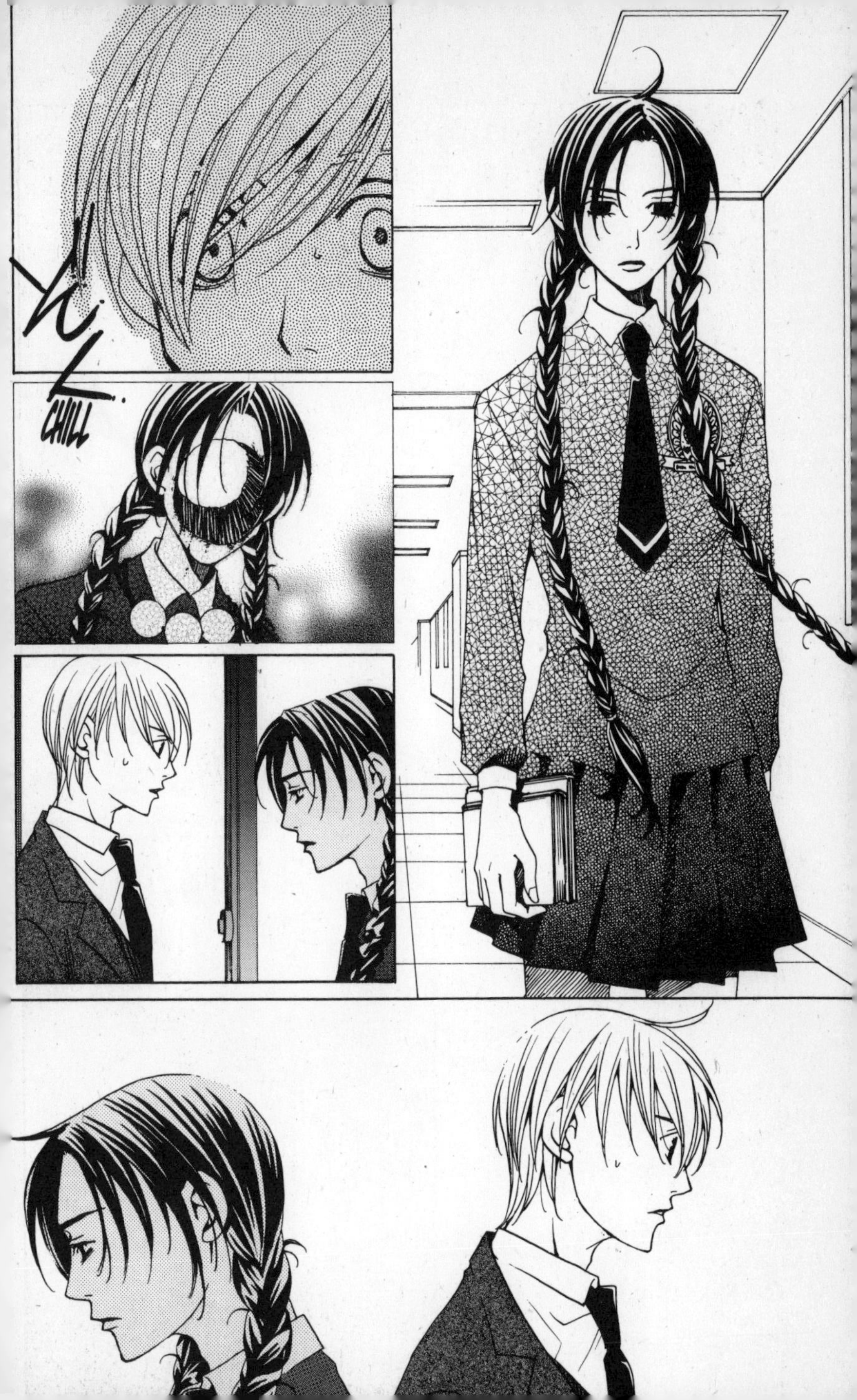
CHILL

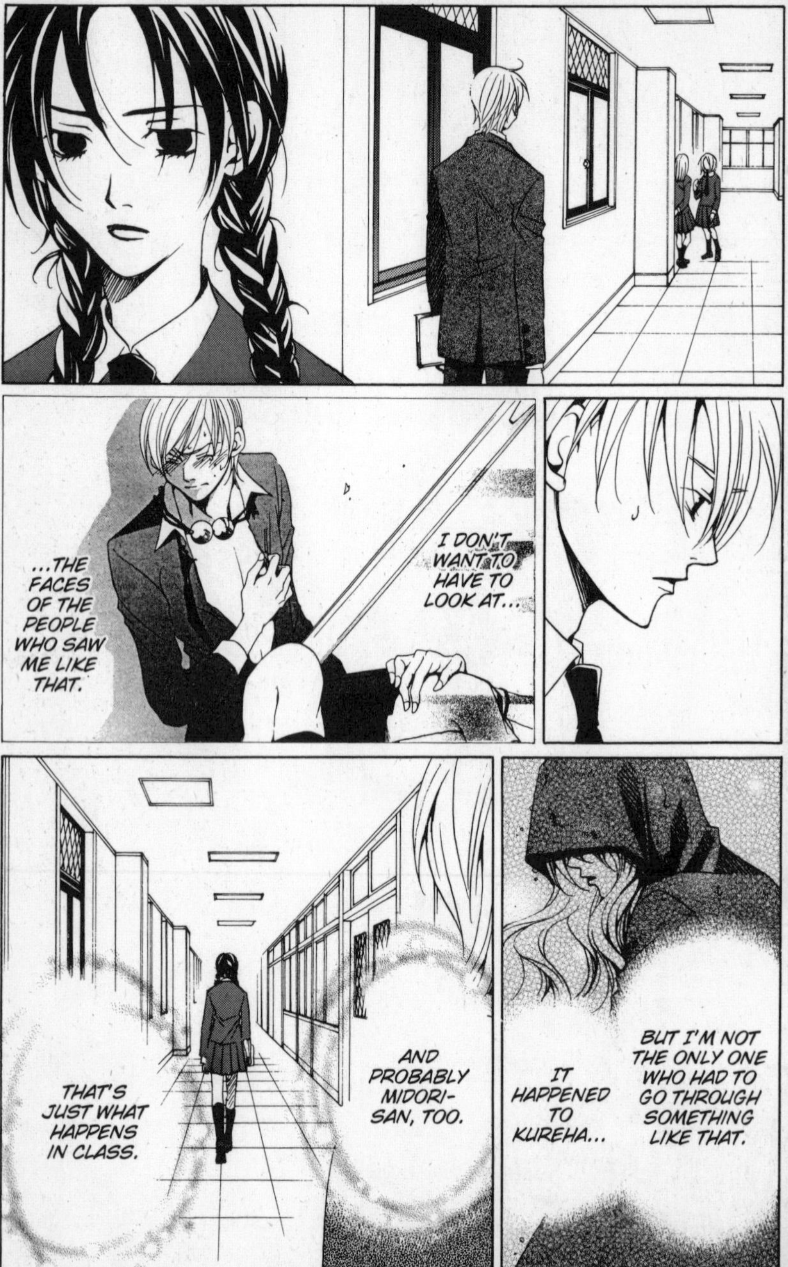
I DON'T WANT TO HAVE TO LOOK AT...
...THE FACES OF THE PEOPLE WHO SAW ME LIKE THAT.
BUT I'M NOT THE ONLY ONE WHO HAD TO GO THROUGH SOMETHING LIKE THAT.
IT HAPPENED TO KUREHA...
AND PROBABLY MIDORI-SAN, TOO.
THAT'S JUST WHAT HAPPENS IN CLASS.

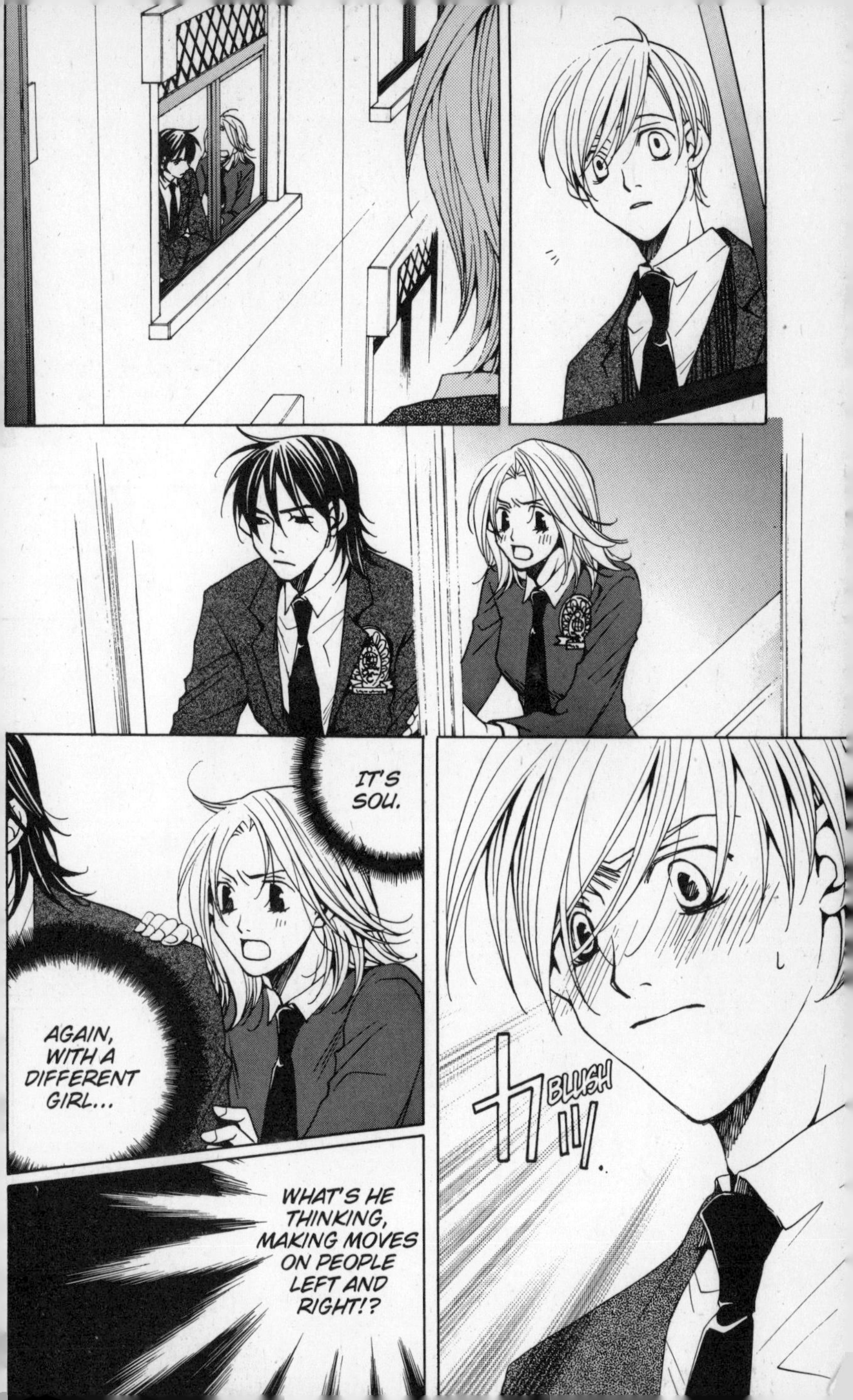
IT'S SOU.
AGAIN, WITH A DIFFERENT GIRL...
WHAT'S HE THINKING, MAKING MOVES ON PEOPLE LEFT AND RIGHT!?
BLUSH

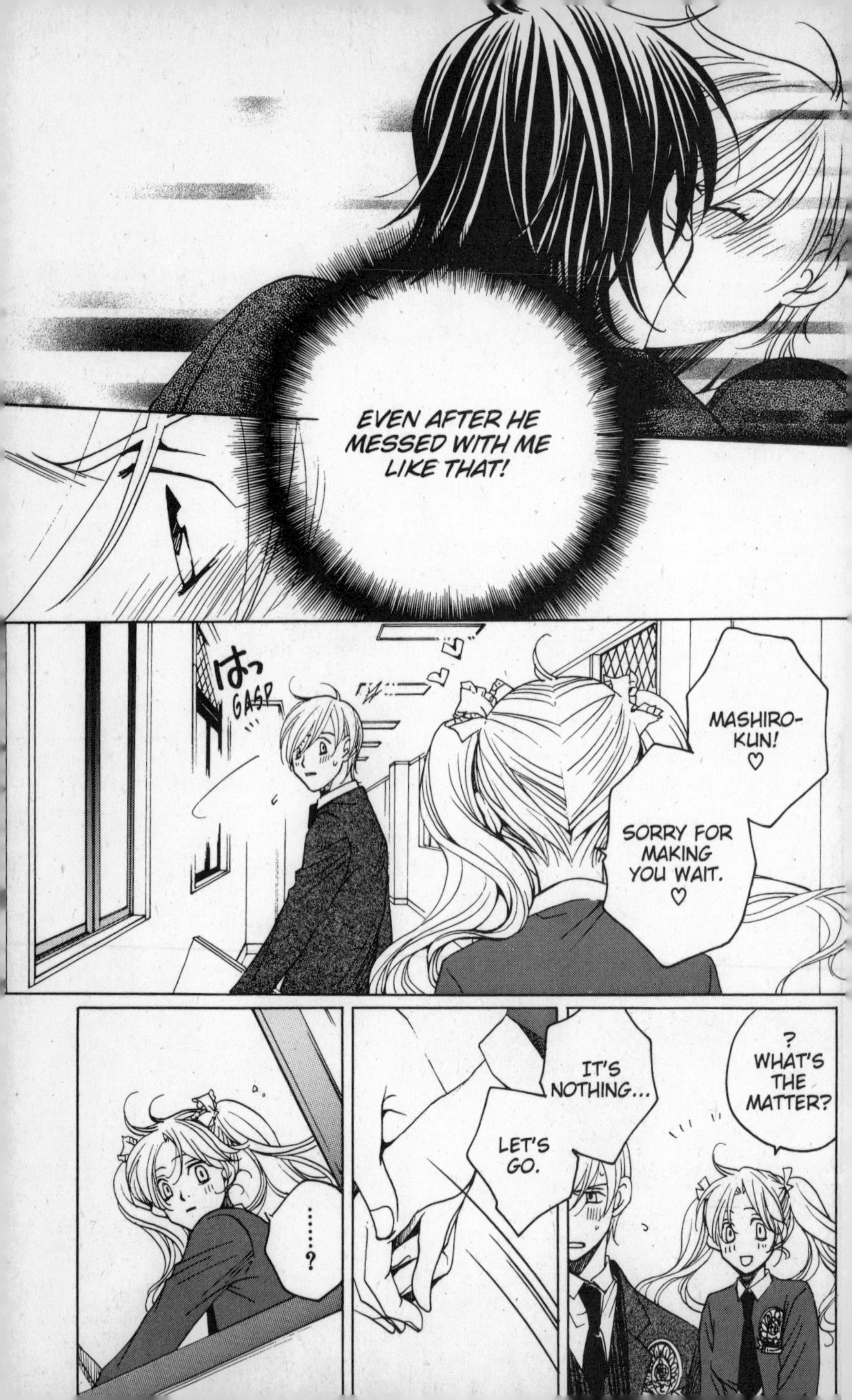
EVEN AFTER HE MESSED WITH ME LIKE THAT!
MASHIRO-KUN! ♡
SORRY FOR MAKING YOU WAIT. ♡
はっ GASP
? WHAT'S THE MATTER?
IT'S NOTHING...
LET'S GO.
......?

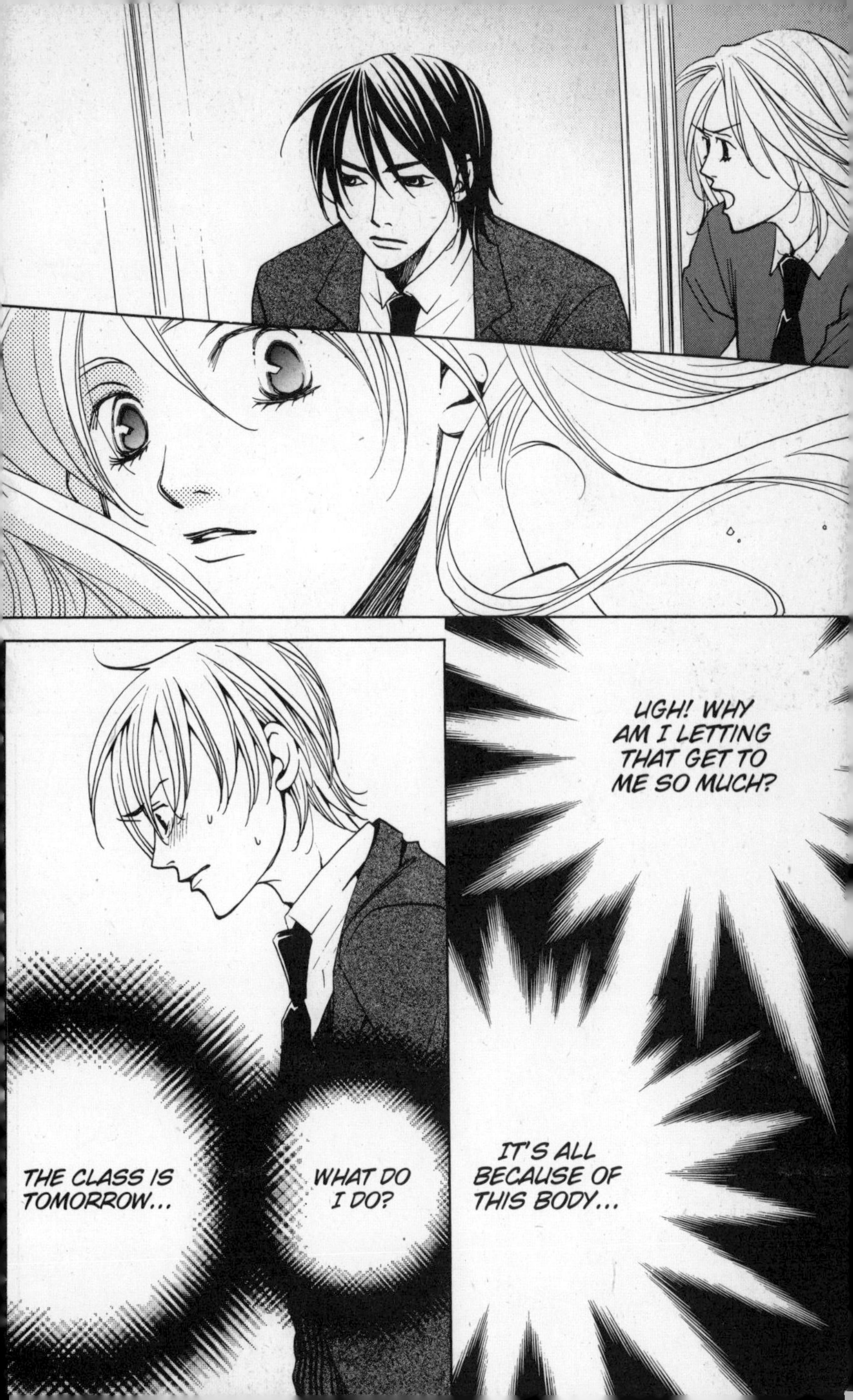
UGH! WHY AM I LETTING THAT GET TO ME SO MUCH?
IT'S ALL BECAUSE OF THIS BODY...
WHAT DO I DO?
THE CLASS IS TOMORROW...

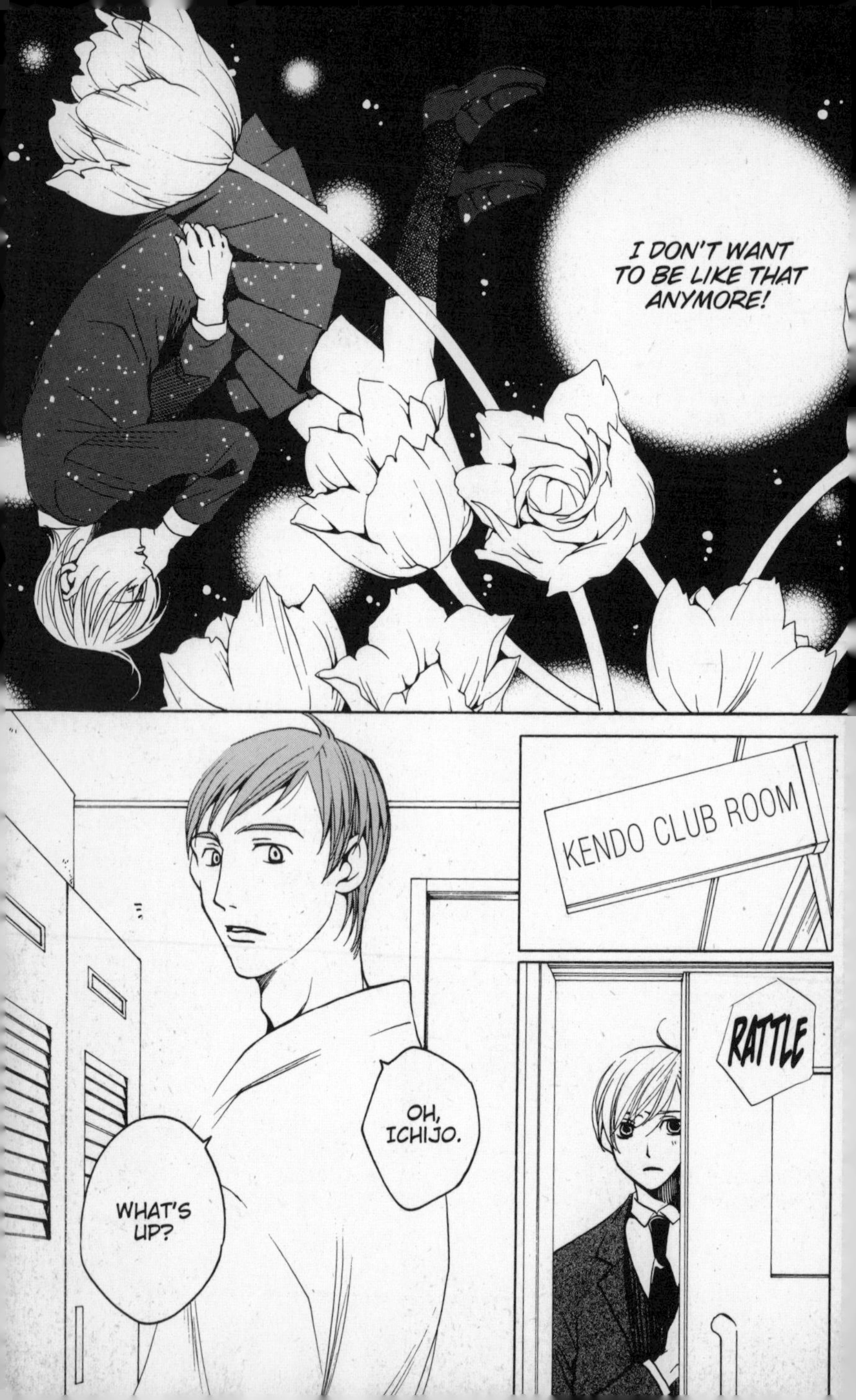
I DON'T WANT TO BE LIKE THAT ANYMORE!
KENDO CLUB ROOM
RATTLE
OH, ICHIJO.
WHAT'S UP?

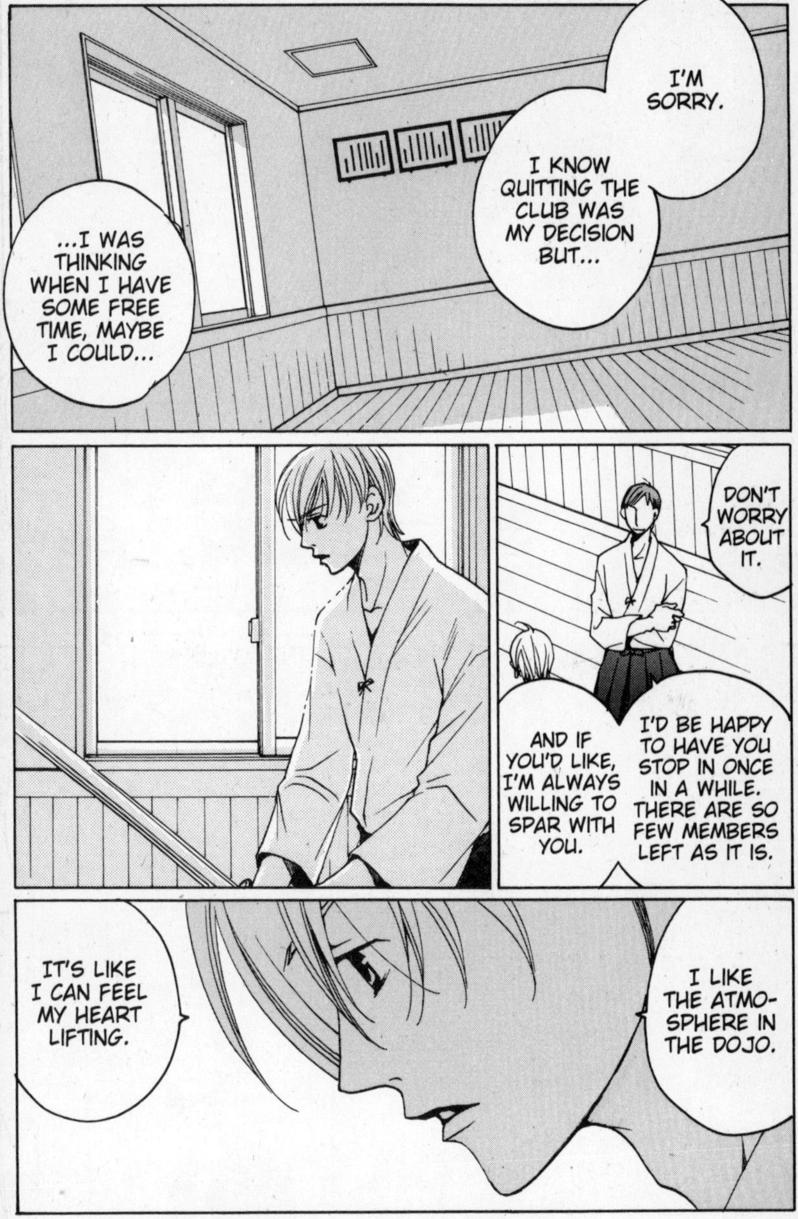
I'M SORRY.
I KNOW QUITTING THE CLUB WAS MY DECISION BUT...
...I WAS THINKING WHEN I HAVE SOME FREE TIME, MAYBE I COULD...
DON'T WORRY ABOUT IT.
I'D BE HAPPY TO HAVE YOU STOP IN ONCE IN A WHILE. THERE ARE SO FEW MEMBERS LEFT AS IT IS.
AND IF YOU'D LIKE, I'M ALWAYS WILLING TO SPAR WITH YOU.
I LIKE THE ATMOSPHERE IN THE DOJO.
IT'S LIKE I CAN FEEL MY HEART LIFTING.

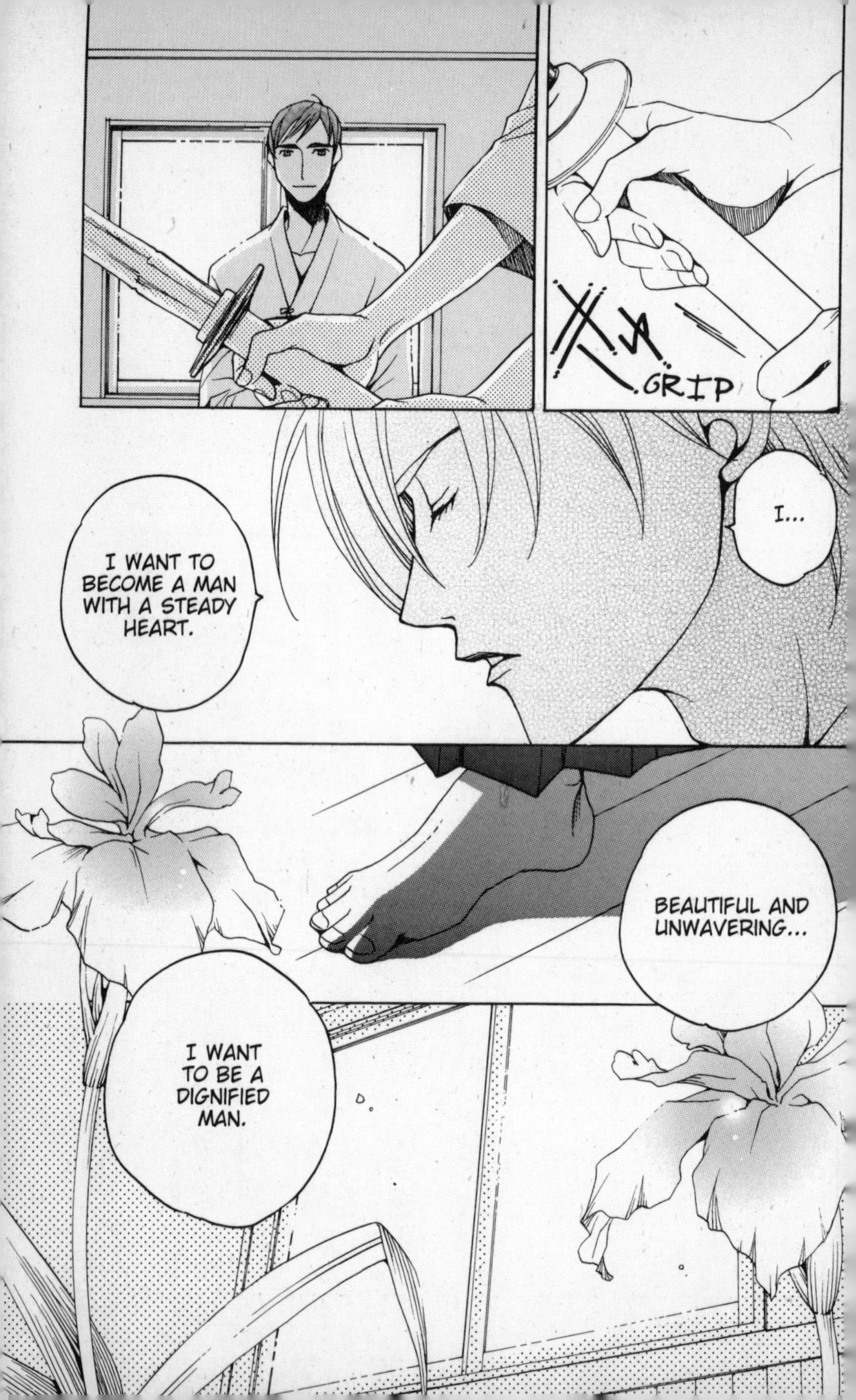
GRIP
I...
I WANT TO BECOME A MAN WITH A STEADY HEART.
BEAUTIFUL AND UNWAVERING...
I WANT TO BE A DIGNIFIED MAN.

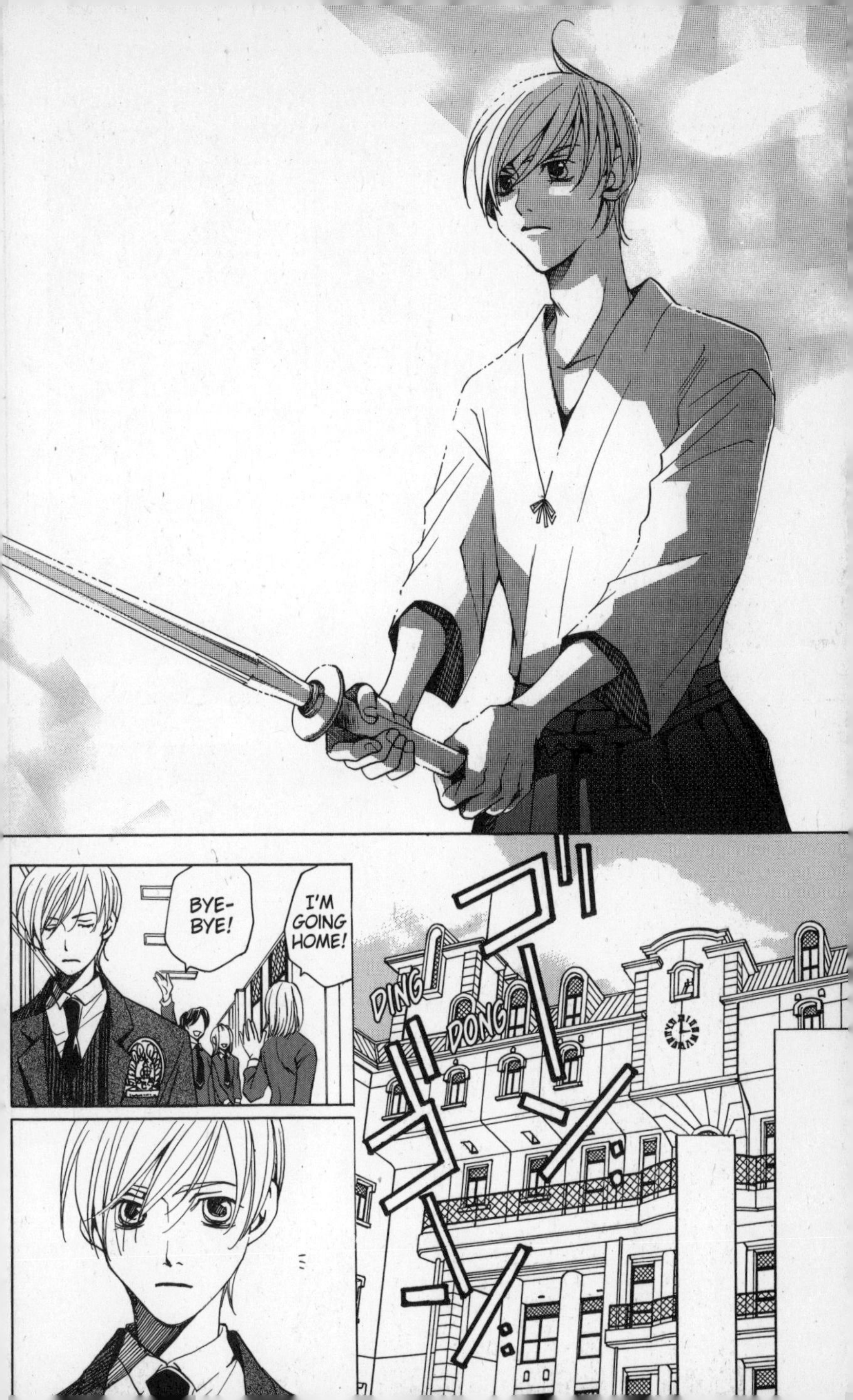
DING
DONG
I'M GOING HOME!
BYE-BYE!

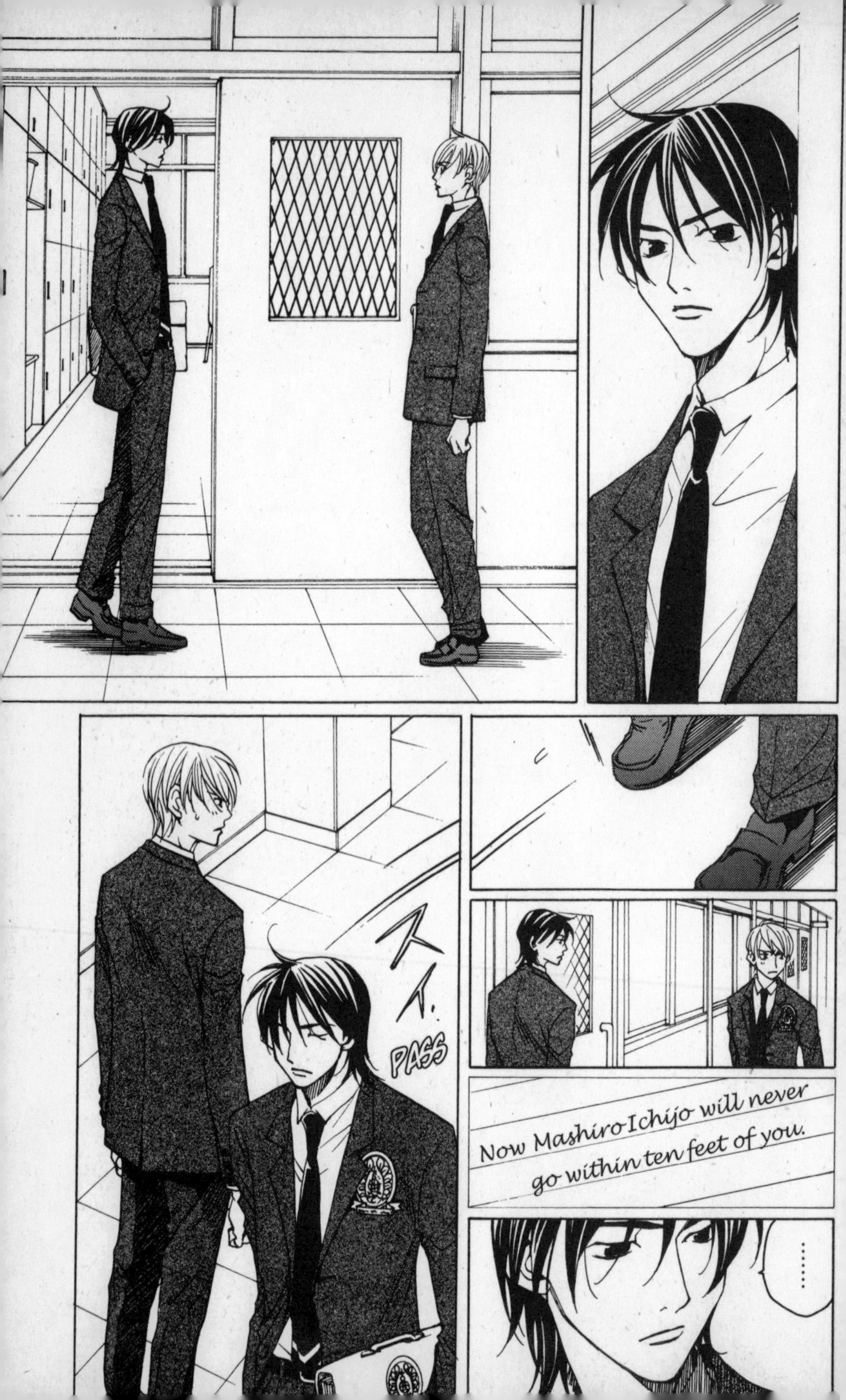
PASS
Now Mashiro Ichijo will never go within ten feet of you.
......

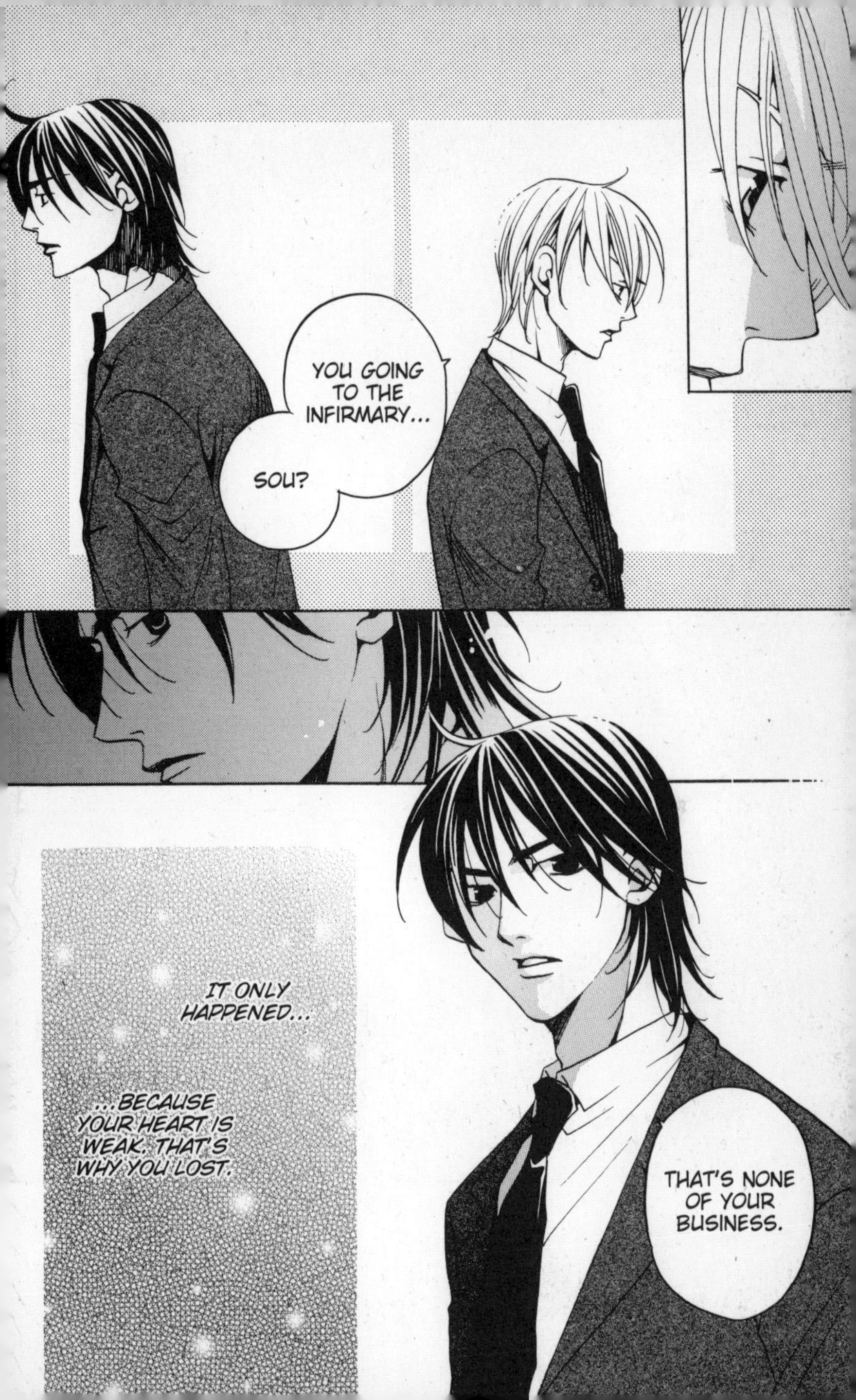
YOU GOING TO THE INFIRMARY...
SOU?
THAT'S NONE OF YOUR BUSINESS.
IT ONLY HAPPENED...
...BECAUSE YOUR HEART IS WEAK. THAT'S WHY YOU LOST.

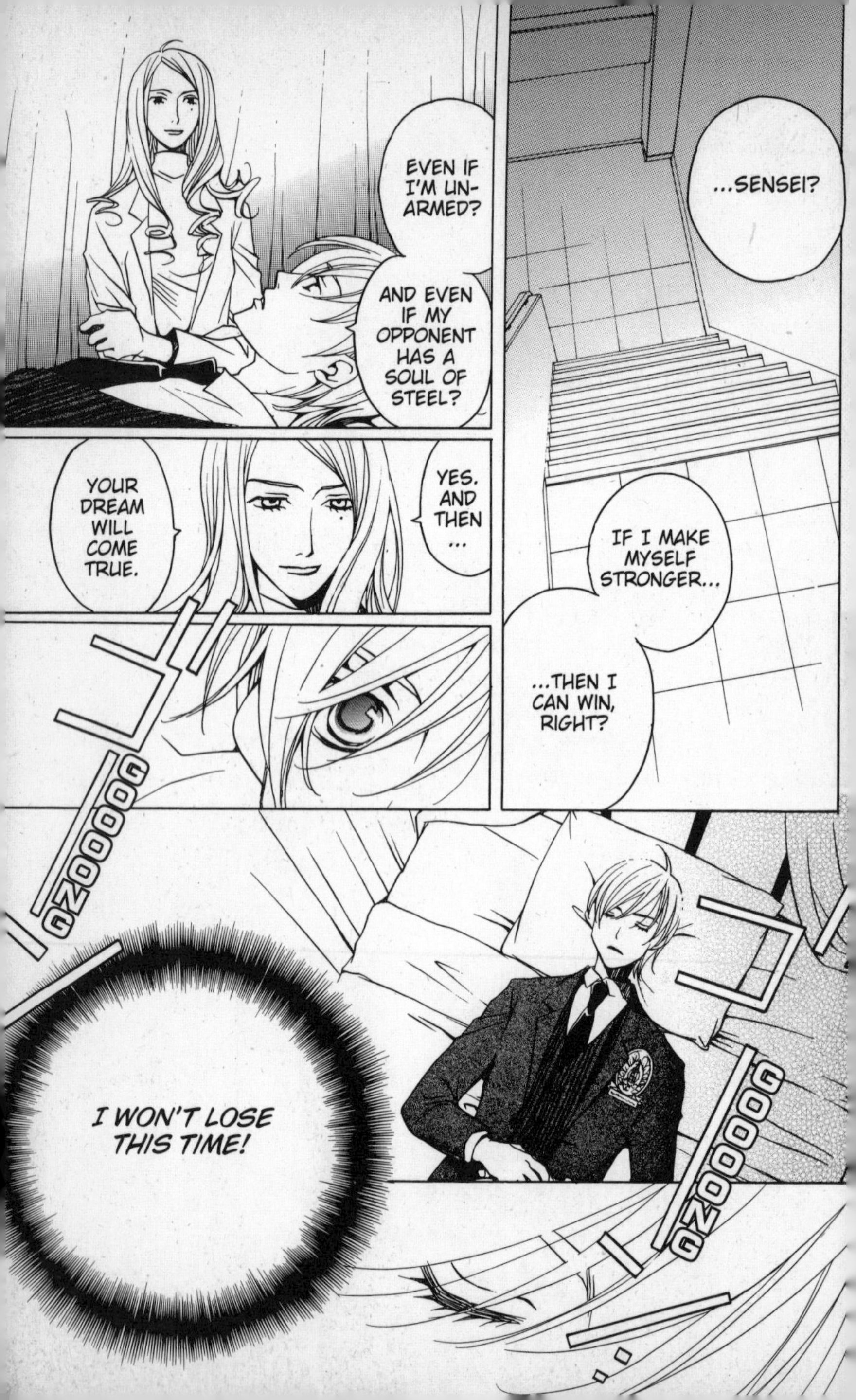
...SENSEI?
IF I MAKE MYSELF STRONGER...
...THEN I CAN WIN, RIGHT?
EVEN IF I'M UN-ARMED?
AND EVEN IF MY OPPONENT HAS A SOUL OF STEEL?
YES. AND THEN...
YOUR DREAM WILL COME TRUE.
GOOOOONG
GOOOOONG
I WON'T LOSE THIS TIME!

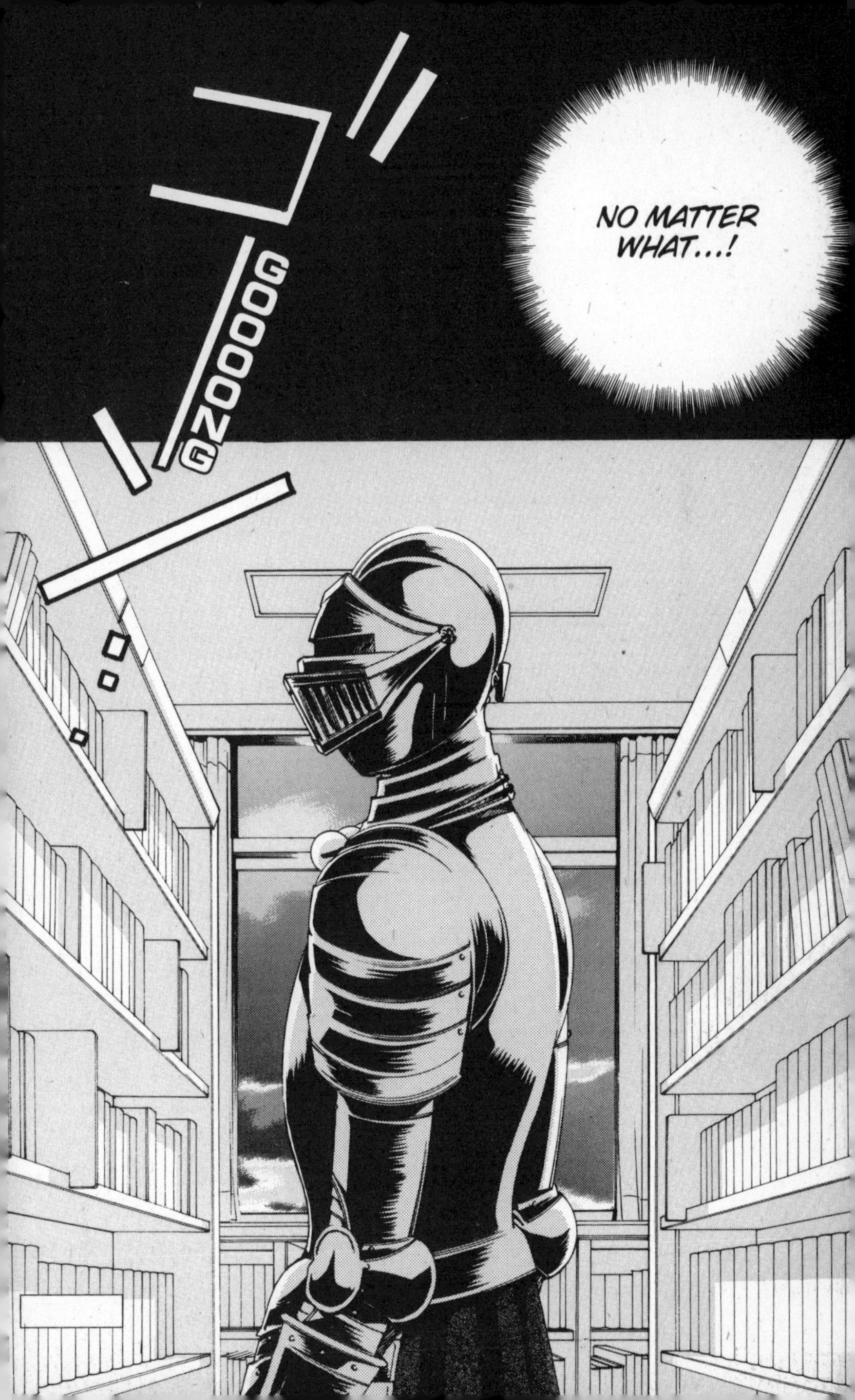
NO MATTER WHAT...!
GOOOOONG

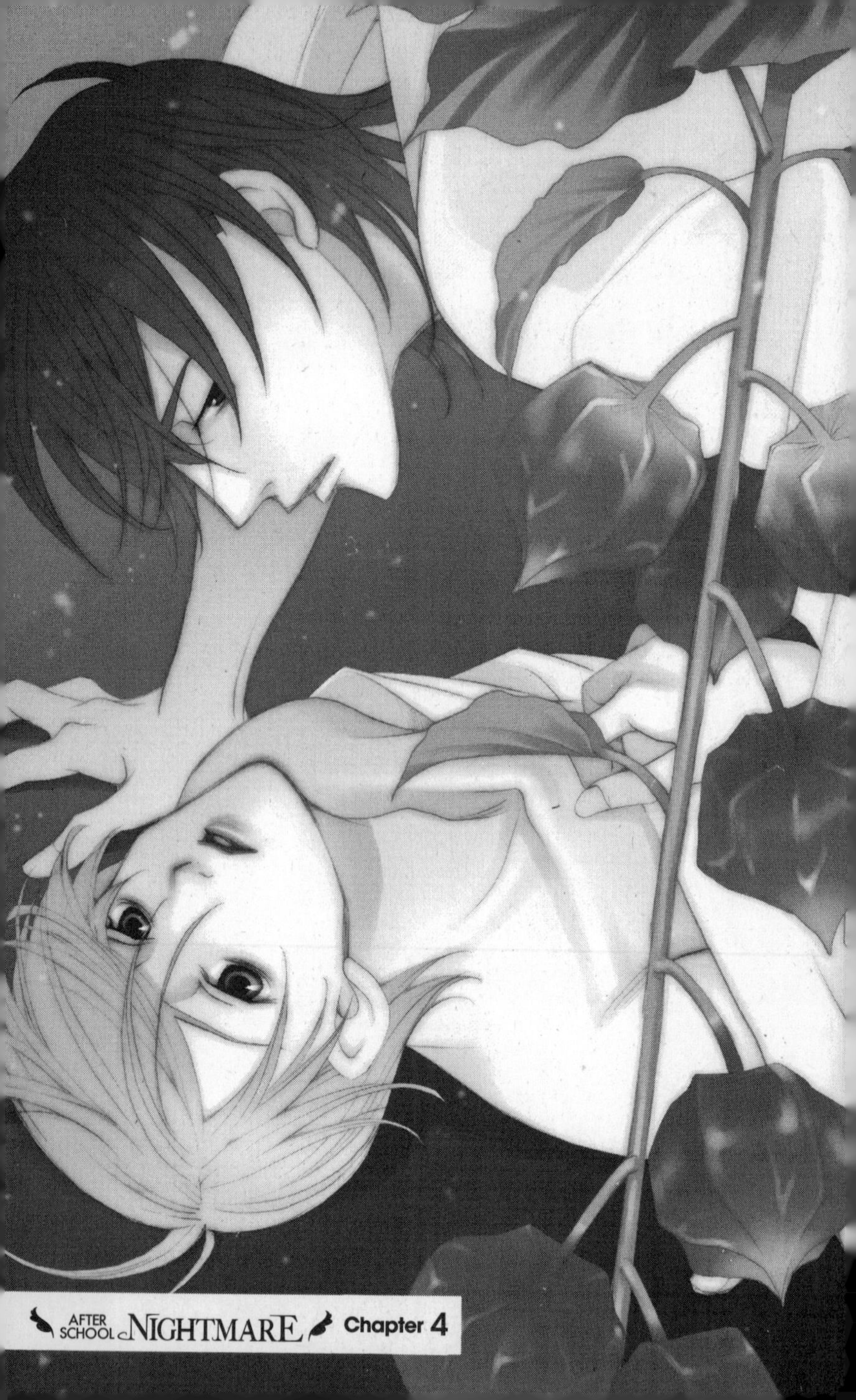
AFTER SCHOOL NIGHTMARE
Chapter 4

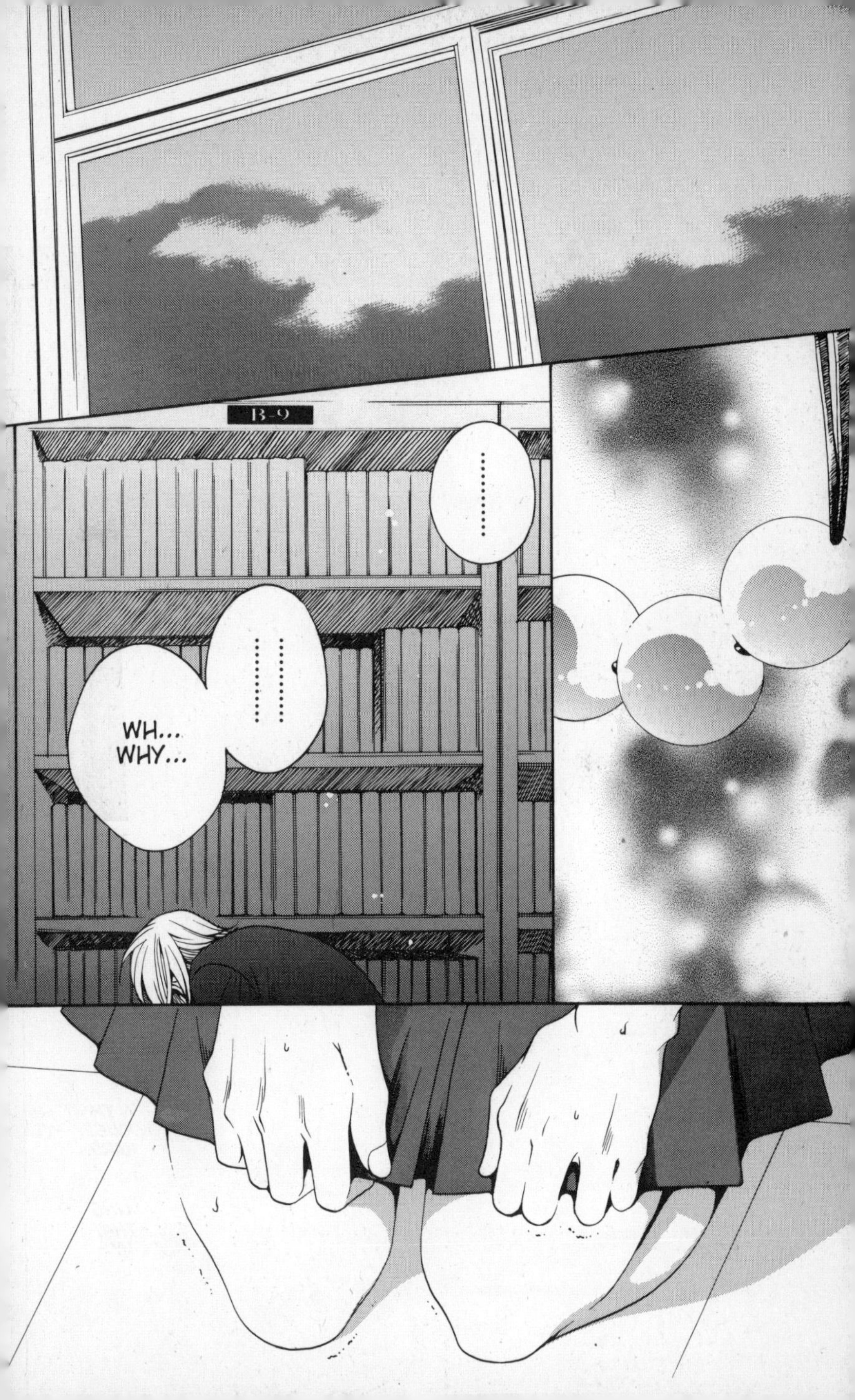
B-9
......
......
......
WH... WHY...

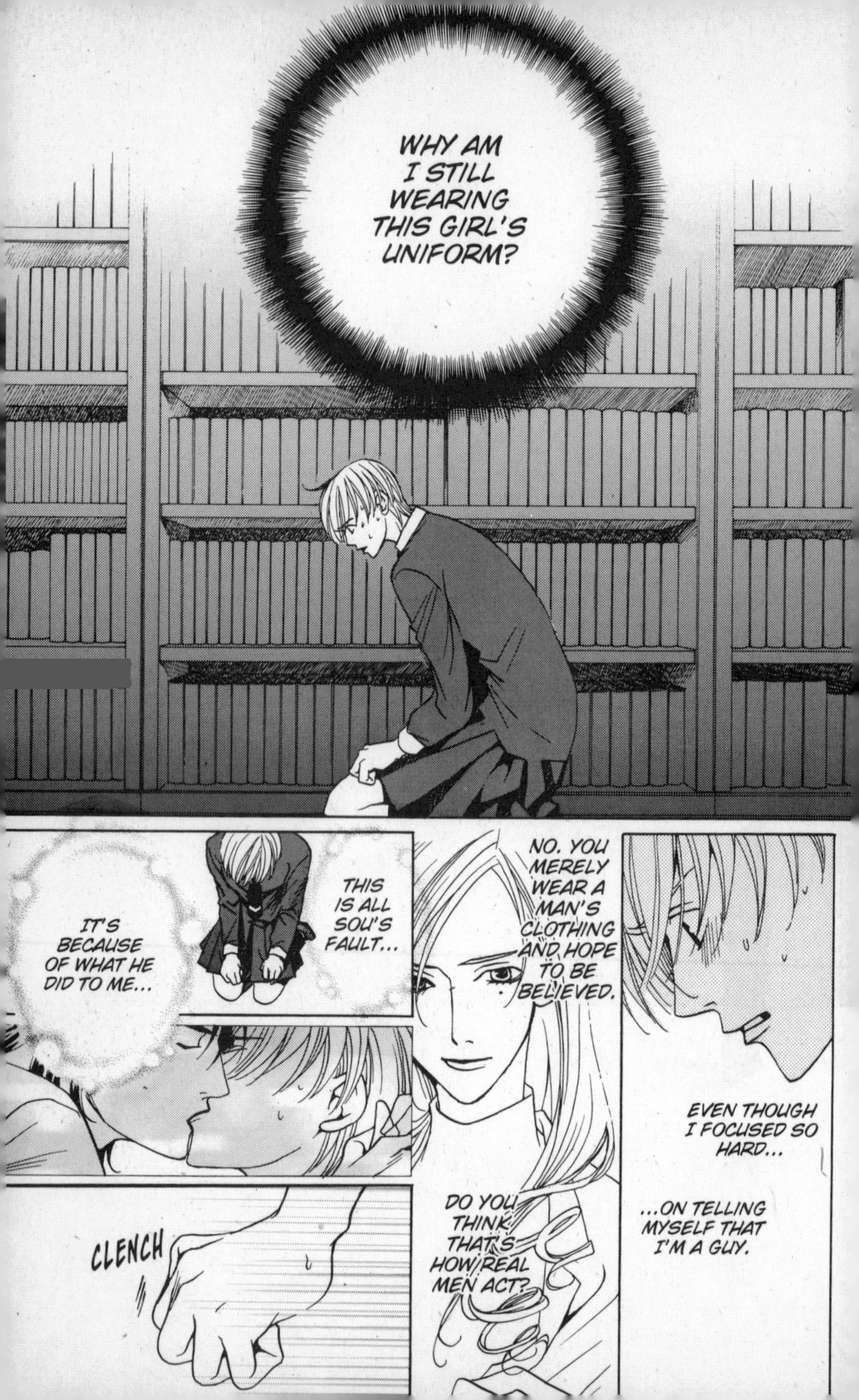
WHY AM I STILL WEARING THIS GIRL'S UNIFORM?
EVEN THOUGH I FOCUSED SO HARD...
...ON TELLING MYSELF THAT I'M A GUY.
NO. YOU MERELY WEAR A MAN'S CLOTHING AND HOPE TO BE BELIEVED.
DO YOU THINK THAT'S HOW REAL MEN ACT?
THIS IS ALL SOU'S FAULT...
IT'S BECAUSE OF WHAT HE DID TO ME...
CLENCH

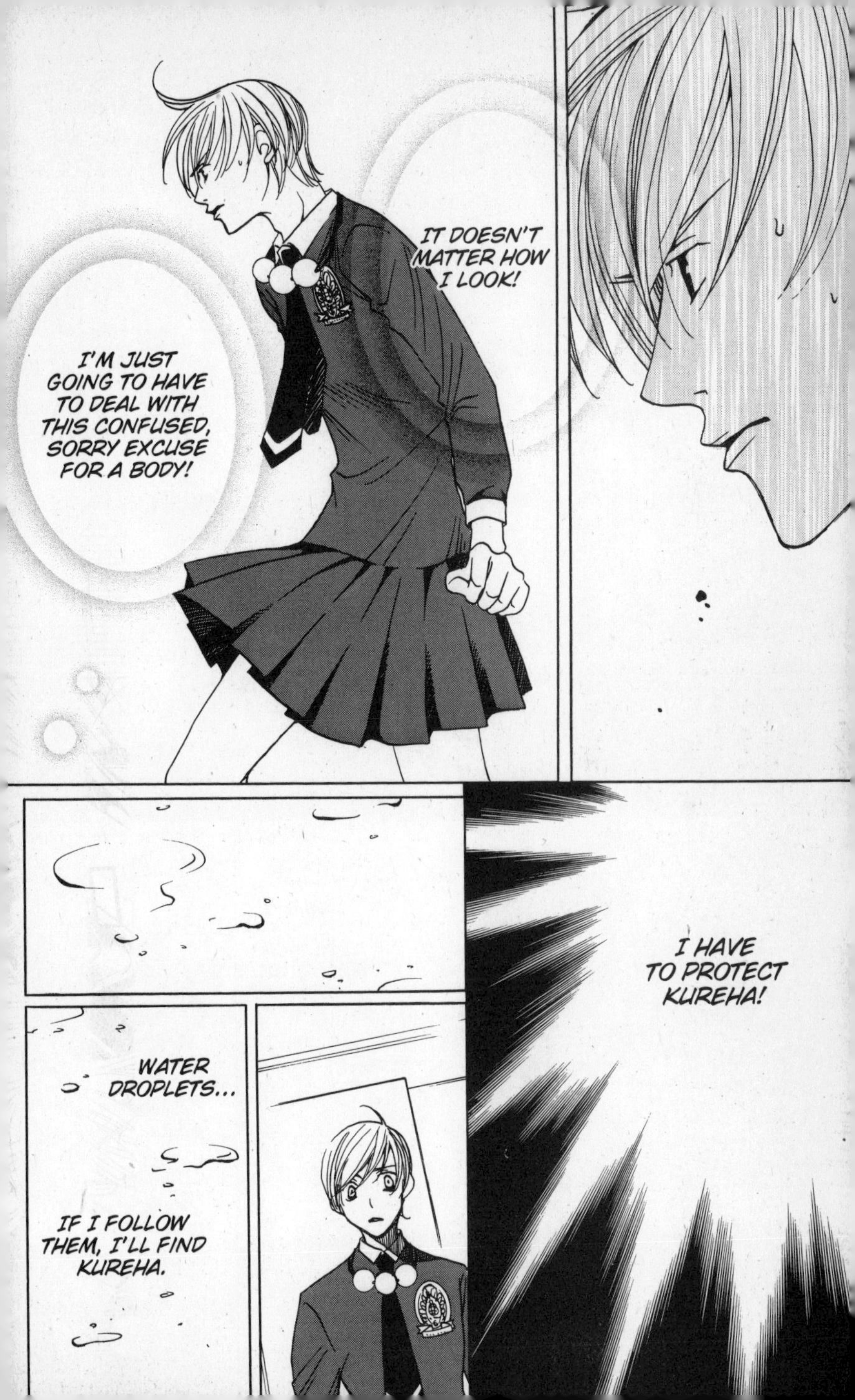
IT DOESN'T MATTER HOW I LOOK!
I'M JUST GOING TO HAVE TO DEAL WITH THIS CONFUSED, SORRY EXCUSE FOR A BODY!
I HAVE TO PROTECT KUREHA!
WATER DROPLETS...
IF I FOLLOW THEM, I'LL FIND KUREHA.

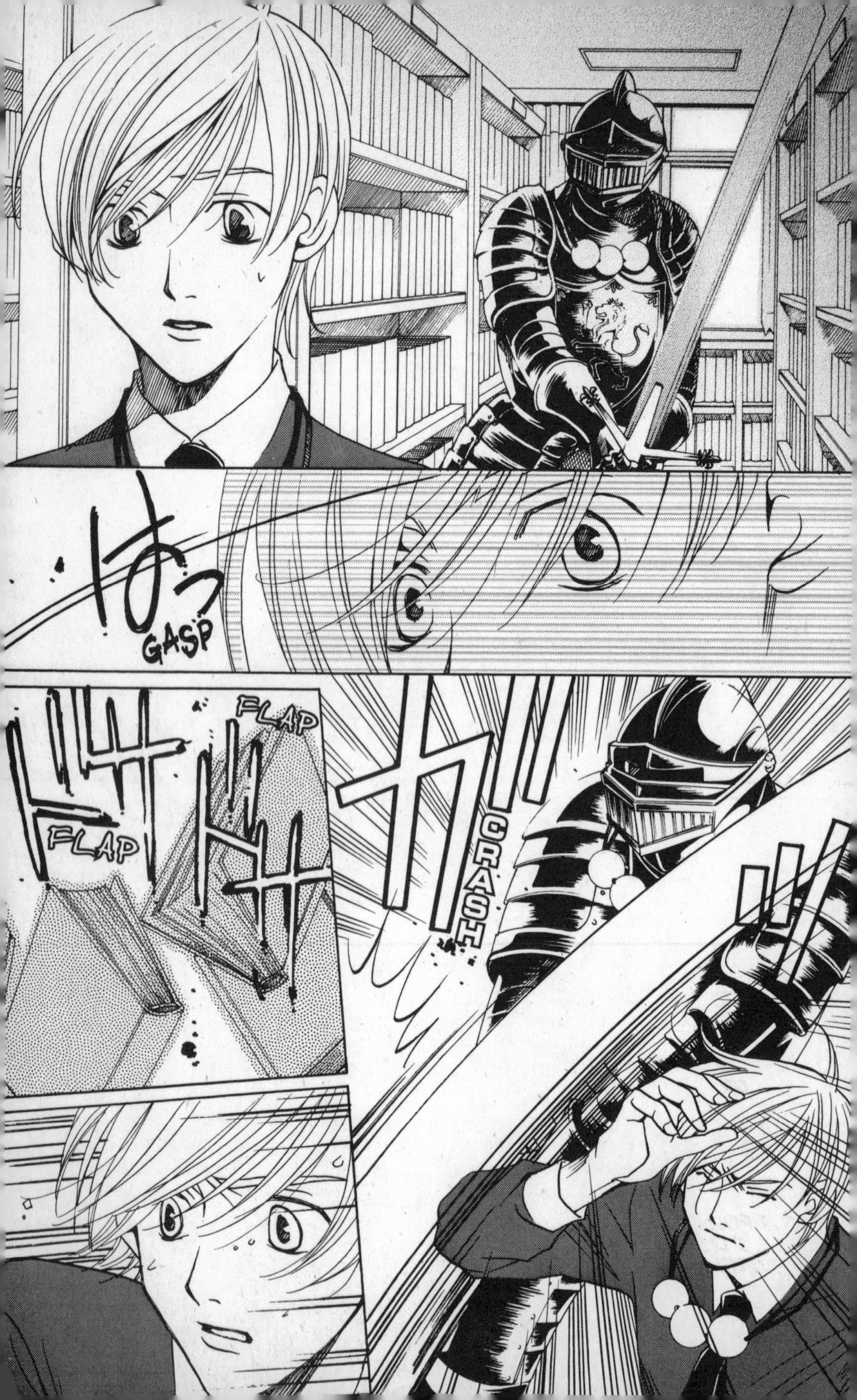
はっ
GASP
ガッ
CRASH
FLAP
FLAP

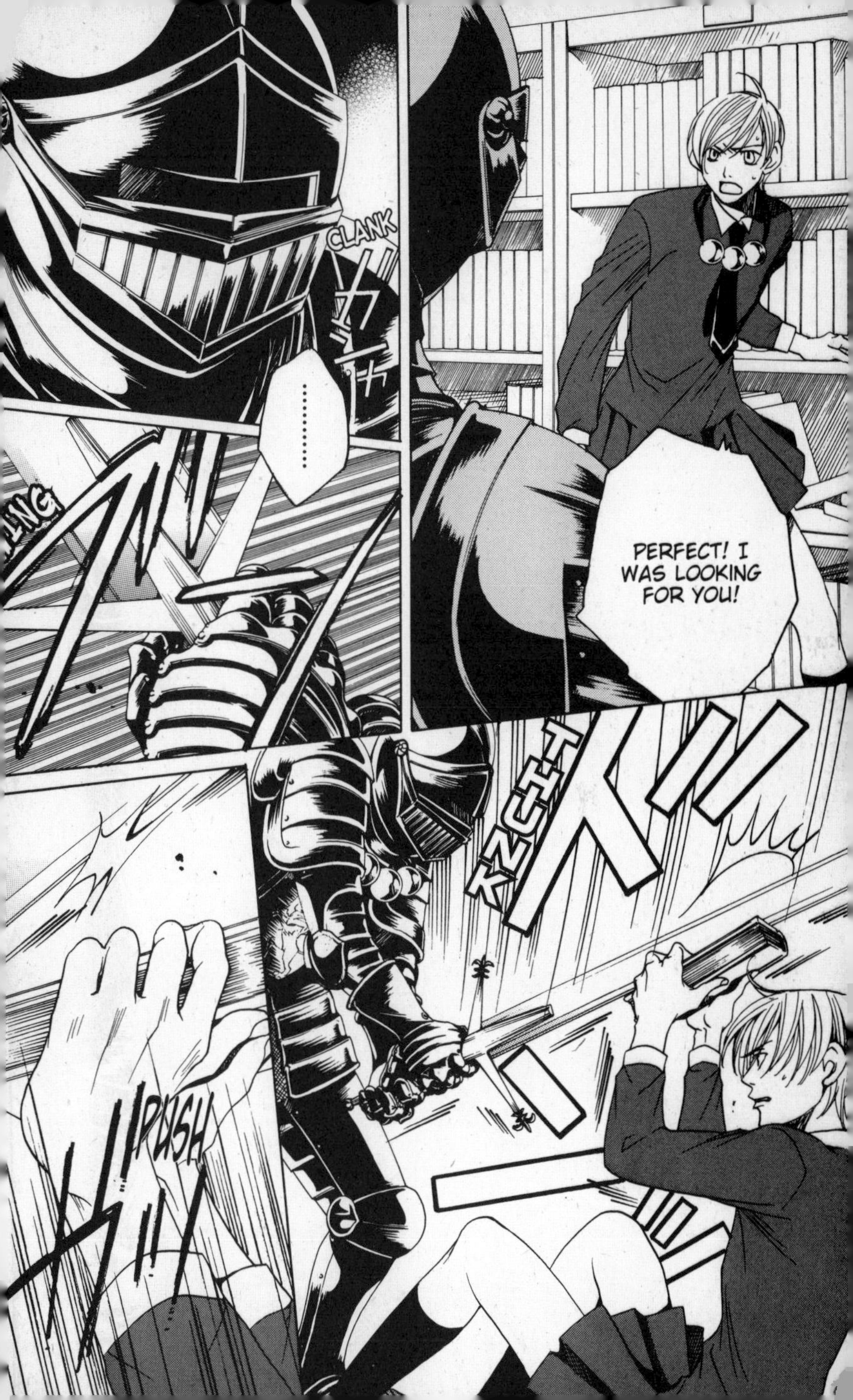
PERFECT! I WAS LOOKING FOR YOU!
CLANK
......
THUNK
PUSH

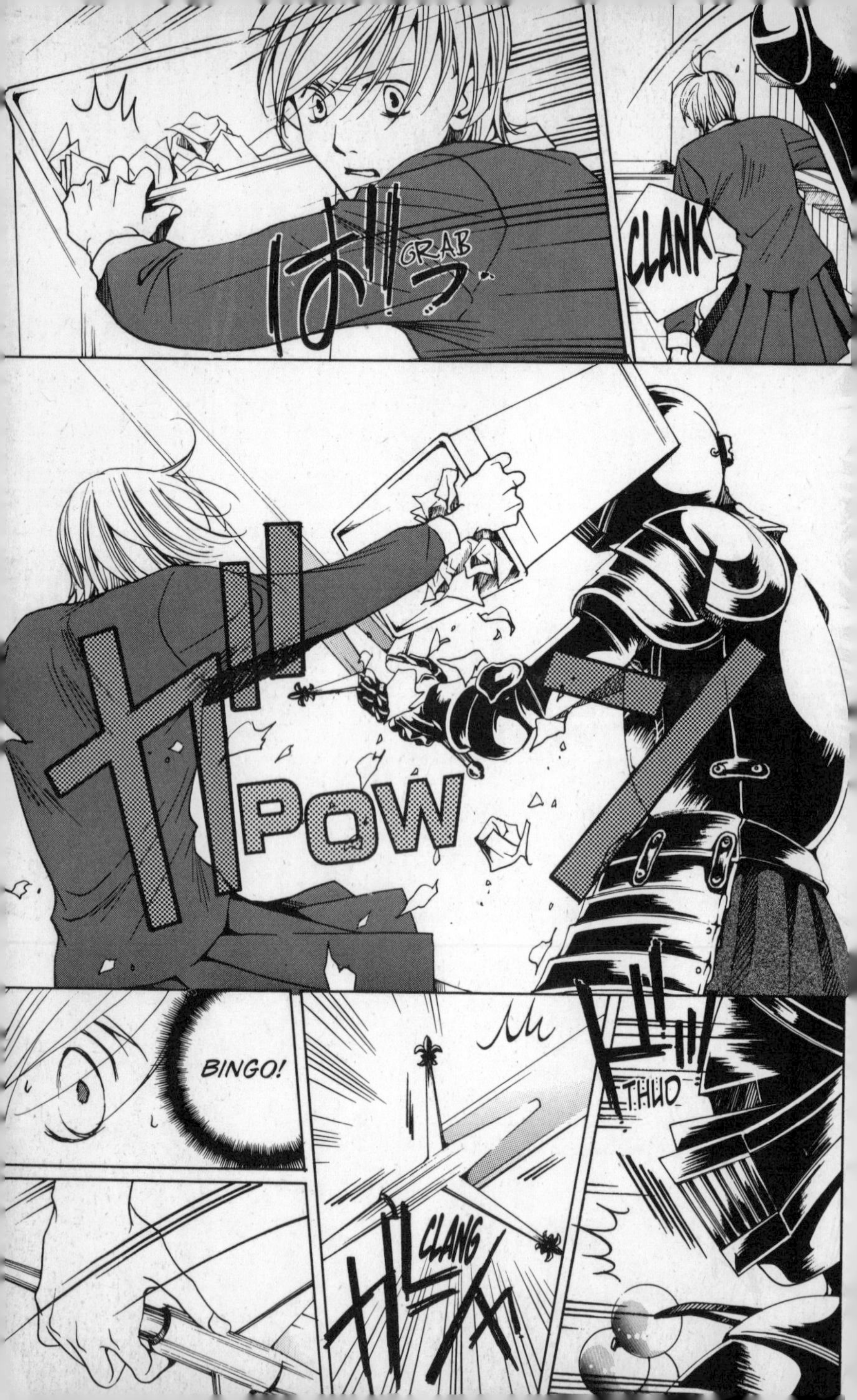
CLANK
GRAB
POW
THUD
CLANG
BINGO!

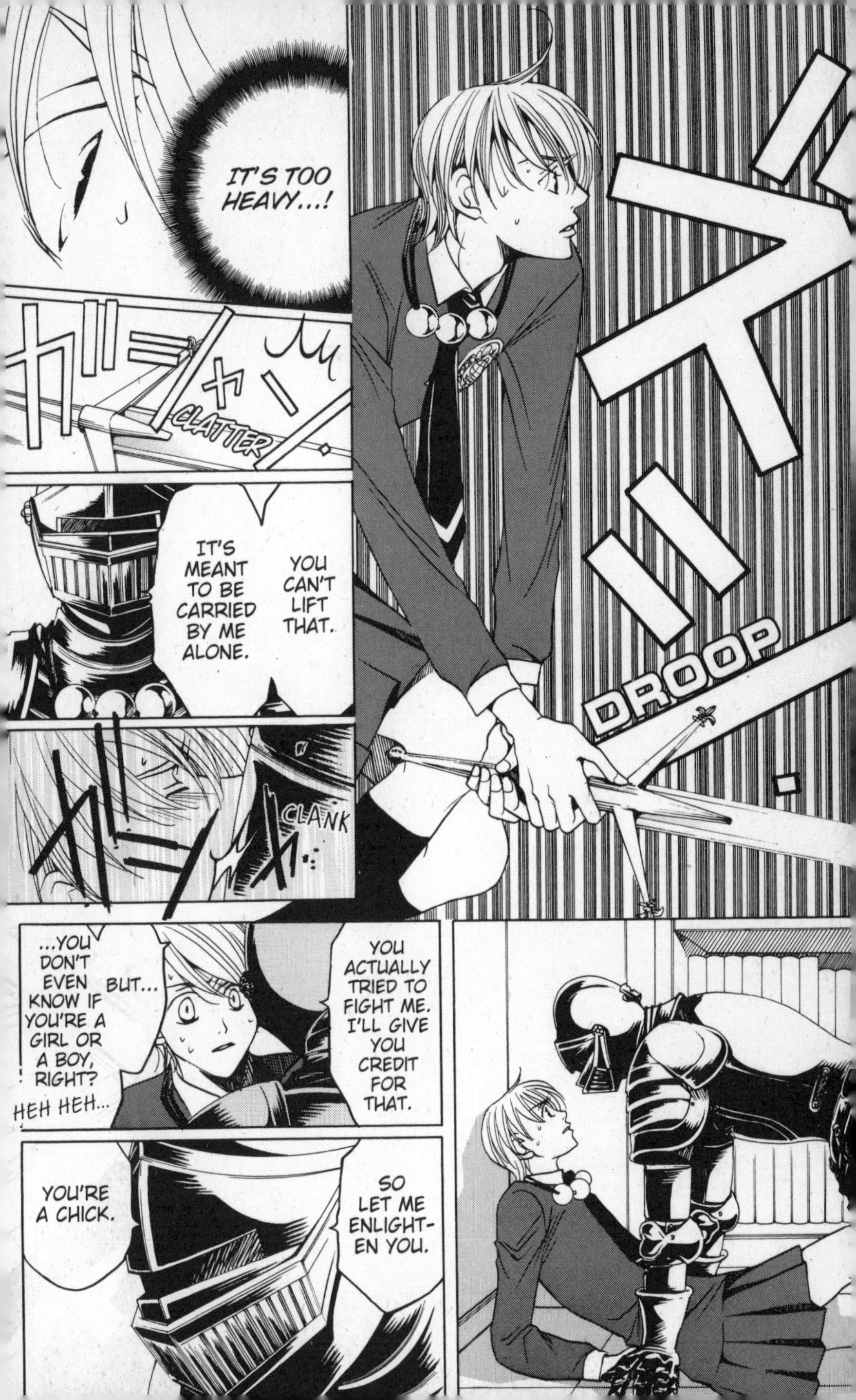
DROOP
IT'S TOO HEAVY...!
CLATTER
YOU CAN'T LIFT THAT.
IT'S MEANT TO BE CARRIED BY ME ALONE.
CLANK
YOU ACTUALLY TRIED TO FIGHT ME. I'LL GIVE YOU CREDIT FOR THAT.
BUT...
...YOU DON'T EVEN KNOW IF YOU'RE A GIRL OR A BOY, RIGHT?
HEH HEH...
SO LET ME ENLIGHT-EN YOU.
YOU'RE A CHICK.

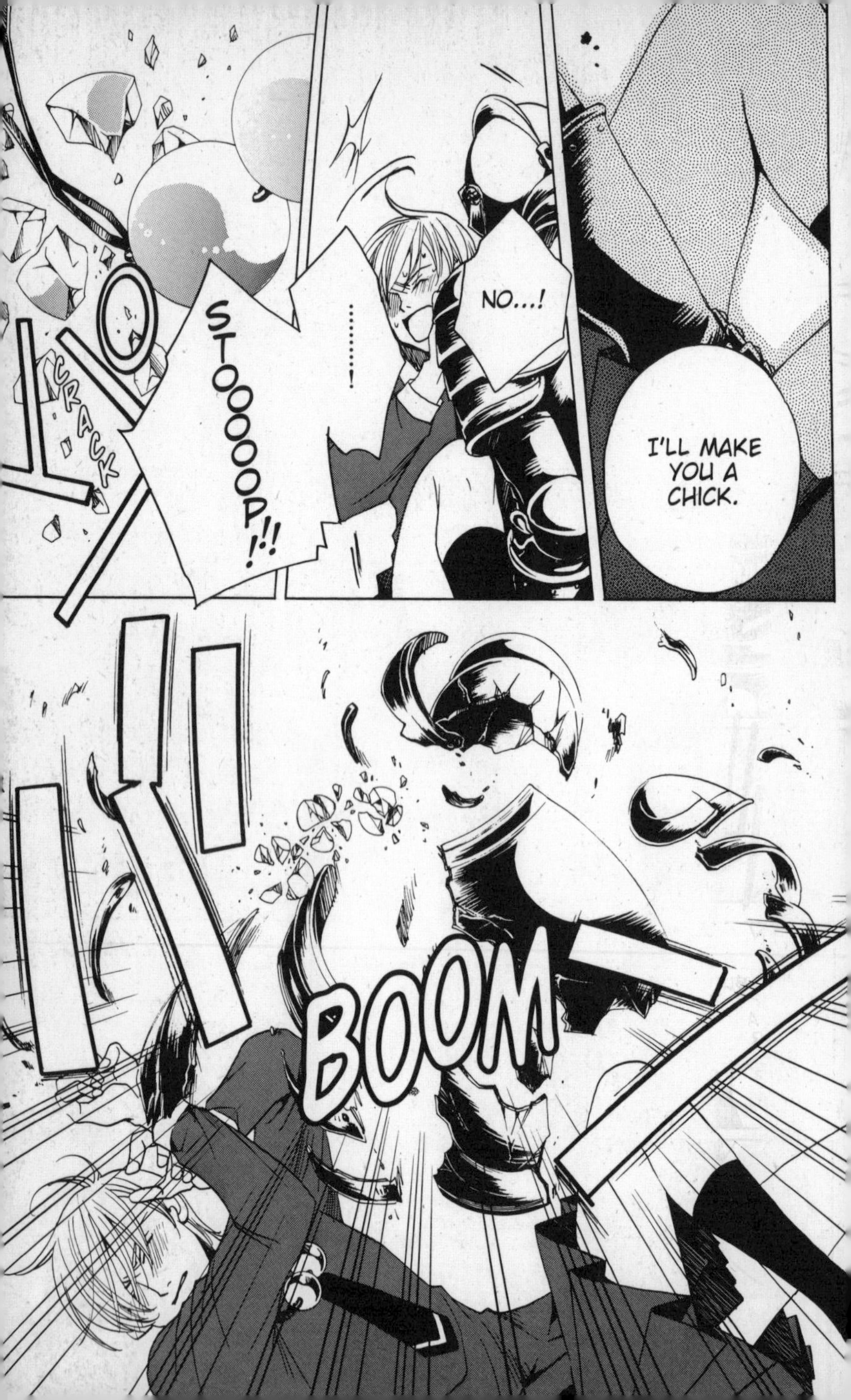
I'LL MAKE YOU A CHICK.
NO...!
......!
STOOOOOP!!!
CRACK
BOOM

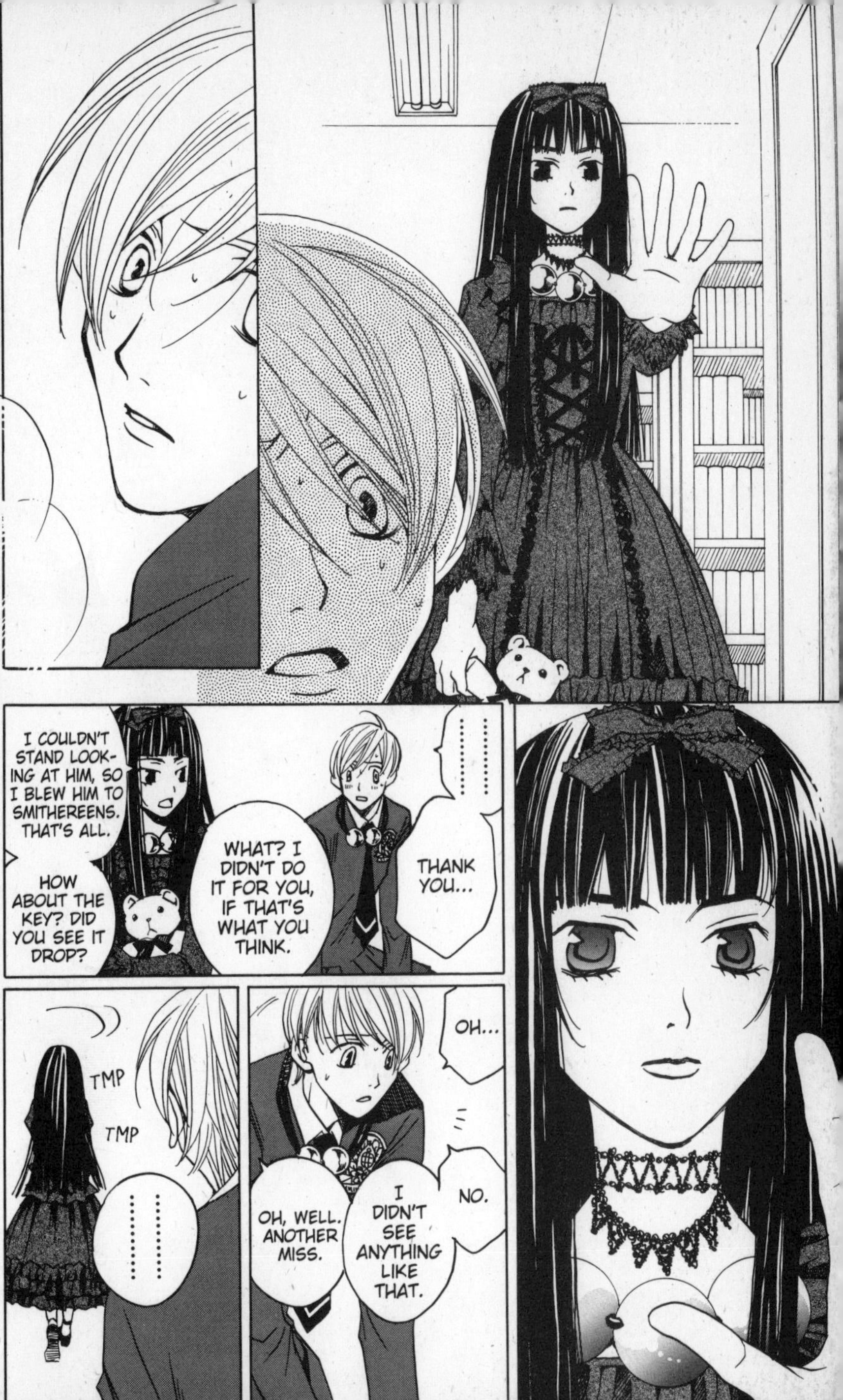
......
THANK YOU...
WHAT? I DIDN'T DO IT FOR YOU, IF THAT'S WHAT YOU THINK.
I COULDN'T STAND LOOKING AT HIM, SO I BLEW HIM TO SMITHEREENS. THAT'S ALL.
HOW ABOUT THE KEY? DID YOU SEE IT DROP?
OH...
NO.
I DIDN'T SEE ANYTHING LIKE THAT.
OH, WELL. ANOTHER MISS.
TMP
TMP
......

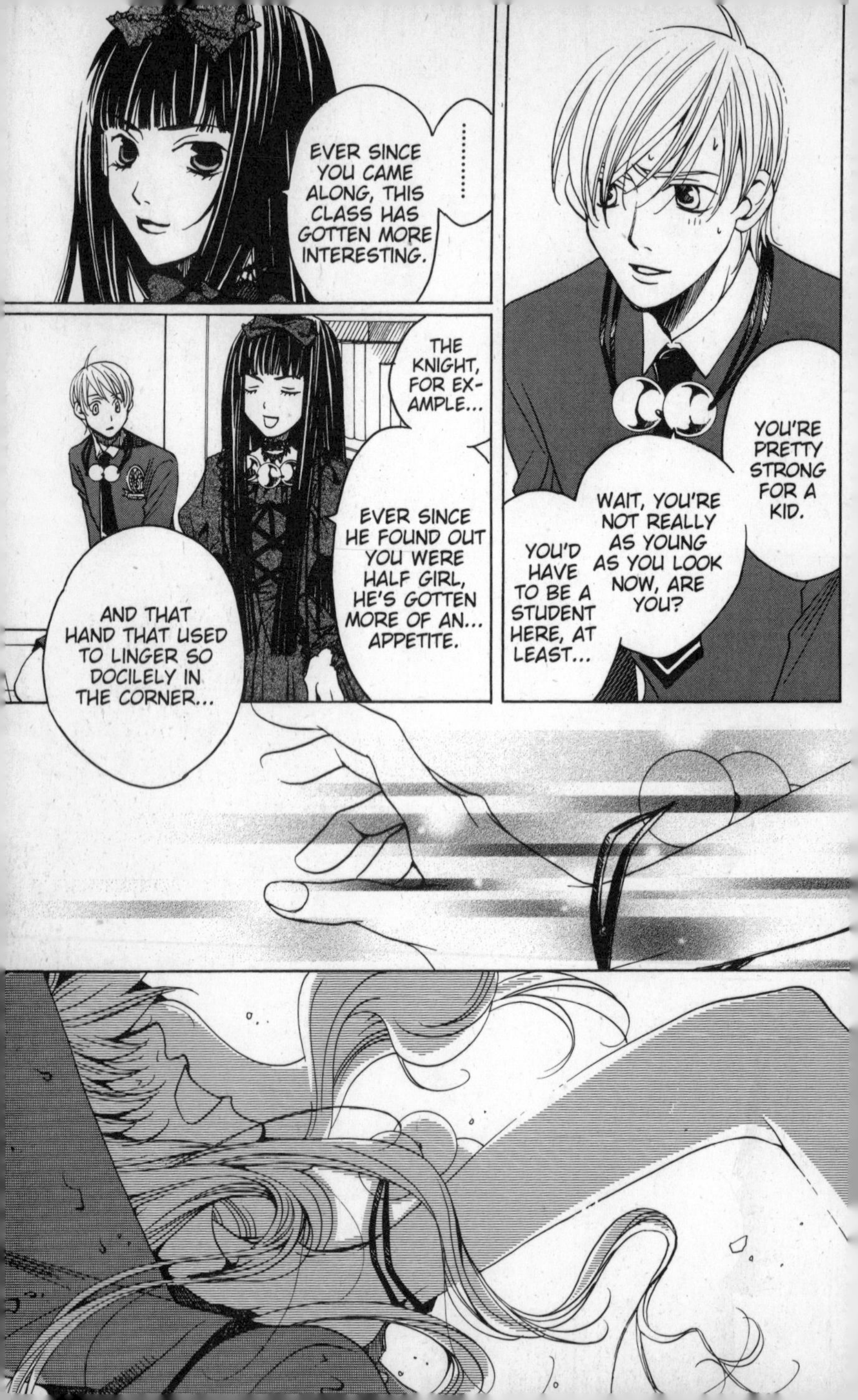
YOU'RE PRETTY STRONG FOR A KID.
WAIT, YOU'RE NOT REALLY AS YOUNG AS YOU LOOK NOW, ARE YOU?
YOU'D HAVE TO BE A STUDENT HERE, AT LEAST...
......
EVER SINCE YOU CAME ALONG, THIS CLASS HAS GOTTEN MORE INTERESTING.
THE KNIGHT, FOR EX-AMPLE...
EVER SINCE HE FOUND OUT YOU WERE HALF GIRL, HE'S GOTTEN MORE OF AN... APPETITE.
AND THAT HAND THAT USED TO LINGER SO DOCILELY IN THE CORNER...

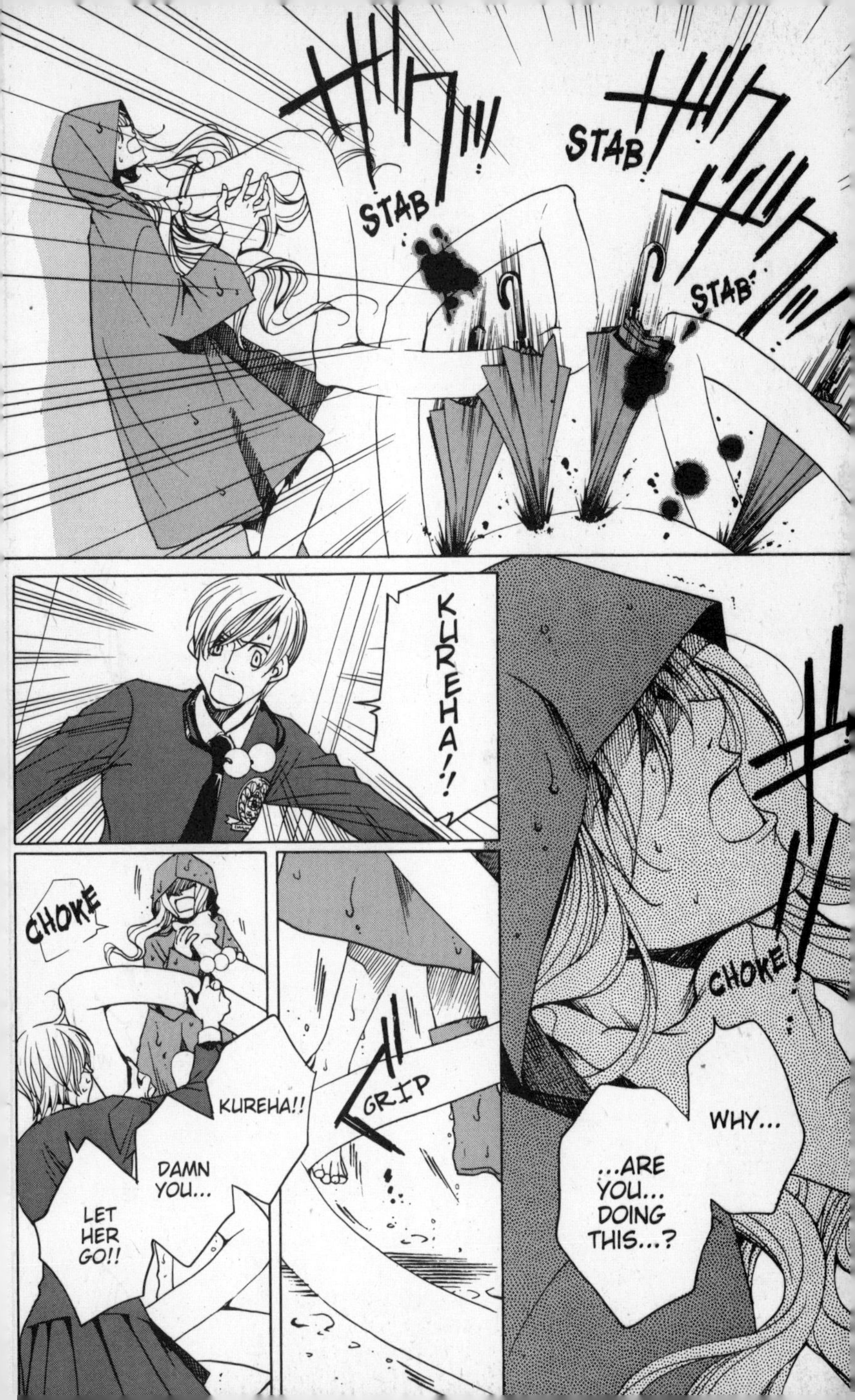
STAB!
STAB
STAB
CHOKE
WHY...
...ARE YOU... DOING THIS...?
KUREHA!!
GRIP
CHOKE
KUREHA!!
DAMN YOU...
LET HER GO!!

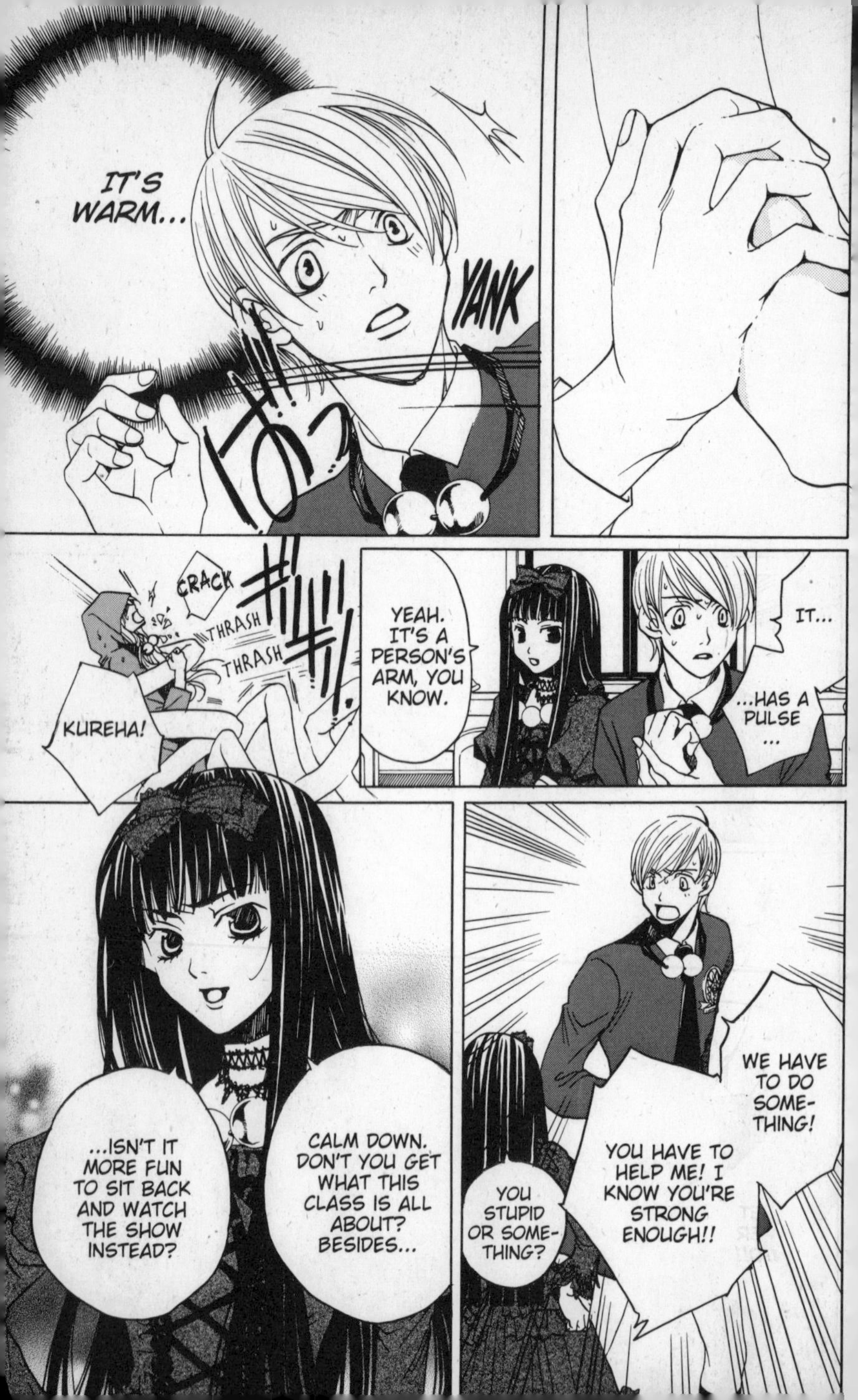
IT'S WARM...
YANK
はっ
IT...
...HAS A PULSE ...
YEAH. IT'S A PERSON'S ARM, YOU KNOW.
CRACK
THRASH THRASH
KUREHA!
WE HAVE TO DO SOME-THING!
YOU HAVE TO HELP ME! I KNOW YOU'RE STRONG ENOUGH!!
YOU STUPID OR SOME-THING?
CALM DOWN. DON'T YOU GET WHAT THIS CLASS IS ALL ABOUT? BESIDES...
...ISN'T IT MORE FUN TO SIT BACK AND WATCH THE SHOW INSTEAD?

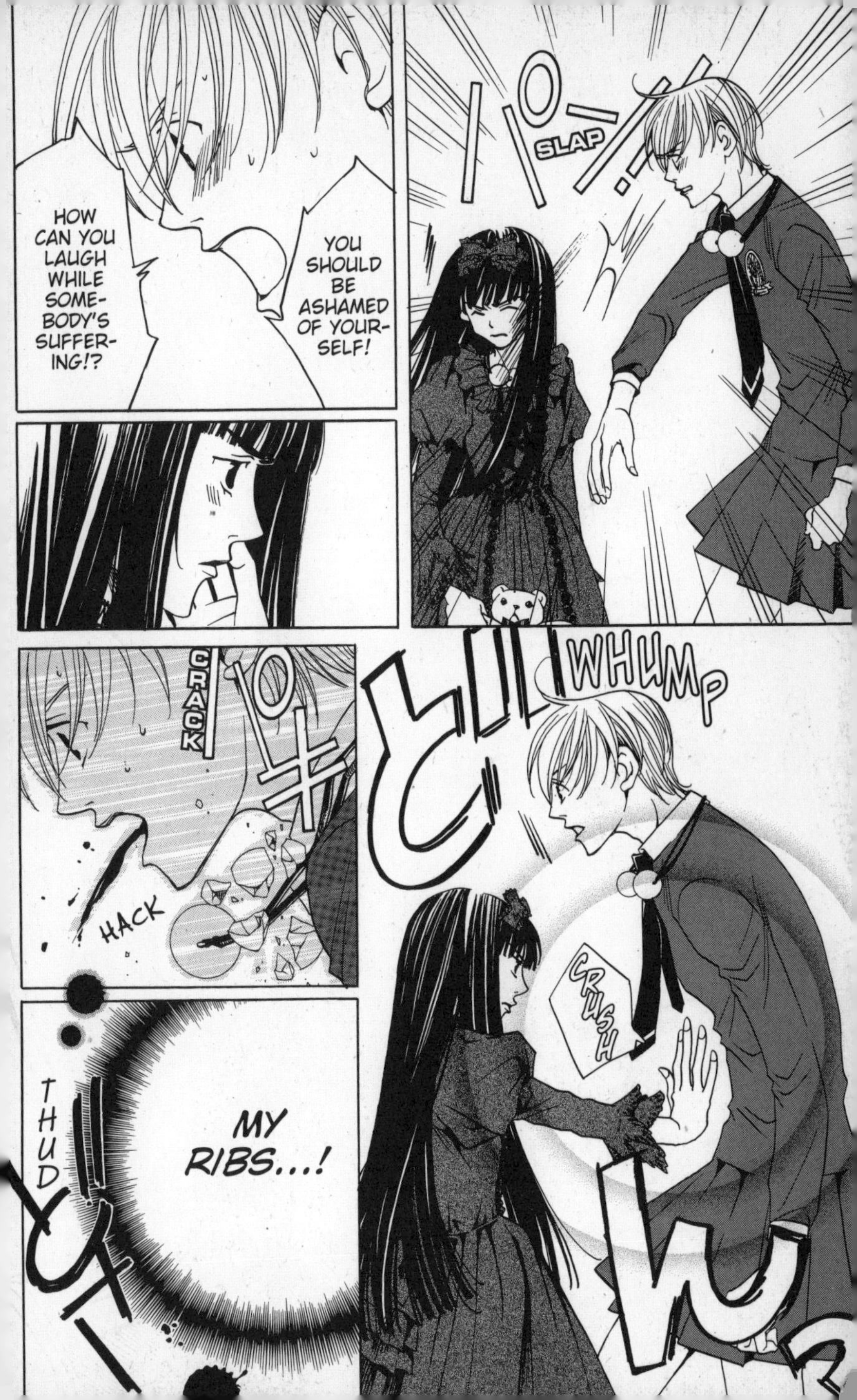
SLAP
YOU SHOULD BE ASHAMED OF YOURSELF!
HOW CAN YOU LAUGH WHILE SOMEBODY'S SUFFERING!?
WHUMP
CRUSH
CRACK
HACK
MY RIBS...!
THUD

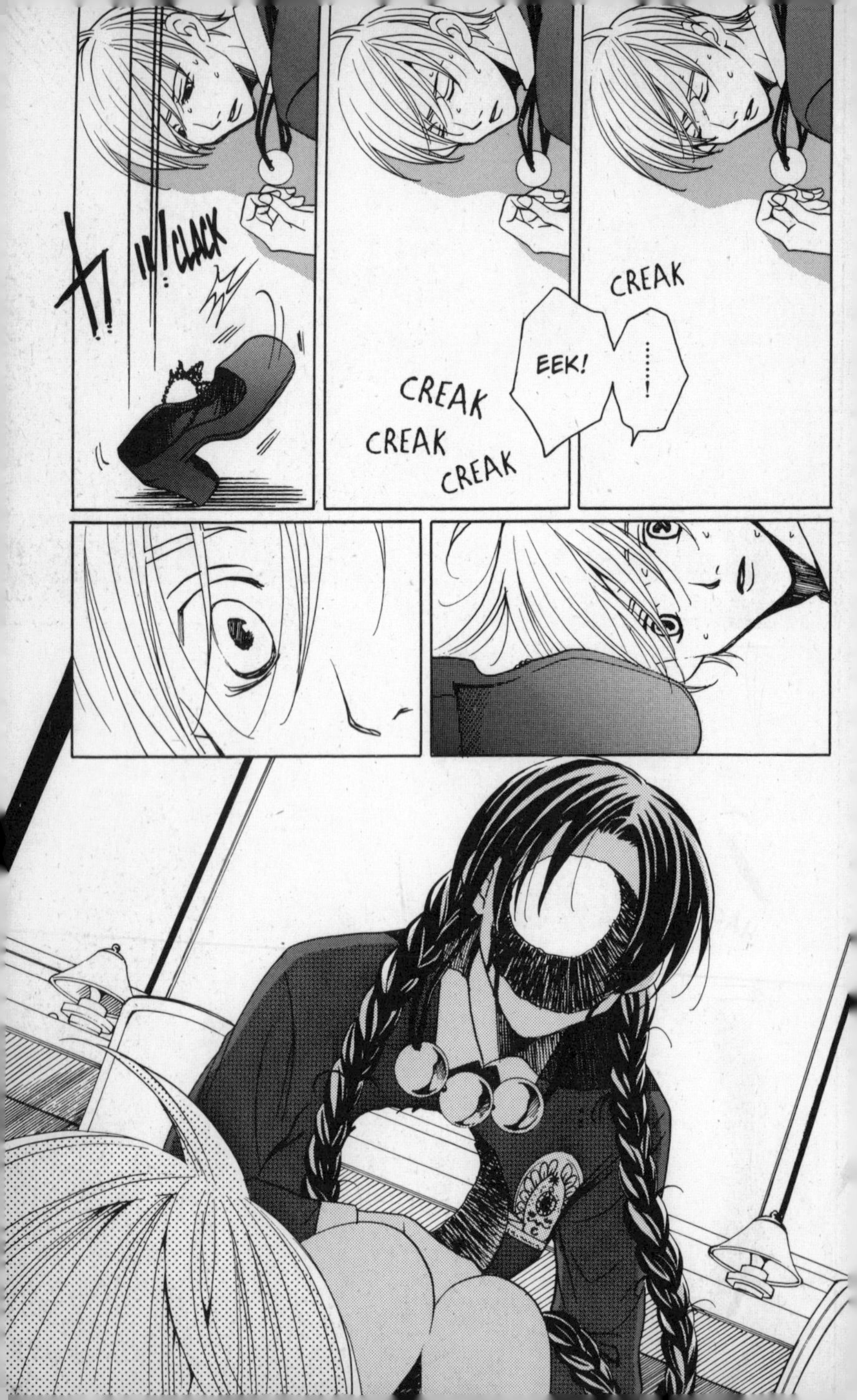

CREAK
......!
EEK!
CREAK
CREAK
CREAK
CLACK

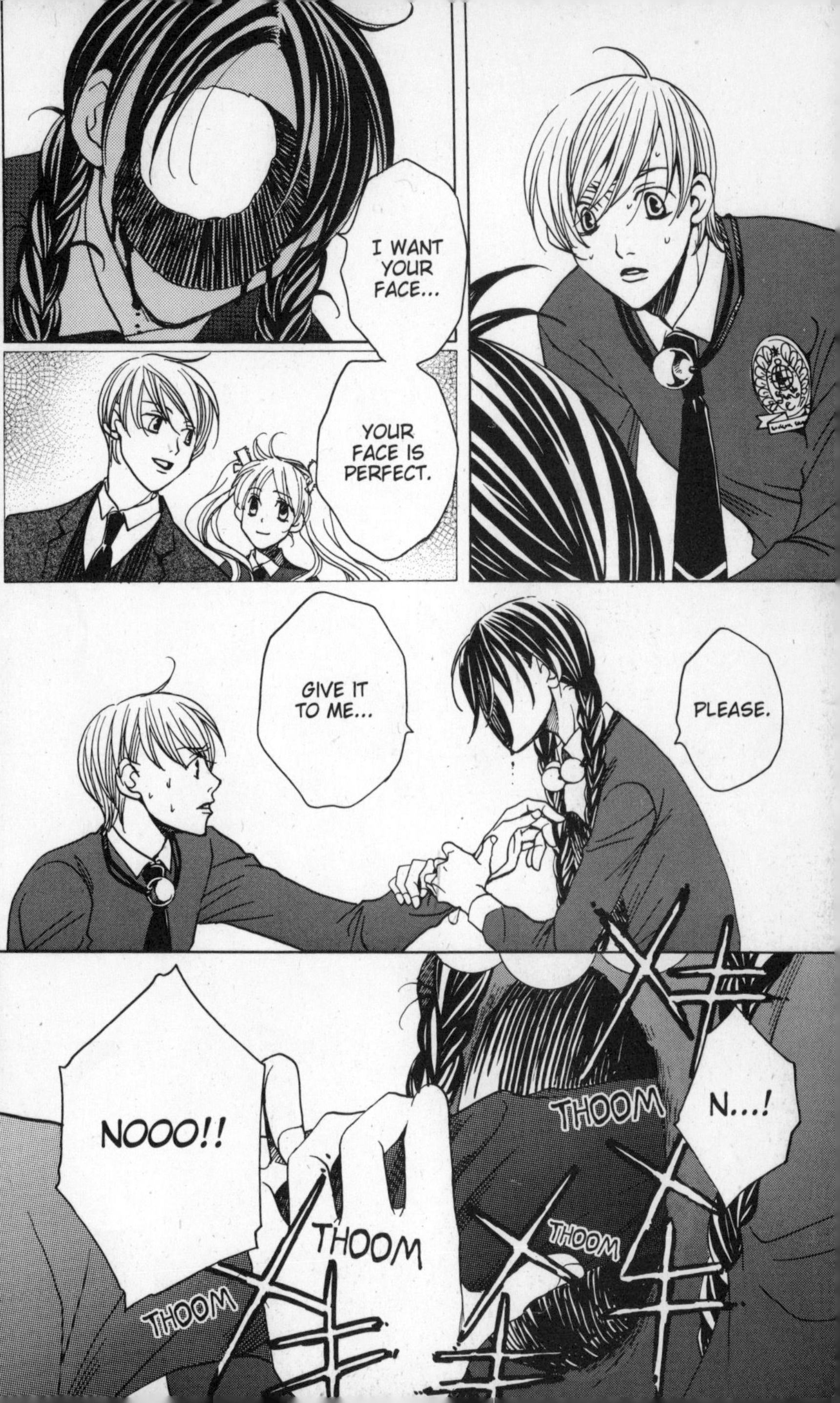
I WANT YOUR FACE...
YOUR FACE IS PERFECT.
GIVE IT TO ME...
PLEASE.
N...!
THOOM
THOOM
NOOO!!
THOOM
THOOM

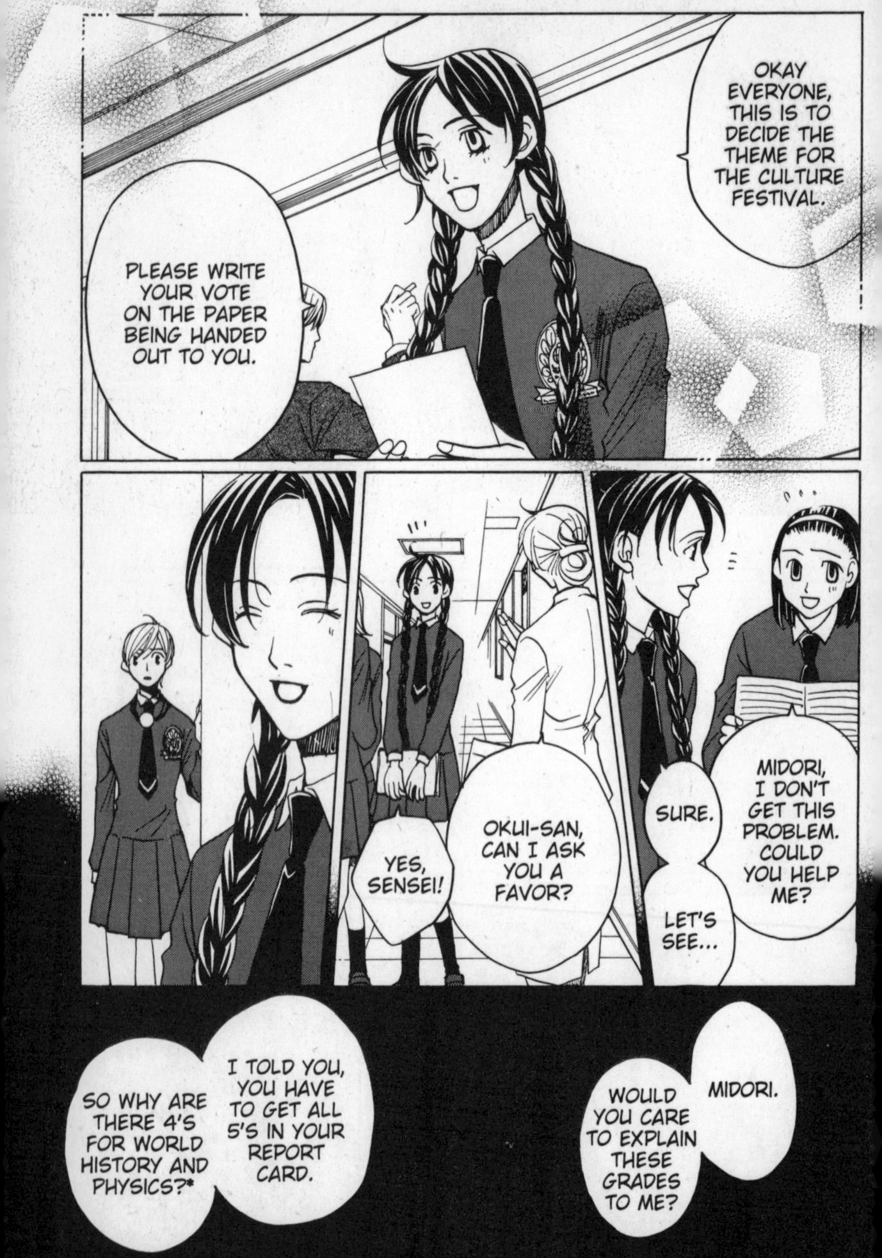
OKAY EVERYONE, THIS IS TO DECIDE THE THEME FOR THE CULTURE FESTIVAL.
PLEASE WRITE YOUR VOTE ON THE PAPER BEING HANDED OUT TO YOU.
MIDORI, I DON'T GET THIS PROBLEM. COULD YOU HELP ME?
SURE.
LET'S SEE...
OKUI-SAN, CAN I ASK YOU A FAVOR?
YES, SENSEI!
MIDORI.
WOULD YOU CARE TO EXPLAIN THESE GRADES TO ME?
I TOLD YOU, YOU HAVE TO GET ALL 5'S IN YOUR REPORT CARD.
SO WHY ARE THERE 4'S FOR WORLD HISTORY AND PHYSICS?*

*SEE TRANSLATOR'S NOTES AT BACK OF BOOK

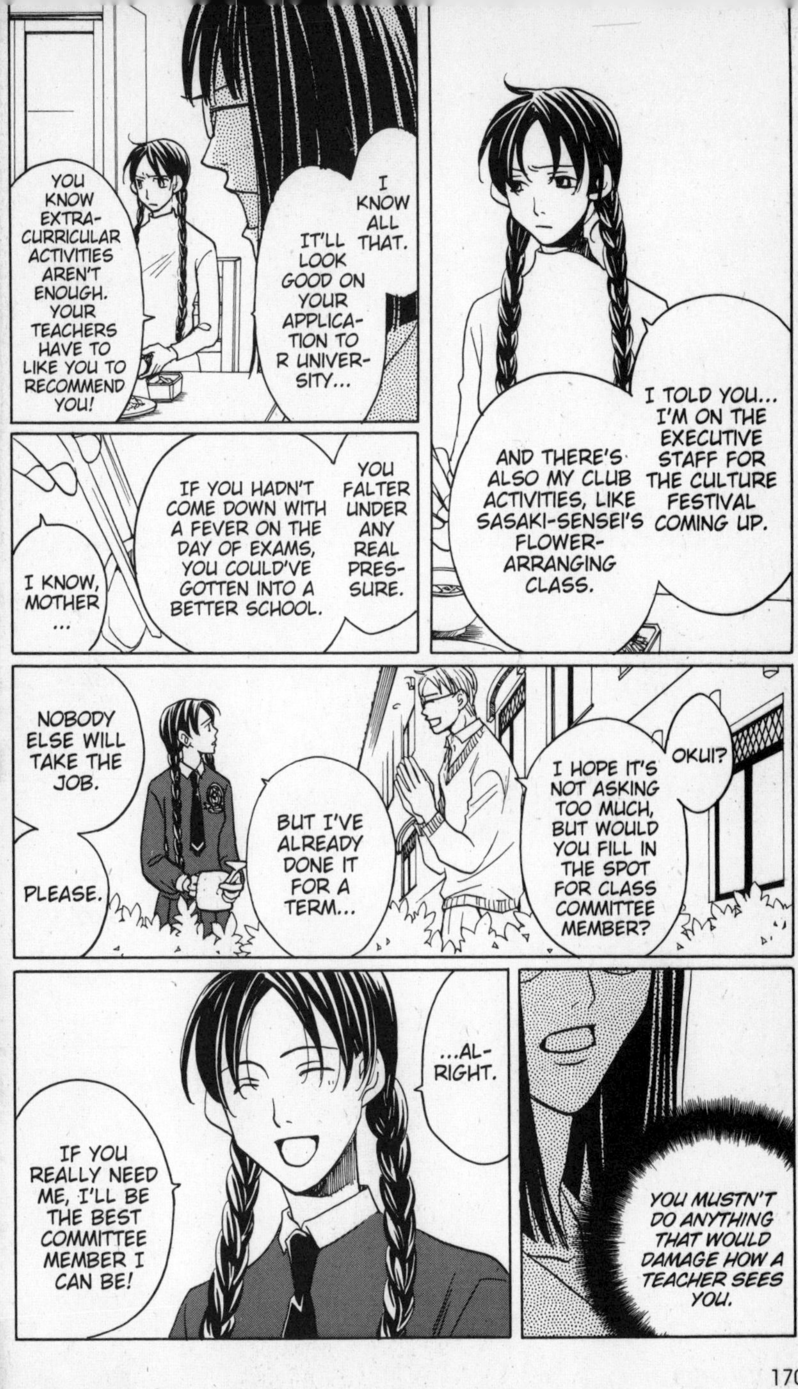
I TOLD YOU... I'M ON THE EXECUTIVE STAFF FOR THE CULTURE FESTIVAL COMING UP.
AND THERE'S ALSO MY CLUB ACTIVITIES, LIKE SASAKI-SENSEI'S FLOWER-ARRANGING CLASS.
I KNOW ALL THAT.
IT'LL LOOK GOOD ON YOUR APPLICATION TO R UNIVERSITY...
YOU KNOW EXTRA-CURRICULAR ACTIVITIES AREN'T ENOUGH. YOUR TEACHERS HAVE TO LIKE YOU TO RECOMMEND YOU!
YOU FALTER UNDER ANY REAL PRESSURE.
IF YOU HADN'T COME DOWN WITH A FEVER ON THE DAY OF EXAMS, YOU COULD'VE GOTTEN INTO A BETTER SCHOOL.
I KNOW, MOTHER...
OKUI?
I HOPE IT'S NOT ASKING TOO MUCH, BUT WOULD YOU FILL IN THE SPOT FOR CLASS COMMITTEE MEMBER?
BUT I'VE ALREADY DONE IT FOR A TERM...
NOBODY ELSE WILL TAKE THE JOB.
PLEASE.
YOU MUSTN'T DO ANYTHING THAT WOULD DAMAGE HOW A TEACHER SEES YOU.
...ALRIGHT.
IF YOU REALLY NEED ME, I'LL BE THE BEST COMMITTEE MEMBER I CAN BE!

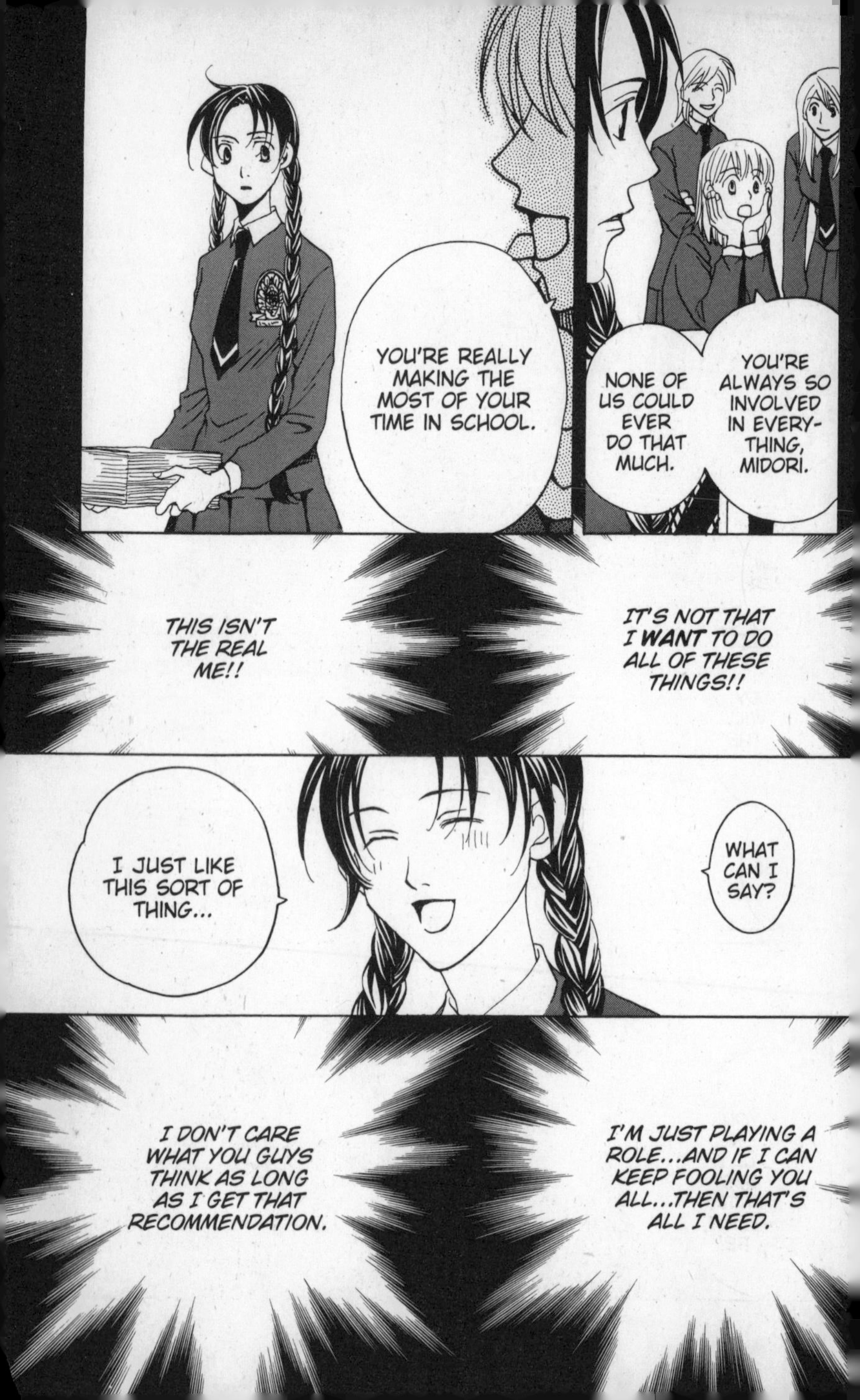
YOU'RE ALWAYS SO INVOLVED IN EVERYTHING, MIDORI.
NONE OF US COULD EVER DO THAT MUCH.
YOU'RE REALLY MAKING THE MOST OF YOUR TIME IN SCHOOL.
IT'S NOT THAT I **WANT** TO DO ALL OF THESE THINGS!!
THIS ISN'T THE REAL ME!!
WHAT CAN I SAY?
I JUST LIKE THIS SORT OF THING...
I'M JUST PLAYING A ROLE...AND IF I CAN KEEP FOOLING YOU ALL...THEN THAT'S ALL I NEED.
I DON'T CARE WHAT YOU GUYS THINK AS LONG AS I GET THAT RECOMMENDATION.

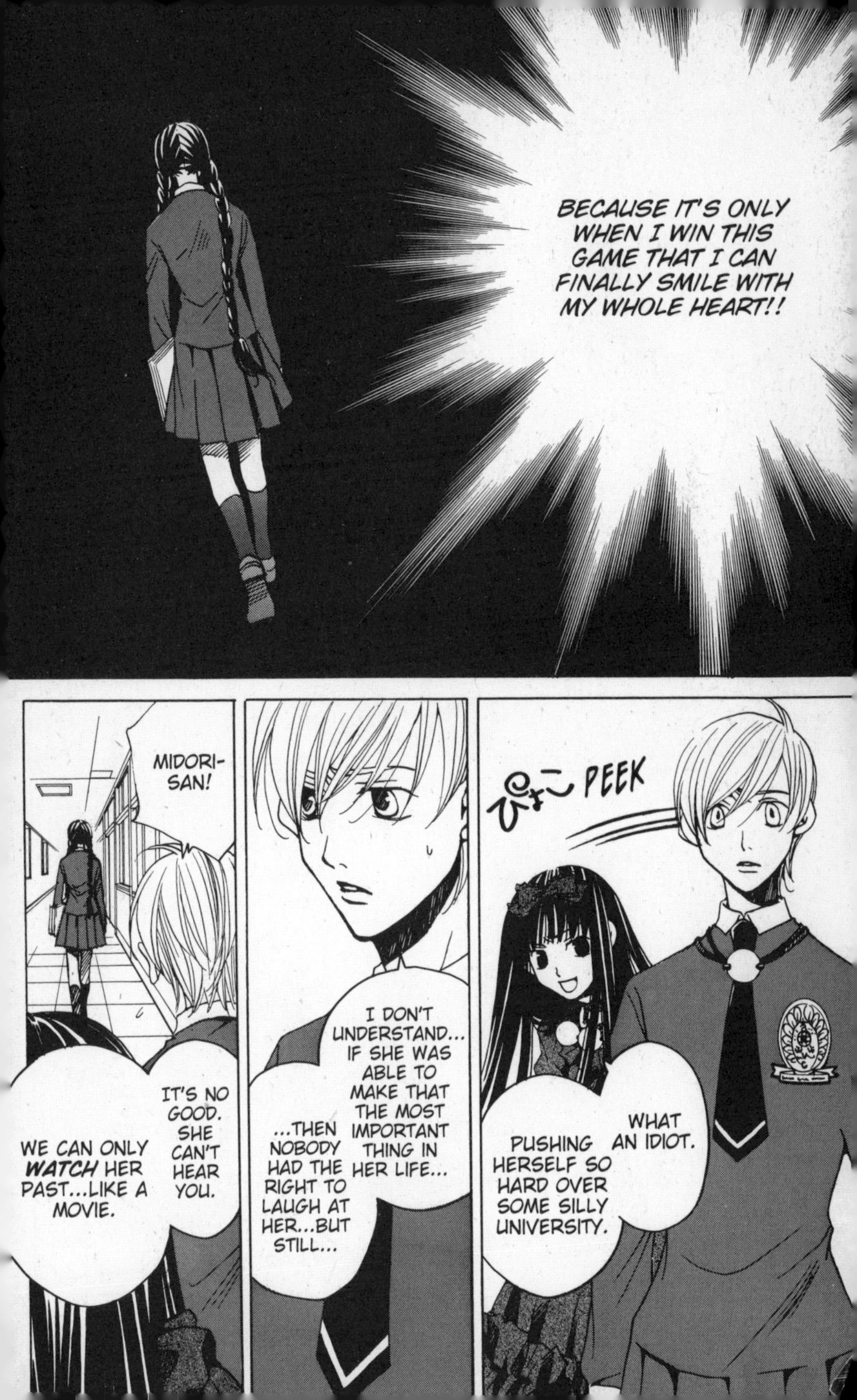
BECAUSE IT'S ONLY WHEN I WIN THIS GAME THAT I CAN FINALLY SMILE WITH MY WHOLE HEART!!
ぴょこ PEEK
WHAT AN IDIOT.
PUSHING HERSELF SO HARD OVER SOME SILLY UNIVERSITY.
I DON'T UNDERSTAND... IF SHE WAS ABLE TO MAKE THAT THE MOST IMPORTANT THING IN HER LIFE...
...THEN NOBODY HAD THE RIGHT TO LAUGH AT HER...BUT STILL...
MIDORI-SAN!
IT'S NO GOOD. SHE CAN'T HEAR YOU.
WE CAN ONLY *WATCH* HER PAST...LIKE A MOVIE.

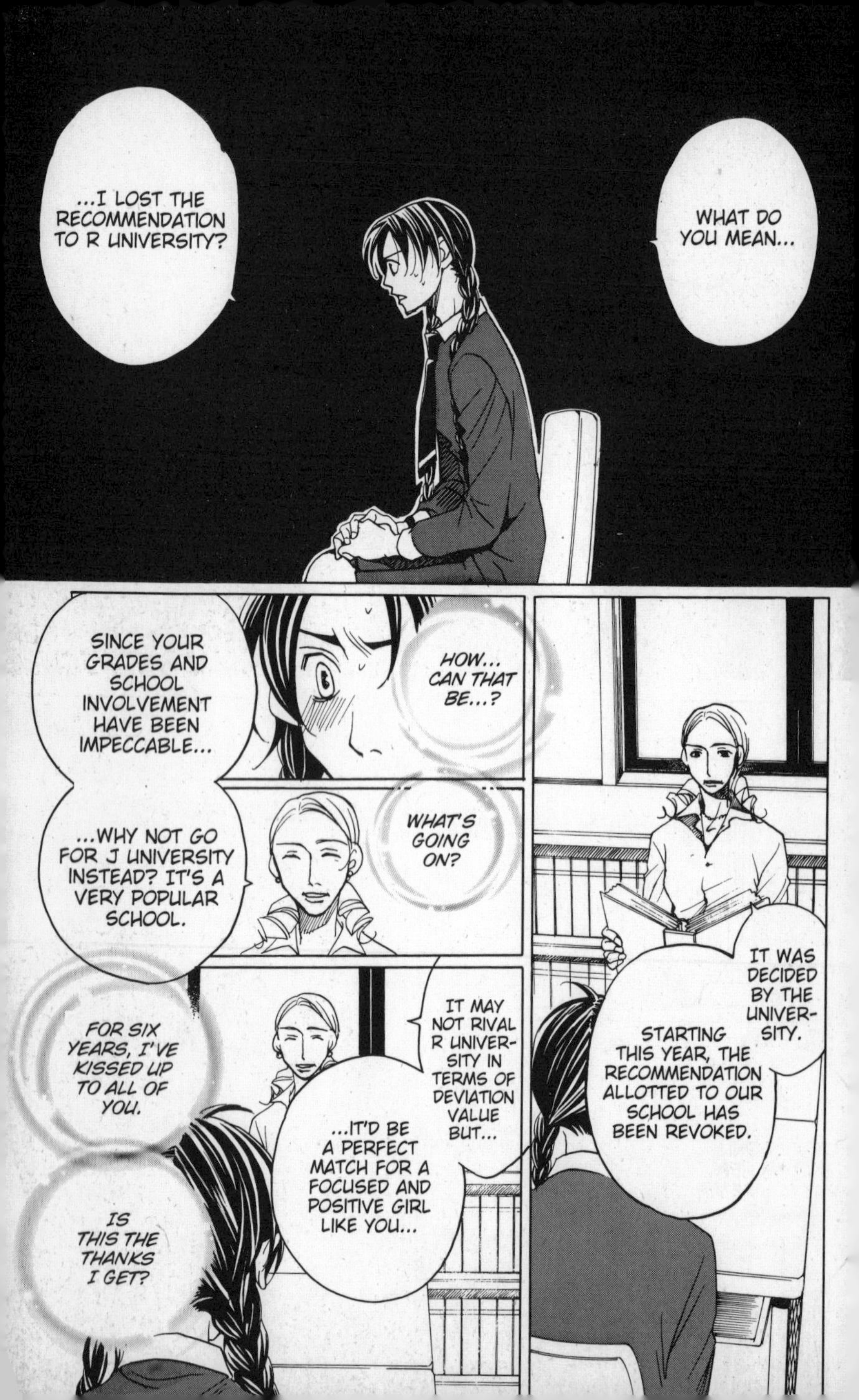
WHAT DO YOU MEAN...
...I LOST THE RECOMMENDATION TO R UNIVERSITY?
IT WAS DECIDED BY THE UNIVERSITY.
STARTING THIS YEAR, THE RECOMMENDATION ALLOTTED TO OUR SCHOOL HAS BEEN REVOKED.
HOW... CAN THAT BE...?
SINCE YOUR GRADES AND SCHOOL INVOLVEMENT HAVE BEEN IMPECCABLE...
WHAT'S GOING ON?
...WHY NOT GO FOR J UNIVERSITY INSTEAD? IT'S A VERY POPULAR SCHOOL.
IT MAY NOT RIVAL R UNIVERSITY IN TERMS OF DEVIATION VALUE BUT...
...IT'D BE A PERFECT MATCH FOR A FOCUSED AND POSITIVE GIRL LIKE YOU...
FOR SIX YEARS, I'VE KISSED UP TO ALL OF YOU.
IS THIS THE THANKS I GET?

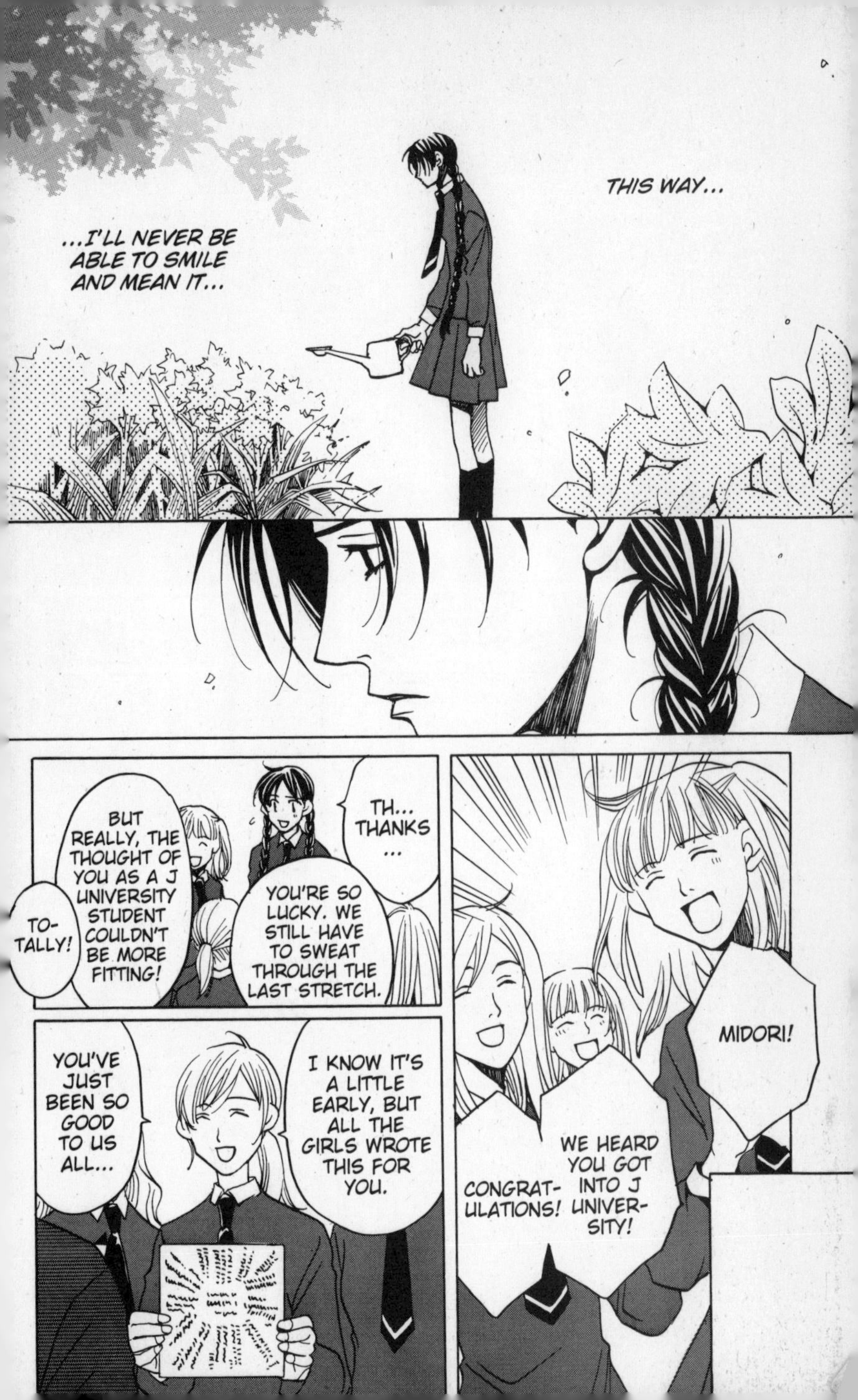
THIS WAY...
...I'LL NEVER BE ABLE TO SMILE AND MEAN IT...
MIDORI!
WE HEARD YOU GOT INTO J UNIVERSITY!
CONGRATULATIONS!
TH... THANKS...
YOU'RE SO LUCKY. WE STILL HAVE TO SWEAT THROUGH THE LAST STRETCH.
BUT REALLY, THE THOUGHT OF YOU AS A J UNIVERSITY STUDENT COULDN'T BE MORE FITTING!
TO-TALLY!
I KNOW IT'S A LITTLE EARLY, BUT ALL THE GIRLS WROTE THIS FOR YOU.
YOU'VE JUST BEEN SO GOOD TO US ALL...

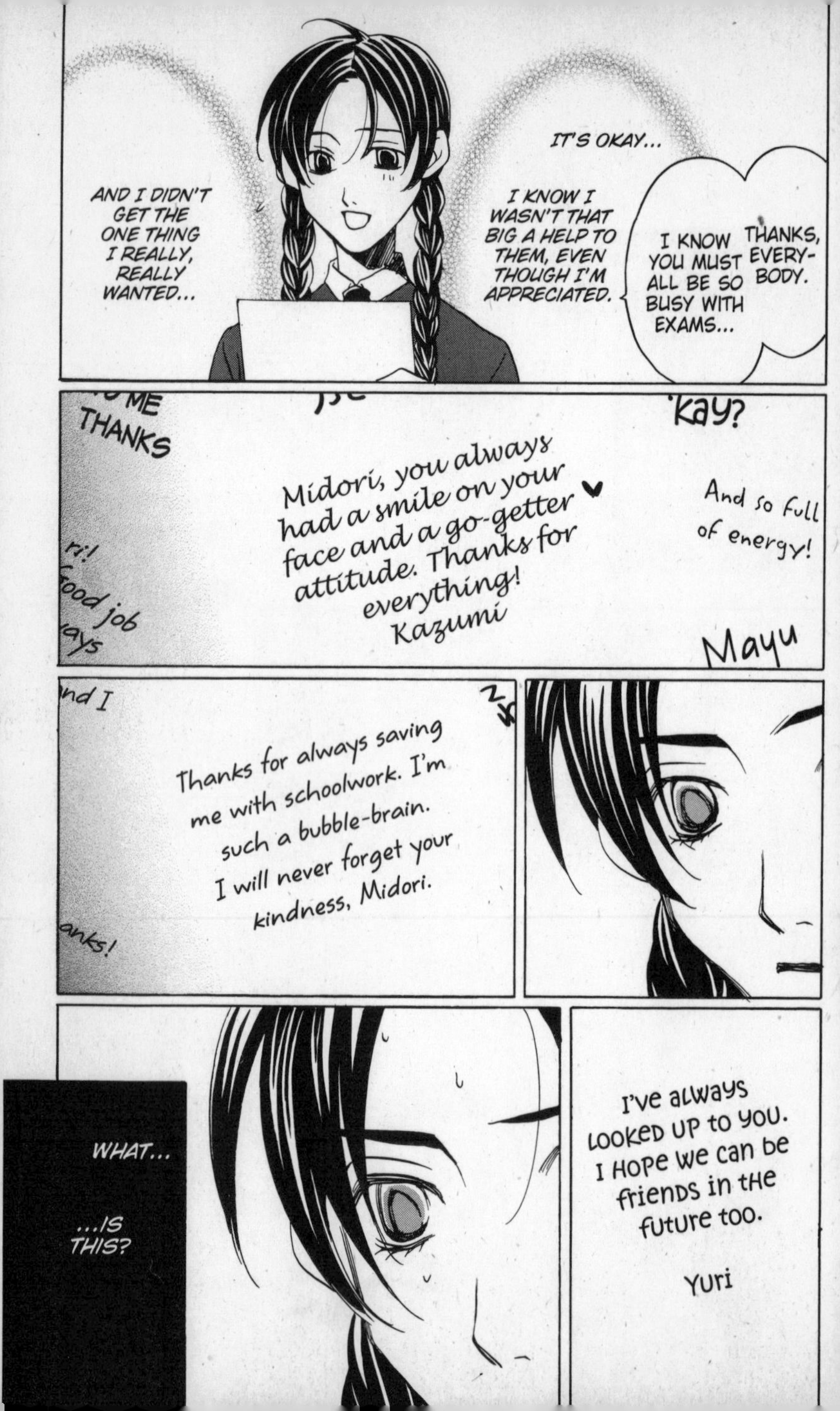
THANKS, EVERYBODY.
I KNOW YOU MUST ALL BE SO BUSY WITH EXAMS...
IT'S OKAY...
I KNOW I WASN'T THAT BIG A HELP TO THEM, EVEN THOUGH I'M APPRECIATED.
AND I DIDN'T GET THE ONE THING I REALLY, REALLY WANTED...
'kay?
And so full of energy!
Mayu
Midori, you always had a smile on your face and a go-getter attitude. Thanks for everything! Kazumi
THANKS
good job
Thanks for always saving me with schoolwork. I'm such a bubble-brain. I will never forget your kindness, Midori.
I've always looked up to you. I hope we can be friends in the future too.
Yuri
WHAT...
...IS THIS?

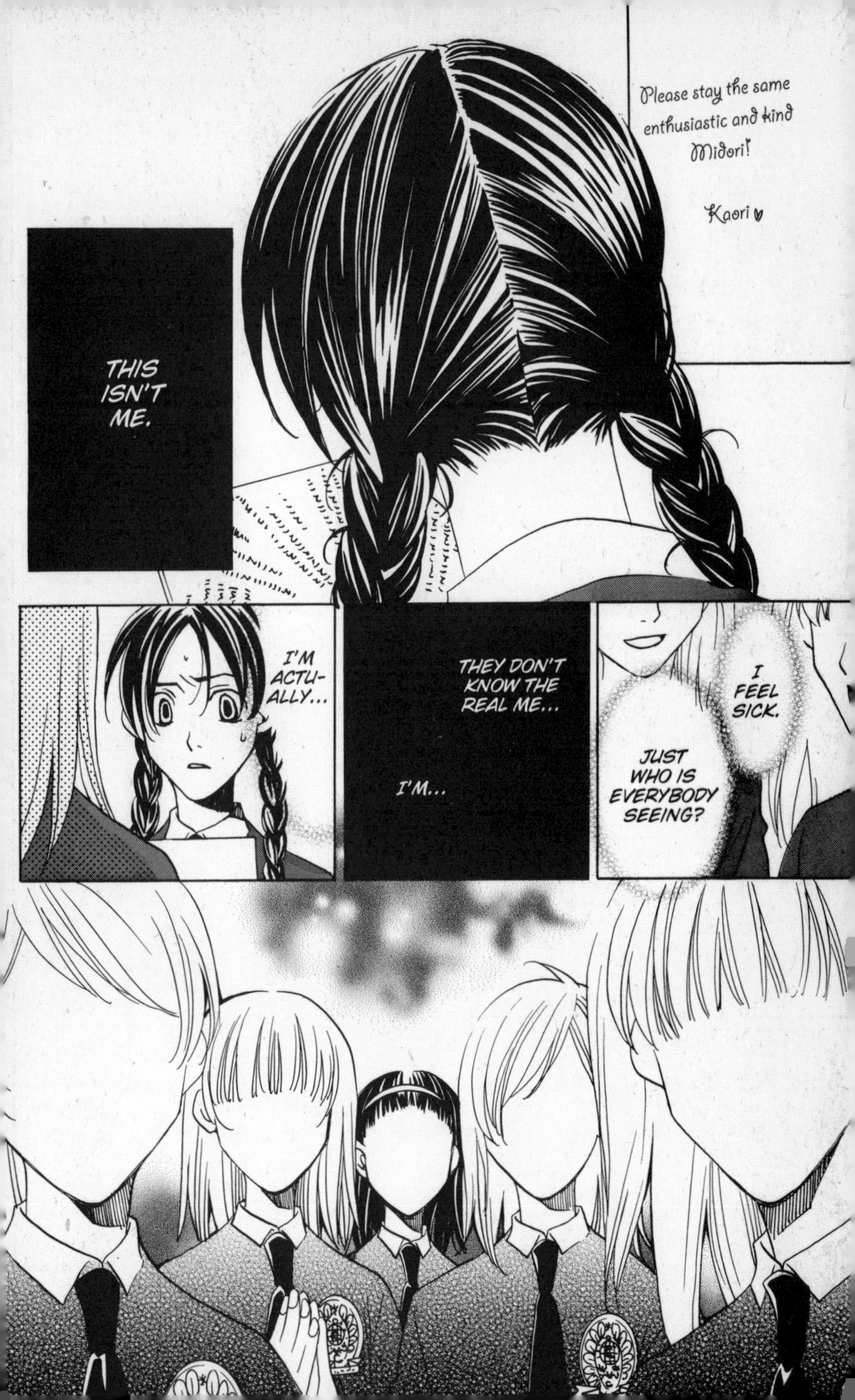
Please stay the same enthusiastic and kind Midori!
Kaori
THIS ISN'T ME.
I FEEL SICK.
JUST WHO IS EVERYBODY SEEING?
THEY DON'T KNOW THE REAL ME...
I'M...
I'M ACTUALLY...

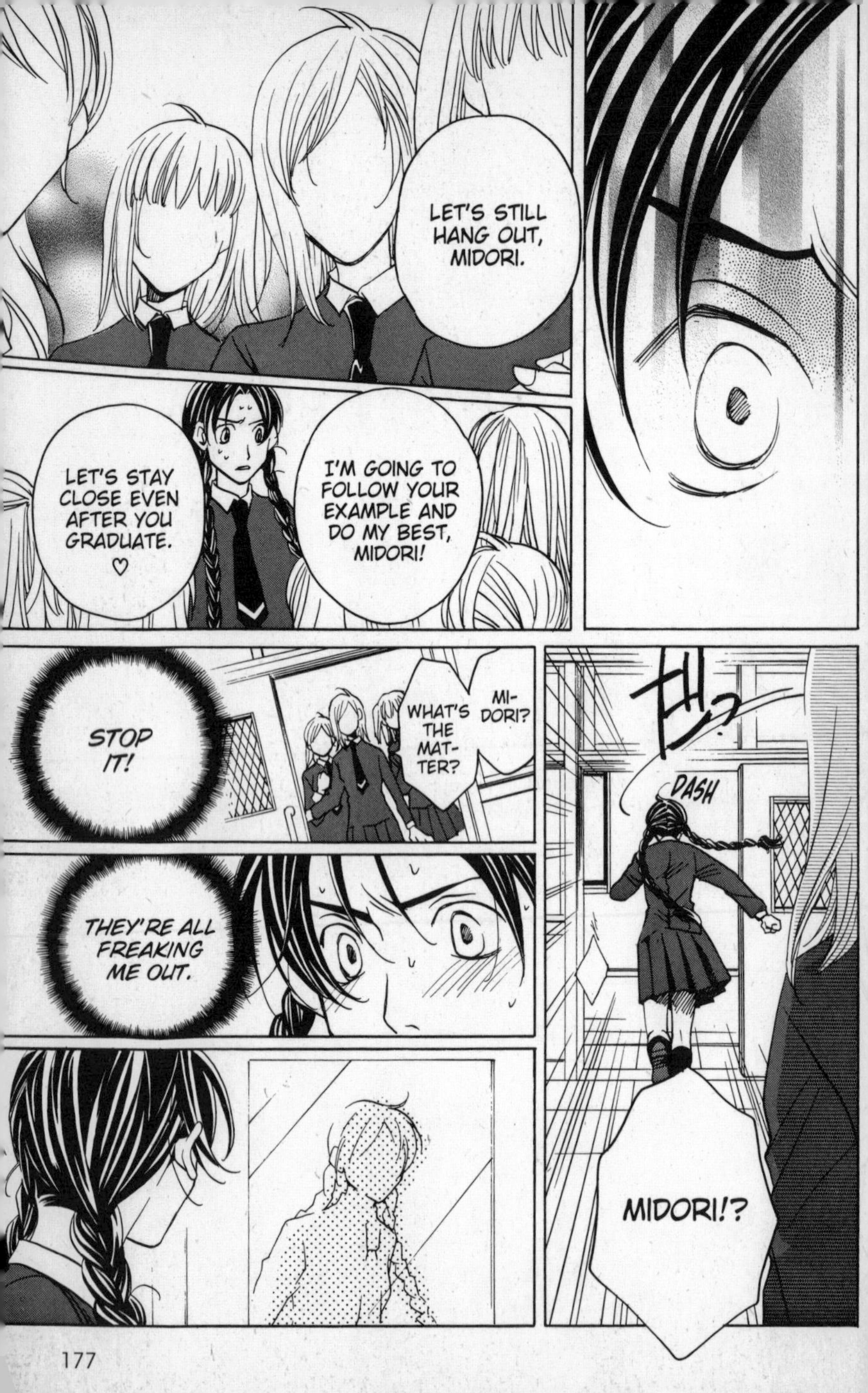
LET'S STILL HANG OUT, MIDORI.
I'M GOING TO FOLLOW YOUR EXAMPLE AND DO MY BEST, MIDORI!
LET'S STAY CLOSE EVEN AFTER YOU GRADUATE. ♡
DASH
MIDORI!?
MI-DORI?
WHAT'S THE MAT-TER?
STOP IT!
THEY'RE ALL FREAKING ME OUT.

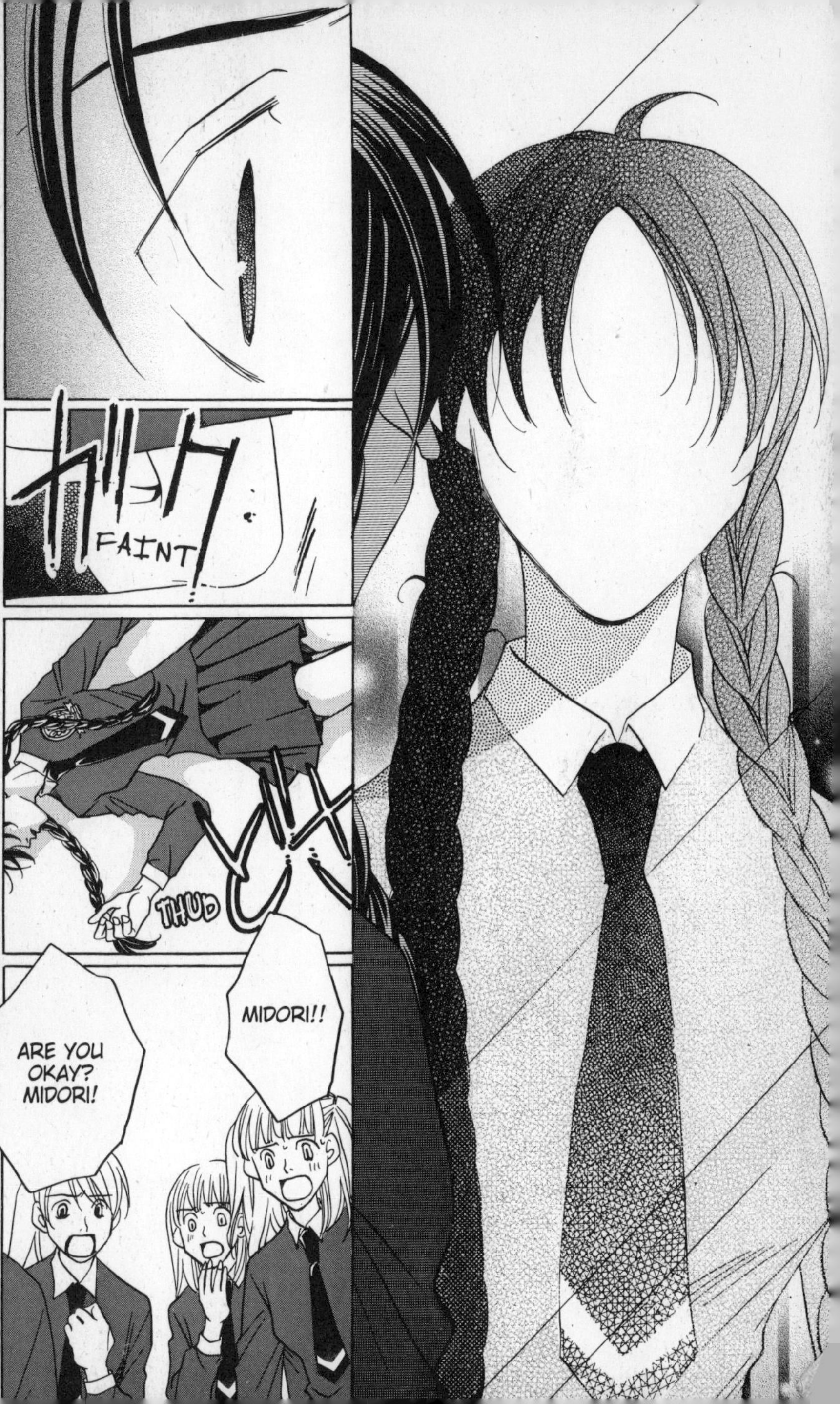
ガリッ
FAINT
ドサッ
THUD
MIDORI!!
ARE YOU OKAY? MIDORI!

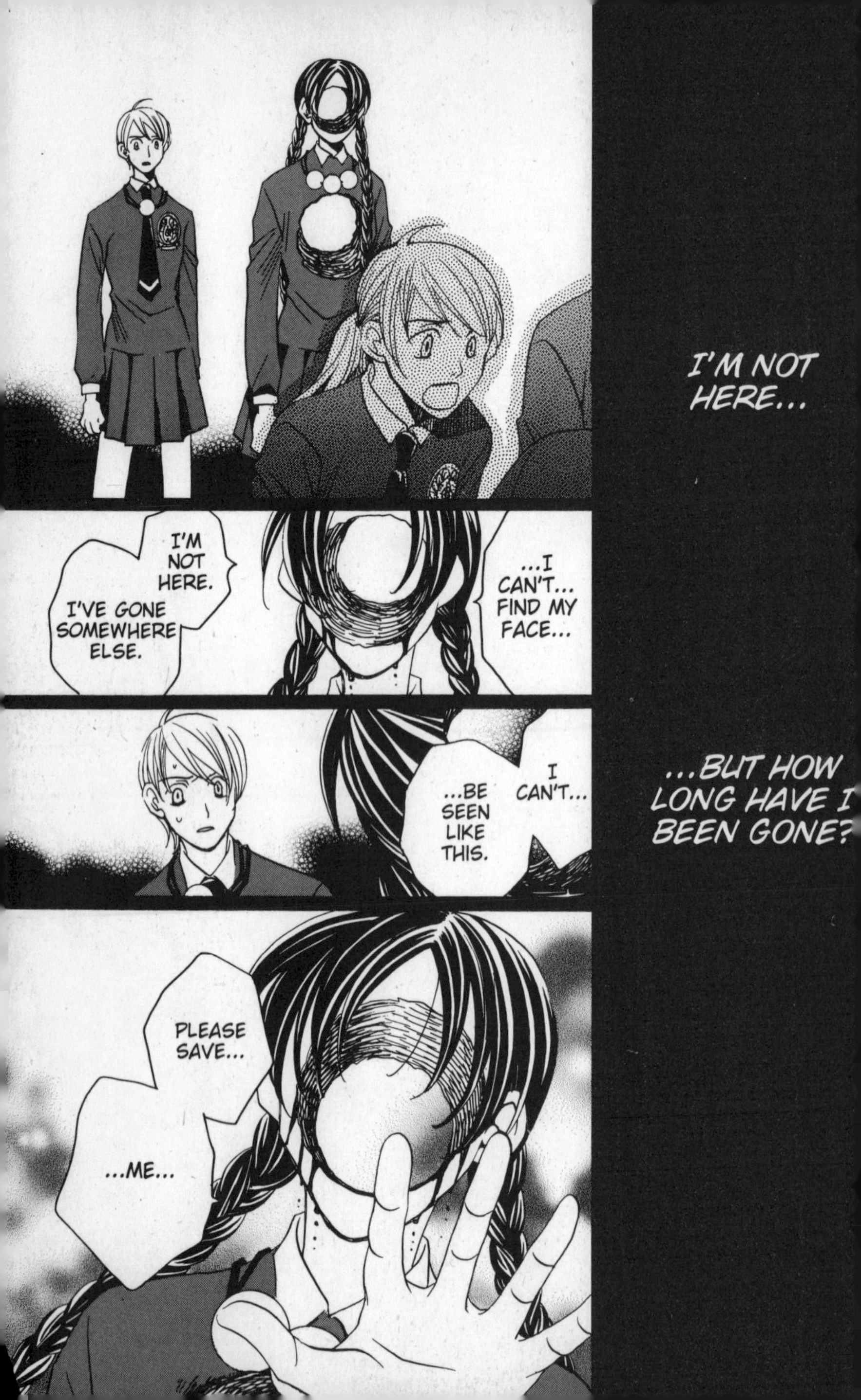
I'M NOT HERE...
...I CAN'T... FIND MY FACE...
I'M NOT HERE.
I'VE GONE SOMEWHERE ELSE.
...BUT HOW LONG HAVE I BEEN GONE?
I CAN'T...
...BE SEEN LIKE THIS.
PLEASE SAVE...
...ME...

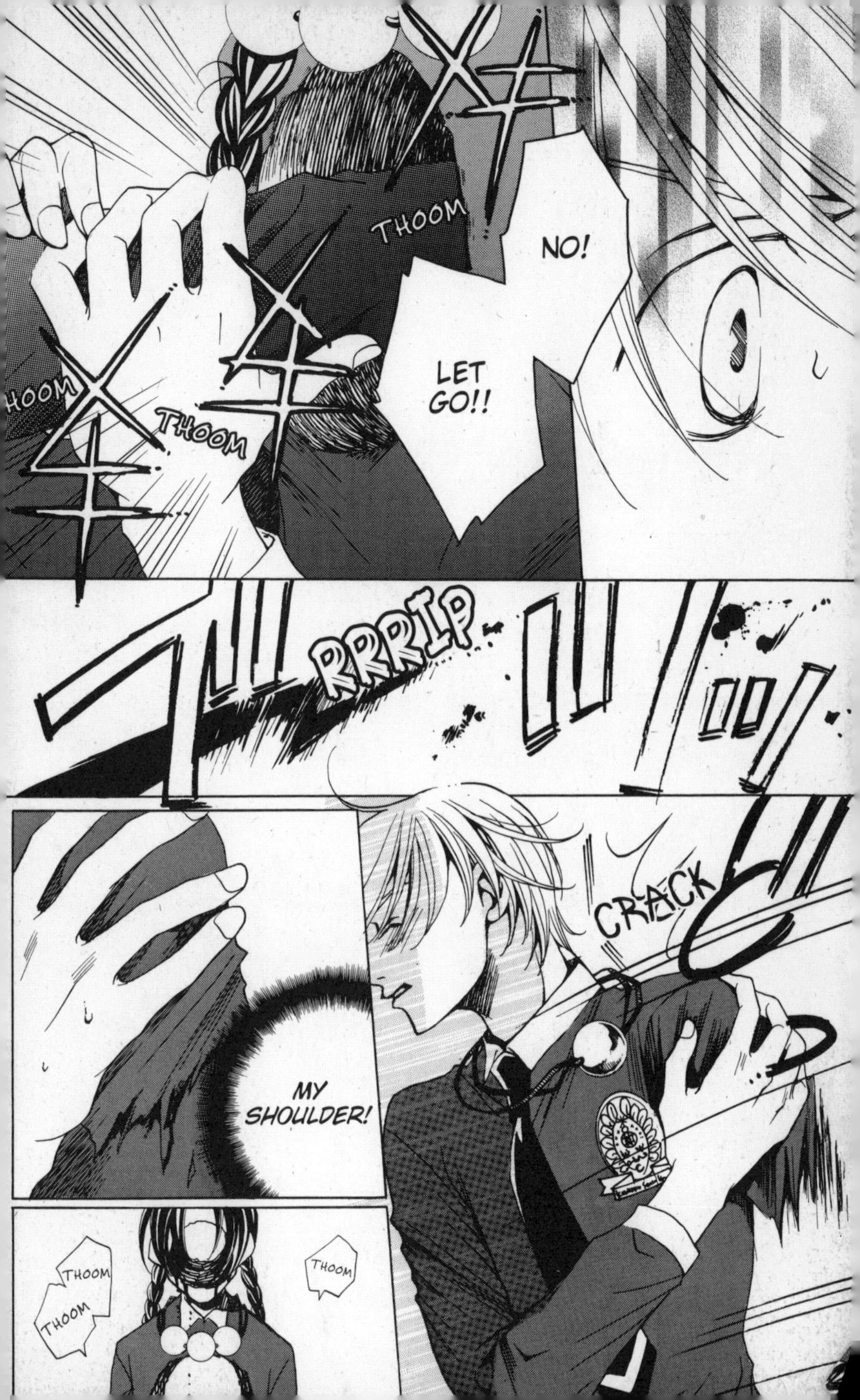
NO!
LET GO!!
THOOM
THOOM
HOOM
RRRIP
CRACK
MY SHOULDER!
THOOM
THOOM
THOOM

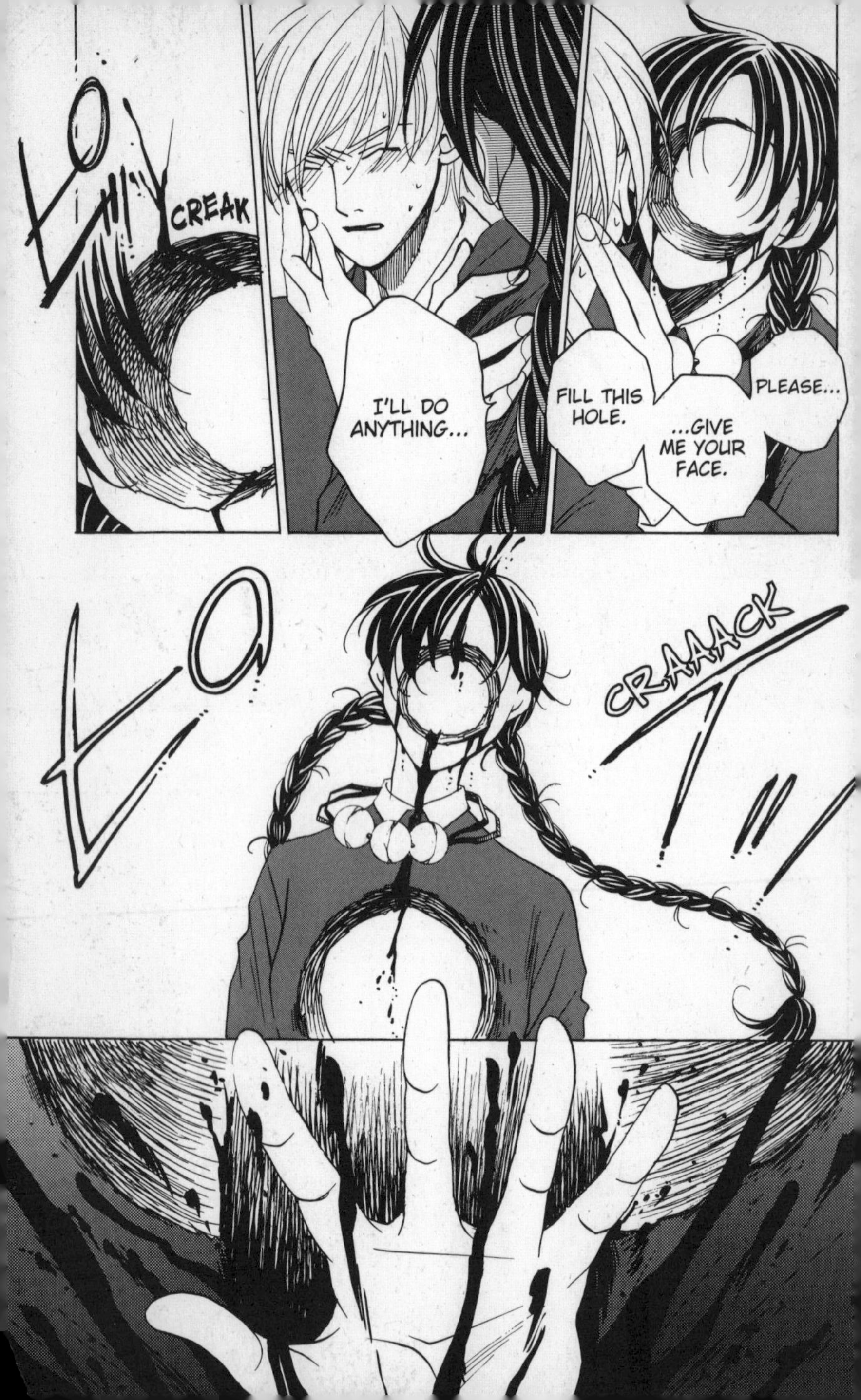
PLEASE...
FILL THIS HOLE.
...GIVE ME YOUR FACE.
I'LL DO ANYTHING...
CREAK
CRAAACK

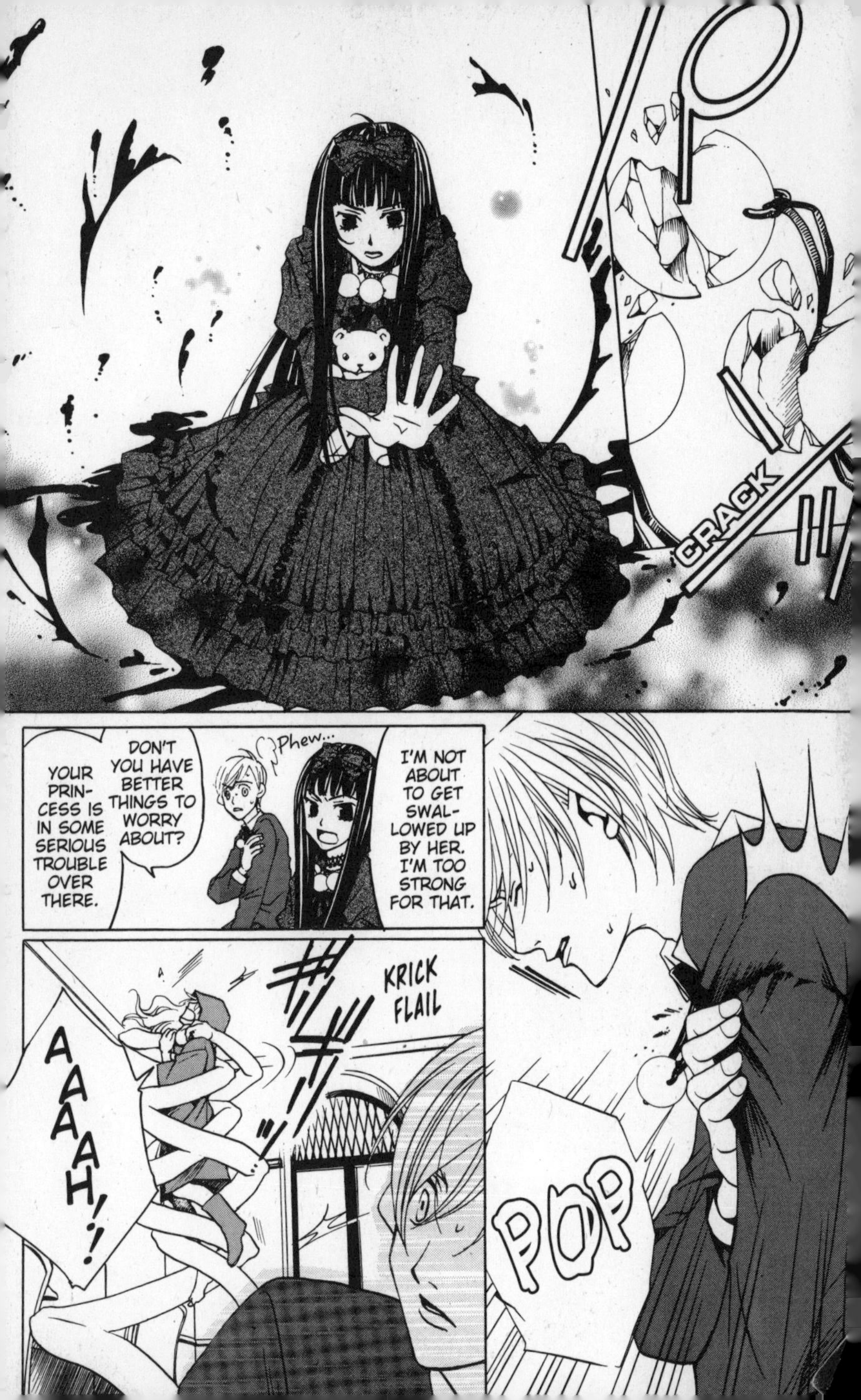
CRACK
I'M NOT ABOUT TO GET SWAL-LOWED UP BY HER. I'M TOO STRONG FOR THAT.
Phew...
DON'T YOU HAVE BETTER THINGS TO WORRY ABOUT?
YOUR PRIN-CESS IS IN SOME SERIOUS TROUBLE OVER THERE.
POP
KRICK FLAIL
AAAAH!!

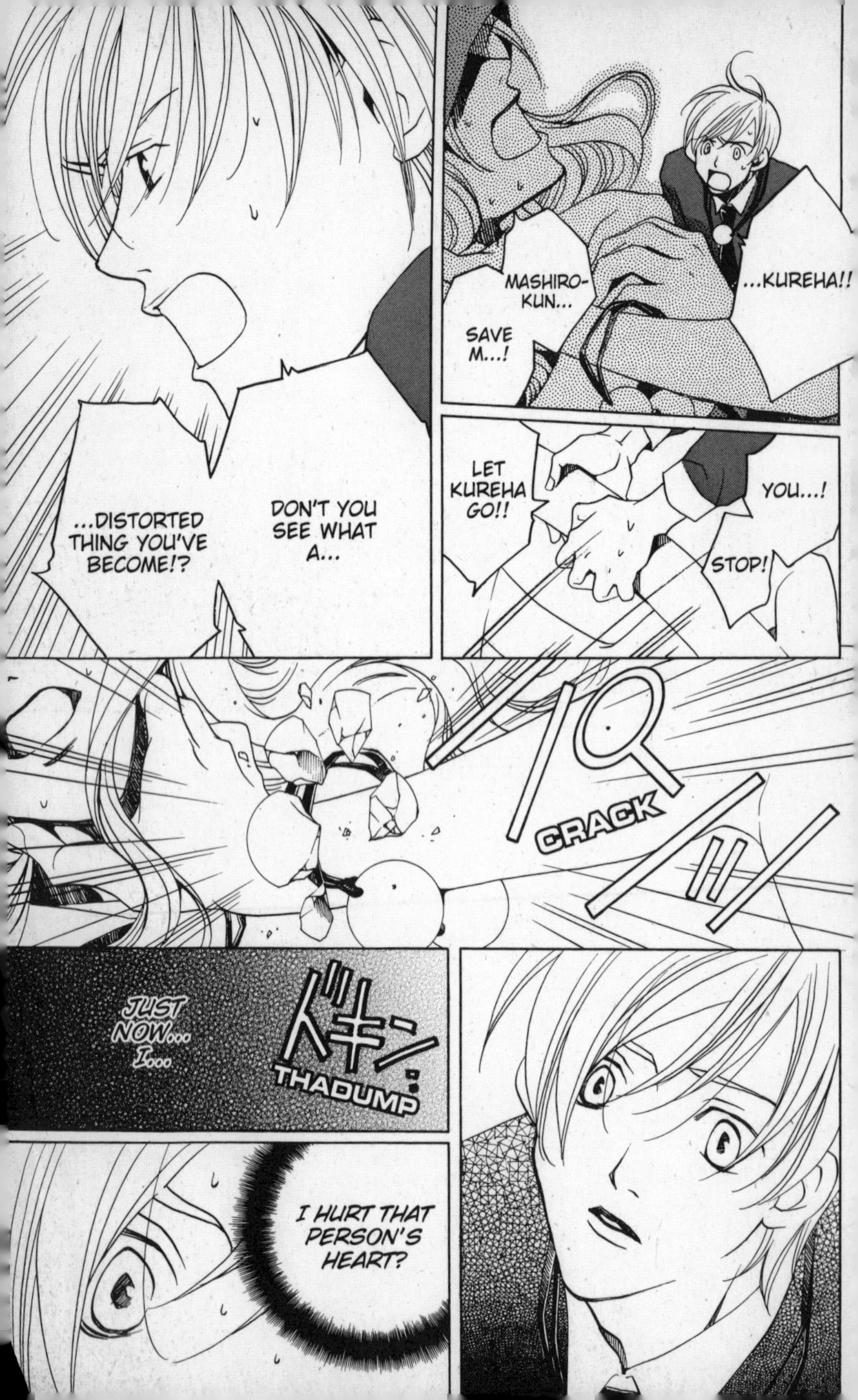
...KUREHA!!
MASHIRO-KUN...
SAVE M...!
YOU...!
LET KUREHA GO!!
STOP!
DON'T YOU SEE WHAT A...
...DISTORTED THING YOU'VE BECOME!?
CRACK
JUST NOW... I...
ドキン
THADUMP
I HURT THAT PERSON'S HEART?

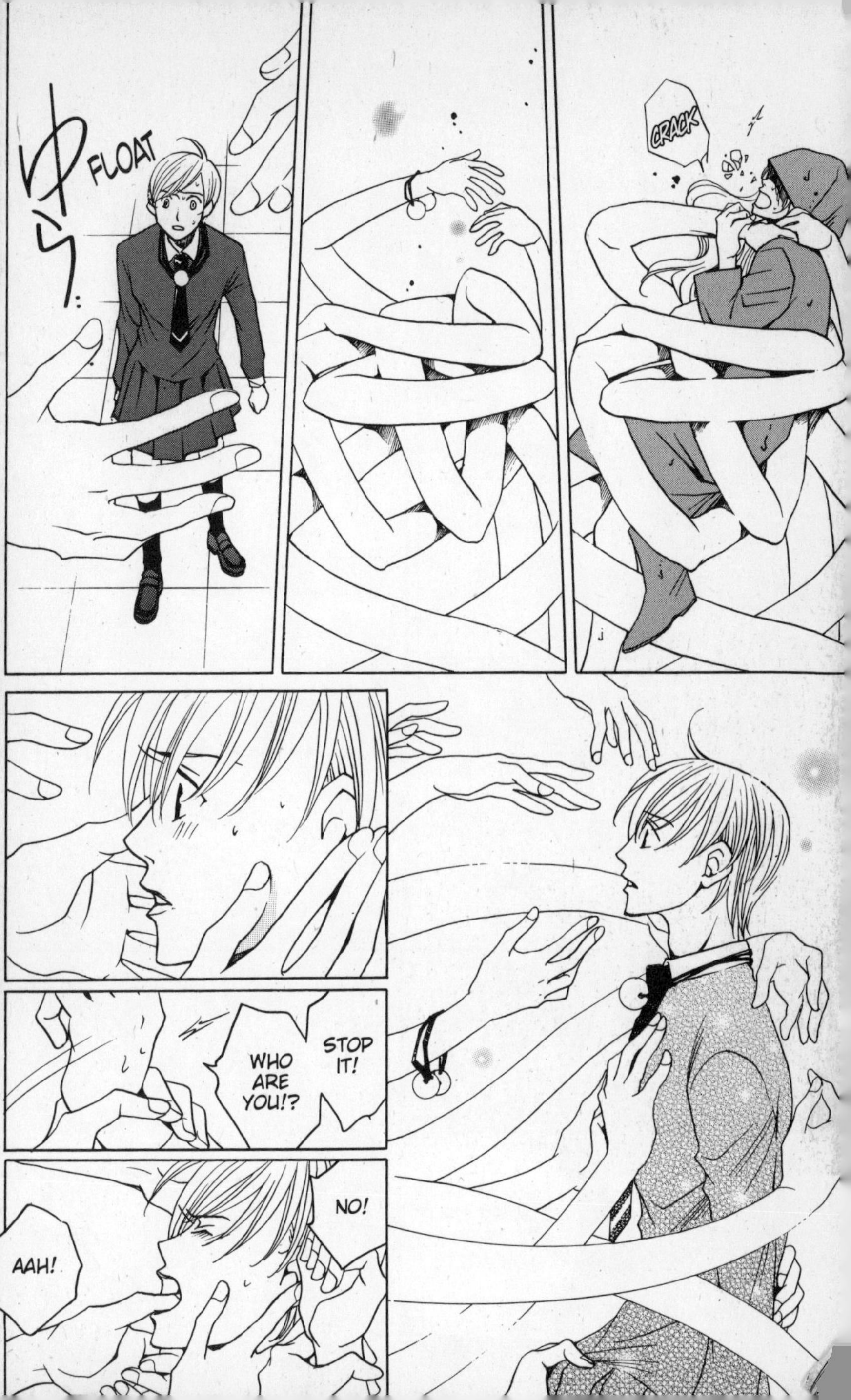
CRACK
FLOAT
STOP IT!
WHO ARE YOU!?
NO!
AAH!

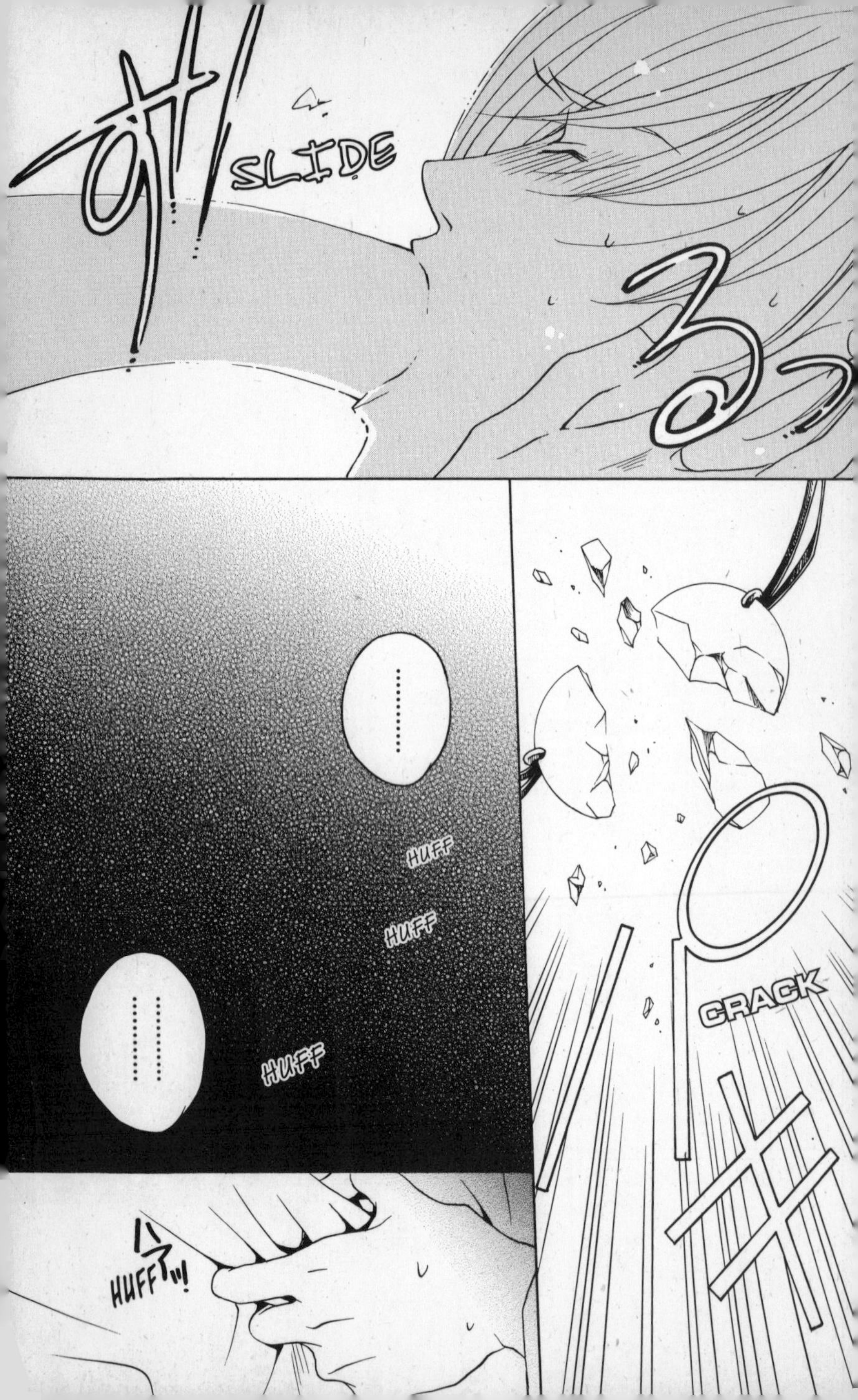
SLIDE
CRACK
....
HUFF
HUFF
....
....
HUFF
HUFF

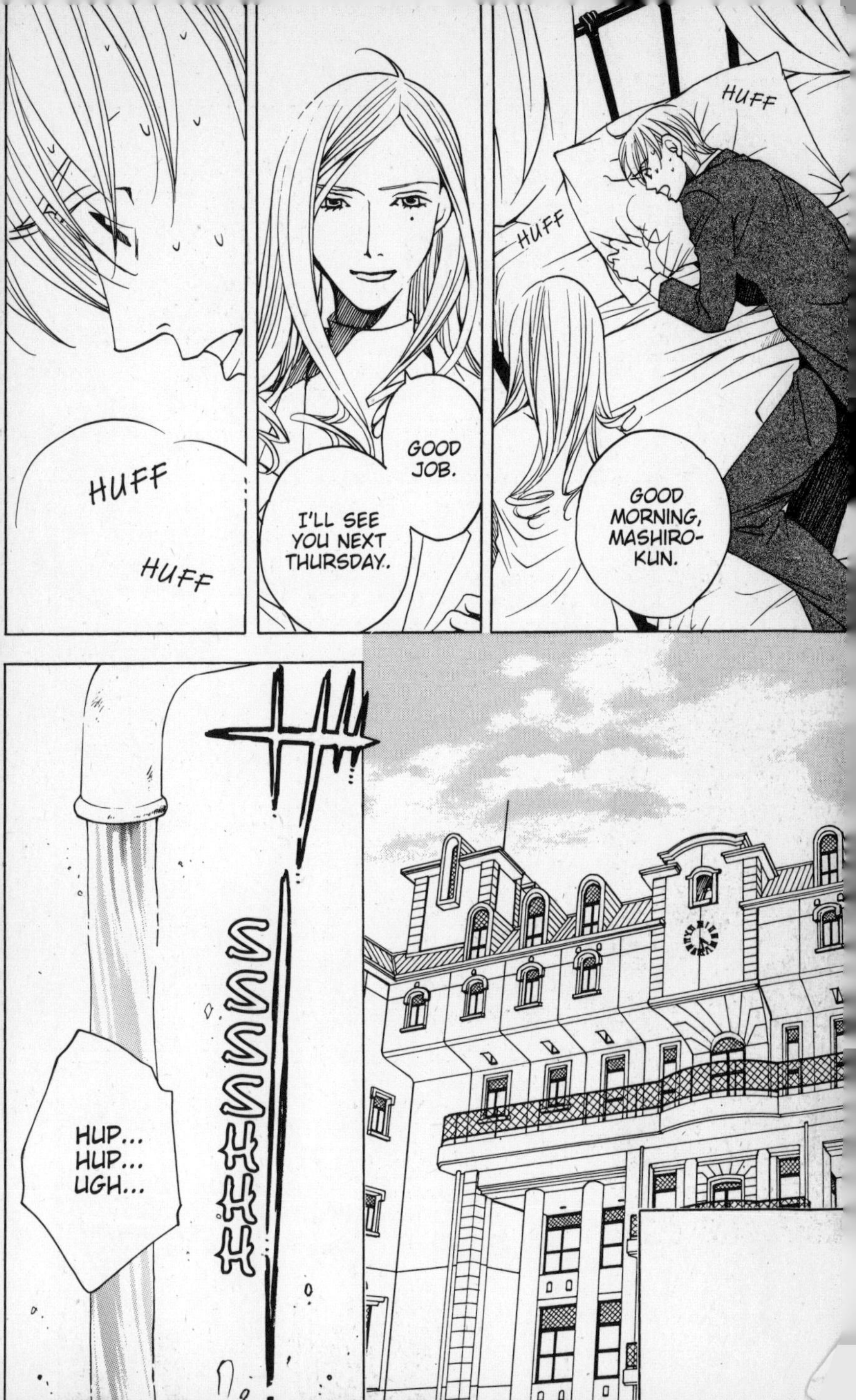
HUFF
HUFF
GOOD MORNING, MASHIRO-KUN.
GOOD JOB.
I'LL SEE YOU NEXT THURSDAY..
HUFF
HUFF
SSSSHHHH
HUP... HUP... UGH...

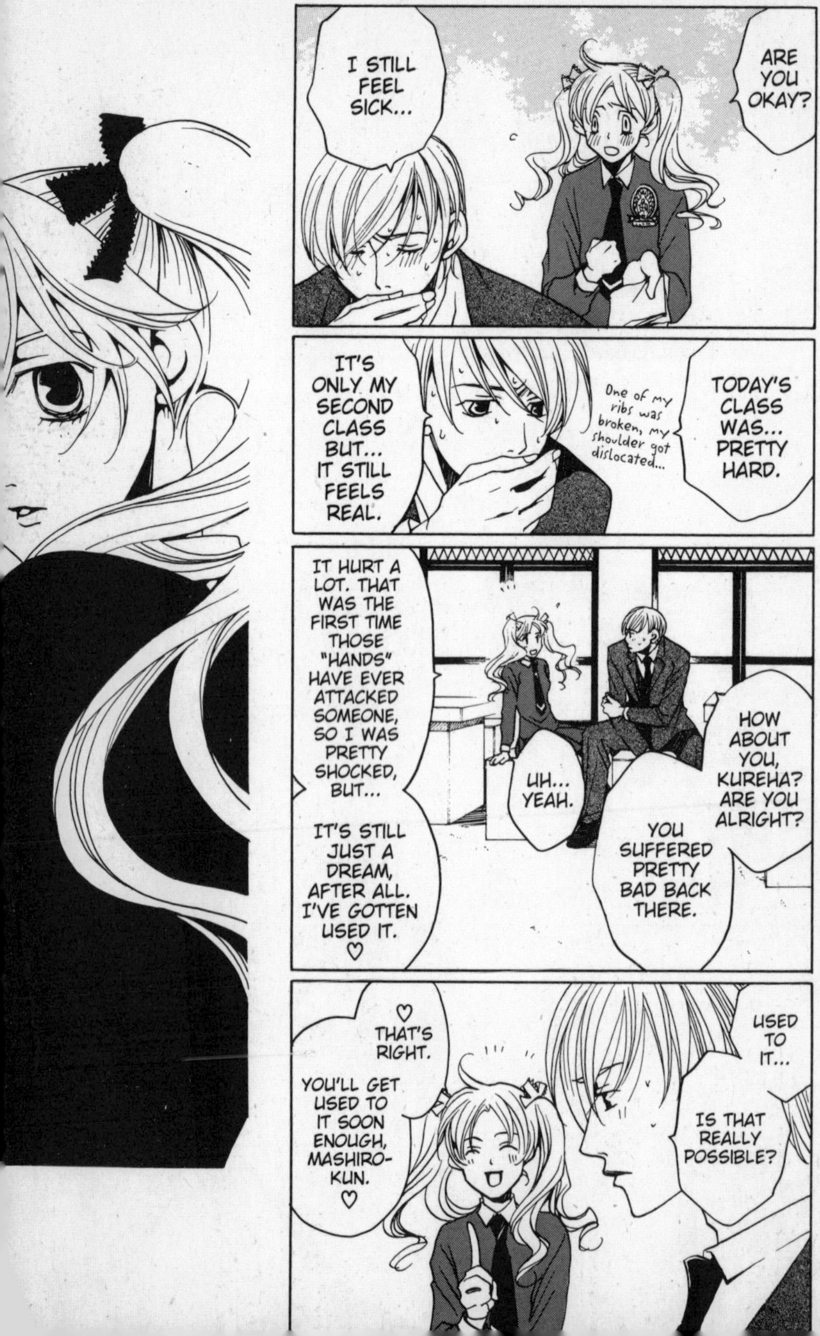
ARE YOU OKAY?
I STILL FEEL SICK...
TODAY'S CLASS WAS... PRETTY HARD.
One of my ribs was broken, my shoulder got dislocated...
IT'S ONLY MY SECOND CLASS BUT... IT STILL FEELS REAL.
HOW ABOUT YOU, KUREHA? ARE YOU ALRIGHT?
YOU SUFFERED PRETTY BAD BACK THERE.
UH... YEAH.
IT HURT A LOT. THAT WAS THE FIRST TIME THOSE "HANDS" HAVE EVER ATTACKED SOMEONE, SO I WAS PRETTY SHOCKED, BUT...
IT'S STILL JUST A DREAM, AFTER ALL. I'VE GOTTEN USED IT. ♡
USED TO IT...
IS THAT REALLY POSSIBLE?
♡ THAT'S RIGHT.
YOU'LL GET USED TO IT SOON ENOUGH, MASHIRO-KUN. ♡

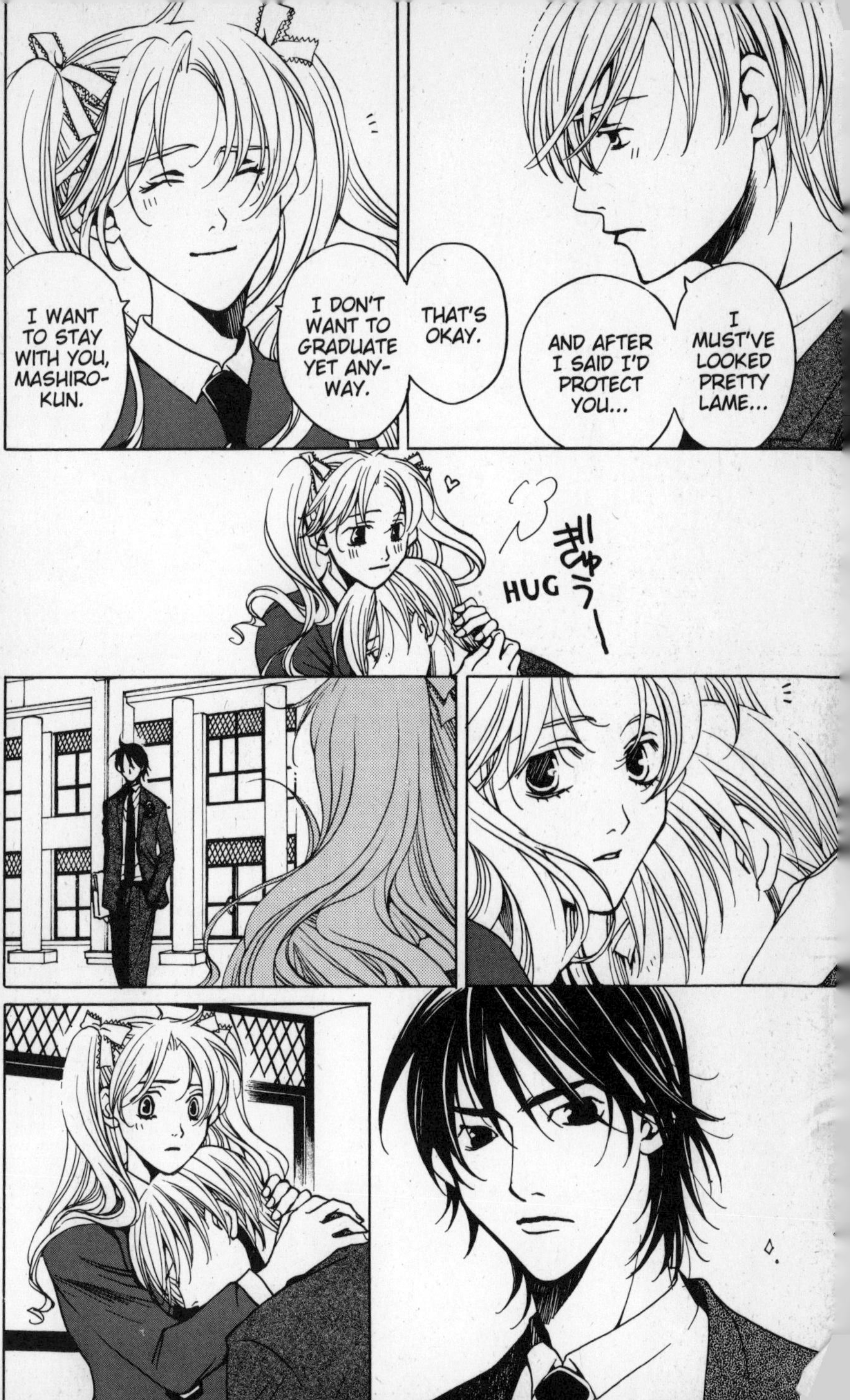

I MUST'VE LOOKED PRETTY LAME...
AND AFTER I SAID I'D PROTECT YOU...
THAT'S OKAY.
I DON'T WANT TO GRADUATE YET ANY-WAY.
I WANT TO STAY WITH YOU, MASHIRO-KUN.
ぎゅう
HUG

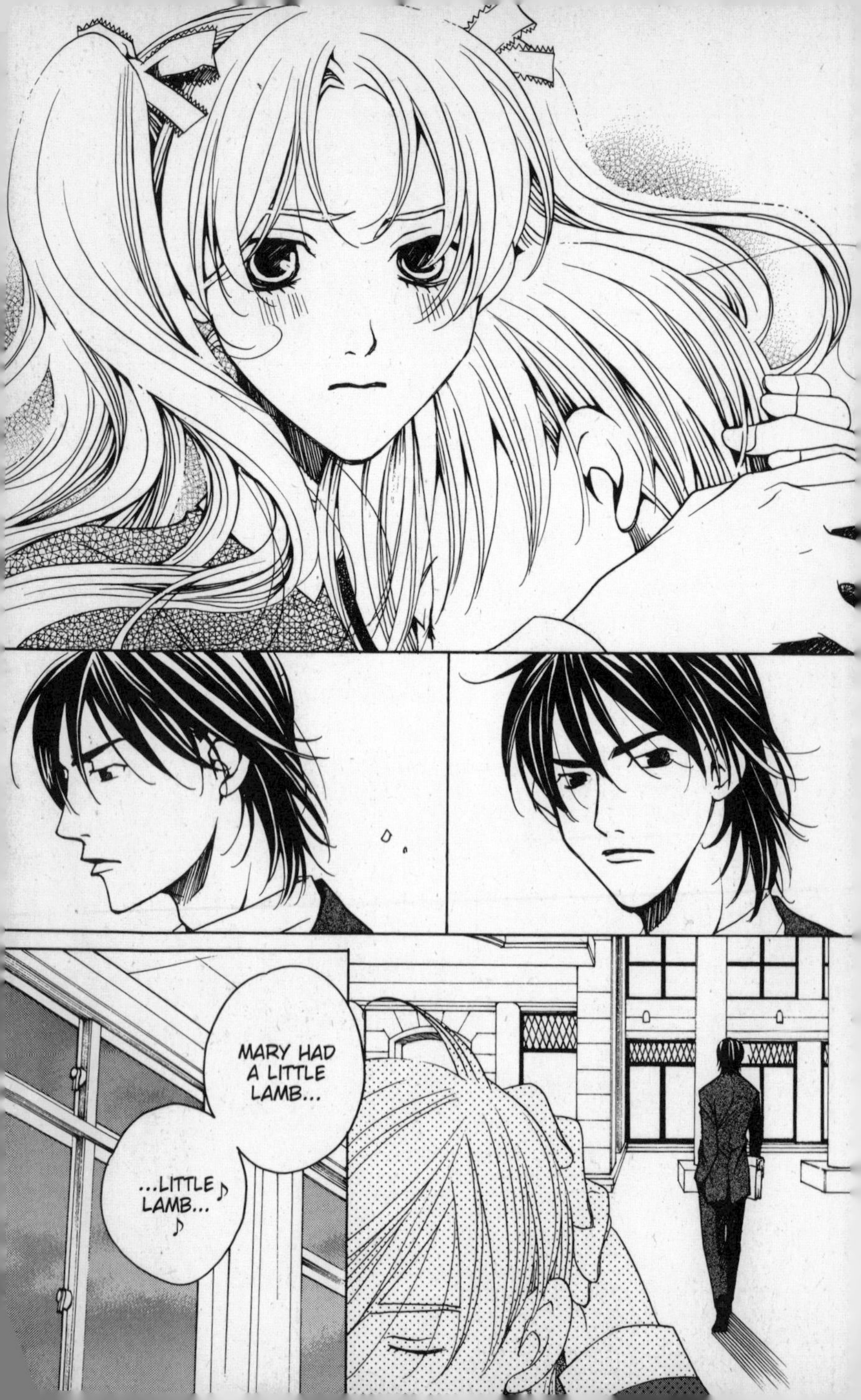
MARY HAD A LITTLE LAMB...
...LITTLE LAMB... ♪ ♪

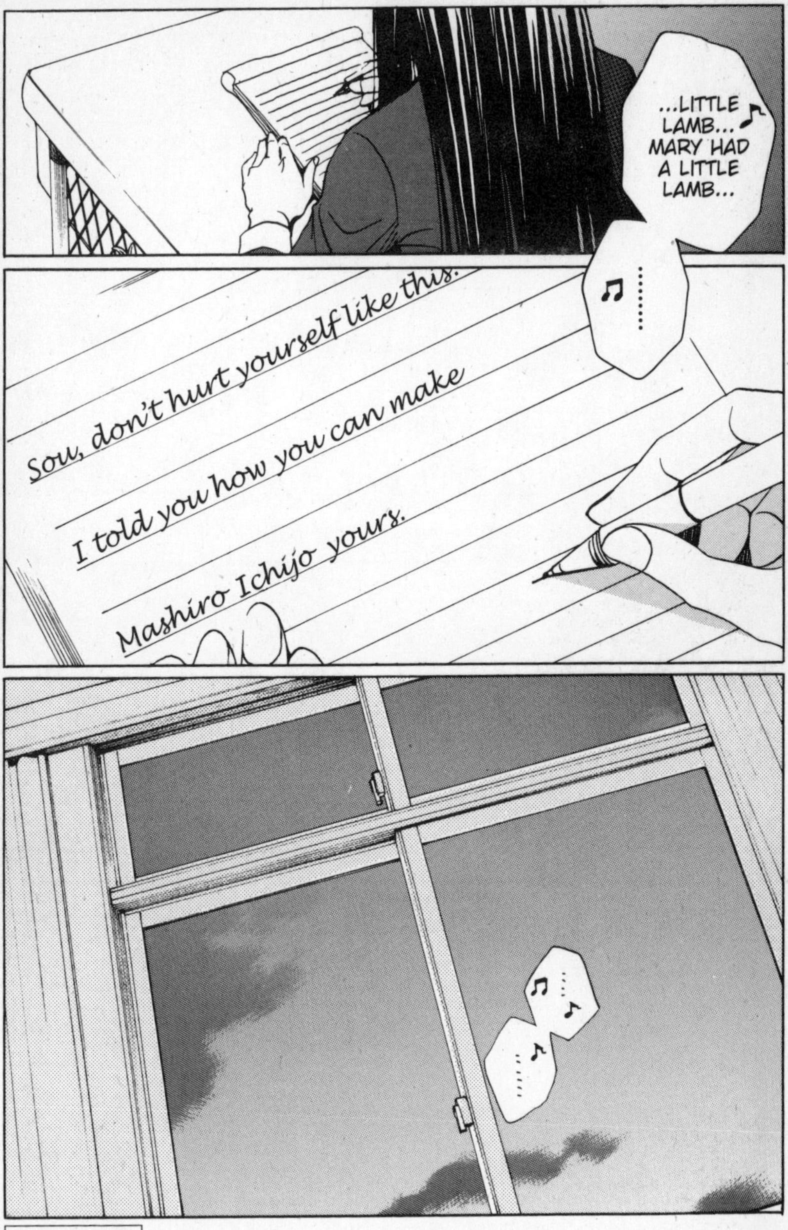
...LITTLE LAMB... MARY HAD A LITTLE LAMB...
Sou, don't hurt yourself like this.
I told you how you can make
Mashiro Ichijo yours.

CHAPTER 4 / OVER

<MIZUSHIRO SETONA'S OFFICIAL WEBSITE> VIEWABLE VIA CELL PHONE TOO!
HTTP://WWW.PAGE.SANNET.NE.JP/SETONA

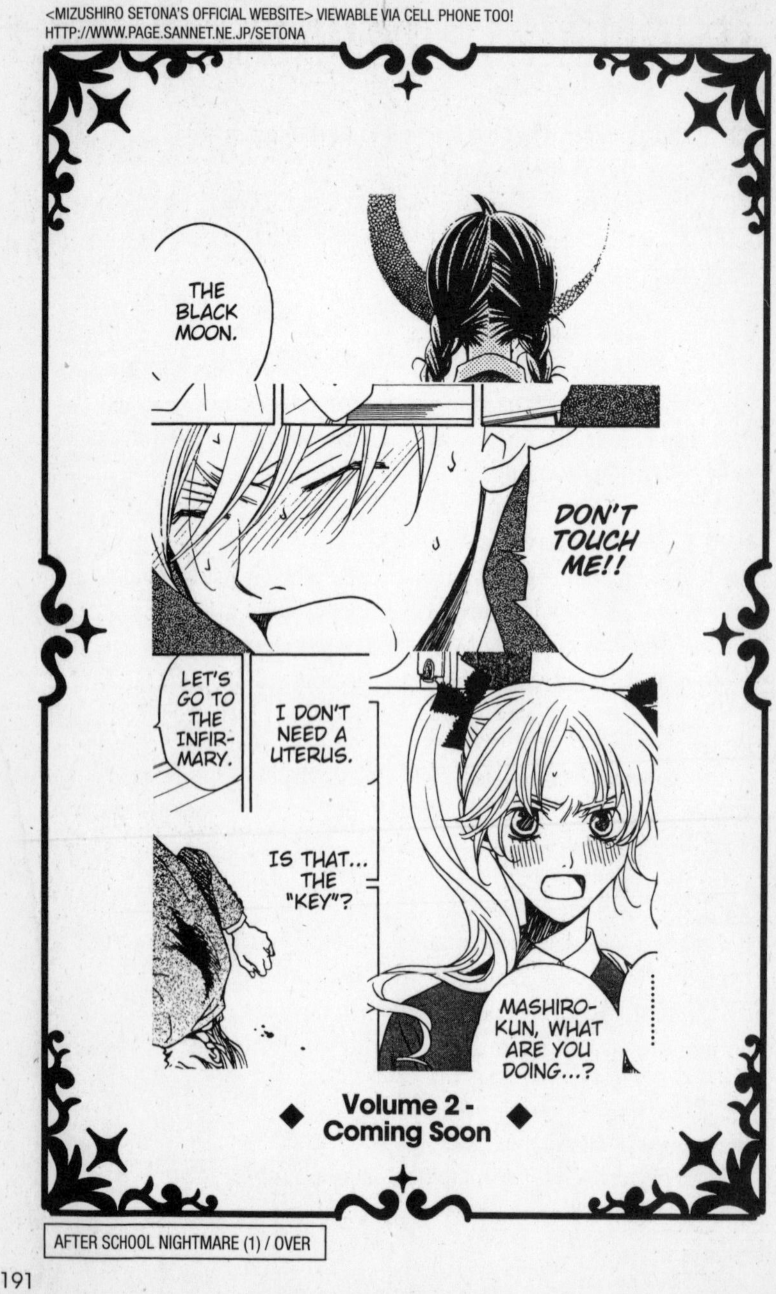
THE BLACK MOON.
DON'T TOUCH ME!!
MASHIRO-KUN, WHAT ARE YOU DOING...?
I DON'T NEED A UTERUS.
LET'S GO TO THE INFIRMARY.
IS THAT... THE "KEY"?

Volume 2 - Coming Soon

AFTER SCHOOL NIGHTMARE (1) / OVER

Translator's Notes:

All of the characters names are colors of the rainbow.

真白 - "mashiro" is pure white

倉 - "sou" is blue

紅葉 - "kure" is crimson

美登里 - "midori" is green

Pg. 21 – *sensei*

Although usually "sensei" conjures up images of teachers and manga-ka, the term is also used when referring to doctors, or in this case, the school nurse. Ironic how she does become a more valid "sensei" in the after school setting.

Pg. 125-6 – The classroom in shock!

The reason that the class was so stunned when Mashiro said Kureha was "cute" is because Japanese students very rarely express any sort of affection in public. A Western equivalent of this would be if Mashiro had said to Kureha in public, "I think you're *really hot*, baby!"

Pg. 135 – *bakkapuru*

In the Japanese version, the girls called Mashiro and Kureha "bakkapuru" -- a convenient combination of the words "baka" and "couple" (stupid couple).

Pg. 137 – *The Tale of Genji*

For these two pages of the manga, Mashiro is reading a passage from the "Murasaki" chapter of *The Tale of Genji* by Murasaki Shikibu. The characters in this scene included a maid talking to a young girl, and Genji, who was watching them both.

Pg. 171 – 4's and 5's

In Japanese schools, the grading system goes up to 5. That means a 5 can be equated to 100, the best score possible, and a 4 can be equated with a score in the 90's.

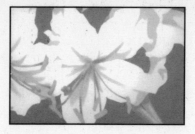

SETONA MIZUSHIRO

Even though I say to myself, "Now this is what I want to draw!" whenever an idea pops into my head, my opportunities to draw ideas are so limited! So countless stories and characters are born and die silently in my head without anyone having a chance to know of them. However, this is the story of how *After School Nightmare* -- one among many doomed stories -- miraculously made it to paper.

It was during a comics free-talk that I let it out that I had wanted to draw this story. After that, time and again, chances to draw it would pop up but every time something would go wrong until I started thinking to myself that this tale would be another lost cause just like the rest of them. But things were not fated to turn out so. Sure, time passed so that the story and characters changed quite a bit, but in the end, they were safely delivered into this world. It was a beautiful thing.

I am most deeply indebted to both those who made this manga possible and those who so graciously read it, and I am invigorated to keep going! (breathe...breathe...) I hope you enjoy it!

ABOUT THE MANGA-KA

Setona Mizushiro's first real dabble in the world of creating manga was in 1985 when she participated in the publication of a dojinshi (amateur manga). She remained active in the dojinshi world until she debuted in April of 1993 with her short single *Fuyu ga Owarou Toshiteita* (Winter Was Ending) that ran in Shogakukan's *Puchi Comic* magazine. Mizushiro-sensei is well-known for her series *X-Day* in which she exhibits an outstanding ability to delve into psychological issues of every nature. Besides manga, Mizushiro-sensei has an affinity for chocolate, her two cats (Jam and Nene), and round sparkly objects.

Concerning Honorifics

At Go! Comi, we do our best to ensure that our translations read seamlessly in English while respecting the original Japanese language and culture. To this end, the original honorifics (the suffixes found at the end of characters' names) remain intact. In Japan, where politeness and formality are more integrated into every aspect of the language, honorifics give a better understanding of character relationships. They can be used to indicate both respect and affection. Whether a person addresses someone by first name or last name also indicates how close their relationship is.

Here are some of the honorifics you might encounter in reading this book:

-san: This is the most common and neutral of honorifics. The polite way to address someone you're not on close terms with is to use "-san." It's kind of like Mr. or Ms., except you can use "-san" with first names as easily as family names.

-chan: Used for friendly familiarity, mostly applied towards young girls. "-chan" also carries a connotation of cuteness with it, so it is frequently used with nicknames towards both boys and girls (such as "Na-chan" for "Natsu").

-kun: Like "-chan," it's an informal suffix for friends and classmates, only "-kun" is usually associated with boys. It can also be used in a professional environment by someone addressing a subordinate.

-sama: Indicates a great deal of respect or admiration.

Sempai: In school, "sempai" is used to refer to an upperclassman or club leader. It can also be used in the workplace by a new employee to address a mentor or staff member with seniority.

Sensei: Teachers, doctors, writers or any master of a trade are referred to as "sensei." When addressing a manga creator, the polite thing to do is attach "-sensei" to the manga-ka's name (as in Mizushiro-sensei).

Onii: This is the more casual term for an older brother. Usually you'll see it with an honorific attached, such as "onii-chan."

Onee: The casual term for older sister, it's used like "onii" with honorifics.

[blank]: Not using an honorific when addressing someone indicates that the speaker has permission to speak intimately with the other person. This relationship is usually reserved for close friends and family.

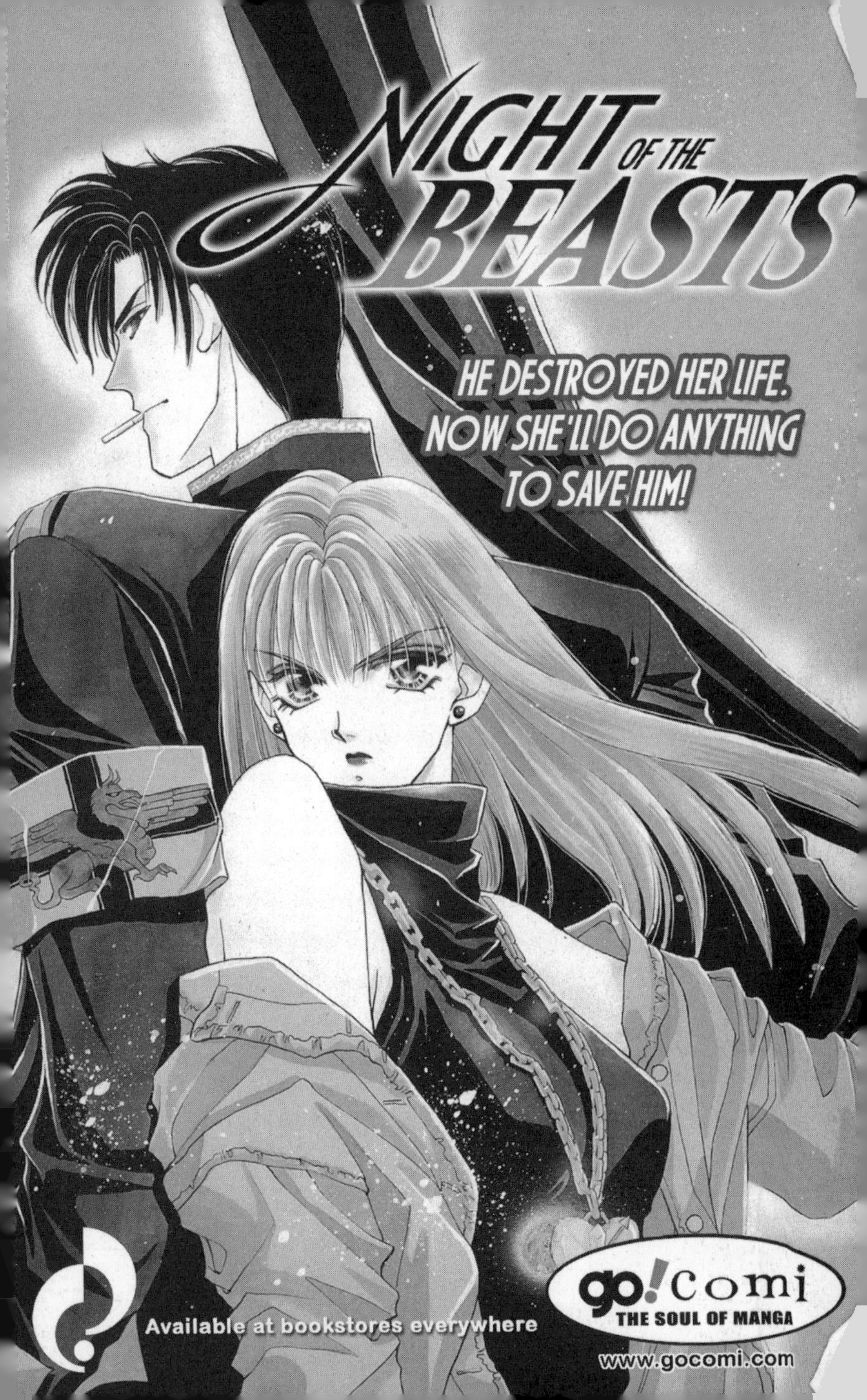
NIGHT OF THE BEASTS
HE DESTROYED HER LIFE. NOW SHE'LL DO ANYTHING TO SAVE HIM!
Available at bookstores everywhere
go!comi
THE SOUL OF MANGA
www.gocomi.com

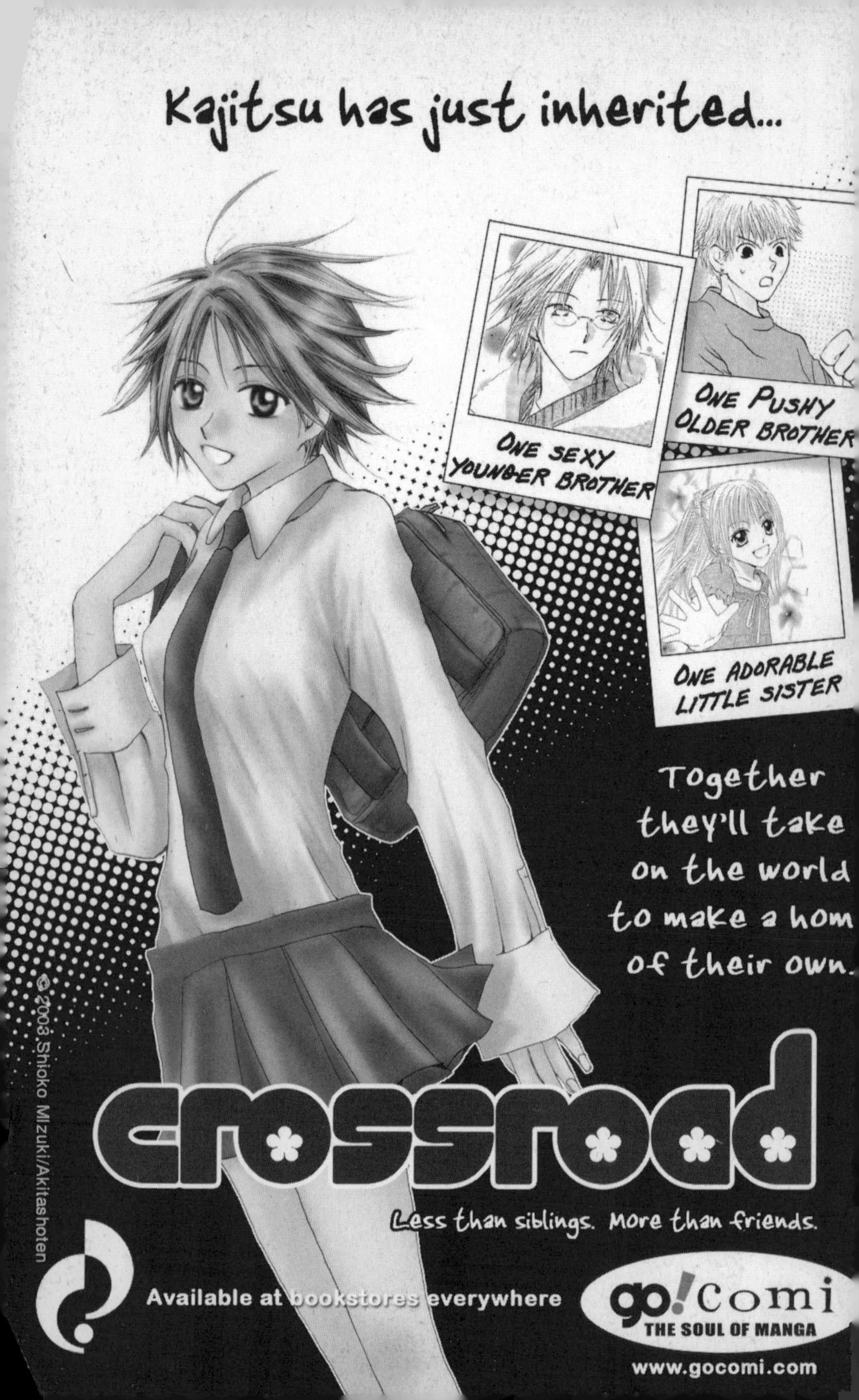

Kajitsu has just inherited...
ONE SEXY YOUNGER BROTHER
ONE PUSHY OLDER BROTHER
ONE ADORABLE LITTLE SISTER
Together they'll take on the world to make a hom of their own.
crossroad
Less than siblings. More than friends.
© 2003 Shioko Mizuki/Akitashoten
Available at bookstores everywhere
go!comi
THE SOUL OF MANGA
www.gocomi.com

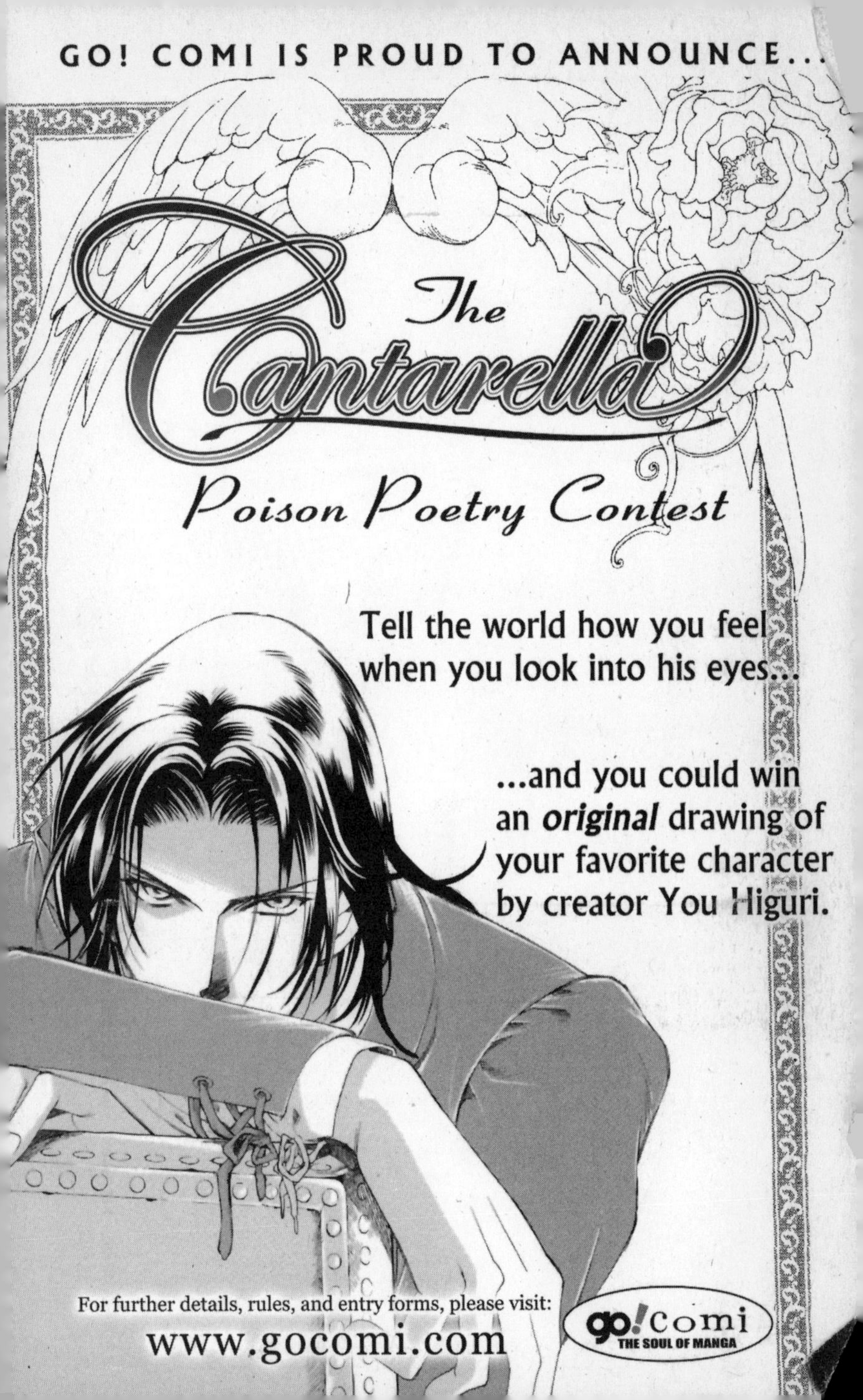
GO! COMI IS PROUD TO ANNOUNCE...
The Cantarella
Poison Poetry Contest
Tell the world how you feel when you look into his eyes...
...and you could win an original drawing of your favorite character by creator You Higuri.
For further details, rules, and entry forms, please visit:
www.gocomi.com
go!comi
THE SOUL OF MANGA

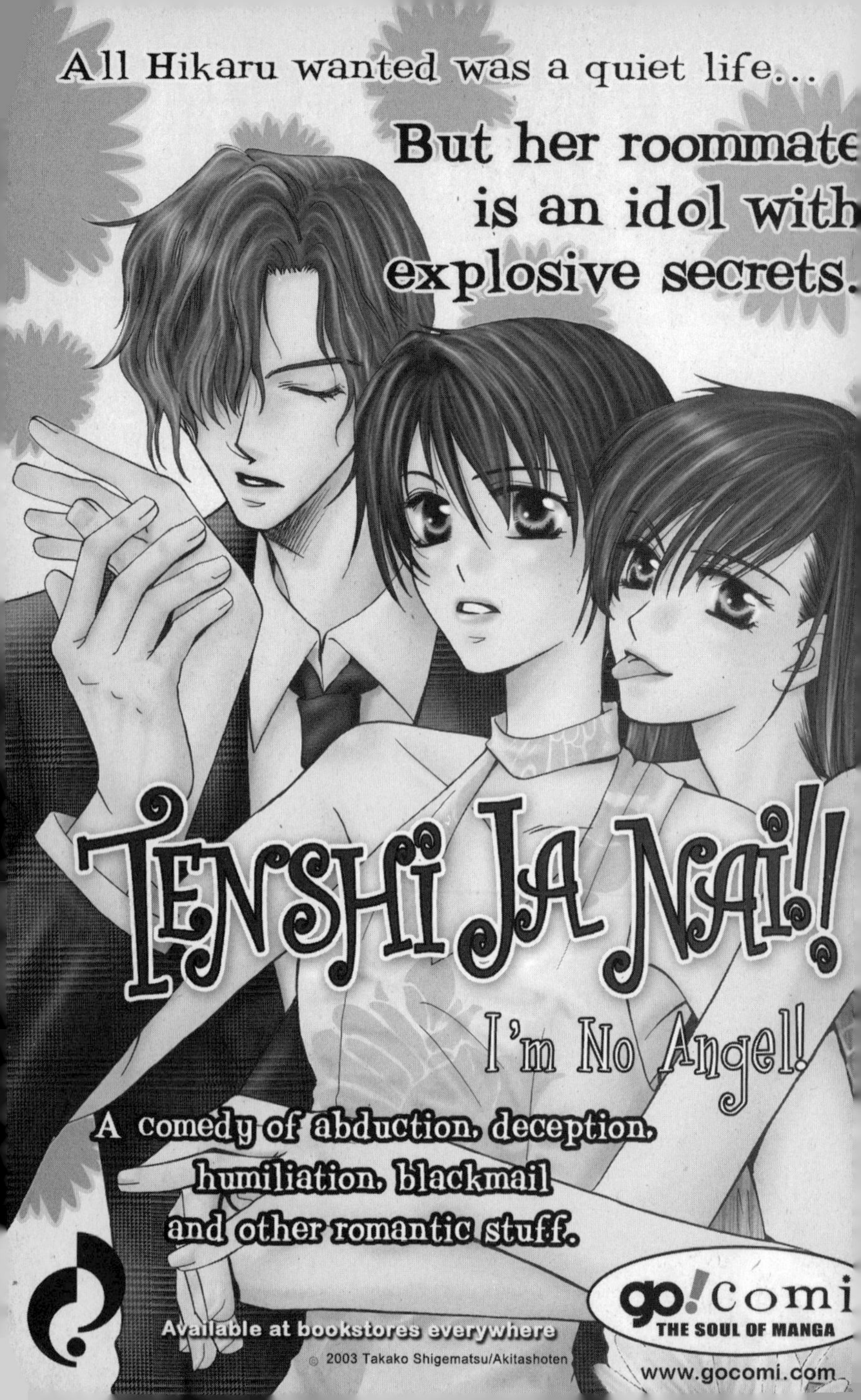

All Hikaru wanted was a quiet life...
But her roommate is an idol with explosive secrets.
TENSHI JA NAI!!
I'm No Angel!
A comedy of abduction, deception, humiliation, blackmail and other romantic stuff.
Available at bookstores everywhere
© 2003 Takako Shigematsu/Akitashoten
go!comi
THE SOUL OF MANGA
www.gocomi.com

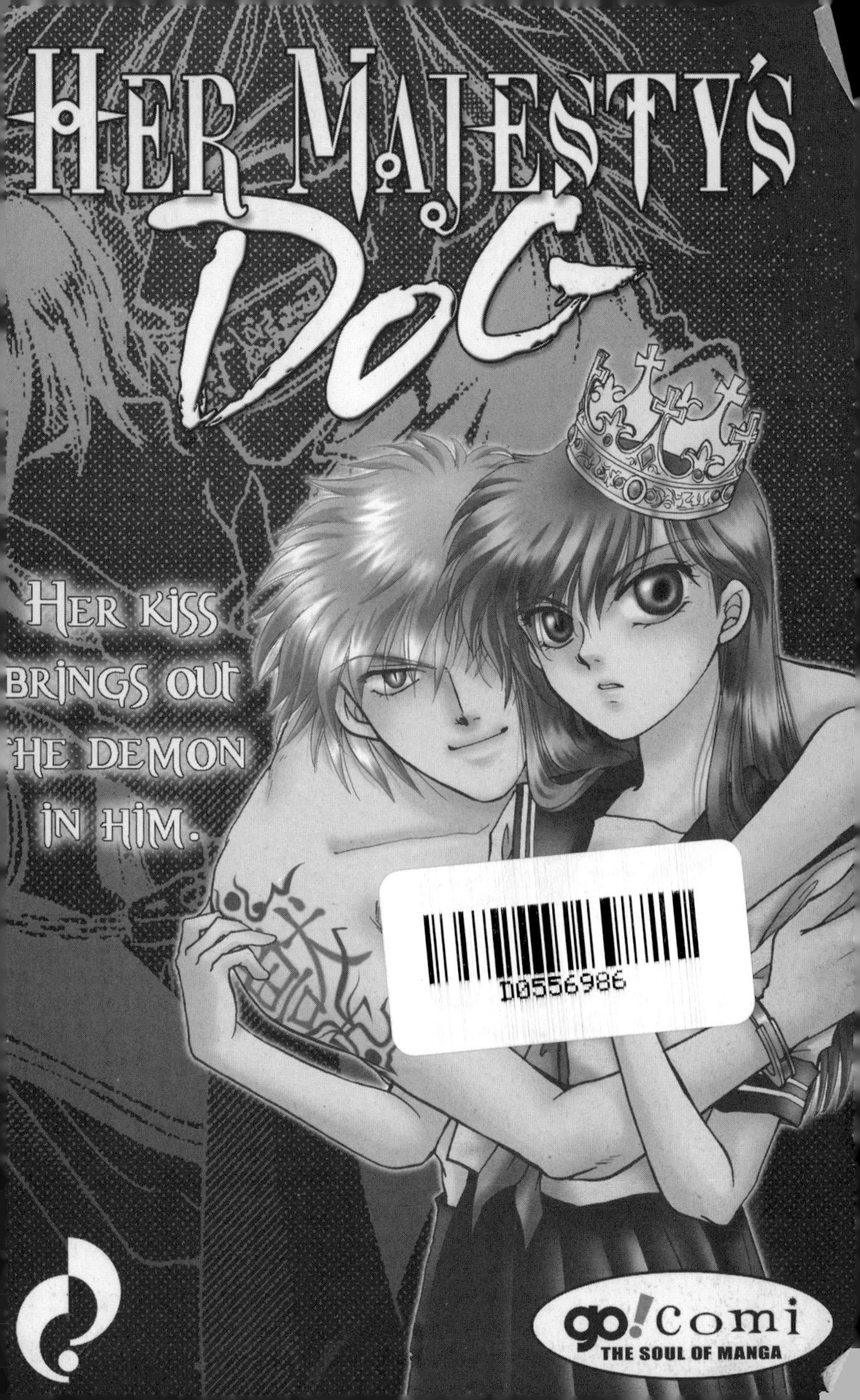
HER MAJESTY'S DOG
HER KISS BRINGS OUT THE DEMON IN HIM.
go!comi
THE SOUL OF MANGA